CONTEMPORARY PROBLEMS IN INTERNATIONAL ARBITRATION

Contemporary Problems in International Arbitration

edited by

JULIAN D.M. LEW

Head of the School of International Arbitration,
Centre for Commercial Law Studies,
Queen Mary College, University of London

1987 **MARTINUS NIJHOFF PUBLISHERS**
a member of the KLUWER ACADEMIC PUBLISHERS GROUP
DORDRECHT / BOSTON / LANCASTER
School of International Arbitration, Centre for
Commercial Law Studies, Queen Mary College

Distributors

for the United States and Canada: Kluwer Academic Publishers, P.O. Box 358, Accord Station, Hingham, MA 02018-0358, USA
for the UK and Ireland: Kluwer Academic Publishers, MTP Press Limited, Falcon House, Queen Square, Lancaster LA1 1RN, UK
for all other countries: Kluwer Academic Publishers Group, Distribution Center, P.O. Box 322, 3300 AH Dordrecht, The Netherlands

Library of Congress Cataloging in Publication Data

ISBN 0-89838-926-7

Book Information

This book was first published in 1986 in a hardcover edition by the Centre of Commercial Law Studies

PRINTED IN THE NETHERLANDS

Contents

Part 3 International arbitration procedure

Part 4 International arbitration involving states and state-entity parties

Glossary of terms

European Convention means the *European Convention on International Commercial Arbitration*, signed in Geneva on April 21, 1961.

ICC means the International Chamber of Commerce, and where appropriate the Court of Arbitration of the International Chamber of Commerce.

ICC Rules means the Rules of Conciliation and Arbitration of the International Chamber of Commerce, in force as from June 1, 1975.

ICSID means the International Centre for the Settlement of Investment Disputes, established by the Washington Convention.

LCIA means the London Court of International Arbitration.

New York Convention means the *United Nations Convention on the Recognition and Enforcement of Foreign Arbitral Awards*, signed in New York on June 10, 1958.

UNCITRAL Model Law means the draft Model Law on International Commercial Arbitration as at March 25, 1985 and as published in United Nations Document No A/CN 9/264.

UNCITRAL Rules mean the Arbitration rules adopted on April 28, 1976 by the United Nations Commission on International Trade Law (UNCITRAL) at its Ninth Session.

Washington Convention means the *Convention on the Settlement of Investment Disputes between States and Nationals of Other States*, signed in Washington, DC, on March 18, 1965.

Glossary of terms

List of contributors

Markham Ball
Attorney-at-Law, Wald Harkrader & Ross, Washington, DC.

Joseph D Becker
J D Harvard; Attorney-at-Law, partner, Fox Flyn & Mela—ed, New York City; Adjunct Professor of Law, New York University.

Giorgio Bernini
Professor of Law, University of Bologna; Chairman-Elect of the International Council for Commercial Arbitration; Advocate, Studio Bernini, Bologna.

Karl-Heinz Böckstiegel
Professor of International Business Law, University of Cologne; President of the Iran–US Claims Tribunal, The Hague.

Stewart C Boyd
One of Her Majesty's Counsel, practising in England.

Philippe Cahier
Professor of the Graduate Institute of International Studies, Geneva.

Jeremy P Carver
Solicitor, partner in Coward Chance, London.

Lawrence Collins
Solicitor, partner in Herbert Smith & Co, London.

Robert Coulson
President of the American Arbitration Association.

Bernardo M Cremades
Practising lawyer in Madrid; Professor of Law, University of Madrid.

Georges R Delaume
Senior Legal Adviser of the International Centre for Settlement of Investment Disputes.

Hazel Fox
Director of the British Institute of International and Comparative Law; formerly Fellow of Somerville College, Oxford.

Ottoarndt Glossner
President of the German Institute of Arbitration, Cologne; President of the ICC Commission on International Arbitration, Paris.

Berthold Goldman
Professor of Law, Université de Droit d'Economie et de Sciences Sociales, Paris.

Roy Goode
Crowther Professor of Credit and Commercial Law; Director, Centre for Commercial Law Studies, Queen Mary College, University of London.

A H Hermann
Consultant on international business law; Legal Correspondent of the *Financial Times*; Editor of the *Financial Times Business Law Brief*.

Gerold Herrmann
Legal Officer in the UNCITRAL Secretariat (International Trade Law Branch office of Legal Affairs, United Nations).

J Martin H Hunter
Solicitor, partner in Freshfields, London.

Sigvard Jarvin
General Counsel of the Court of Arbitration of the International Chamber of Commerce.

Pierre Lalive
Professor of Law, Geneva University and the Graduate Institute of International Studies, Geneva; Counsel, Lalive and Budin, Geneva; President of the ICC Institute of International Business Law and Practice, Paris; President of the Swiss Arbitration Association.

Ole Lando
Professor of European and Comparative Law, Institute of European Market Law, Copenhagen, School of Economics and Business Administration.

Julian D M Lew
International Lawyer, Partner in S J Berwin & Co, London; Senior Visiting Fellow and Head of the School of International Arbitration, Centre for Commercial Law Studies, Queen Mary College, University of London.

Werner Melis
Chairman of the Arbitral Centre of the Federal Economic Chamber of Austria.

Jan Paulsson
Practising Lawyer, Partner in Coudert Frères, Paris.

Kenneth S Rokison
One of Her Majesty's Counsel, practising in England.

Samir Saleh
Attorney-at-Law (Beirut), Law Consultant (London), Islamic and Middle Eastern Law, Vice-Chairman of the Court of Arbitration, ICC, Paris.

Pieter Sanders
Professor Emeritus, Law Faculty of the Erasmus University, Rotterdam; Chairman, International Council for Commercial Arbitration.

Clive M Schmitthoff
Barrister, Visiting Professor of International Business Law, City University and of Kent at Canterbury; Joint Vice-Chairman of the Committee of Management, Centre for Commercial Law Studies.

David W Shenton
Solicitor, Senior Partner of Lovell, White & King, London; Chairman of Committee D (Procedures for Settling Disputes) of the Section on Business Law of the International Bar Association.

Kenneth R Simmonds
Professor of International Law, Queen Mary College, University of London; Former Dean of the Faculty of Laws, Queen Mary College, London.

John A Tackaberry
One of Her Majesty's Counsel, practising in England.

Albert Van den Berg
Partner, Messrs Van Doorne & Sjollema, Rotterdam.

Table of Cases

Table of Statutes

Table of Treaties and Conventions

Draft Legislation

Rules

Resolutions

Declaration

Draft Convention

EEC Secondary Legislation (Regulations)

Miscellaneous

Introduction

The establishment of a School of International Arbitration was a sufficiently important occurrence to have brought to London, for its inaugural conference, most of the world's leading experts on international arbitration. The three-day Symposium on March 25–27, 1985 sought to identify and consider the contemporary problems affecting international arbitration. It was not the aim of the Symposium to develop, propose or agree solutions to these problems, but rather to discuss the issues and alternative solutions. The success of the School will be measured in the future by its contribution, through research and teaching, to the development of solutions to the difficulties and uncertainties which reduce the effectiveness of international arbitration agreements and awards and the conduct of international arbitral proceedings.

This book reproduces the papers presented at the Symposium (amended and varied by several contributors). It is not considered appropriate here to comment on or analyse paper by paper the ideas presented or discussions which ensued. However, it would be appropriate to make reference to specific developments in the short period since the Symposium directly relevant to the papers reproduced and the discussions which ensued. The pertinence of the subject-matter selected becomes clear from these subsequent developments.

The internationalisation or denationalisation of international arbitration is recognised as one of the most vital and necessary elements for the development and acceptance of arbitration as the most suitable and effective mechanism for the resolution of disputes arising out of international commercial arrangements. Specifically, the elimination of the restrictions and prejudices of national laws and the ability to transcend national, political and cultural differences is fundamental for the future of international arbitration.

In its traditional form, the concept and practice of arbitration was fashioned and used principally by the western trading nations. Although no statistics are available, it is apparent that there is today an increasing acceptance and use of arbitration by governments and trading entities from the developing and Third World. These countries have adopted national legislation, in many cases influenced by contemporary views and practice, have become party to the New York and Washington Conventions, and have participated in the development of international instruments relating to arbitration. These developing and Third World countries have accepted the philosophy and concept of arbitration as generally understood in the developed countries with comparatively little compromise on the part of the latter.

The extent to which arbitration can be denationalised has long been in dispute. Clearly, rules acceptable to the international business community can and have been developed, but parochial criteria have invariably required compromises for their adoption by or implementation in national law. Nonetheless there is an increasing recognition of the need for an internationalisation of arbitration, as well as a practical movement in this direction. Since the end of the Second World War there have been a plethora of international instruments, including the New York and Washington Conventions, and the UNCITRAL Arbitration Rules 1976. Each instrument, in its own way, has contributed towards the resolution of the specific difficulties which exist between the arbitrants, but more significantly have been developed by experts from and representing the governments of countries with different legal, political, economic and cultural backgrounds, all of whom have sought to identify and agree on areas of common ground and standards.

On June 21, 1985, the most recent and perhaps most significant step towards the internationalisation of the law relating to international arbitration was taken with the adoption of the UNCITRAL Model Law on International Commercial Arbitration. UNCITRAL's pedigree in this area has been proved over ten years with the acceptance of the UNCITRAL Arbitration Rules and Conciliation Rules, but those are for optional use by parties submitting future or existing disputes to arbitration or conciliation. The Model Law, by contrast, is intended to be the pro forma for the national law of as many countries as possible. Ambiguous and unclear in parts, the Model Law is essentially a compromise: it contains the basic and essential rules to govern the arbitration of international commercial disputes. On the other hand, without the ambiguities the Model Law would never have been accepted. The success of the Model Law is still to be seen, but the participation of delegates from 62 countries is encouraging and in many countries there have been and are feasibility studies to determine the extent to which the Model Law is compatible with or could be adopted in place of the existing national legislation. This, in itself, is a major step towards the internationalisation of arbitration.

It is noteworthy that Belgium (the only country to adopt the Uniform Law on Arbitration in the Council of Europe Convention 1966), adopted on March 27, 1985 an amendment to its law which effectively denies litigants access to the Belgian courts for the purposes of annulling an arbitration award, even if that award has taken place in Belgium, where neither of the arbitrants is a resident in or a citizen or corporation of Belgium, or being a foreign entity does not have a branch or working office there. Although the object may appear to be nationalistic, the overt intention of the law is to prevent the Belgian courts being used for the purposes of abusing the arbitration mechanism, where neither party has a significant connection with Belgium.

As important as the unification of arbitration laws is the need to develop common or accepted standards and practices for arbitration. The authority and jurisdiction of arbitrators are frequently discussed as an example where law, attitudes and practices differ. In the past decade these differences have also become less pronounced. It is now generally accepted that party autonomy through the arbitration clause or agreement is the primary source of the arbitrator's authority and jurisdiction, subject only to mandatory or public policy regulations of the law governing the arbitration and the place of arbitration. Where the parties have not agreed or are unable to agree on specific issues the law governing the arbitration will prevail.

What subject-matters can properly be submitted to arbitration and whether the arbitrators can themselves decide on issues of jurisdiction continue to be contentious questions. When the authority of the arbitrator is questioned, should he stay his proceedings and refer the parties to the court, or should he decide the issue and leave the parties to challenge it in the courts after his award has been made? Specifically, can an arbitrator hear a dispute and render an award if the base contract concerns either bribery and corruption, or a matter of national mandatory (public policy, *ordre public*) law, or more specifically, anti-trust rules?

On the issue of a contractual arrangement involving bribery, the decision of the California Federal District Court in *Northrop Corporation* v *Triad Financial Establishment*[1] is now pending appeal to the Supreme Court of California. In that case the California Federal District Court refused to enforce an award where the base contract was contrary to the United States and Saudi Arabian anti-corruption legislations. The California Federal District Court here adopted the internationally accepted view that arbitration should not be the vehicle for resolving disputes arising out of illegal, immoral and unethical commercial arrangements. Even if the arbitrators allow the matter to pass and render an award, national courts will deny its effect.

With respect to the issue of anti-trust law, the decision on July 2, 1985 of the United States Supreme Court in the matter of *Mitsubishi Motors Corporation* v *Soler Chrysler-Plymouth Inc*[2] is perhaps one of the most important national court decisions affecting international arbitration for many years, and may well influence the policy of the European and Japanese anti-trust authorities. In this case the Supreme Court recognised that where a contract concerns international commerce arbitrators could decide issues involving United States anti-trust legislation provided the arbitrators respected those anti-trust laws. The effect of this decision is to allow an arbitrator to investigate an allegation by one party that the contract violated the United States anti-trust laws. This is the generally accepted view in the European Community. The Supreme Court decision effectively overruled what has for many years been considered the legal position in the United States, based on the Supreme Court decision in *American Safety Equipment Corporation* v *J P McGuire & Co*,[3] and limited non-arbitrability of anti-trust issues to domestic contracts.

The majority decision in the *Mitsubishi Motors* case has raised several issues which will no doubt be discussed and analysed in depth in the future. Here reference needs to be made specifically to the internationalist approach adopted by the majority in the Supreme Court in explaining and justifying their decision. They followed the 1974 approach and decision in *Scherk* v *Alberto-Culver Co*,[4] stating:

> '... we conclude that concerns of international comity, respect for the capacities of foreign and transnational tribunals, and sensitivity to the need

1 593 F Supp 928 (1984).
2 24 *ILM* 1064 (1985).
3 391 F 2d 821 (2nd Cir 1968).
4 417 US 506 (1974).

of the international commercial system for predictability in the resolution of disputes require that we enforce the parties' agreement, even assuming that a contrary result would be forthcoming in a domestic context.

Even before *Scherk*, this Court had recognised the utility of forum-selection clauses in international transactions. ... Notwithstanding the possibility that the English court would enforce provisions in the towage contract exculpating the German party which an American court would refuse to enforce, this Court gave effect to the choice-of-forum clause.

Recognising that "agreeing in advance on a forum acceptable to both parties" is an indispensable element in international trade, commerce, and contracting ". . . the decision in *The Bremen* clearly eschewed a provincial solicitude for the jurisdiction of domestic fora".[5]

The *Bremen* and *Scherk* established a strong presumption in favor of enforcement of freely negotiated contractual choice-of-forum provisions. Here, as in *Scherk*, that presumption is reinforced by the emphatic federal policy in favor of arbitral dispute resolution. And at least since this Nation's accession in 1970 to the (New York) Convention, ... and the implementation of the Convention in the same year by amendment of the federal Arbitration Act, that federal policy applies with special force in the field of international commerce. Thus, we must weigh the concerns of *American Safety* against a strong belief in the efficacy of arbitral procedures for the resolution of international commercial disputes and an equal commitment to the enforcement of freely negotiated choice-of-forum clauses.'[6]

Finally, after analysing the Supreme Court decision in *American Safety Equipment* case, Justice Blackmun for the majority stated:

'As international trade has expanded in recent decades, so too has the use of international arbitration to resolve disputes arising in the course of that trade. The controversies that international arbitral institutions are called upon to resolve have increased in diversity as well as in complexity. Yet the potential of these tribunals for efficient disposition of legal disagreements arising from commercial relations has not yet been tested. If they are to take a central place in the international legal order, national courts will need to "shake off the old judicial hostility to arbitration" ... and also their customary and understandable unwillingness to cede jurisdiction of a claim arising under domestic law to a foreign or transnational tribunal. To this extent, at least, it will be necessary for national courts to subordinate domestic notions of arbitrability to the international policy favoring commercial arbitration.'[7]

This internationalist approach is increasingly to be found in national laws and national court decisions, at least where matters of international commerce are involved. Notwithstanding the divergences which have appeared in the interpretation which national courts give to the New York Convention when

5 24 *ILM* 1072.
6 *Ibid*, at 1073.
7 *Ibid*, at 1076–7.

asked to enforce foreign awards, the increasing number of states party to the Convention manifest the general view as to its importance. It is for this reason that lawyers and arbitrators should and do, in fact, try to determine in advance where the award will have to be enforced and the practicality of enforcement in that place.

Whilst the law as it applies to the recognition and enforcement of awards has reached a degree of basic uniformity, great divergences still exist with respect to the effect of state and state entity participation in international commerce and accordingly in international arbitration. Notwithstanding the adoption in the United States and in the United Kingdom of the Foreign Sovereign Immunities Act 1976 and the State Immunity Act 1978 respectively to bring those laws into line with contemporary practice with respect to sovereign immunity, the practical effects of a state and state entity being party to an arbitration agreement remain uncertain, and the enforceability of awards against state or state entities also present considerable difficulties.[8]

ICSID, through its public international character, appears to offer an attractive vehicle to overcome some of the problems, but whilst all the necessary mechanisms appear to be present and effective, there is still an absence of practical actual cases, there having been only 20 cases to date and only five awards. With the passage of time and a liberal interpretation of 'investment disputes' ICSID or a similarly constituted arbitration institution may be the structure to overcome the abuses of sovereign immunity. The establishment of the US–Iran Claims Tribunal in The Hague through a public international law instrument and the provision of funds from which the arbitrators can order an award to be honoured, may also point the way to the future.

Truly effective arbitration requires willing participants: businessmen, lawyers, arbitrators and national laws. This necessitates a willingness and desire to overcome the political, legal, economic and cultural differences which divide the nations of the world, and to transcend the national and parochial distinctions between the systems, views and concepts. This is also considered one of the essential requirements for a good international lawyer and international arbitrator. In this respect comparative law can provide an insight into and an understanding of different systems and attitudes which they can use in the context of an international arbitration.

It is the aim of the School of International Arbitration to provide an entry to the subject of international arbitration, both from the perspective of national law, that is the comparative view of how different systems consider and deal with international arbitration, and from the transnational perspective, with a view to how the arbitrant sees himself in arbitration, divorced fully or in part from national law. In this task, the encouragement of all the participants at the Symposium and, in particular, those who have contributed to this publication, has provided an incentive and stimulus for the functions, role and future activities of the School of International Arbitration.

8 See for example *South Pacific Properties* v *Arab Republic of Egypt*, X *Yearbook: Commercial Arbitration* 504 (1985).

I wish to acknowledge the efforts of all the contributors to the Symposium and to this publication. These papers which provide an erudite and scholarly discussion of arbitration law and practice and original thoughts on the contemporary problems facing arbitration. The role of Mrs Nicola Jones, Administrator of the Centre of Commercial Law Studies, was crucial to the success of the Symposium, communicating with contributors and participants, ensuring that all the papers were received on time, and that the Conference programme proceeded efficiently as arranged and without any mishaps. To her go our particular thanks.

My thanks also to my secretary, Miss Jane Relf, who typed and retyped large parts of the final manuscript. Finally, Mr Adam Samuel has assisted with editing and Mr Robert Spicer with the indexing of this publication.

Julian DM Lew

Part 1

The School of International Arbitration

The birth of the School of International Arbitration 1

Pieter Sanders*

I am most honoured to speak on this happy occasion, and a happy occasion it is, indeed. We celebrate the birth of a new institute: the School of International Arbitration. This conference has been very promising. Many fairy godmothers well known in the world of international arbitration stood at the cradle of the School. You have heard them speak these past few days. There was no wicked fairy amongst them. On the contrary, they all wholeheartedly welcomed the newborn and contributed to her their gifts of arbitration-wisdom.

From fairyland to reality

Reality begins in October when, as announced, the first courses start for post graduates, interested in arbitration as a means of settlement for international commercial disputes. The origin of this remarkable initiative certainly is to be found in the increasing use made of arbitration in the international field. This is no wonder if we compare international arbitration with its alternative: going to court and submitting the case to court proceedings, the rules of which may be unfamiliar to at least one of the parties. Instead of going to court, maybe in a remote country, parties may prefer to submit their case to arbitrators, chosen by themselves and acting under arbitration rules equally known to both of them like, for example, the UNCITRAL Arbitration Rules. The place of arbitration, convenient to both parties, may be another attraction like, last but not least, the simplified procedure for enforcement of an award, once rendered, under the New York Convention 1958 which today has been ratified by more than 60 countries, world-wide.

Developing countries

These countries also show a growing interest in international arbitration, provided they too can have a piece of the arbitration cake. For this it is indispensable to find qualified arbitrators in those countries as well. I refer to a well known saying 'an arbitration is as good as the arbitrators'. In view of the trend of increased use of arbitration in international matters and the growing interest from the side of developing countries I must express the hope that the

* Speech delivered at the dinner in the Hall of the Middle Temple, on March 26, 1985 to celebrate the establishment of the School of International Arbitration.

School will also attract participants from developing countries and perhaps will stimulate their presence by grants.

The programme of the School is not yet known to me. However, I am convinced that it will be *truly international*. That means that students should be made aware of different systems of arbitration and different systems of substantive law existing in the world of today.

The curriculum will certainly deal with *procedural problems* of international arbitration. They are manifold, ranging from the conclusion of a valid arbitration agreement to the end, the award. To mention only a few examples, different systems exist as to the choice of arbitrators and, during the proceedings, the taking of evidence. Problems may arise in respect of the competence of arbitrators; I would also refer to the question of separability of the arbitration clause. Or in the making of the award: refusal to sign by an arbitrator, dissenting opinions, and the reasons to be given. Also, the problems of how to reduce the costs of international commercial arbitration and how to prevent protracted proceedings, should not be neglected.

Apart from these procedural problems which can easily be multiplied – think of multi-party arbitration in the construction business – there are also problems of *substance*. The choice of applicable law or even no specific law at all but rather the *lex mercatoria*. This has to do with the rules to be applied to the substance of the dispute. Here again, the students should be aware of the fact that different systems of law exist. An introduction to *comparative law* may well be included in the curriculum of the School.

The distinction I have made between procedural and substantive aspects is, when dealing with arbitration, a useful one. It is also reflected in the programme of the next ICCA Congress in New York, in May 1986. Two subjects will be dealt with. The first is 'Comparative Arbitration Practice' on the basis of a hypothetical case, arbitration as practised in different parts of the world, will be considered. The second subject is more of a substantive nature: 'The Role of Public Policy in International Commercial Arbitration'. Both these subjects require a great deal of *research*, a task the School also has ahead of it.

The *comparative approach*, both on procedural questions and on substantive issues, leads to an *open mind*. One becomes aware of other systems than the system with which one is familiar. It may even lead to the conclusion that other systems, both procedural or in substance, may be as good or even better than one's own. The students who graduate from the School should leave the School with an open mind to different approaches on substance as well as forms of procedure. They, like the School, should be *truly international* in spirit.

Although it may seem that my remarks were in particular aimed at lawyers being trained as international arbitrators, I would not exclude a *businessman* or *engineer*. Their practical knowledge, their travels around the world, combined with a perfect natural feeling for justice which I have often noticed, may prepare them as well for being good international arbitrators. As far as arbitration is concerned, non-lawyers are also in a position to render legally sound awards. In the application of law, common sense may be the deciding element, and common sense is not a privilege of lawyers alone. I do not know what the School's policy on this matter is, but I would imagine and urge that non-lawyers also be welcome to participate in its courses.

So far, I have let my fantasy run as to *who* could participate and become students of the School: lawyers and non-lawyers, as well as participants from developing countries where arbitration is in the full process of development. I have also ventured to launch some ideas about the *curriculum*: a comparative approach as well in regard to questions of arbitral procedure as to questions of substance that may arise in arbitration. All this to achieve the goal of training truly international arbitrators.

Permit me to make one final remark. We celebrate the birth of the School of International Arbitration. However, arbitration is not the only way to solve disputes. There are large parts of the world where *conciliation* comes as the preferred dispute settlement mechanism. Also, arbitration could lead to a settlement, reached during arbitral proceedings. Then you have the link between the two. The UNCITRAL Arbitration Rules recognised this and introduced in one of the rules the *award on agreed terms*. Whether this can be obtained depends also on the atmosphere that may reign during meetings of the arbitrators with the parties, and this atmosphere, in its turn, depends largely upon the tact of the arbitrators and their chairman. Of course, not every case lends itself to such a solution. The only thing I wanted to say is that, when teaching arbitration, the technique of conciliation should not be neglected.

Queen Mary College has been very courageous in starting this new venture. It is an academic approach, but an approach very closely connected with the realities of the international business world. Arbitration in the sense I have described, is a *service* to the international business community looking for a speedy, efficient, fair and, if possible, less expensive solution for disputes that may always arise out of international relations. I am sure that I speak in the name of all of you, in wishing the School good luck and great success in the fascinating task it has undertaken.

2 The School of International Arbitration: aspirations and objects

Roy Goode

Introduction

The huge growth in the volume and complexity of international arbitration has led to a host of initiatives at national, regional and international level to facilitate the arbitration process. New laws have been enacted, new procedures devised, new arbitral institutions established. The world's leading arbitration centres – London, Paris, Geneva and New York – have highly developed arbitration services and facilities, and around the globe new national and regional centres are coming into being to provide a service to the business community and assistance to the arbitrators.

But hitherto one important element has been lacking. There has been no institution devoted to advanced and systematic teaching, research and scholarly publication in the field of arbitration law and practice. It is this deficiency which the School of International Arbitration is designed to repair. Created with the enthusiastic support of the world's leading arbitration experts and arbitral institutions and launched at this its inaugural international conference, the new School will be a major component of the Centre for Commercial Law Studies here at Queen Mary College, one of the largest multifaculty Schools of the University of London. The Centre, which has acquired an international reputation for its courses, conferences and publications in commercial law, and for its annual Commercial Law Summer School, is itself part of a strong Faculty of Laws engaged in undergraduate and postgraduate teaching and research and in continuing legal education.

The international character of the School

The purpose of this paper is to describe briefly the *raison d'être* of the new School, its philosophy and objectives and the way in which it intends to achieve these – in short, the why, the what and the how of the School of International Arbitration. But first I should like to make a preliminary point which is central to our conception of the School. Though located in London, the School is international in character and outlook. Its function is not to promote any particular national arbitration system or service but to inculcate, through its teaching and research activities, a greater knowledge and understanding of the arbitration processes and underlying principles and rules of law in the world's major legal systems. Its outlook will be international and its method comparative. To that end, it will draw on the knowledge and experience of the distinguished experts from this country and overseas who have agreed to serve on the School's International Advisory Panel and who will be actively involved in the shaping of the School's programmes and curricula.

The involvement of practising experts

From its very inception the Centre for Commercial Law Studies has attached the greatest importance to collaboration with business and the professions, and practising lawyers, bankers and other experts regularly contribute to the Centre's post-experience courses and its Commercial Law Summer School. We regard such collaboration as particularly important in the field of arbitration, and hope to establish close links both with individual experts and with arbitral institutions.

WHY?

It may be asked whether such a practical subject as arbitration merits scholarly study at all. There are several reasons why the answer to this question must be a positive 'yes', and some of these apply equally to other branches of law. The practitioner, be he an arbitrator, a lawyer acting for one of the parties, a technical expert or a party to an arbitration, is at the sharp end of the arbitration process. The academic cannot hope to match the day-to-day working knowledge of the professional, and in the practical handling of arbitration there is no substitute for experience. It is the practitioner who in the first instance receives the raw material from which the law is fashioned. But his role is essentially problem-oriented. He is concerned with that part of arbitration law which is relevant to the solution of the particular problem confronting him. This fact, coupled with the general pressure of work, makes it difficult for even the experienced practitioner either to find the time or to develop the method to survey the subject as a whole, to stand back and examine the present law and evolving practice in a systematic way.

It is here that the scholar can make a contribution, by laying out the subject in a structured fashion, by surveying current practice, by identifying problems and suggesting solutions and by disseminating knowledge through his teaching, research and writings.

International arbitration is particularly appropriate as a subject of academic study because so much of the law is uncertain and derives from evolving practice and from international consensus. Indeed, it is in this area, which involves not only private parties but states, that doctrinal writings can have a particularly powerful influence.

WHAT?

What do we mean by arbitration law? The question is as difficult to answer as the question what is commercial law? My own conception of arbitration law is that it encompasses all principles of law, from whatever source, which bear upon the resolution of disputes referred to arbitration.

Obviously, arbitration law in its narrow sense covers such matters as the arbitration agreement, the appointment, jurisdiction, powers and duties of arbitrators, the relationship between arbitrators and the courts and the enforcement of arbitral awards. But in my view the subject is much broader and more fundamental than a mere collection of technical rules and procedures. For underlying all arbitral disputes are principles of the general law of obligations. Time and again at this conference we have come back to principles of the laws of contract, tort, conflict of laws and public international law. I do not believe that any school of international arbitration worthy of the name can neglect the comparative study of these fundamental subjects upon which the rights of the parties to a dispute so much depend. I therefore regard it as of paramount importance for the new School to develop a body of expertise in the fundamentals of the law of obligations in the major legal families, and in relevant aspects of public and private international law, and for that purpose to engage scholars trained in the civil law and socialist legal systems as well as in the common law.

We must be concerned also with practical questions such as the speed and efficiency of arbitration proceedings. The large international commercial arbitration, involving parties and arbitrators in several countries, raises acute problems of management, and there is much useful work that can be done to identify weaknesses in practice and procedure and to suggest methods of keeping down expense and of speeding up the arbitral process.

Our objectives, then, are to promote a greater knowledge and understanding of the law and practice of national and international arbitration in different legal systems; to help identify ways in which the arbitral process can be improved to the benefit of the parties; and to foster the international exchange of academic and practising experts in this field.

HOW?

Activities

Among its other activities, the School of International Arbitration will:

- offer full-time postgraduate courses in arbitration law and practice, both for law graduates and for non-law graduates (the first such course, a component of the University's LLM programme began in October 1985);
- arrange short courses, conferences and seminars on current legal developments affecting arbitration and specific aspects of arbitration law and practice;
- host meetings of specialists drawn from different disciplines – law, architecture, engineering, finance, among others – to discuss present and emerging problems in the field of international arbitration;
- develop links with national and international organisations involved in arbitration and with universities and research institutes here and overseas interested in this field (we look forward in particular to collaborating with the Chartered Institute of Arbitrators in this country and with the ICC's Institute of International Business Law and Practice in Paris);
- provide international exchanges among scholars and students in the field of arbitration;
- build up a specialist library collection in arbitration law and practice and

collate materials relating to legislation, rules, legal developments and arbitration institutes of different countries;
- in due course, organise an information service on legal developments in arbitration;
- undertake practical studies into ways of making international commercial arbitration faster, cheaper and more effective.

Staffing

The School of International Arbitration will consist of a nucleus of permanent staff headed by an established scholar in the field, together with additional research staff engaged for specific projects and part-time and visiting academics and practitioners from different parts of the world.

These, then, are the aspirations of the new School of International Arbitration within the Centre for Commercial Law Studies at Queen Mary College. I should like to express my indebtedness for the enormous support and good wishes we have received from all over the world and for the invaluable advice given (and, I trust, to be given in the future) by the members of our International Advisory Panel and other good friends, whose involvement and guidance we greatly value.

3 International arbitration – teaching and research

Pierre Lalive

Professor Roy Goode has asked me to say a few words, presumably both as a practitioner of arbitration and as a professor, on the teaching of international arbitration. When wondering on how best to approach such an interesting but rather difficult subject, I thought that a convenient (and perhaps dangerous) starting point might be to try to establish the profile of the 'ideal' international arbitrator – perhaps a suicidal pursuit bound to lead to my immediate disqualification in a few pending cases!

Now, you all know the qualities traditionally mentioned of the 'good' international arbitrator: character, independence, common sense, etc, and, on the professional level (assuming as I do that the international arbitrator should normally be a lawyer) a good general legal training and practical experience in *at least one* national legal system. The arbitrator should have a good command of contract law, commercial law, procedure, private international law and preferably also public international law. On top of this, he should have a certain amount of training in and experience of *comparative law* and the comparative method, while having a good working knowledge and understanding in at least two of the great legal systems of the world, common law, civil law, Moslem law, etc.

While this observation may well seem somewhat abstract or theoretical, it is in my submission of great practical importance. As I have stated elsewhere, 'the arbitrator of today must show proof of a comparative or comparatist mind, open to legal pluralism, to various cultures and various political and social systems'.[1] Let me quote again a great master of arbitration, René David, who wrote: 'arbitration will hardly be regarded by a party as a suitable way of solving the case if it is to be administered by an arbitrator who is imbued with the ways of thinking and the prejudices of another culture'.

Contrary to a view which seems still to be held by many practitioners, I believe that, in the case of an international dispute, *the arbitration also must be 'international'*, which does imply, as a general rule, that it must take place preferably in a third, neutral country ('neutral' in relation to both parties), before an 'international' panel of arbitrators, ie, including arbitrators of different nationalities and backgrounds, and this is not enough, for it should preferably be argued by an 'international' team of lawyers or at least internationally-minded and trained lawyers.

1 Lalive 'Enforcing Awards', in *Sixty Years of ICC Arbitration* 317, at 350.

A common saying, well known to all of you, is that 'an arbitration is worth what the arbitrator is worth'! It expresses an undeniable but very *partial* truth, and I would like to add that 'an arbitration is also worth what *counsel* for the parties are worth' (not to mention what the arbitral institution is worth!).

Yesterday, someone rightly remarked that it was sometimes quite a problem for a party to 'communicate' with an arbitration tribunal, and not easier for a 'common law' counsel to communicate with a 'civil law' arbitrator, and vice versa. And he added that this type of difficulty made it especially necessary for each party to have, inside the tribunal, one 'party-designated arbitrator', able and willing to act 'as a bridge'.

I certainly agree but would like to submit two additional observations:

(a) one should not overestimate (nor of course underestimate) the difficulty of communication between so-called 'civil law' lawyers and so-called 'common law' lawyers; more and more young practitioners, in civil law countries, have spent one or two years in the United States of America or, less frequently, in the United Kingdom and have acquired some knowledge and understanding of the common law, and the converse situation is also true, though perhaps, and regrettably so, to a lesser extent.

(b) Equally (or more) important than to have, inside the arbitration panel, an arbitrator able, while independent, to act 'as a bridge' is for a party to have at least one *counsel* sufficiently trained in foreign law or having a sufficiently 'comparative outlook'. Lack of time unfortunately prevents me from quoting the many examples which come to my mind of cases in which, either as counsel or arbitrator, I noticed the difficulties or damage caused by the fact that very able counsel arguing before an international panel were conducting their case just as if they were appearing before a local court and had visibly no idea that their own national law was neither the sole legal system in the world nor necessarily the most perfect! If I had (which God forbid) to write a book on 'how *not* to win an international case', I would certainly insert at least one chapter on legal nationalism.

To sum up on this point, it seems a fair generalisation to say that, in any important or complex international arbitration case, each side should preferably be represented by an 'international' team of counsel (and/or consultants), by which I do *not* mean only a team composed of counsel of different nationalities or legal backgrounds, but also and foremost counsel trained in comparative and foreign law and specially trained to deal with international arbitral cases.

Many international arbitrators I know frequently note with regret the lack of 'international and comparative outlook', the lack of 'arbitral feeling and diplomacy' evinced by too many counsel, who merely transpose into international arbitration proceedings their traditional national recipes and the 'aggressive' tactics which they use in their own courts.

And this leads me to the School of International Arbitration which, in the light of my preceding observations, is clearly going to fill an important gap. I therefore welcome whole-heartedly Professor Roy Goode's remarkable and timely initiative.

True it is that a lot of valuable work in the same direction is already being done in various countries and, for instance, in some universities or affiliated institutions: the Graduate Institute of International Studies in Geneva, the

Parker School of Foreign and Comparative Law of Columbia University are but two examples I happen to know well, among many others. Professional organisations, on the national or international level (like the International Bar Association or the International Law Association) are increasingly active also in that field of 'permanent education'. As you may know, the ICC sponsored the creation, some five years ago, of the Institute of International Business Law and Practice. There is now in Rome an Institute of International Development Law (IDLI) which has the advice and support of such well-known experts as Messrs Shihata and Delaume, of ICSID, and the list could no doubt be extended. However that may be, a great deal remains to be done and a great deal will doubtless be achieved by the School of International Arbitration of Queen Mary College, London.

Professor Goode has referred to the change – a most unfortunate change – that had occurred in many universities, where the teaching of the law, because of, *inter alia*, the frightening growth of national legislation, has become less and less 'international'. The undeniable fact is that, in most countries today, the part played in a student's *curriculum* by what I would call 'non-national' subjects (ie, public and private international law, comparative law, international trade law and the like) has steadily diminished over the years, paradoxically, at the very time when everyone can observe and should know that the world is becoming more and more international.

In this connection, may I advise you to read carefully an important but too little known text, the Resolution adopted by the Institute of International Law at its Athens session in 1979.[2] After a detailed study of the 'Teaching of International Law' (prepared by a Committee chaired by Professor Zourek), the Institute unanimously passed a resolution which noted with regret that

> 'In many countries law is still taught essentially or even exclusively along the lines of national considerations and methods and that the teaching of international law, whether public or private, is often quantitatively and qualitatively inadequate to meet the demands of our times and is not provided in a sufficiently international perspective, ... [which] entails a host of unfavourable consequences which are often not appreciated or are underestimated and leads, in particular, to inadequate preparation for the needs of contemporary international life in the relations between both individuals and States'.

The text of the whole Resolution would deserve to be quoted in full and should be born in mind by all practitioners and teachers, especially if interested in international arbitration. I shall content myself with mentioning Article 1 of the Athens Resolution which considers it

> 'essential that specific measures be taken in universities, faculties or similar institutions teaching law, economics, political science or international relations to promote development and coherence of all subjects of international relevance ... [and it stresses] the value of the comparative method and its potential contribution towards better international understanding ...'.

To sum up, I should stress again that there remains a great deal to do to

2 See 58–II *Annuaire de l'Institut de Droit International*, 204–209 (1979).

improve first the basic and then the professional training of lawyers (and I dare not speak, before so many representative of those professions, of the training of businessmen or of civil engineers). And I believe that this conclusion applies to legal practitioners from both industrialised and developing countries.

The initiative taken by Professor Goode and Queen Mary College, London, is therefore especially to be welcomed. All the more since, to quote Sir John Donaldson's opening speech on Monday, the intention is to create, not an English school, but an international or rather a 'transnational' school (which is a quite different thing from a national school with a little coat of 'international painting' on top). Professor Goode has made that intention totally clear and this, in my respectful submission, is going to be a key to the School's future and international influence.

One of the great obstacles to a smooth functioning of international arbitration and to its success is the narrow national (not to say nationalist) outlook of many practitioners and the misconception that international arbitration is by and large nothing more than an extension of national, domestic methods, which they try consciously or not to impose on others. Some of you may recall that, a few years ago, in another London conference, I observed with typical lack of tact that, for some of my English friends, the *ideal* international arbitration seemed to be arbitration in London by parties represented by English counsel arguing before English arbitrators applying English law and supervised by English judges! And a similar remark could doubtless be made in my own country. While this may admittedly be a good solution in some cases, I venture to think that, for most parties, it would hardly be a true and satisfactory 'international arbitration'. It is indeed most gratifying to hear that Professor Goode and the Master of the Rolls have emphasised the necessary *transnational* character of the School of International Arbitration, to which we all extend our warmest congratulations and wishes of success.

Part 2

The jurisdiction and authority of arbitrators

ICSID arbitration 4

Georges R Delaume

The International Centre for the Settlement of Investment Disputes (ICSID) provides international methods for the settlement of disputes between states and investors.

ICSID differs from other arbitration institutions in several respects:

(a) Unlike commercial arbitration institutions, ICSID is a specialised international organisation created by the Washington Convention, which came into force in 1966.[1]

(b) ICSID is an organisation closely associated with The World Bank. This association entails two important consequences. Like The World Bank, the paramount objective of ICSID is to promote a climate of mutual confidence between states and investors favourable to increasing the flow of resources to developing countries under reasonable conditions. ICSID, therefore, cannot be viewed solely as a dispute settlement machinery. It must be regarded instead as an instrument of international policy for the promotion of economic development.

Another consequence of the association between ICSID and The World Bank is that, because The World Bank subsidises ICSID, the cost of ICSID arbitration is significantly lower than that of commercial arbitration.[2]

(c) ICSID arbitration proceedings take place in the context of truly international norms set forth in the ICSID Convention and the Regulations and Rules adopted for its implementation.[3] Unlike

1 Convention on the Settlement of Investment Disputes between States and Nationals of Other States, October 14, 1966.

2 Unlike commercial arbitration institutions, which require at the outset the deposit of funds calculated to cover full administrative charges, ICSID's practice is to request from time to time from the parties advance payment to cover estimated expenditure for periods of three to six months (Administrative and Financial Regulations 14(3)(a)). Also with a view toward economy, the fees of arbitrators are set at a stated amount (at present SDR600) per day of work.

ICSID also performs a number of services free of charge. Such is the case with regard to services supplied by the Secretariat prior to the constitution of the arbitral tribunal and on request, the appointment of arbitrators by the Chairman of the Administrative Council of ICSID. See text and note 42 *infra*.

3 The ICSID Regulations and Rules were originally issued in 1968. They were revised in 1984. The text of the Convention and of the Revised Regulations and Rules is published in a single brochure: Doc ICSID/15 which can be obtained on request addressed to: International Center for Settlement of Investment Disputes, 1818 H Street, NW, Washington, DC 20433. Telephone: (202) 477 4943.

commercial arbitration, which can never be fully insulated from the reach of domestic law and the control of domestic courts, ICSID constitutes a self-contained machinery operating in total independence from domestic legal systems. In the context of ICSID, the sole role of domestic courts is one of judicial assistance intended to facilitate the recognition of ICSID awards and to increase their effectiveness.

(d) ICSID arbitration is compulsory arbitration. Once the parties have consented to ICSID arbitration, each of them is assured that neither of them can unilaterally withdraw its consent. If one of the parties defaults or does not cooperate in the conduct of the proceedings, the ICSID Convention provides the means for the proceedings to go on and to lead eventually to an award whose recognition is assured in all of the 87 states that have ratified the Washington Convention.[4]

(e) ICSID arbitration is intended to maintain a careful balance between the interests of investors and those of Contracting States.

The Washington Convention gives investors direct access to an international forum and enables investors to provide in an investment agreement that disputes will be decided under rules of international law.[5]

In exchange, the Washington Convention protects Contracting States from other forms of foreign or international litigation. Because consent to ICSID arbitration is just as binding upon the investor as it is on the state party to the dispute, that state is assured that the investor cannot bring suit in a non-ICSID forum whether in the investor's state or elsewhere.[6] Furthermore, the Washington Convention expressly provides that when an investor and a Contracting State have agreed to have recourse to ICSID, the state whose national is the investor may not espouse the case of its national, give that national diplomatic protection, or bring an international claim in respect of the dispute.[7]

ICSID arbitration has significant and original implications both as to matters of substance and of procedure. The point is well illustrated by ICSID's record as well as by the new activities that ICSID has assumed in order to be of further assistance to transnational litigants in quest of a smooth and effective settlement of disputes between them.

ICSID's record

ICSID's caseload

The caseload of ICSID has significantly and steadily increased in the last few years. ICSID had a relatively slow start. Between 1966 and 1981, only nine disputes had been submitted to ICSID arbitration. From 1981 to the time of

4 The number of ICSID members exceeds by far that of states parties to the New York Convention.

5 See text and notes 31–38 *infra*.

6 Article 26 of the Washington Convention. The exclusive character of ICSID arbitration has been acknowledged recently by a French court. See Court of Appeal of Rennes October 26, 1984. For discussion of this feature of the Washington Convention, see Delaume, 'ICSID Arbitration and the Courts', 77 *Am J Intl L* 784 (1983).

7 Washington Convention, Article 27. In this connection, see Shihata, 'ICSID and Latin American', *News from ICSID*, Vol 1, No 2 (Summer 1984), p 203.

writing, thirteen new proceedings have been instituted, ten of which relate to arbitration, two to conciliation and one concerns the annulment of an award.[8]

At this time, ten proceedings are pending. Of the twelve proceedings that have been concluded, only five resulted in an award on the merits and seven were either discontinued or amicably settled. This high proportion of settlements is a characteristic feature of the ICSID machinery. It is consistent with the objectives of ICSID and should increase as a result of the availability of new procedures intended to facilitate such settlements.[9]

The effectiveness of ICSID cannot, however, be assessed only on the basis of the number of disputes that have been submitted to arbitration under its rules. Because the Washington Convention provides for compulsory arbitration, it is to be assumed that the prospect of involvement in proceedings from which there is no escape is a deterrent to the institution of proceedings and cannot but encourage the parties to settle their differences by agreement. There are, of course, no statistics in point, since the parties have no obligation to disclose such arrangements to the Secretariat. Nor is it possible, for the same reason, to assess the number of ICSID arbitration clauses in existence. In this respect, however, it is clear that that number must exceed by far that of the clauses which have been communicated to the Secretariat.[10] As a matter of fact, it is to be noted that the majority of ICSID proceedings have been based on consent clauses of which the Secretariat was not aware before the institution of the proceedings. In the same connection, it is also significant that clauses not previously disclosed to the Secretariat appear from time to time in specialised publications,[11] or surface on the occasion of queries addressed to the Secretariat regarding matters of drafting and other issues.

Issues that have been considered in the context of proceedings

The 'jurisdiction' of ICSID

Pursuant to Article 25 of the Washington Convention, ICSID arbitration is open to the parties to investment disputes provided that three basic conditions are fulfilled. First, the parties must agree to submit their dispute to ICSID. Second, the dispute must be between a Contracting State (or one of its subdivisions or agencies) and a national of another Contracting State. Third, the dispute must be a legal dispute arising out of an investment.

Consent, the identity of the parties and the nature of the dispute are thus the three basic conditions that must be present to satisfy the requirements of the Washington Convention and to give ICSID 'jurisdiction'.[12]

8 A recent brochure (ICSID/16) entitled *ICSID Cases: 1972–1984*, consolidates information on ICSID proceedings and references to published awards, and the relevant literature.

9 See text and notes 60–2 *infra.*

10 More than three hundred clauses are found in the archives of ICSID.

11 In particular Barrows, *Petroleum Legislation (Basic Oil Laws and Concession Contracts).*

12 The term 'jurisdiction' of ICSID 'is used in the Convention as a convenient expression to mean the limits within which the provisions of the Convention will apply and the facilities of the Centre will be available for conciliation and arbitration proceedings' (report of the Executive Directors of The World Bank on the Convention, paragraph 22).

Under Article 41(1) of the Washington Convention an ICSID arbitral tribunal is judge of its own 'competence'. That term includes the determination of the question whether the requirements of the Washington Convention are satisfied and issues relating to whether the tribunal is 'competent' in the sense that it is properly constituted or that the dispute is not already *alibi pendens.*

Interestingly enough, one of these conditions, ie, that relating to the nature of the dispute, has raised no serious problem. In this respect, it should be recalled that the Washington Convention does not define the term 'investment'. This lack of definition, which was deliberate, has enabled the Convention to accommodate both traditional types of investment in the form of capital contributions and new types of investment, including service contracts and transfers of technology.[13]

A number of disputes submitted to ICSID arbitration relate to the modern concept of investment. Since no objection to the jurisdiction of ICSID has been raised in these proceedings, it must be inferred that the parties subscribe to the view that, for the purposes of the Convention, the term 'investment' should be broadly construed and should include contemporary types of association between investors and states, even when those are limited to the supply of technology or other services.

In contrast, the issue of consent has been raised in several proceedings. The first of these concerned a dispute between Jamaica and foreign investors.[14] Before it is considered, it should be noted that ratification of the Washington Convention is, on the part of a Contracting State, only an expression of its willingness to make use of the ICSID machinery. As such, ratification does not constitute an obligation to use that machinery. That obligation can arise only after the Contracting State concerned has specifically agreed to submit a particular dispute or classes of disputes to ICSID arbitration. In other words, the decision of a state to consent to ICSID arbitration is a matter of pure policy and it is within the sole discretion of each Contracting State to determine the type of investment disputes that it considers arbitrable in the context of ICSID.

Under Article 25 of the Convention, any Contracting State may notify ICSID, either at the time of ratification or at any time thereafter, of the class or classes of disputes that it would or would not consider arbitrable under ICSID. So far only five Contracting States have made such a notification.[15] Jamaica is one of these states. However, Jamaica's notification was made after it had already concluded investment agreements with foreign companies for the mining and the processing of bauxite. Each of these agreements provided for ICSID arbitration.

In 1974, contrary to a provision regarding the 'stabilisation' of the relevant tax system, Jamaica decided unilaterally to increase significantly the taxes

13 The type of investments involved in ICSID disputes are listed in *ICSID Cases: 1972–1984*. See also, Delaume 'ICSID Clauses: Some Drafting Problems', *News from ICSID*, Vol 1, No 2 (Summer 1984), 16, at 18–19.

14 *Alcoa Minerals of Jamaica Inc/Kaiser Bauxite Co/Reynolds Jamaica Mines Ltd and Reynolds Metals Co* v *The Government of Jamaica* (1975) *ICSID ARB* 74/2, an unpublished award. See Schmidt, 'Arbitration under the Auspices of the International Centre for Settlement of Investment Disputes (ICSID): Implications of the Decision on Jurisdiction in Alcoa Minerals of Jamaica Inc v Government of Jamaica', 17 *Harv Intl L J* 90 (1976).

15 Saudi Arabia has stated that it intends to exclude investment disputes relating to 'oil and pertaining to acts of sovereignty'; Guyana and Jamaica have excluded disputes concerning their 'minerals and other natural resources'. Papua-New Guinea has specified that 'it will only consider submitting those disputes to the Centre which are fundamental to the investment itself' and Israel has declared that it shall consider submitting to ICSID only disputes related to an approved investment under one of the Israeli laws for the Encouragement of Capital Investments. See *Doc ICSID/8* (revised as of March 1, 1984).

payable by the investors. One month before that decision was published, Jamaica notified ICSID that it intended to exclude from its consent disputes arising out of 'an investment relating to mineral and other resources and sought to give retrospective effect to that notification. Immediately after the enactment of the new tax legislation, the investors affected by it instituted ICSID arbitration proceedings. The arbitral tribunals, despite objections to their jurisdiction formulated by Jamaica, held that the disputes concerned 'investments' and that since the initial consent of Jamaica had been unconditional and unqualified, no retrospective effect could be given to the 1974 declaration.[16]

In *Amco-Asia et al* v *The Republic of Indonesia*,[17] the respondent objected to the jurisdiction of the tribunal on the ground, *inter alia*, that consent to ICSID arbitration by a state should be construed 'restrictively' since it constituted a limitation to the state's sovereignty. The tribunal disagreed and held that the agreement to arbitrate:

> '... is not to be construed restrictively, nor as a matter of fact, broadly or liberally. It is to be construed in a way which leads to find out and to respect the common will of the parties: such a method of interpretation is but the application of the fundamental principle pacta sunt servanda, a principle common, indeed, to all systems of internal law and to international law.'[18]

A matter of great practical significance has been raised in certain proceedings. Investment agreements are often concluded in stages, over a protracted period of time. Several arrangements may thus be concluded, the sum of which constitutes the 'agreement' between the parties. If, for some reason, an ICSID clause is stipulated in one agreement and the clause is not repeated, or expressly incorporated by reference in the other agreements, it is not excluded that one of the parties may, at the time of a dispute, challenge the jurisdiction of an ICSID tribunal in regard to disputes concerning such other agreements. This is an issue which was raised in the case of *Holiday Inns/Occidental Petroleum Corporation* v *The Government of Morocco*, which will be discussed in another context.[19] In that case, the tribunal held that:

> 'It would not be consonant either with economic reality or with the intention of the parties to consider each of [the agreements] in complete isolation from the others.'[20]

Substantially the same approach was followed in *Klockner et al* v *United*

16 As stated in one of the decisions:

> 'In the present case the written consent was contained in the arbitration clause between the Government and Alcoa ... This consent having been given could not be withdrawn. The notification under Article 25 only operates for the future by way of information to the Centre and potential future investors in undertakings concerning minerals and other natural resources of Jamaica.'

Any other conclusion:

> 'would largely, if not wholly, deprive the Convention of any practical value.'

(Quoted from Schmidt, *op cit*, note 14 *supra*, at 103.)

17 23 *ILM* 351 (1984).

18 Paragraph 14 of the award. The tribunal upheld its jurisdiction not only with regard to the original investor but to an assignee of the investor; see paragraphs 27 to 31 of the award.

19 P Lalive, 'The First "World Bank" Arbitration (Holiday Inns v Morocco) – Some Legal Problems', 51 *British Yearbook of International Law* 123 (1980).

20 *Ibid*, at 159.

Republic of Cameroon et al,[21] which involved a number of interrelated agreements. A similar issue has arisen in a proceeding which is pending and cannot, therefore, be disclosed.

Another series of jurisdictional objections have been formulated in certain proceedings in connection with the nationality requirement specified in the Washington Convention in regard to juridical persons.[22]

Within the framework of the Washington Convention, the nationality of a corporation is determined on the basis of its *siège social* or place of incorporation. Consequently, a business association incorporated in Contracting State A and investing in Contracting State B is eligible to be a party to an ICSID clause and to avail itself of ICSID facilities if the need arises. Conversely, a juridical person incorporated in the Contracting State party to the dispute would not be so eligible.

Although this is the principle, it is qualified in the sense that a juridical person incorporated in the host state can still be regarded as the national of another Contracting State if 'because of foreign control', the parties have agreed that it should be treated as such for the purposes of the Convention. This provision is intended to account for the rather common situation in which a host government insists that foreign investors channel their investment through a locally incorporated company. In the absence of this qualification of the general rule, such a company could not resort to ICSID facilities, notwithstanding its foreign elements.

This is an issue which arose in the case of *Holiday Inns/Occidental Petroleum Corporation* v *The Government of Morocco*.[23] In that case, a Swiss and a US corporation had entered in 1966 into a Basic Agreement with the Government of Morocco. The Agreement provided for the construction and operation of four hotels in Morocco through subsidiaries, incorporated in Morocco, of the parent companies. A dispute arose and the parent companies submitted to ICSID a request for arbitration not only in their own name but also on behalf of their subsidiaries.

The ICSID arbitration clause did not expressly state that the Moroccan subsidiaries were to be treated as foreign entities because they were under the 'foreign control' of the parent companies. Morocco took the position that, since it had not agreed to treat the subsidiaries as foreign nationals, the tribunal had no jurisdiction to hear their claims. This argument succeeded. The tribunal held that Article 25(2)(b) makes an exception to the general rule that the Convention does not apply to disputes between a Contracting State and one of its nationals and that, under the circumstances, one would expect that an agreement regarding the foreign control of a local company should be explicit.

However, in *Amco-Asia et al* v *The Republic of Indonesia*,[24] the tribunal held

21 Award of October 21, 1983. The award has not been published in full. However, exerpts appear in *News from ICSID*, Vol 1 No 2 (Summer 1984), p 7; 111 *Clunet* 409 (1984). See also Paulsson, 'The ICSID Klockner v Cameroon Award: The Duties of Partners in North–South Economic Development Agreements', 1 *Journal of International Arbitration* 145 (1984).

22 According to the Washington Convention, the investor must be a 'national' of another Contracting State. The term 'national' applies to both natural and juridical persons. However, so far all ICSID proceedings have involved corporations only.

23 See note 19, *supra*.

24 See note 17, *supra*.

otherwise. In that case, an American investor had submitted an application to the Government of Indonesia relating to the establishment of a 'foreign business', in the form of an Indonesian company. The company was established but was not expressly acknowledged as being the national of another Contracting State for the purposes of the Washington Convention and, the respondent relied on the *Holiday Inns* case to argue that the requirement set forth in Article 25(2)(b) of the Convention was not satisfied, and that, therefore, the tribunal lacked jurisdiction.

The tribunal disagreed and distinguished the *Holiday Inns* award. The tribunal noted that the Convention does not require that the agreement of the parties as to the 'foreign control' of a locally incorporated company be stated in formal fashion. The tribunal said:

> 'What is needed, for the final provision of article 25(2)(b) to be applicable, is, 1° that the juridical person party to the dispute be legally a national of a Contracting State which is the other party and 2° that this jurisdictional person being under the foreign control, to the knowledge of the Contracting State, the parties agree to treat it as a foreign juridical person.'[25]

In the tribunal's view these two conditions were fulfilled, because the application submitted by the applicant referred to the establishment of a 'foreign business' and was, therefore, acknowledged to be under 'foreign control'. By agreeing to the application, the respondent knew that the local company would be under foreign control. By approving the application and the ICSID clause in it, it was 'crystal clear' that the respondent 'agreed to treat the local company as a national of another Contracting State, for the purpose of the Convention.' In this connection the tribunal said also:

> 'To refer to the *Holiday Inns* award – in spite of the same not being a binding precedent in this case – here, this agreement is by no means implied; it is expressed, and clearly expressed, no formal or ritual clause being provided for in the Convention, nor needed in order for such an agreement to be binding on the parties.'[26]

The lack of specificity of the ICSID clause regarding the specific nationality of the foreign interests controlling the local company was also considered irrelevant in the circumstances of the case.

The tribunal noted that:

> '[T]here is no provision in the Convention imposing a formal indication, in the arbitration clause itself, of the nationality of the foreign juridical or natural persons who control the juridical person having the nationality of the Contracting State, party to the dispute.'[27]

The tribunal found that in view of the facts, and in particular of the content of the application which referred to the applicant as a United States corporation, represented by its President, a United States citizen, and to the fact that the local company would be managed under the control of the applicant, the

25 Award, paragraph 14(ii).
26 *Ibid.*
27 Paragraph 14(iii).

nationality of the local company had been clearly identified in a document approved by the respondent.[28]

Similar solutions have obtained in two other decisions of ICSID tribunals on matters of jurisdiction, which, however, have not been published and must, therefore, remain confidential.

A novel issue may arise in *Maritime International Nominees Establishment (MINE)* v *The Republic of Guinea*. The issue concerns the nationality of MINE and was the object of attention in the context of proceedings between the parties in United States courts.[29] MINE is a Lichtenstein company. However, the ICSID arbitration clause provides that: 'The parties hereby precise [sic] that the investor is Swiss'. The provocative question is whether the parties to an ICSID clause may agree upon the nationality of a company which (unlike in the case of a company incorporated in the state party to the dispute but under 'foreign control') is a company incorporated in a third state. All that can be said at this time is that a request for arbitration submitted by MINE was registered on September 18, 1984, however 'without prejudice' to the issue of MINE's nationality.[30]

Issues of applicable law

Much has been written about Article 42 of the Washington Convention.[31] This provision acknowledges party autonomy in the choice of the legal rules, whether domestic or international, applicable to the relationship arising out of

28 In the same connection, the tribunal was asked to consider another argument of the respondent, namely that the true 'controller' of the local company was not the applicant but a Mr X, a Dutch citizen residing in Hong Kong, who himself controlled the applicant. It refused:

> 'To take this argument into consideration, the Tribunal would have to admit first that for the purpose of Article 25-2(b) of the Convention, one should not take into account the legal nationality of the foreign juridical person which controls the local one, but the nationality of the juridical or natural persons who control the controlling juridical person itself: in other words, to take care of a control at the second, and possibly third, fourth or *x*th degree.
>
> Such a reasoning is, in law, not in accord with the Convention. Indeed, the concept of nationality is there a classical one, based on the law under which the juridical person has been incorporated, the place of incorporation and the place of the social seat. An exception is brought to this concept in respect of juridical persons having the nationality, thus, defined, of the Contracting State party to the dispute, where said juridical persons are under foreign control. But no exception to the classical concept is provided for when it comes to the nationality of the foreign controller, even supposing – which is not at all clearly stated in the Convention – that the fact the controller is the national of one or another foreign State is to be taken into account.'

Paragraph 14(iii).

29 Delaume, 'ICSID Arbitration and the Courts', 77 *Am J Intl L* 784 (1983).

30 *News from ICSID*, Vol 2, No 1 (Winter 1985).

31 Article 42 reads as follows:

> '(1) The Tribunal shall decide a dispute in accordance with such rules of law as may be agreed by the parties. In the absence of such agreement, the Tribunal shall apply the law of the Contracting State party to the dispute (including its rules on the conflict of laws) and such rules of international law as may be applicable.
>
> (2) The Tribunal may not bring in a finding of non liquet on the ground of silence or obscurity of the law.
>
> (3) The provisions of paragraphs (1) and (2) shall not prejudice the power of the Tribunal to decide a dispute ex aequo et bono if the parties so agree.'

an investment. In addition, Article 42 provides that, in the absence of an express stipulation of the applicable law, the arbitral tribunal shall apply the law of the Contracting State party to the dispute (including its rules on the conflict of laws) and such rules of international law as may be applicable.

However, if one leaves scholarly discussion aside, one must acknowledge that, in the light of experience, this provision has not been the object of dramatic contractual or arbitral developments.

An analysis of the stipulations of applicable law in agreements providing for ICSID arbitration shows that these stipulations do not substantially differ from those found in other economic development agreements. Depending upon the circumstances, the parties provide for the application of domestic law or seek to 'internationalise' the relationship.[32]

Out of five ICSID awards on the merits, only three have been published.

The award in *AGIP SpA* v *Government of the People's Republic of the Congo*,[33] shows clearly the importance of precise drafting in relation to effective conflict avoidance. In that case, the investment agreement between AGIP, an Italian company, and the Congolese Government provided that the agreement was governed by:

> 'la loi congolaise, complétée le cas échéant par tout principe de droit international. (Congolese law supplemented, if needed by any principle of international law).'

The agreement included also a 'stabilisation' clause freezing Congolese law in point of time.

In 1975, the Congolese Government nationalised AGIP. In October 1977, AGIP instituted ICSID proceedings. The arbitral tribunal rendered a unanimous award in November 1979.

According to AGIP the expression *complétée* (supplemented) following the reference to Congolese law in the above quoted provision meant not only that international law might be relied upon to fill gaps in the Congolese legislation, but implied that both Congolese and international law should be applicable.

The award, although it does not precisely solve this issue of interpretation, nevertheless notes:

> 'le caractère irrégulier, au regard de ce droit (international law) des mesures de nationalisation intervenues dans la présente affaire. (The irregular character in regard to (international law) of the measures of nationalization involved in this case.)'[34]

The dispute was settled in favour of AGIP on the ground that the measure of nationalisation was contrary to the stabilisation clause in the investment agreement.

Klockner Industries et al v *Republique Unie du Cameroun*,[35] also raises an

32 Delaume, *Transnational Contracts*, Chapter XV, paragraph 15.24. For other issues of applicable law, see *ibid*, Chapter I, paragraph 1.01; Chapter II, paragraph 2.03; Chapter III, paragraph 3.03 and Chapter IV, paragraph 4.06.

33 Award of November 4, 1977, 64 *Rivista di Diritto Internazionale* 863 (1981) (French original); 21 *ILM* 762 (1982) (English translation); VIII *Yearbook: Commercial Arbitration* 133, (1983) (English translation).

34 Paragraph 88 of the Award.

35 See note 21, *supra*.

interesting issue. The agreement between the parties did not contain a stipulation of the applicable law. The tribunal held that the law applicable was that of Cameroon. The tribunal was then faced with an additional question. The Cameroonian legal system is not unified. As a result of Cameroon's colonial heritage, both English common law and French law continue to apply respectively in the anglophonic and francophonic parts of that country. The tribunal had, therefore, to determine which system of law was applicable.

Referring to Article 42 of the Convention, the tribunal noted that it should apply the law of Cameroon 'including its rules on the conflict of laws'. Considering that the agreements involved had been executed in Yaoundé and that the investment was also located in the francophonic part of Cameroon, the tribunal concluded that, in accordance with the domestic conflicts rules of Cameroon, French law was the applicable law.[36]

Société Benvenuti & Bonfant SARL v *Government of the People's Republic of the Congo*,[37] concerned the issue whether, in the absence of an initial stipulation of the applicable law, the parties may subsequently exercise their option and determine the applicable law either before the institution of the proceedings or during the proceedings. In that case, the investment agreement contained no stipulation of the applicable law. During the proceedings the parties agreed that the tribunal should decide the case *ex aequo et bono*. The tribunal complied with this agreement.

Procedural issues

As already mentioned, the Washington Convention provides a self-contained dispute settlement machinery governed by truly international rules. To review the application of these rules in detail would require a separate study.[38] A few significant issues can, however, be identified.

Issues regarding the constitution of arbitral tribunals illustrate both the flexibility of the ICSID Rules and the effectiveness of the ICSID machinery.

In order to provide for the many situations that may arise in arbitration proceedings, most of the provisions of the Washington Convention regarding the number of arbitrators and the method for their appointment are permissive and apply only in the absence of specific agreement between the parties.[39]

36 Notwithstanding its reference to Article 42 of the Convention, this decision does not quite fit under that provision. The reference in Article 42 to the conflicts rules of the host State relates, rightly or wrongly, to a case of *renvoi*, ie, to the law of another State. See Delaume, *Transnational Contracts*, Chapter IV, paragraph 4.06.

In *Klockner*, the tribunal was faced simply with the issue of 'internal' or 'domestic' conflicts within a federation.

37 Delaume, *Transnational Contracts*, Chapter II, paragraphs 2.04–2.05.

38 This study will appear in Delaume, *Transnational Contracts*, Chapter XV.

39 The only mandatory provisions found in the Washington Convention are those according to which: (1) an arbitral tribunal composed of more than a sole arbitrator must include an uneven number of arbitrators (Washington Convention, Article 37(2)); and (ii) the majority of the arbitrators must be nationals of a State other than the State party to the dispute or the State whose national is a party to the dispute (Washington Convention, Article 39). Exceptions to this last rule are possible, however, if the parties agree jointly to appoint each and every member of the tribunal. This was done in the case of *Société Ouest Africaine des Betons Industriels (SOABI)* v *The State of Senegal* (Case ARB/82/1), in which one arbitrator had the nationality of the claimant (Belgian), another arbitrator was a national of the respondent State, and the President of the tribunal was a national of a third country (The Netherlands).

In the selection of arbitrators, the parties are free to choose persons whose names appear on the Panel of Arbitrators maintained by the ICSID Secretariat or from outside the Panel. In practice, both options have been used.

Anticipating the possibility that one of the parties may refuse to cooperate in the appointment of arbitrators, the Convention provides that the Chairman of the Administrative Council of ICSID,[40] shall at the request of either party, and after consulting both parties so far as possible,[41] appoint the arbitrator or arbitrators not yet appointed. In practice, the Chairman has acted as appointing authority in the majority of ICSID proceedings either at the time of the constitution of the tribunal or during the proceedings, following the death or resignation of arbitrators. Unlike the parties, the Chairman's freedom of choice is limited, since he must appoint persons whose names appear on the Panel of Arbitrators.[42]

The self-contained character of the ICSID machinery entails a number of consequences, three of which deserve mention.

In the context of ICSID arbitration, the seat of arbitration does not have the same significance as it has in regard to other types of arbitration, be it *ad hoc* or institutional arbitration, which remain subject to a greater or lesser extent to domestic law. In fact, in the case of ICSID, the place of arbitration is legally immaterial and its determination is one of pure convenience.

Under Article 62 of the Washington Convention, the seat of arbitration is normally situated in Washington, DC, where ICSID has its headquarters. However, pursuant to Article 63, the parties may agree that the proceedings take place in another location. Two situations must be distinguished. The parties are free to decide that the proceedings may be held at the seat of the Permanent Court of Arbitration, in The Hague, or at the seat of any other institution with which ICSID may make appropriate arrangements.[43] The parties may also choose any other location, subject, however, to obtaining the approval of the arbitral tribunal and after consultation with the Secretary-General of ICSID.[44] In practice, the location of ICSID proceedings has been about equally distributed between Washington, DC and European cities.[45]

Because of the exclusive character of consent to ICSID arbitration, the parties are assured that neither of them can have recourse to proceedings other

40 The Administrative Council is the plenary organ of ICSID. The Chairman is, *ex officio*, the President of The World Bank.

41 Consultation with the parties is the rule and, in most cases, the parties have responded by cooperating with the Chairman. In this respect, ICSID's practice contrasts favourably with that of other arbitration institutions, such as the ICC. Under the ICC Rules, appointments are made by the ICC Court of Arbitration upon recommendations from national committees. See Craig, Park and Paulsson, *International Chamber of Commerce Arbitration* (New York 1984), paragraph 12.03.

42 Washington Convention, Article 38 and 40(1).

43 These type of arrangements have been made with the Asian-African Legal Consultative Committee's Regional Offices in Kuala-Lumpur and in Cairo. See 22 *ILM* 522 (1984), at p 524.

44 On occasion, the parties to ICSID clauses provide in the clause itself that the seat of arbitration shall be located in a certain city (such as London, Paris, or Geneva, or in a city in the territory of the State party to the clause). This type of provision could not be enforced as such, but is clearly to be given consideration by arbitral tribunals at the time of the preliminary procedural consultation with the parties (see Arbitration Rule 20).

45 *ICSID Cases: 1972–1984.*

than those that they have voluntarily provided for. This rule has now been acknowledged by the courts of the United States and France.

The American decisions in point, which involved the dispute between MINE and Guinea,[46] are not as clear as they should have been because they are based on considerations of domestic law (in this case the Foreign Sovereign Immunities Act 1976)[47] rather than on the Convention itself. However, the recent decision of the Court of Appeal of Rennes in the case of *République Populaire Révolutionnaire de Guinée et al* v *Société Atlantic Triton*,[48] is squarely in point. In that case, Atlantic Triton, a Norwegian company, and Guinea had entered into an agreement for the conversion of vessels into fishing vessels and for the training of crews. In accordance with an ICSID arbitration clause in the contract, Atlantic Triton submitted to the Secretary-General of ICSID a request for the institution of proceedings. The request was registered on January 19, 1984. An ICSID tribunal was constituted on August 1, 1984. On October 12, 1983, ie *before* the submission of the request, Atlantic Triton obtained from a French commercial court an order of attachment concerning three Guinean vessels under repairs in a French port. The order was confirmed on April 6, 1984, ie *after* the registration of the request. On appeal, the Court of Appeal of Rennes vacated the attachment on the ground that the arbitral tribunal had 'general and exclusive competence to decide not only in regard to the merits, but also in respect of any provisional measures' and that, consequently, the French courts had no jurisdiction on the matter.

The third illustration of the self-contained machinery provided by the Washington Convention is found in the annulment proceeding that has been instituted against the *Klockner* v *Cameroon* award.[49] Under the Washington Convention, an award is final and binding upon the parties.[50] The only remedies against an award are limited to revision (on the ground of newly discovered facts 'of such a nature as decisively to affect the award,'[51]) and annulment, on specific and limited grounds.[52] Consistent with the system set up in the Convention, these remedies must be exercised under the auspices of ICSID. In other words, and in contrast with awards within the scope of other international conventions,[53] ICSID awards are not open to attack on any ground (not even on the ground of public policy) in the courts of Contracting States. At the time of writing, an annulment proceeding (the first in the history of ICSID) is pending and no more can be said about it.

The effectiveness of ICSID awards

Under the Washington Convention, awards are not only binding on the parties, but each Contracting States is bound to recognise any such awards and enforce the pecuniary obligations imposed by the award as if it were a final judgment of a court in the recognising state.[54]

46 See text and note 29, *supra*.
47 *Ibid*.
48 See note 6, *supra*.
49 See *ICSID Cases: 1972–1984*.
50 Washington Convention, Article 53(1).
51 *Ibid*, Article 51.
52 *Ibid*, Article 52.
53 See, eg, the New York Convention, Article V.
54 Washington Convention, Article 54(1).

The procedure for the recognition and enforcement of ICSID awards is made as simple as possible. Under Article 54(2) of the Convention, any party to an ICSID award may obtain recognition and enforcement of the award by furnishing to the competent court or other authority designated for the purpose by each Contracting State, a certified copy of the award.[55]

An illustration of the effectiveness of this procedure is found in a French decision giving recognition to the award rendered in the case of *Benvenuti & Bonfant* v *Congo*,[56] in which the Court said that:

> '[The provisions of the ICSID Convention] offer a simplified procedure for recognition and enforcement (*exequatur simplifié*) and restrict the function of the court designated for the purposes of the Convention by each Contracting State to ascertaining the authenticity of the award certified by the Secretary-General of the International Centre for Settlement of Investment Disputes.'

The court proceeded to recognise the award.[57]

Once it is recognised, an ICSID award becomes an executory title. As such it can be enforced readily against an investor or its assets.

The situation might be otherwise if enforcement is sought against the state party to the dispute. The reason is that the Convention,[58] does not alter or supersede the rules of immunity from execution against a state which would fail to comply with an ICSID award. The effectiveness of measures of execution against a state depends therefore, upon the immunity rules prevailing in the country in which execution is sought. Suffice to say that so far the problem has remained theoretical and is likely to remain so for the foreseeable future.

New initiatives of ICSID

The pre-hearing conference

The fact that more than one-half of ICSID proceedings that have been terminated have been amicably settled lends support to the consideration that ICSID arbitration is not limited to providing effective means of dispute settlement but seeks to achieve a wider objective, namely to restore confidence between investors and States when differences arise between them.

With a view to increasing the effectiveness of ICSID in the pursuit of this objective, the Revised Arbitration Rules adopted by the Administrative Council in September 1984 now offer a new procedure in the form of a 'pre-hearing conference' which may be called by the Secretary-General or by

55 The ICSID Secretariat keeps a currently updated list of the juridical or other authorities designated by Contracting States. These States include those in which leading commercial and financial centres are located. In practice, therefore, the parties should experience no real difficulty in identifying countries in which recognition and enforcement may be usefully sought, because of the presence of local assets of the borrower, for example.

56 Court of Appeal of Paris, June 26, 1981, *SARL Benvenuti & Bonfant* v *Gouvernment de la Republique Popularie du Congo*, 108 *Clunet* 843 (1981); 20 *ILM* 878 (1981). For further analysis, see Delaume, *op cit*, note 29 *supra*, at 796–800.

57 Following recognition of the award, the Congolese Government complied with it. See *News from ICSID*, Vol 1, No 1 (Winter 1984), 2.

58 Article 55.

the President of an ICSID tribunal. The object of such a conference is to expedite the proceedings by permitting early identification of undisputed facts, thereby limiting the proceedings to the real areas of contention.[59]

In a similar spirit, the Revised Rules also give the parties the right to request the convening of a pre-hearing conference between the tribunal and the parties, in the hope that it will give their authorised representatives the opportunity to reach an amicable settlement.[60] Such a settlement could take the form of an agreement between the parties or be recorded in an award in accordance with the ICSID Rules.[61]

ICSID and multipartite arbitration

Due to the complexities of contemporary transnational contracts, it may happen that disputes involving different parties will be the object of separate proceedings even though the issues involved bear a close connection to one another. This problem arises both in regard to commercial transactions and to contractual arrangements relating to investments and the carrying out of large economic development projects.

It was unavoidable that the problem would arise in the context of ICSID arbitration. An example is found in the three parallel proceedings that were instituted against Jamaica by *Alcoa Minerals of Jamaica/Kaiser Bauxite Co/Reynolds Jamaica Mines Ltd and Reynolds Metals Co.*[62] The proceedings were instituted pursuant to ICSID arbitration clauses stipulated in each individual agreement between the claimants and Jamaica. The nature of the disputes was identical: it concerned the imposition of new taxes by Jamaica contrary to stabilisation clauses in the agreements.

In this case, the claimants appointed the same person as arbitrator.

Jamaica having failed to appoint an arbitrator, the claimants requested the Chairman of ICSID's Administrative Council to appoint, for each proceeding, two arbitrators and to designate one of them as President of each tribunal. The Chairman made the necessary appointments and selected for the purpose the same two persons to serve on each arbitral tribunal.

On July 5–6, 1975, the three arbitrators considered each dispute and held in respect of each of them that the dispute fell within their 'competence'. The disputes were subsequently settled amicably.

More recently, new situations have been submitted to ICSID. One of these concerned the *Klockner* v *Cameroon* case.[63] In that case, the original request had been submitted not only by the applicant, but also by its Dutch and

59 Arbitration Rule 21(1) reads as follows:
'At the request of the Secretary-General or at the discretion of the President of the Tribunal, a pre-hearing conference between the Tribunal and the parties may be held to arrange for an exchange of information and the stipulation of uncontested facts in order to expedite the proceeding.'

60 Arbitration Rule 21(2) reads as follows:
'At the request of the parties, a pre-hearing conference between the Tribunal and the parties, duly represented by their authorised representatives, may be held to consider the issues in dispute with a view to reaching an amicable settlement.'

61 Arbitration Rule 43. This was the case in *Guadaloupe Gas Products Corporation* v *Federal Military Government of Nigeria* (Case ARB/78/1).

62 See note 14, *supra*.

63 See note 21, *supra*.

Belgian subsidiaries. At the first hearing of the tribunal, counsel for Cameroon argued that since Article 25(1) of the Washington Convention refers to a 'national' of another Contracting State, multipartite participation in the proceedings seemed excluded. The President of the tribunal informed the parties that the tribunal had considered the issue, but from another viewpoint, namely the question whether the applicant had authority to represent its two affiliates. The issue was settled after the tribunal and the parties agreed that the applicant could act on behalf of its affiliates if it obtained proper powers from them and supplied the tribunal with evidence of such powers, which was done.

Whether, as argued against by counsel in the Cameroon case, the Washington Convention should be construed restrictively as excluding multipartite arbitration is a debatable question. To be true, the Convention when it refers to the parties to investment disputes, uses the singular. There is, however, nothing in the Convention which would exclude a broader construction. Since recourse to the ICSID arbitration is based on consent, it would seem within the realm of possibility that the parties agree to submit to a single proceeding a dispute involving a plurality of participants. This, of course, might require various contractually agreed amendments to the ICSID Rules, which are also drafted with a view to litigation between individual parties, but that such amendments are possible results clearly from the spirit as well as the letter of the Washington Convention.

This is an issue as to which there is no known precedent. However, the issue is worth keeping in mind. So much the more, since the problem of multipartite arbitration is not likely to receed into the background, whether in an ICSID context or in the context of other forms of arbitration.[64]

In this connection, it may be appropriate to mention certain new situations that have been submitted to the ICSID Secretariat for advice. These include cases in which investment agreements, containing an ICSID arbitration clause, are intimately related to other arrangements, such as supply or sales contracts, which fall outside the scope of the Washington Convention. In cases such as these, the Secretariat has suggested to the parties that they provide in the relevant arrangements for *ad hoc* arbitration incorporating, to the extent necessary, the ICSID Rules and designating the Secretary-General as appointing authority. It is quite clear that awards rendered under such arrangements could not be considered 'ICSID awards'. Nevertheless, this contractual machinery may have considerable advantages in coordinating the ICSID and the non-ICSID proceedings, particularly if both are administered by the same arbitrators.

ICSID and non-ICSID proceedings

ICSID as a designating authority for arbitration purposes

In an increasing number of cases, the Secretary-General of ICSID has accepted to act as 'designating authority' in connection with *ad hoc* arbitration agreements which do not fall within the scope of the Washington Convention.

The most consistent use of ICSID as a designating authority has been made

64 See, eg, in the context of ICC Arbitration, Craig, Park and Paulsson, *International Chamber of Commerce Arbitration*, paragraph 8-14.

in connection with the borrowings made on the Euro-market by Brazilian public entities, guaranteed by the Brazilian Government.[65]

Other examples relate to disputes between contractors and states, which did not qualify as investment disputes under the Washington Convention.[66] Recently, the Secretary-General has also been designated as appointing authority in the relevant provisions of a power supply contract between the Province of British Colombia and the City of Seattle concluded within the context of a Treaty between Canada and the United States for the economic use of international rivers.[67]

ICSID additional facility

In 1978, ICSID was entrusted with the administration of an Additional Facility regarding proceedings falling outside the scope of the Washington Convention because the state party to the dispute or that of the national party to the dispute is not a Contracting State, or the dispute is not an investment dispute, or the type of proceeding involved concerns fact finding.[68]

Reference to the Additional Facility appears in several bilateral investment treaties between both the United States and the United Kingdom, and other countries.[69] It can, therefore, be expected that ICSID, as Administrator of the Additional Facility, may provide increased services to interested parties.

Conclusion

ICSID is an institution in progress. The increasing number of disputes submitted to ICSID shows the vitality of the organisation and the confidence of the parties in the impartiality and effectiveness of ICSID proceedings. As a result of the publication of certain ICSID awards and of the disclosure by the Secretariat of non-confidential information about ICSID proceedings, it can be expected that the international community will become more than ever aware of the merits of the ICSID machinery and show increasing willingness to make use of its facilities.

Another factor to take into account is that, in recent years, the flow of funds from developed to developing countries has decreased significantly. If developing countries are to attract foreign capital they must find new ways to give assurances to foreign private investors regarding the safety of their

65 Delaume, 'The ICSID and the Banker', *Intl Financial L* (October 1983) 9, at 13; 'L'Arbitrage CIRDI et le Banquier', *Revue Banque*, juillet–aout 1983, 889, 894.

66 *News from ICSID*, Vol 1, No 1 (Winter 1984), 4.

67 *Ibid*, and No 2 (Summer 1984), 13. Contrary to the case of other arbitration institutions which charge a fee when they act as designated authority, ICSID performs that service free of charge.

68 Broches, 'The Additional Facility of the International Centre for Settlement of Investment Disputes', IV *Yearbook: Commercial Arbitration* 373 (1979); Toriello, 'The Additional Facility of the International Centre for Settlement of Investment Disputes', 4 *The Italian Yearbook of International Law* 59 (1980). On September 26, 1984, the administrative Council decided to continue the Additional Facility, initially approved for a five-year term, indefinitely. See *News from ICSID*, Vol 2, No 1 (Winter 1985).

69 Delaume, 'ICSID and Bilateral Investment Treaties', *News from ICSID*, Vol 2, No 1 (Winter 1985).

investments. ICSID membership is one of the ways in which this can be accomplished.

In this connection, the fact that ICSID membership now includes certain Latin American countries, traditionally hostile to international (and not only ICSID) arbitration is significant.[70] It shows an awareness on the part of these countries of ICSID as an organisation capable of reconciling the interests of states and private foreign investors by bringing between them a climate of mutual confidence and by restoring that climate in the event that differences arise between the interested parties.

70 Paraguay and El Salvador have ratified the Washington Convention, and Costa Rica has signed it but not yet ratified it. See, Shihata, 'ICSID and Latin America', Editorial in *News from ICSID*, Vol 1, No 2 (Summer 1984), 2–3. See also in the same issue (3–4) a report on the conference on ICSID held on April 6, 1984 in Sao Paulo under the auspices of the Research Centre of the Sao Paulo Bar Association.

5 States in the international arbitral process

Karl-Heinz Böckstiegel

The general context of dispute settlement between and with states

In the international arbitral process, two categories of parties can be distinguished. The first may be called 'private parties' and includes natural persons as well as legal entities of private law, especially enterprises. The second category may be called 'state parties' and includes states, subdivisions of the state, legal entities of public law formed by the state, and also international governmental organisations. Though still the majority of parties appearing in international arbitral procedures are private parties, the international arbitral process has always been used and is increasingly being used by state parties as well. To mention just one illustration, according to statistics of recent years, one third of the many cases submitted each year to ICC arbitration involves state parties.

Since I have dealt in recent publications[1] extensively with the special considerations relevant if and when state controlled enterprises are parties in international arbitrations, I will concentrate here on the role of arbitration in disputes directly involving states themselves as parties.

The basic legal framework is first of all formed by general international law, as set forth in Article 2, paragraph 4 of the Charter of the United Nations, prohibits states from using force or the threat of force and obliges them to settle their disputes in a peaceful way. And Article 33 of the Charter further clarifies this obligation and also mentions expressly arbitration:

> 'The Parties to any dispute, the continuance of which is likely to endanger the maintenance of international peace and security, shall, first of all, seek a solution by negotiation, enquiry, mediation, conciliation, arbitration, judicial settlement, resort to regional agencies or arrangements or other peaceful means of their own choice. The Security Council shall, when it deems necessary, call upon the parties to settle their disputes by such means.'

1 K H Böckstiegel, *Arbitration and State Enterprises – A Survey on the National and International State of Law and Practice*, Kluwer Publishers (Deventer) and International Chamber of Commerce (Paris) 1984; Böckstiegel, 'The Legal Rules Applicable in International Commercial Arbitration Involving States or State-Controlled Enterprises', in *ICC Court of Arbitration 60th Anniversary Conference Proceedings*, Paris 1984, 117.

While on one hand we find here the express mention of 'arbitration' as a means of dispute settlement among states, Article 33 on the other hand states that it does not deal with all disputes, but only with those, the continued existence of which is likely to endanger the maintenance of international peace and security, and that neither the Charter of the United Nations nor general international law obliges states to submit their disputes to a machinery of third party settlement, be it courts or arbitration. As a matter of legal policy, one has of course no difficulty in subscribing to the unanimously adopted 1959 resolution of the Institut de Droit International[2]:

> 'In an international community the members of which have renounced recourse to force and undertaken by the Charter of the United Nations to settle their international disputes by peaceful means in such a manner that international peace and security, and justice, are not endangered, recourse to the International Court of Justice or to another international court or arbitral tribunal constitutes a normal method of settlement of legal disputes.'

But here again, as in other fields, the resolution of the Institut de Droit International has not been realised in international law and practice.

As is well known, states have been especially reluctant to submit to the jurisdiction of the International Court of Justice. Since its start in 1946 the Court has had relatively few cases to deal with and even less in which the procedure was concluded by a judgment on the merits. This is true, though the Court has had more cases in recent years than in the periods before.

In comparison, international arbitration has been used much more widely by states for the settlement of their international disputes. But before we go into this in more detail, a short note may be appropriate on the distinction between international arbitration and international courts. Both have in common that a decision is found on the basis of law and that this decision is binding on the parties. Though, at first sight, a basic distinction seems to be that judges are appointed in a different way from arbitrators, further examination proves this distinction not to be so important, since even for the International Court of Justice the parties have a certain influence on the selection of the judges. Nevertheless, the view still prevails that international arbitral bodies and international courts are something fundamentally different and one has tried to develop more sophisticated criteria for this distinction. If one examines those criteria in more detail – which cannot be done here – one soon finds out how fluid the borderlines between those two categories have become.[3] Faced with this difficulty, one has tried to define as international arbitration any third party dispute settlement outside the International Court of Justice or, as has been suggested, to abolish this traditional distinction altogether.[4]

I must admit that I have some sympathy for the latter suggestion. First of all I find it difficult to see any other justification for this distinction than that of academic categorisation, and academic categories should at least not be upheld

2 48 II *Annuaire de l'Institut de Droit International* 359 (1959).

3 For further details and references see: von Mangoldt, 'Judicial Settlement of International Disputes', in *Proceedings of an International Symposium of the Max Planck Institute for Comparative Public Law and International Law*, Heidelberg 1974, 417, 424.

4 Sohn, ILA Reports, 52nd Sess, 326.

once it becomes clear that they do not conform to factual and legal realities. Furthermore, the International Court of Justice has been moved even closer to traditional concepts of arbitration when – in addition to the traditional option of state parties to appoint: a judge *ad hoc* – an option for Ad-Hoc Chambers was institutionalised in 1978 and then in fact used in two procedures.[5] It would even be a further illustration of the arbitral element if it was true – as has been indicated by some sources – that the United States and Canada when introducing their recent case to a Chamber of the ICJ indicated a preference for certain judges to be nominated for that Chamber and also indicated that otherwise they might consider submitting this case to an arbitral tribunal which might contain the judges indicated.

While the International Court of Justice is moving closer to traditional concepts of arbitration, on the other hand international arbitration shows certain developments which move it closer to permanent international courts. First, one has to remember that for decades already, administered or institutionalised arbitration, rather than *ad hoc* arbitration, has mostly been used, as is illustrated by the well known international and national arbitration institutions whose arbitration rules are referred to in the majority of international contracts. As indicated before, states have not seldom been involved as parties in such arbitration procedures. A further step in this direction has been the institution of a specific arbitration machinery for investment disputes with states by the Washington Convention which established ICSID in 1965.

The arbitral process moved even closer to a permanent court when Iran and the United States in 1981 agreed to establish an arbitral tribunal for disputes involving the two states and their nationals. On the one hand this solution was characterised by traditional criteria of arbitration, for the Algiers Claims Settlement Declaration between the two states includes a general reference to the UNCITRAL Arbitration Rules[6] and the tribunal was set up for a limited number of disputes. On the other hand this 'Iran–United States Claims Tribunal', as it is now called, contains many traditional criteria for permanent international courts, eg, one tribunal is called upon to deal with the almost 4,000 cases submitted; the two states may submit further disputes to the tribunal in the future regarding the interpretation or performance of the Algiers instruments of public international law; the tribunal has its own permanent premises in The Hague and has been recognised by the Dutch government with the status and privileges of an international governmental organisation in the Netherlands. At least in practical terms a further distinction to traditional arbitration is also that the sums in dispute before the tribunal which are at present calculated without counterclaims in the region of US$60 billion go far beyond the scope of any former arbitration procedure and that – besides the enforceability of awards which is also a normal feature of international arbitration – a special security account of US$1 billion was set up in the Netherlands from which awards can be payed upon notification by the president of the Tribunal.

5 Text: International Court of Justice, Acts and Documents concerning the organisations of the Court, No 4, 1978, 92. Jiminez de Arechaga, 'The Amendments to the Rules of Procedure of the ICJ,' 67 *Am J Intl L* 1 (1973), at 21.

6 Article III, para 2.

Probably the most important illustration for the acceptance of international arbitration in modern state practice as a subsidiary means of dispute settlement can be found in the new Law of the Sea Convention. The general provisions on the settlement of disputes are contained in its Articles 279–299. They give priority to the disputes settlement procedure agreed to by the state parties involved in a dispute (Articles 280 and 282). If the state parties do not come to such a specific agreement, Article 287 gives them a choice between the following means for the settlement of disputes:

> '(a) the International Tribunal for the Law of the Sea established in accordance with Annex VI;
> (b) the International Court of Justice;
> (c) an arbitral tribunal constituted in accordance with Annex VII;
> (d) a special arbitral tribunal constituted in accordance with Annex XIII for one or more of the categories of disputes specified therein.'

Paragraphs 3 and 5 of Article 287 then provide for arbitration as the compulsory subsidiary means of dispute settlement:

> '3 A State Party, which is a party to a dispute not covered by a declaration in force, shall be deemed to have accepted arbitration in accordance with Annex VII.'
> '5 If the parties to a dispute have not accepted the same procedure for the settlement of the dispute, it may be submitted only to arbitration in accordance with Annex VII, unless the parties otherwise agree.'

In view of the fact that certain sections of the Law of the Sea Convention are highly disputed in some countries, especially some western industrialised countries, it should be noted that the provisions on dispute settlement found general agreement at a rather early state of the Law of the Sea Conferences and have not been disputed since. They can therefore be considered as a genuine indication of what modern state practice is most ready to accept as a procedure for dispute settlement between and with states.

Finally it should be noted that this trend has been confirmed by the work of the International Law Association since it started first the discussion on and then the preparation of a draft convention for the settlement of disputes regarding space activities. Paragraph 3 of the 1982 Montreal resolution[7] of the ILA provides:

> 'The Convention should provide States with a choice among different settlement methods which, for binding settlement, should include adjudication by the International Court of Justice as well as administered and ad hoc arbitration.'

And indeed, the first draft for the convention elaborated for the 1984 Paris ILA conference[8] and accepted in principle, follows the example set by the Law of the Sea Convention. Article 6, paragraph 4 of the draft convention provides:

> 'If the parties to a dispute have not accepted the same procedure for the settlement of the dispute, it may be submitted only to arbitration in accordance with Section V, unless the parties otherwise agree.'

7 ILA, Report of the 60th Conference, 12.

8 ILA Paris Conference (1984), Space Law Committee Report.

Thus, again arbitration is chosen as the compulsory subsidiary settlement procedure, if the parties do not agree otherwise.

Finally it should be noted that both the Law of the Sea Convention as well as the ILA draft convention permit to a certain extent that not only states and international governmental organisations, but also private persons and private enterprises, are parties in the respective disputes.

The diminishing relevance of traditional distinctions

We already have seen that the traditional distinctions between the International Court of Justice and international arbitral tribunals are diminishing. It has also already been indicated that, while private enterprises traditionally were and still are today the typical parties in an international arbitration, states as well as state subdivisions and state enterprises make increasing use of international arbitration. We will deal with this practice of states submitting to arbitration in more detail later in this paper. In the context of the diminishing relevance of traditional distinctions, one cannot but notice that the very distinction between state parties and private parties is itself losing some of its relevance.

First, states are directly or indirectly involved nowadays in a much greater part of international trade quantitatively and have taken up many fields of international trade qualitatively which traditionally were the realm of private enterprises. As is well known, in many socialist countries a state monopoly on foreign trade is part of the national economic and legal system, and foreign trade enterprises are the exclusive instruments from such states to participate in international commerce. Though generally these foreign trade enterprises have a separate legal personality from the state, there is a differing degree of control by the respective states or the Ministries of Foreign Trade by selecting the management, influencing the budget and the policy within the planning of the national economy. And in developing countries with a principally private economy system, the specific know-how or size of enterprises necessary for the participation in international trade and investment may lead to at least a major part of foreign trade being reserved in fact for the state or state controlled corporations. Even in the industrialised private economy countries, if one takes a closer look at the degree of state involvement in the industry, one is often surprised as to the extent of such an involvement. By tradition or by earlier or recent nationalisations, as in France, many branches of industry and commerce are partly or dominantly or even exclusively controlled by the state. This development to a quantitatively and qualitatively greater state involvement in international trade has necessarily had its consequences on legal principles which were based on the traditional basic distinction between the state and private parties. Without going into details here, at least major illustrations of such legal consequences in the practice of international arbitration should be noted. The possibility of a state party to claim immunity has been restricted considerably, partly by specific national legislation, partly by the doctrine that states can only claim immunity for their *acta jure imperii*, and partly by interpreting the acceptance of an arbitration clause in an international contract as a waiver of immunity with regard at least to the arbitration proceedings, perhaps also for enforcement of an eventual arbitration award.[9] And another illustration is that practice and doctrine has emerged for circumstances under which acts of state cannot be accepted as *force majeure* where the state is indirectly involved in international trade.[10]

The growing participation of states in the international arbitral process has also led to a diminishing relevance of traditional distinctions with regard to the applicable law. This is both true for the distinction between national and international law and for the distinction between private and public law.

We still do have, of course, arbitrations which are exclusively based either in the field of public international law or national law. Examples for the first category are bilateral air transport agreements and investment protection treaties, as well as multilateral treaties establishing international organisations, all of which normally include arbitration clauses for eventual disputes. Examples for the exclusive application of national law are especially those many contracts in international trade which, on the one hand, provide for international arbitration in case of a dispute, but on the other hand also include a choice of law clause referring to a specific national law, not seldom the national law of the contracting state party.

But there is now also a great number and a great variety of instruments in international trade and investment which reject the traditional exclusive application of either public international law or national law and combine the arbitration clause with choice of law clauses referring in different ways to either none or both of these two traditional fields of law or to other sources of law, either alone or in combination with one or both of these traditional fields. Again, it is not possible within the framework of this paper to go into much detail here. But as an illustration I should perhaps at least mention some of the choice of law clauses I found in former research on this matter.[11] One finds clauses referring:

1 to two systems of national law;
2 to a national law and, in addition, to the 'principle of good will and good faith';
3 to a national law in combination with 'the general principles of law and justice';
4 to the principles of law common to the national legal systems of the contracting partners;
5 to the 'principles of law recognised by civilised nations';
6 exclusively to the contract itself, possibly in addition to *bona fides*;
7 to legal principles or combinations of legal principles which go beyond any specific category;
8 to the arbitrators themselves, asking them to act as '*amiable compositeur*' or decide '*ex aequo et bono*';
9 and – to allow arbitrators to 'decide all cases on the basis of respect for law, applying such choice of law rules and principles of commercial and international law as the Tribunal determines to be applicable, taking into

9 For further details and references: Böckstiegel, *op cit*, in *ICC Court of Arbitration 60th Anniversary Conference*, at 145.

10 *Ibid*, at 130.

11 Sources, examples and references can be found in: Böckstiegel, *Der Staat als Vertragspartner auslandischer Privatunterenhmen*, Frankfurt 1971, 86.

account relevant usages of the trade, contract provisions and changed circumstances'. (Article V of the Claim Settlement Declaration for the Iran–United States Claims Tribunal.)

Traditional distinctions are also diminishing if and when a contract between a state and a foreign private enterprise is directly subject to public international law as the applicable law either due to a respective express choice of law clause in the contract or because the contract has to be qualified as a 'public international law contract'.[12] And traditional distinctions with regard to the applicable law are, of course, also at stake in the discussion of the possible relevance of a *lex mercatoria* in international arbitration.[13]

The traditional distinction between public law and private law, which at least in civil law countries is a fundamental one, has also proved to be subject to change. While in civil law countries the borderline between these two fields of law has become fluid and transparent, it seems that in some common law countries one now finds a greater appreciation of the specific character of public law rules. In international arbitration, especially in the field of investment, but also in the field of trade, arbitrators find it more and more necessary to decide disputes not exclusively on the traditional basis of private and commercial law, but also to take into consideration rules of public or at least mandatory law. In fact, already with regard to the arbitration procedure, it is sometimes not easy to identify mandatory rules. And with regard to the applicable substantive law, public law rules may have to be taken into account not only from a chosen national law, but also from other national legal systems which are in some way relevant for the fulfilment of the contract. And especially, when states are involved in an arbitration procedure, additional public law rules dealing with specific state activities, competences of institutions, etc, may come in.

Finally it should be noted that the traditional distinctions between national courts and arbitration have changed. On the one hand the legally possible and factual influence of state courts on arbitration proceedings has been reduced considerably. Specific national legislation such as the United Kingdom Arbitration Act 1979 and the recent French arbitration legislation illustrate this, as well as the draft UNCITRAL Model Law, Article 5 of which expressly says that 'no court shall intervene except where so provided in this law'. On the other hand, the more liberal approach of the national legislator and of national courts to arbitration and especially international arbitration has made cooperation between courts and arbitral tribunals easier in fields where such cooperation is useful or even necessary in the interest of an effective dispute settlement. An important example for the practice of international arbitration are interim measures which may have to be granted by courts either because the arbitral tribunal has not yet been constituted or because interim measures

12 Details of this category of contract would again go beyond the limits of this paper so that reference must be made to: Böckstiegel, *op cit*, *ICC Court of Arbitration 60th Anniversary Conference*, at 165.

13 Goldman, *Frontières du droit et lex mercatoria*, Archives de philosophie du droit, Paris 1964; Goldman, 'La lex mercatoria dans les contrats et l'arbitrage internationaux: réalité et perspectives', 106 *Clunet* 475 (1979). Also in *Etudes offertes à Berthold Goldman*, Paris 1982, contributions by Battifol, Kahn, von Mehren, Rigaux, Weil; and recently: Cremades and Plehn, 'The New Lex Mercatoria and the Harmonisation of the Laws of International Commercial Transactions' 3 *Boston Univ Intl LJ* 317 (1984).

by the arbitral tribunal itself cannot be enforced since the New York Convention may not be applicable.

State practice submitting to arbitration

In the preceding sections of this paper it has already been indicated in general terms that nowadays states play a much greater role in the international arbitral process than used to be the case. The different aspects and examples of this greater involvement shall now be considered more closely though a detailed description is not possible within the limited framework of this paper.

As far as the fields of international business activities are concerned, both international trade and international investment practice show, first of all, a greater use of arbitration as the method to settle disputes, and secondly, within these arbitrations agreed to or actually carried through, states play a greater role as contractual partners or arbitration parties respectively.

The greater involvement of states in international arbitration is mainly due to an overlapping effect of two more general developments. The first is the growing use of arbitration as the preferred dispute settlement machinery for international business relations which can be noticed throughout the world in recent decades, including western industrialised countries, socialist countries and developing countries, and even noticeable in traditional 'difficult' regions such as Latin-America and the Arab world. The second contributing general development, as has already been indicated, is the greater participation of states in international trade, directly and indirectly, which again can be noticed not only in industrialised socialist and developing countries, but also, though to a lesser extent, in industrialised private economy countries.

As regards international investment, contracts and especially arbitrations are much less than those in international trade, but on the other hand state involvement is relatively greater, because in many countries, especially again in the developing world, the state is more directly concerned and therefore active in relation to foreign investors. Agreement on arbitration in the field of foreign investment is found in two sorts of relationships involving state parties. First, treaties between states may provide for arbitration, and secondly, contracts between the host state and the foreign investor may also provide for arbitration. In addition to the well known general reasons which lead to the choice of arbitration in international business relations, in the field of investment arbitration is often chosen because foreign investments are specially open to the risk of interference by public authorities of the host state and legal procedures of protection may either not or not sufficiently be available in that host state or may at least not be satisfactory for the confidence of the prospective investor. Since submission to the jurisdiction of the International Court of Justice is not found too often, the foreign investor or his home state may feel without adequate legal protection so that agreeing on arbitration is an obvious solution.

International investment is a field in which we find an especially great number of state treaties providing for arbitration. This is a remarkable difference from most other fields of public international law where one finds a considerable weakness to be the absence of a machinery for enforcement of treaty obligations. Several hundreds of bilateral treaties for the promotion and protection of foreign investment have been concluded in the last 25 years; most are between western European industrialised states and developing countries, and most provide for arbitration in case of disputes. While most of these treaties, however, only provide for arbitration between the respective states, direct arbitration between the investor and the host state is provided for by the Washington Convention 1965 creating ICSID. More than 80 states have now ratified this Convention, but it must be noted, of course, that ratification of the Convention by a state does not yet make concrete investments subject to the arbitration of ICSID. Submission to that arbitration procedure still requires specific agreement in every contract. In that respect it has been indicated that in spite of the relatively few arbitration cases, ICSID has been chosen in many investment contracts.

In addition to the foregoing and outside the scope of the Washington Convention, there is a long tradition and an increasing practice to include arbitration clauses in contracts between a state and a foreign investor. Concession contracts in particular show the tradition,[14] which started by an arbitral award certified by Emperor Barbarossa in 1156.[15] The tradition of agreeing on arbitration in contracts by which foreign investors receive concessions from states is continuing, as can be seen from concession contracts that have become known in recent years either by themselves or due to arbitral disputes.

A hurdle that a number of states have to get over before agreeing to arbitration is the restriction provided by many national laws to the effect that the state and/or certain of its corporations may not or only under certain specific circumstances submit to commercial arbitration. Sometimes these restrictions are only applied for contracts in disputes of a national character, but not for those of an 'international' character. These restrictions vary widely between the different states where they are found. As an illustration, mention may be made of Article 1676 of the Belgian Judicial Code according to which the Belgian State may only agree to arbitration where an international treaty ratified by Belgium so provides. This restriction has recently been the object of an award in a large international arbitration procedure which has recently been published.[16] In view of the fact that most Latin-American countries also have restrictions with regard to arbitration, I may perhaps add at least in general terms that I participated very recently as arbitrator in an award in which the arbitral tribunal upheld its jurisdiction since it felt that the legal restrictions in that large Latin-American country did not interfere with the submission to arbitration in the respective international contract even though the national law of that Latin-American country was the applicable law for the contract. It should be added that looking at the restrictions in the written law may by itself not be the full picture, since sometimes administrative measures may still lead to restrictions while in other countries courts may apply the written restrictions to only national contracts and admit submission to arbitration in international commercial contracts.

14 Fischer, *A Collection of International Concessions and Related Instruments*, New York, 10 volumes so far.

15 Reprinted in Fischer, *op cit*, Vol 1, 153.

16 *Journal des Tribunaux*, Brussels, 31.3.1984, 230. English translation in: 1 *Journal of International Arbitration* 184 (1984).

Finally, if one discusses the state practice of submission to arbitration, it may be permitted to point out that one cannot disregard the Iran–United States Claims Tribunal in this context, since this is an arbitration system with a number of historically specific features. Two states in a deep crisis of their bilateral relations and representing fundamentally different values and beliefs agreed on arbitration to settle their disputes. They did this in the most general sense, including issues of the interpretation of public international law treaties, the legal consequences of nationalisations and other acts of state as well as normal commercial contracts and investments. For many of these disputes this meant that they were withdrawn from the jurisdiction of the national courts of the two states. Besides the fact that this is with regard to the number of cases and the amounts involved one of the largest arbitrations in history, these specific features of the Iran–United States Claims Tribunal make it, of course, more difficult to proceed with this arbitration in an efficient and adequate way. These and other unique characteristics of this arbitration put a greater burden on the two governments, their agents, the private enterprises involved, their lawyers, the international staff of the Tribunal and – not the least – the arbitrators themselves. After only about three years of functioning of the Tribunal it is certainly too early to evaluate whether this new venture of states into the international arbitral process has been able to contribute to the peaceful settlement of disputes involving states and to the development of the law.

6 The sources and limits of the arbitrator's powers

Sigvard Jarvin

Introduction

The arbitrator dealing with an international commercial dispute has important powers. He need not follow the procedure laid down for actions in a court of law, provided that the procedure followed does not lead to unfairness between the parties. He has power to order pleadings and particulars, to fix dates for hearings, to grant postponements, to proceed with a hearing in the absence of a party duly notified, to order discovery, to order inspection of documents, property and premises, to order security for costs, to appoint experts, to delegate duties to secretaries, to refer costs to be taxed and consult with other persons and adopt their views as his own (after having formed his own judgment).

These powers may seem awesome and the discretion of the arbitrator without limits. The exercise by the arbitrator of his procedural powers can rarely be tested by the courts during the arbitration procedure. In general national courts have no power to supervise the arbitrator who exercises or refuses to exercise his jurisdictional powers within wide limits.[1]

However, the arbitrator's authority is derived from the law and his jurisdiction is based on the will of the parties, whether expressed in a contract in general terms covering a future dispute or in a separate agreement covering an existing dispute. The authority to hear the parties and make an award exists only through the agreement of the parties. It stems from a voluntary act. The arbitrator's authority is no broader than that defined by the parties and some of his duties are defined by law. Not only national legislators set the limits inside which the arbitrator must act, but international customs, usages and conventions also play an important role. The arbitrator's authority is an area of the law subject to extensive changes and rapid development.

It is the purpose of this paper to discuss the sources and limits of the arbitrator's powers, not by identifying every national or international source or framework, which is being done elsewhere, but by taking examples from the practice of the ICC Court of Arbitration and the working bodies of the ICC dealing with arbitration. Most of the paper will deal with procedure, since, in the words of Mr J Gillis Wetter[2] 'arbitration as a subject *is* procedure'. In doing

1 Russell on *The Law of Arbitration*, 19th Edition, London, at 233.

2 J Gillis Wetter, *The International Arbitral Process, Public and Private*, New York 1979, Vol II, 288.

this I gladly endorse his statement that the arbitral process is
liberal, flexible and open-minded, an informal system for the re
international commercial disputes. There is no uniform internatio
procedure, and let's hope that there never will be one. But if the sc
particular problems can be enhanced by the publicity given to the fi
individual arbitrators, then this paper may serve a purpose.

The arbitration agreement

Express and implied agreement

Since arbitration is based upon agreement, and steered by the will of the parties, and has the important effect of creating a barrier to court litigation both parties have an interest to prove its existence by safe and easy means. An agreement to arbitrate is therefore usually made in writing.[3] It is unusual to find an agreement to refer *future* disputes to arbitration completely isolated from any other contractual relationship.[4] Agreements to refer an *existing* dispute to arbitration are likely to have been drawn up as a separate contract. Where there is no express written agreement, an agreement to arbitrate may in some jurisdictions be inferred from the conduct of the parties.[5]

This may be the case when parties have ratified the arbitration provisions of an invalid main contract or have sought to enforce them.[6] In ICC arbitration the question of the existence or validity of the arbitration agreement comes up at an early stage in the proceedings. Article 7 of the Rules[7] prevents arbitration from being set in motion where there is no *prima facie* agreement to arbitrate.[8] The defendant may choose however to respond to a request for arbitration notified to him by the Court's secretariat and if he answers on the merits the Court would interpret this behaviour as an acceptance of ICC arbitration and let the case proceed. By not responding in a case where there is no *prima facie* agreement, the defendant bars the case from proceeding further. This decision does not prejudice a national court from determining whether there in fact exists an agreement to arbitrate under the ICC Rules, since the decision of the ICC is of an administrative nature only.[9]

If the ICC Court finds in favour of a *prima facie* agreement, its existence is not definite until the arbitrator has examined the problem and decided

3 The New York Convention includes an exchange of letters or telegrams as made 'in writing'.
4 Mustill and Boyd, *The Law and Practice of Commercial Arbitration in England*, London 1982, at 75.
5 *Ibid*, at 102.
6 *Ibid*, at 77.
7 Rules for the ICC Court of Arbitration, version 1975. ICC Publication No 291.
8 Article 7 reads: 'Where there is no prima facie agreement between the parties to arbitrate ... and if the Defendant does not file an answer within 30 days or refuses arbitration by the International Chamber of Commerce, ... the arbitration cannot proceed'.
9 Article 12, second paragraph, of the Internal Rules of the Court stipulates: 'This decision is of an administrative nature. If the Court decides that the arbitration solicited by the Claimant cannot proceed, the parties retain the right to ask the competent jurisdiction whether or not they are bound by an arbitration agreement in the light of the law applicable.'

whether he has jurisdiction.[10] The *prima facie* criterion is a filter through which many agreements pass all of which do not stand up to the final test. In ICC Case No 4402 the Court held that there was a *prima facie* agreement to arbitrate binding a party who had not signed the agreement entered into between its subsidiary and third parties. The arbitrators however rejected this position and denied jurisdiction after having heard the parties' submissions. Applying Swiss law and the Concordat, the arbitrators decided to make a partial award on the jurisdictional issue, in which they did not find enough evidence that the parent company had agreed to arbitrate, either expressly or through its conduct. Consequently there was no implied agreement to arbitrate.[11]

An implied agreement to arbitrate was held to exist in Case No 4131 (*Dow Chemical et al* v *Isover Saint-Gobain*),[12] involving a similar situation, where some but not all of the entities of a group of companies had signed an arbitration agreement. The arbitrators, who deliberately excluded any national law in reaching their decision, found that the common intention of all the parties, as evidenced by their participation in the formation, performance and termination of the contract justified the application of the arbitration clause even to those entities who had not signed the contract.

Interpretation of the arbitration agreement

If the existence of an arbitration agreement is asserted or even confirmed, there sometimes remains to be decided how it should be interpreted, and notably by applying what law? The first duty of the arbitrator confronted with this problem as a preliminary issue when deciding what powers the arbitration agreement confers upon him, is to study the arbitration agreement. Does it contain a choice of law clause on the validity or interpretation of the arbitration agreement or not? If it does, such a clause would be valid[13] even if different from the law applicable to the merits of the contract and the rules governing the arbitration procedure.

Where no express choice of law on the interpretation of the arbitration agreement has been made, the arbitrator should look for a possible choice by the parties as to the law applicable on the merits; parties may assume that this choice governs the validity and interpretation of the arbitration agreement as well. If such an assumption can be proven, the arbitrator would apply the same law as that on the merits.[14]

10 Article 12, third paragraph of the Internal Rules of the Court stipulates: 'If the Court of Arbitration considers "prima facie" that the proceedings may take place, the arbitrator appointed has the duty to decide as to his own jurisdiction and, where such jurisdiction exists, as to the merits of the dispute'.

11 The case has been published in VIII *Yearbook: Commercial Arbitration* 204 (1983) – the *prima facie* decision of the ICC Court, and IX *Yearbook: Commercial Arbitration* 138 (1984) – the arbitrator's decision.

12 *Dow Chemical et al* v *Isover Saint-Gobain*, IX *Yearbook: Commercial Arbitration* 131 (1984).

13 With respect to English law, see Mustill and Boyd, *op cit*, at 89.

14 In ICC Case 4131, IX *Yearbook: Commercial Arbitration* 131 (1984) the arbitrators held that 'the sources of law applicable to determine the scope and the effects of an arbitration clause providing for international arbitration do not necessarily coincide with the law applicable to the merits of a dispute submitted to such arbitration. Although this law or these rules of law may in certain cases concern the merits of the dispute as well as the arbitration

The problem may be more delicate where the parties' underlying agreement contains no express stipulation on any law, whether as regards the merits, the procedure nor the validity or interpretation of the arbitration agreement; and this is not unusual (at least in ICC arbitration). In ICC Case No 4392[15] the arbitrator held that when deciding on his jurisdiction he should examine the arbitration agreement by applying the law applicable at the place of arbitration (which was Zürich). In choosing the law at the place of arbitration an arbitrator avoids the difficulties that might arise at the stage of enforcement or recognition under the New York Convention, which rejects awards made according to agreements that are not valid under the law of the country where the award was made (still presuming the parties have not made an express choice of law).[16]

Scope of the arbitration agreement

Since the arbitrator derives his powers from the arbitration agreement he is bound by the wording of the agreement when deciding what authority he has to decide a particular dispute. Parties are not totally unrestricted in drawing up clauses submitting disputes to arbitration (or rather they may be unrestricted in what they agree but the effects of their agreement may be limited). First, arbitration rules applicable may restrict the kind of disputes for which the rules have been envisaged and by referring to the rules of an institution the parties' agreement will include the limitations contained in the rules proper. By way of illustration it is worth mentioning two examples: the UNCITRAL and the ICC Arbitration Rules. The former set of Rules is recommended for use in the settlement of disputes 'arising in the context of international commercial relations' but seem to be adoptable for any type of disputes.[17] The ICC Rules are appropriate only for business disputes having an international character.[18]

There are some general rules as to the types of disputes that may be submitted to arbitration.

---

agreement, it is perfectly possible that in other cases, the latter, because of its autonomy, is governed – not only as to its scope, but also as to its effects – by its own specific sources of law, distinct from those that govern the merits of the dispute. This is particularly the case – unless the parties have expressly agreed otherwise – with respect to an arbitration clause referring to the ICC Rules' (at 133). The Court of Appeal in Paris approved this observation by the arbitrators (at 132).

15 110 *Clunet* 907 (1983).

16 New York Convention, Article V 1(a).

17 Resolution 31/98 adopted by the UN General Assembly on December 15, 1976. The UNCITRAL Arbitration Rules themselves do not contain the restriction to commercial disputes, since Section 1: Scope of Application, Article 1, stipulates: 'Where the parties to a contract have agreed in writing that disputes in relation to that contract shall be referred to arbitration under the UNCITRAL Arbitration Rules, then such disputes shall be settled in accordance with these rules subject to such modification as the parties may agree in writing'.

18 Article 1 of the Internal Rules of the ICC Court of Arbitration provides however that the Court may accept jurisdiction over business disputes not of an international nature, if it has jurisdiction by reason of an arbitration agreement. The restriction to business disputes remains and, eg, labour disputes, family affairs, liability out of medical malpractice, traffic accidents, would not fall within the ICC jurisdiction.

Does the formula used in the arbitration agreement cover the dispute?

The arbitration agreement may use a formula that is narrow or broad, conferring jurisdiction for specific types of claims, or for specific damages only, regarding events occurring in the course of the contract but not after its expiration, etc.[19] The importance of careful drafting can be illustrated by the following ICC cases. In Case No 4491 (unpublished) a licensing agreement between Finnish and Australian parties referred to arbitration 'possible disagreements between (the Finnish plaintiff) and (the Australian defendant)'. The arbitrator's jurisdiction was challenged by the defendant who agreed that some of the claims were not within the scope of the arbitration provisions. The arbitrator (English, sitting in London) held:

> 'The expression "possible disagreements" is an unusual one and a wide one. The Plaintiff's claims can be divided into claims for royalties due under the Licensing Agreement prior to its termination and claims for damages and injunctive relief in respect of the period after the termination of the Licensing Agreement. The former claims for royalties are clearly within the arbitration provisions, even though the claims were only made after the termination of the Licensing Agreement. But the latter claims are "passing off" claims or otherwise based upon intellectual property rights claimed by the Plaintiff. As such they could only arise after the termination of the Licensing Agreement and do not concern anything done or not done under that Agreement. Whether or not the expression "possible disagreements" might cover a claim in tort, if there were a sufficiently close connection between the claim and a dispute arising out of the contract containing the arbitration clause – and I have some doubt about that – I certainly do not consider that the expression can cover tortious claims arising subsequently to the termination of the Licensing Agreement. It follows that I find that the Plaintiff's claims for damages and injunctive relief after the termination of the Licensing Agreement are not within the scope of the arbitration provisions of the Licensing Agreement and I cannot entertain or arbitrate upon such claims.'

In Case No 4753 (unpublished) a contract for sale of movable property by an Indian seller to a German buyer contained the following arbitration provision:

> 'In amendment of I-5, it is agreed upon that final settlement of any arising dispute, which could not be cleared by (the Seller) and (the Buyer) themselves, should be effected through an Arbitration Committee of the International Chamber of Commerce in Zürich, Switzerland.'

When the Buyer requested arbitration regarding losses after an alleged breach of contract, the Seller objected that only disputes regarding the quality of the products were covered but that any other dispute should be referred to state courts. In support hereof he held that the words 'in amendment of I-5' introducing the clause, referred to provisions in the Seller's offer regarding replacement of defective parts. Therefore only such disputes were covered.

19 Mustill and Boyd, *op cit*, at 86–8, cite a variety of examples such as 'claims, differences, disputes, in connection with, in relation to, in respect of, with regard to, arising out of, under, during the execution of'.

The Arbitrator (Swiss, sitting in Zürich) decided that the wording 'any arising dispute', and the placement of the clause under the heading 'General' in the seller's order, favoured an interpretation that all contractual provisions be governed by arbitration. He added that it would be 'odd and rather rare to have in the framework of extensive written agreements an arbitration clause which is very limited in its scope. *The contrary is the usual practice. All kinds of disputes arising out of a specific contract between the parties are referred to arbitration*'. (Emphasis added.)

Does a dispute exist?

Arbitration agreements usually refer to the existence of a dispute, meaning that an arbitrator will have jurisdiction only if a dispute exists at the time a request is made. It is unusual, although not excluded, that the defendant admits the claim, but it happens in practice that the reasons for non-payment are as simple as a lack of funds or the impossibility to obtain a government authorisation to transfer money abroad.

In ICC Case No 4265 (unpublished), an Egyptian commission agent claimed damages from its Dutch principal for two agreements concluded on its exclusive territory. The Dutch defendant alleged that there was no dispute as to the existence of the claim for commission, which it had admitted, at least partly, after the arbitration proceeding had started. Since the defendant had proposed to the claimant that a conciliation procedure be commenced, and since this proposal had been made before the claimant's request for arbitration, the arbitrator held this fact was evidence enough of existence of a dispute, and retained jurisdiction.

In Case No 4705 (unpublished) where the respondent did not dispute the sum claimed or the liability to pay interest thereon (and where the only reason for not having paid was financial difficulties), the arbitrator defined the issue to be determined as 'the manner in which the admitted debt and interest should be discharged'.

Procedural powers

The parties' agreement, which is the arbitrator's prime source when determining his powers to conduct the proceedings, may be more or less specific as to what powers the arbitrator has, and may circumscribe the degree of discretion he has in the absence of agreement. Most jurisdictions give broad discretion to parties to determine the conduct of private arbitrations, and many give especially wide latitude with respect to disputes that are international.[20] The parties' will may be expressed indirectly by a reference to a set of rules which should be applied, such as those of the UNCITRAL or the ICC.

The UNCITRAL arbitration rules contain an entire section (No III) on the proceedings, in which the powers and duties of the arbitrator are set out in some detail. Thus out of the 16 articles of the section, 15 give directions or discretionary power to the arbitrator on how to conduct the proceedings. The powers are however usually subject to the proviso that the parties have not

20 Craig, Park and Paulsson, *International Chamber of Commerce Arbitration*, New York 1984, No 61.01.

made an agreement which regulates the matter, and do not therefore impose a uniform procedure.

The ICC Rules are less detailed on procedure. Apart from basic rules laid down in Article 14 (parties' right to be heard, arbitrator's right to appoint experts, the possibility of deciding the case on the documents only), and Article 15 (summoning parties to hearings, proceeding *ex parte*, language of the proceedings, restriction on non-parties' right to be present, representation by counsel), which are mandatory,[21] the parties and the arbitrator are completely free to agree and direct how the hearings shall be conducted. The rules empower the arbitrator, in the absence of agreement, to establish rules completely detached from statutes, decrees or municipal law. The arbitrator is free to choose the best of different rules, to combine municipal procedural rules with his own rules based on previous experience. Consequently the framework of the ICC Rules allows for an important development and refinement of international arbitration procedure to take place. Below are some examples of procedural power given to the arbitrator by the parties and/or issued by virtue of the power embodied in Article 11.[22]

- Le siège de l'arbitrage a été fixé à Francfort sur le Main. *Les audiences pourront se dérouler en tout autre lieu choisi.* (Case No 4165, German sole arbitrator.)

- At any time during the Arbitration, the Tribunal may, upon request of a party or on its own motion, direct a party to *produce such additional documentation* as it may deem appropriate.
- *Parties and witnesses will be heard by the Tribunal* and will reply to questions posed by the Arbitrators and/or counsel for the parties.
- *The Tribunal may extend time limits* or otherwise modify the procedures set out above.
- *Procedural questions* arising in the course of the Arbitration not resolved by these Terms of Reference *shall be resolved by decision of the Tribunal applying* the ICC Rules or, where these are silent, *any other procedural rules or standards which the Tribunal considers appropriate in furtherance of fairness and justice.* (Case No 3998, Tribunal of three arbitrators, Swedish Chairman, sitting in France.)

- La langue de l'arbitrage est le français. *Le tribunal arbitral peut cependant autoriser des tiers* (témoins, experts, . . .) *à produire des documents rédigés dans une autre langue* ou à s'exprimer en une autre langue, sauf le droit pour chacune parties d'en demander, et pour le tribunal arbitral d'en ordonner la traduction. (Case No 4697, Tribunal of three, Belgian Chairman, sitting in Paris.)

- *The language of the arbitration shall be English. Parties may use Spanish or German for their pleadings and written statements*, but each party must furnish

21 Article 11 of the Rules provides: 'The rules governing the proceedings before the arbitrator shall be those resulting from these rules and, where these rules are silent, any rules which the parties (or, failing them, the arbitrator) may settle, and whether or not reference is thereby made to a municipal procedural law to be applied to the arbitration.'

22 Emphasis added by the author in these extracts.

an English translation thereof if the other party so requests. *Parties may be accompanied* at their expense *by their own interpreters.* (Case No 4451, Belgian sole arbitrator, sitting in Paris.)

- The parties agree that partial awards may be made *inter alia* on the following issues:
  . . .
- Within the limits of these Terms of Reference the Arbitral Tribunal shall be free to *define the exact subject-matter to be covered by each partial award.* (Case No 4928, Tribunal of three, Swiss Chairman, sitting in Geneva.)
- *All procedural measures* (relating to time limits, hearings, etc) *shall be ordered by the chairman* on behalf of the tribunal after consultation with the other arbitrators and, *if urgency so requires, without it.* (Case No 4873, Tribunal of three, Swiss Chairman, sitting in Geneva.)
- Le tribunal arbitral pourra, par simple lettre adressée aux parties, leur poser des questions et les inviter à produire tout document qu'il estimerait indispensable ou utile à l'accomplissement de sa mission. En cas *de refus de production des pièces demandées, le tribunal arbitral en tirera telle conséquence qu'il jugera approprié.* (Case No 4820, Tribunal of three, Belgian Chairman, sitting in Paris.)
- The procedural rules to be followed by the Tribunal will be *the rules of procedure applicable to an ICC arbitration in Paris.* (Case No 4620, Tribunal of three, English Chairman, sitting in Paris.)
- Le Tribunal arbitral *peut tenir toute réunion interne en tel lieu qui plaira au président* avec l'accord des co-arbitres. (Case No 4502, Tribunal of three, Swiss Chairman, sitting in Geneva.)

These examples have been picked at random and represent powers of the arbitrator that will typically be found in ICC arbitration. The following characteristics are noteworthy:

Flexibility
Arbitrators are allowed and show great flexibility with regard to language. Typically more than one language is used in an international arbitration. (Case Nos 4697, 4451)
Arbitrators may modify the procedure in order to make it effective in the particular case. (Case No 3998) The procedure is left to the arbitrator's discretion provided he applies what is required at the place of arbitration. (Case No 4620)

Detachment
The arbitrator decides the procedure that corresponds to international expectations of fairness and justice (Case No 3998). The place of arbitration is not always the place where the parties involved meet. (Case Nos 4165, 4502)

Adaptability
The chairman may take urgent decisions alone. (Case No 4873) The tribunal may decide on the need for and subject to partial awards. (Case No 4928)

Liberty of decision
The tribunal may evaluate parties procedural behaviour as evidence. (Case No 4920)

Active role
Arbitrators can order parties to produce documents and hear parties and witnesses on their own motion. (Case No 3998)

Terms of reference

Some legal systems do not give recognition to a general agreement to refer future disputes to arbitration.[23] A separate agreement to refer the dispute that has arisen to arbitration will then be the source of the arbitrator's power.

But generally speaking the drafting of terms of reference is not a requirement in arbitration of international business disputes.[24] If it is one of the characteristics of ICC arbitration (it has survived several amendments of the Rules because it has been considered to be an invaluable element).

The purpose of the Terms of Reference, as emerges from Article 13.1 of the ICC rules, is to define the context of the dispute to specify the claims of the parties and to list the points at issue. The Terms of Reference shall help the arbitrator and the parties to plan the proceedings and the Court to check that the arbitrator's award deals with the claims defined. The drafting of the Terms of Reference affords an (initial) opportunity for the parties and arbitrator to meet, and may result in a settlement of the dispute at an early stage.

The Terms of Reference must state:

- the full names and addresses of the parties and the arbitrator;
- a summary of the parties' respective claims;
- a definition of the issues to be determined. This list includes those questions which the arbitrator believes essential to decide in order to assess the parties' claims;
- the indication of the place of arbitration.

According to the ICC Rules the Terms of Reference must be signed by the arbitrator(s) and the parties, and once signed constitutes an agreement to arbitrate which either confirms an original, general clause to submit future disputes or is the evidence of an agreement to arbitrate where no earlier agreement had been made.

In theory an arbitrator might refuse to sign the Terms of Reference (this happens very rarely in practice) and a party (mostly the defendant) may refuse to sign the document. (This happens to some extent in practice.) Should a member of the arbitral tribunal refuse to participate in drawing up the Terms of Reference owing to exceptional circumstances or to sign it following agreement by the parties, the Chairman of the tribunal must inform the Court of Arbitration. The Court then takes the necessary measures and may apply Article 2.8 of the Rules.

23 S Saleh, *Commercial Arbitration in the Arab Middle East*, London 1984, at 25.

24 Neither the UNCITRAL Arbitration Rules nor other well-known rules – *ad hoc* or institutional – have this requirement. In the UNCITRAL systems parties state their claim and defence (Articles 18, 19) and the arbitrator decides to what extent a party subsequently may amend its claim or defence (Article 20).

Should one of the parties refuse to sign the draft Terms of Reference after having had the opportunity to state his comments, the draft must be submitted to the Court of Arbitration for approval (Article 13.2 of the Rules). The Court fixes a time-limit within which the defaulting party is invited to add his signature. The arbitration proceeds as soon as the party has signed or, upon the expiry of the time-limit, without the party's signature. A refusal by a party to sign the Terms of Reference does not affect the validity of the proceedings, nor does it prevent that party from taking part in the hearings of the case. The party concerned must in all respects be treated as if he had signed.

The Terms of Reference are not intended to be a solution of the dispute. Rather they should be a true statement of the parties' respective claims and defence but not at this stage an analysis by the arbitrator as to what solution shall be given to the dispute; that will be done in the award. If the arbitrator tries to suggest solutions in the Terms of Reference he can be sure of encountering difficulties from the parties, who will be hesitant to sign the Terms of Reference, and delays will inevitably occur.

On the other hand, the points at issue must be determined by the arbitrator, with the assistance of the parties, and defined in the Terms of Reference. It is the arbitrator's task to define the points at issue on the basis of the claims presented by the parties. The parties' opinion as to what the points at issue are may only serve as guidelines for the arbitrator who himself must define them; he is thus not bound by the parties' opinion in this respect.

The claims set forth in the Terms of Reference have important consequences for the proceedings that follow. According to Article 161 of the Rules the parties may make new claims or counter-claims before the arbitrator only if these remain within the limits of the Terms of Reference or if they are specified in a rider to the Terms of Reference, signed by the parties and communicated to the Court.

Multi-party disputes

It is axiomatic, given the contractual basis of arbitration, that the powers of the arbitrator, given to him by the parties can only emanate from the parties. Where in addition to the original claimant and defendant the involvement of a third party is proposed, the contractual sources of the arbitrator's power must be extended to include the will of all the parties concerned.

In practice the following situations involving more than two parties are frequent:

- *Assignment* The first party has assigned all its rights to a third party. The arbitration clause remains valid and enforceable against the assignee and the parties to the original contract. This situation may create problems as to the right of the assignor to participate in an arbitration between the assignee and the second party to the original contract.
- *Guarantee* Where a bank or other guarantor has guaranteed the performance of the defendant in the arbitration, does the guarantor have a right to join in the proceedings, and conversely can the defendant compel the guarantor to participate, and does the arbitrator have power to make an award binding the guarantor? The answer should be sought by examining the arbitration clause, which may have foreseen such a dilemma. In the

absence of agreement by all three parties, the arbitrator has no authority or duty to deal with an arbitration involving more than the two original parties to the arbitration agreement.

- *Subcontracting* In construction projects, the contractor frequently sublets work to another party. Upon a claim from the owner the contractor may wish to have the responsibility of the subcontractor tried in the same proceeding. There is no contract between the owner and the subcontractor, but only between the owner and the contractor on the one hand and between the contractor and the subcontractor on the other. Even if both contracts were to stipulate arbitration, the arbitrator nominated for one of the disputes must seek authority for dealing with the two disputes in one and the same proceeding from all three parties concerned, unless the arbitration clause in either agreement is of a multi-party kind which envisages the right to join in, and to be joined in, as a third party.[25]
- *Several defendants* An owner who has contracted separately with a building firm and an architect relating to a building project, may find it difficult to decide against which of the two to direct his claim for damages since the facts giving rise to the damages claim cannot clearly be attributable to one or the other party. The owner generally prefers to sue both of them simultaneously to establish liability and to avoid that arbitrators in two separate actions come to different findings of fact or law. The solution to this problem is the same as in the foregoing example: the arbitrator's source of authority lies with an agreement between all three parties concerned. Without such authority he may not join the two cases even if he were to be nominated by the parties in two separate proceedings, since none of the parties need suffer the extra costs, lack of confidentiality and other disadvantages entailed in proceeding in a multi-party arbitration.

In ICC Case No 4806 a Hungarian company, A, requested arbitration against a US company by virtue of an agency agreement concluded between them. This agency agreement was one of three agreements entered into by the US company concerning a project for which it had further concluded one principal agreement with four other Hungarian parties, B, C, D, E, and one know-how agreement with D. Now the US company, defendant in the arbitration, requested the joinder as counter-defendants of B, C, D and E, since the three agreements were interrelated (they referred to each other) there was a close legal relationship between A, B, C, D and E, all parties were factually involved in the dispute and in order to avoid that similar claims were subsequently brought by B, C, D and E. The additional Hungarian companies all objected to being joined since, allegedly, there was no agreement to arbitrate between them and the US company.

The Court of Arbitration denied the request to join B, C, D and E. Later the US company motioned that B only be joined in the first proceedings. The Court of Arbitration maintained its decision and held that any request for the introduction of additional parties must be submitted to the arbitrators (who have in the meantime been appointed).

25 The ICC Commission on International Arbitration has set up a working party with the task of drafting such multi-party arbitration clauses. A draft was presented at the Commission's meeting in November 1984, Doc No 420/263, which is still being worked on and has not been adopted by the Commission.

National law

A commercial arbitration based on an arbitration agreement must comply with the law. National law is the source which governs not only the fundamental questions of the possibility of having recourse to arbitration as such, but also the various aspects of the conduct of an arbitration.

As to the content of national law, which will not be treated here, reference is made to the reports published in the Yearbooks, the ICC series and specific national texts.[26]

The impact of national law is primarily one of exercising control over the arbitrator, thus setting up limits within which the arbitrator must act. This is done in two ways: by deciding what matters are not arbitrable and by establishing a system of procedure (which in most instances is far from complete). Within the wide limits fixed by the national law, the arbitrator enjoys a certain degree of discretionary powers for the conduct of the reference. These aspects will be treated in more detail below under the heading 'public policy' and in other papers.[27] Suffice it to recall here some of the mechanism by which the national laws come into play, and the role of parties acting on the international arbitration scene in setting the mechanisms in motion.

1 Parties to international commercial transactions frequently make express provisions in their contract on the law that shall govern their relations. The source of the arbitrator's power is hence being fixed without his assistance and before his appointment. The arbitrator's first task will be to examine the scope of the national law with regard to the arbitration he is about to commence in order to ascertain the arbitrability of the dispute, possible rules governing the procedure, etc.
2 The parties may by reference to a national law, which differs from that of the law applicable to the merits, have made an agreement on the procedure to be followed. Again the arbitrator's authority is based on a national law which has been decided independently of his own will. The *lex arbitri* so fixed must be checked by him with regard to its compatibility with mandatory rules at the place of arbitration.
3 The parties may have stipulated a place of arbitration only and nothing more. In this situation the national law which will be the source of the arbitrator's authority will depend on the locality chosen: whereas some countries impose a set of procedural rules of the place (eg, the Swiss Concordat), others leave complete freedom of choice, except for a few mandatory provisions (eg, France). In the latter case the parties and the arbitrator have a greater say in the choice of procedural law, and thus the source.
4 Where the parties have made no choice of law, procedural rules or locale, the arbitrator and – under the rules of some institutions – the institutions are able to influence and decide the source of the arbitrator's powers.

26 See, ICCA, *Yearbook: Commercial Arbitration*, since 1976; ICC, *Arbitration Throughout the World*, ICC Publication No 353, concerning Western Europe; a further issue will cover the Far East and the Pacific countries.
27 See Lew, 'Determination of Arbitrators' Jurisdiction and the Public Policy Limitations on that Jurisdiction', Chapter 7, *infra*, at 73.

With respect to the *place* of arbitration the arbitrator decides it in the absence of an agreement by the parties[28] or the Court of Arbitration does so in the absence of agreement by the parties.[29]

The arbitrator's influence over the choice of the national law that will be the source of his powers is manifest when it comes to the choice of the *law on the substance*. Where the ICC Rules apply the following situation prevails:

Drawing its inspiration from the 1961 European Convention, Article 13.3 of the ICC Rules stresses the freedom of the parties to determine the law applicable to the merits of the dispute. In the absence of any indication by the parties as to the applicable law, the arbitrator shall apply the law designated as the proper law by the rule of conflict which he deems appropriate. An arbitrator acting within the framework of the ICC Rules of Arbitration is therefore under no obligation to apply the system of conflict of laws in force at the place of arbitration. If he does so it can only be by virtue of his own choice. Nor is he under any obligation to take the rule of conflict he chooses from a national system of conflict of laws. One may venture that the freedom of the arbitrators in this respect merely amounts to expressing the will of the parties, whose role in choosing the law applicable in contractual matters is widely recognised. Increasingly ICC arbitrators choose the applicable law directly, that is without passing through a conflict of laws rule.[30]

International usages

Conventions

International, regional, multilateral and bilateral conventions are more than usages and constitute an important source for the determination of the arbitrator's powers and duties. The New York Convention, for example, contains precise provisions in Article V regarding the circumstances in which the recognition and enforcement of an arbitral award may be refused, *inter alia* because of the conduct of the arbitrator.

Habitual conduct of proceedings in various trades

Mustill and Boyd state that 'many trades have developed their own, often idiosyncratic, ways of conducting arbitrations',[31] which have been recognised by the English Courts.

Arbitrators seeking guidance on what procedure to apply in a particular dispute should examine whether the trade has already developed a habitual way of conducting the reference. Such is said to be the case, eg, in the shipping and commodity trades where the arbitrations are said to be informal and in engineering and building disputes which are said to be conducted in a manner comparable to proceedings in the High Court.[32]

28 UNCITRAL Arbitration Rules, Article 16.
29 ICC Arbitration Rules, Article 12.
30 See Lando, 'The Law Applicable to the Merits of the Dispute', Chapter 9, *infra*, at 104.
31 Mustill and Boyd, *op cit*, at 59, 249.
32 *Ibid*, at 249.

Rules of conduct in international arbitrations

Without having been suggested by national legislators or sanctioned by courts of law, international arbitrators have developed a number of rules which apply to the conduct of an arbitration. These rules are generally addressed to the parties and may be qualified as an emerging source of rules of good conduct in international arbitration, the breach of which would give the arbitrator good reasons to penalise the party in breach.

Below are some examples from the ICC practice:

Parties have an obligation to cooperate in good faith for the presentation of evidence[33]

The arbitrators, faced with parties and counsel from different legal systems, used to different principles with regard to the burden of proof and presentation of evidence, should try to find a middle way which can be applied by both sides and thus achieve fairness for both of them. The strict distribution of the burden of proof applied by national courts does not apply in international arbitration. In another case,[34] the arbitrators stated that the parties have a general duty to cooperate in determining the truth.

Parties must abstain from acts that make enforcement more difficult or aggravate an on-going arbitration[35]

The arbitrators were faced with a request to declare null and void certain bank guarantees issued in favour of one of the parties to the dispute, which bank guarantees the party wanted to draw on while the arbitration was under way. The arbitrators stated that it was a well established rule in international arbitration that parties should abstain from any act that might endanger the effective enforcement of the future award and, in a general sense, that no party must do anything that might aggravate or prolong the dispute between them.

The arbitrator may freely evaluate the evidence[36]

The arbitrators held that an arbitrator dealing with an international case has the power to make a free evaluation of the evidence and may base his award on circumstantial evidence or take into account facts which have not been referred to if they are notorious or generally known. He may also base his judgment on (his) experience.[37]

Appointing authority

Arbitration agreements often provide for the appointment of an arbitrator by a third party, such as by a court, an organisation, a society, etc. This may be the

33 Case No 1434, 103 *Clunet* 982 (1976).
34 Case No 3410, unpublished.
35 Case No 3896, 110 *Clunet* 914 (1983).
36 Case No 3410, unpublished.
37 French original: 'Dans sa libre appreciation des preuves, l'Arbitre international peut fonder son jugement sur des indices ou prendre en consideration même des faits non allegues s'ils sont notoires ou generalement connus et s'appuyer sur les donnees de l'experience'.

case in default of agreement by the parties as to the sole or presiding arbitrator, to fill a vacancy, when one of the parties fails to appoint 'his' arbitrator, or after an arbitrator has been removed. The identity of the appointing authority may have been agreed by the parties in advance[38] or will be proposed by one party to the other for agreement only when the question of the appointment arises.[39]

Whereas a court of law generally has power to appoint an arbitrator where the parties are unable to agree, or fail to fill a vacancy, or where one party fails to make his appointment, etc, an appointing authority which is not a court has power to intervene only where there exists an agreement providing for such appointing authority and then only in the instances covered by the parties' agreement. Limiting the discussion to the latter category, the party-designated appointing authority, the sources and limits of the arbitrator's powers originate from the parties' agreement, and the appointing authority can neither vest the arbitrator with greater authority than that provided in the parties' agreement or narrow his powers. The appointing authority is merely executing the will of the parties to have an arbitrator appointed, and cannot add to, or deduct from, the arbitrator's authority.

The appointing authority cannot heal a defect in the parties' agreement and the arbitrator appointed by the appointing authority is under the same duty as someone appointed by the parties or by an arbitral institution, to decide on his own jurisdiction. Taking the example of the ICC acting as appointing authority under the UNCITRAL Arbitration Rules or otherwise outside the ICC Rules of Arbitration,[40] the ICC acts on a simple party request, accompanied by a copy of the document (agreement) to which the party refers in support of the ICC's authority to act. The request is notified to the other party who may submit observations within a certain period of time, whereupon the ICC proceeds to the appointment if it is *prima facie* satisfied that it has been designated as appointing authority by agreement.

The extent of the arbitrator's jurisdiction and the limits of his power to determine his own jurisdiction

The problem can briefly be described as follows. Some types of dispute cannot be decided by means of arbitration but only by courts of law. In international business relations it is generally accepted that the arbitrators themselves have a wide authority to decide their own jurisdiction. But if the arbitrator's decision does not comply with the law, the court of a particular country may refuse enforcement of the arbitral award or the court at the place of arbitration may in some countries intervene during the arbitration to stop the arbitration proceedings.

Separability and Kompetenz-Kompetenz

Where the business agreement entered into by the parties, containing an arbitration clause, is invalid, is *ipso facto* the arbitration clause also invalid since it is an integral part of the main agreement?

38 See, ICC as appointing authority under the UNCITRAL Arbitration Rules, ICC publications No 409.
39 UNCITRAL Arbitration Rules, Article 7.
40 Appendix III to the Rules for the ICC Court of Arbitration, Article 4.

The answer would seem to be yes, if it were not for the doctrine of separability that has developed, whereby the main agreement and the arbitration clause are regarded as two separate agreements. When two parties enter into a business agreement containing an arbitration clause they enter into not one but two agreements, one regarding the business deal and one regarding arbitration in case a dispute arises. Although this theory probably is far from the minds of businessmen when they sign a contract, it has become widely accepted since the arbitral process would otherwise be ineffective.[41] A plea by one party that there is no valid arbitration agreement can therefore be tried by the arbitrator and must not be referred to court, which would delay the result of the matter. But even in accepting the separability doctrine a logical difficulty remains, namely, what authority arbitrators have to decide their own jurisdiction if the arbitration agreement itself was invalid (and thus both the main contract and its arbitration clause are struck with invalidity).

The arbitrator's authority to determine his own jurisdiction (*Kompetenz-Kompetenz*) is supported by conventions and the rules of several arbitration institutions, eg, the European Convention 1961, Article 5.3; the Washington Convention 1965, Article 41; the Rules of the ICC Court of Arbitration, Article 8.4; UNCITRAL Arbitration Rules, Article 21. It is also recognised by a large number of national legislations.

The arbitrator of an international business dispute has thus, by virtue of the above described doctrines, a duty to proceed with the arbitration based on the parties' arbitration agreement and to avoid a petition by the party to a national court seeking to declare the procedure invalid. He should also proceed, in order to make arbitration effective, if a judicial order has been issued by a court, except of course if issued by a court at the place of arbitration or otherwise if the order has a compelling force over the arbitral tribunal. The latter may be the case if one of the arbitrators resides in the country where the order was made.[42]

Court control

The arbitrator's freedom to decide on his own jurisdiction does not exclude court control. This can be exercised either during an arbitration or later when a party seeks recognition or enforcement of the arbitral award. The extent to which the courts at the place of arbitration may intervene varies from country to country; for example, a partial award on jurisdiction made in Switzerland may be challenged in a Swiss Court.[43]

The courts at the place of execution of an arbitral award will exercise an effective control of the arbitrability of the dispute. I shall not deal with the subject of arbitrability here other than to recall some subjects that one often

41 Gillis Wetter, 'Salient Features of Swedish Arbitration Clauses', in [1983] *Yearbook of the Arbitration Institute of the Stockholm Chamber of Commerce* 34; Craig, Park and Paulsson, *op cit*, No 5.04.

42 In international arbitrations where three arbitrators are appointed both parties will normally appoint one of them, the third being appointed by agreement, by the institution or by the appointing authority.

43 *Concordat suisse*, Article 9.

considers to be non-arbitrable: contracts *contra bonos mores*, fraud, competition and anti-trust issues, patents and trademarks, bankruptcy, securities, and public order issues (which will be discussed below). The non-arbitrable character of a dispute will be decided by the judge in consideration of the law at the place of enforcement.[44] The judges of some countries may apply a wider definition of arbitrable matters to international business disputes as compared to national.

However, the arbitrator's authority to determine his own jurisdiction is not dependent on the question whether the award will be enforceable or not. These are separate questions and the enforcement does not constitute a limit in the arbitrator's decision on his jurisdiction. An arbitrator may be well advised to consider the possible difficulties that may arise at the time of enforcement, as he is obliged to do according to the ICC Rules.[45] The uncertainty of where an award may ultimately be enforced and the difficulty of foreseeing how a judge in such a country might determine the questions of arbitrability at a future date, must not limit the arbitrator's authority to decide his own jurisdiction according to the parties' agreement.

Public policy and the arbitrator

Generalities

Public policy is not a fixed concept and it is hard to define. It varies from country to country and develops with time. The judge determines and upholds the public policy by ensuring that 'those principles and standards which are so sacrosanct as to require maintenance at all costs and without exception',[46] are respected.

The public policy can be either national or international and its scope varies accordingly. The national judge must respect the public policy expressed in the legislation of his country or otherwise accepted as being the norm. In applying the public policy norms the judge may refuse to accept a foreign law or to recognise or enforce an arbitral award. By the creation of community law such as that of the EEC, the judges in the member countries apply the community public policy since EEC law is directly applicable.[47] On the other hand, in dealing with an international arbitration, does the arbitrator have a duty to apply public policy, and if so what public policy?

The national public policy at the place of arbitration will decide, for instance, the arbitrability of certain types of dispute, the procedure in the reference, and the arbitrator's powers. When mandatory, these provisions must be followed. Otherwise the arbitrator runs the risk of an attack or the setting aside of an ensuing award, either at the place of arbitration or at the place where enforcement will be sought.[48]

44 New York Convention, Article V(2)(a).

45 See, Article 26 which provides: 'In all matters not expressly provided for in these rules, the arbitrator shall make every effort to make sure that the award is enforceable at law.'

46 Julian D M Lew, *Applicable Law in International Commercial Arbitration*, New York, 1978, at 532.

47 For example, the rules against restraint of competition, Treaty of Rome, Articles 85 and 86.

48 New York Convention, Article V, 1(e) and 2(b).

For reasons of enforceability at a place other than that of the *situs*, the same care should be taken by the arbitrator to ensure that his award does not offend the public policy at the place of enforcement.[49]

International public policy

Along with the special status that has developed with regard to international arbitration, an international public policy has evolved. This international public policy has a more limited impact than national public policy and national courts have accepted international contracts providing for arbitration which would have been unenforceable under pure national law.[50] The United States Supreme Court accepted in the landmark case *Scherk* v *Alberto-Culver*[51] that questions relating to the securities laws could be arbitrable in an international context.[52]

Julian Lew holds[53] that as a result of the special position of international arbitrators, who have become the judges of international trade, the arbitrators and the institutions have a special responsibility to international commerce.

49 New York Convention, Article V, 2(b).
50 Craig, Park and Paulsson, *op cit*, No 5.07.
51 417 US 506 (1974).
52 In ICC Case No 4219 (unpublished) the defendant had undertaken to provide structures, elements and other material for the construction of a hotel in Egypt. The plaintiff alleged that the defendant was in breach of contract and claimed damages. The defendant argued that the arbitration proceedings should be dismissed on two principal grounds:

(i) that the Claimant's conduct in connection with the procurement and performance of the contract was fatally poisoned and permeated throughout by moral corruption, extortion and criminality, and violated the ICC's own 'Rules of Conduct to Combat Extortion and Bribery' governing international commercial dealings and that this corrupt conduct offends basic United State's public policy and that the United States courts would refuse to enforce any award, and
(ii) that the ICC Court of Arbitration has no jurisdiction over subject-matters involving criminality.

The allegation behind the conduct complained of was that commissions had been paid.

The arbitrators (two French with an English Chairman) considered the enforceability of any final award, which 'in any event, (was) a duty imposed upon it by Article 26 of the ICC Rules of Arbitration'. The Tribunal was satisfied that the substantive matter in dispute was subject to an arbitration clause which was valid. It went on:

> 'The Tribunal is satisfied that it is in a position to make an enforceable award. It is fortified in this view by its consideration of leading cases which have been before the United States Supreme Court and other United States courts. These United States decisions reflect the international nature of international arbitration agreements and indicate and reflect the reluctance of national courts generally to set aside arbitration awards made in accordance with the contractual arrangements, agreements and obligations entered into between commercial parties. This recognition of the special considerations arising in regard to international contracts is reflected in the leading United States Supreme Court case of *Fritz Sherk* v *Alberto-Culver Co* (June 17, 1974: US No 4).
>
> The Tribunal has considered the extent to which its jurisdiction may be affected by the defendant's allegations as to the conduct of the claimant in connection with the procurement and performance of the contract. The Tribunal is of the opinion that matters relating to criminal conduct may involve penal action elsewhere but do not affect the Tribunal's duty to determine issues of civil liability.
>
> The unanimous decision of the Tribunal is accordingly, that it does have jurisdiction to continue to adjudicate upon the substantive matters at issue between the parties.'

53 Lew, *op cit*, at 540.

> 'They are the guardians of the international commercial order: they must protect the rights of participants in international trade; give effect to the parties' respective obligations under the contract; imply the presence of commercial *bona fides* in every transaction; respect the customs followed in international trade practice and the rules developed in relevant international treaties; uphold the commonly accepted views of the international commercial community and the policies expressed and adopted by appropriate international organisations; and enforce the fundamental moral and ethical values which underlie every level of commercial activity.'

Arbitrators acting within the framework of the ICC Rules disapprove of agreements arrived at by means of corruption and bribery. Recently several cases have been decided where the arbitrators considered that they had jurisdiction to deal with such matters and penalised the reproachable behaviour. A development has taken place where corruption and bribery, as being contrary to public policy (both national and international) is considered arbitrable, which was not the case earlier. An allegation by a defendant that the agreement is contrary to public policy is no longer sufficient to escape the arbitrator's jurisdiction.[54]

This development should be welcomed. It proves that arbitration is not an escape system for contracts which would not be upheld in a trial in court. International arbitrators are, after all, better informed than national judges to know the practices and malpractices of international business and to create an internationally acceptable public policy with respect to business behaviour.

Competition law

Competition law has in many countries been considered an area excluded from the jurisdiction of the arbitrators. Where an arbitrator's jurisdiction is not *a priori* excluded, his powers are however limited.[55] An arbitrator may not apply administrative or penal sanctions or powers exclusively reserved to a public authority, such as granting an exemption under Article 85(3) of the Treaty of Rome.[56]

A claim that a contract is unenforceable due to the non-arbitrability of issues concerning competition laws raises the question whether the arbitrator has jurisdiction to deal with the dispute or whether he should refer the decision on jurisdiction to a court of law as a preliminary issue. By making such a reference the arbitrator reduces the efficacy of arbitration, since the allegation of non-arbitrability may have been formed *mala fide* to delay the proceedings. The arbitrator's dilemma has been well described by Jacques-Michel Grossen[57] as 'the triple conviction'. First that the arbitrator should do everything possible to make the award enforceable. Second that an arbitration in Switzerland should not be allowed to serve as escape from the constraints of

54 See ICC Cases Nos 2730, 3913, 3916 in 111 *Clunet* 914, 920, 930 (1984).

55 For the situation in Switzerland see Jacques-Michel Grossen, 'Arbitrage et droit la concurrence', in *Receuil de travaux suisses sur l-arbitrage international*, Zurich 1984, 38.

56 See, eg, B Goldman, 'The Complementary Roles of Judges and Arbitrators in Ensuring that International Commercial Arbitration is Effective', *Sixty Years of ICC Arbitration*, Paris 1984, at 271.

57 *Op cit*, at 42.

a legal system to which the parties would normally be submitted. Third that an arbitrator sitting in Switzerland has no automatic duty to make himself an agent for the application of economic policy of foreign states. Therefore Mr Grossen recommends that in case of an evident non-compatibility with the competition law normally applicable or with that of the place of enforcement, the arbitrator should advise the parties that he cannot pursue his reference. Where the arbitrator has a doubt only as to the compatibility, he should let the parties decide whether they want him to pursue the arbitration. In any event he should abstain from notifying the award to an authority, since he is not an agent for a foreign state.

The EEC Commission recently issued a block exemption for patent licensing agreements. In a draft text it had been suggested that arbitral awards deciding matters relating to the interpretation or appreciation of patent licensing agreements be notified by the parties to the EEC Commission so that the Commission could check their conformity with the Treaty of Rome. The ICC objected to such a notification duty,[58] (and it was abandoned by the EEC), in pointing out that any control of arbitrators dealing with issues of competition matters should be exercised by the courts at the time of enforcement of the award.[59] The EEC abandoned the notification obligation in the final patent licence regulation.[60]

A better way to obtain a coherent competition policy would be, it seems, to allow arbitrators to submit questions relating thereto for guidance by the European Court of Justice, if such a 'case stated' procedure could be done expeditiously and keeping the parties' identity confidential. The 'Nordsee' decision does not go this way.[61]

The United States Supreme Court held in July 1985 that a Sherman Act anti-trust claim can be subjected to arbitration where the dispute arises out of a contract for international commerce.[62]

58 ICC Report dated 1984–04–06 'Arbitration and Competition', Doc No 420/259.

59 Arbitrators are bound to respect public policy since they do not want to risk their awards being nullified. A notification procedure would not help since the arbitrator's award is final, binding and the matter *res judicata* whatever the EEC Commission, when notified, might think about its compatability with its competition policy. The fact that an award has been notified would not stop it from becoming binding since the EEC Commission has no jurisdictional powers with regard to setting aside an arbitral award.

60 See, *Official Journal*, L 219. Commission Regulation (EEC) No 2349/84 of July 23, 1984 on the Application of Article 85(3) of the Treaty to certain categories of Patent Licensing Agreement.

61 *Nordsee Deutsche Hochseefischerei Nordstern GmbH* v *Reederei Mond Hochseefischerei Nordstern AG & Co* [1982] ECR 1095. Also reported in [1983] *Revue de l'Arbitrage* 389.

62 *Mitsubishi Motors Corp* v *Soler Chrysler-Plymouth Inc* 24 *ILM* 1064 (1985), United States Supreme Court. When sued by Mitsubishi for breach of contract (non-payment for ordered vehicles), Soler counter-claimed asserting the dealership agreement violated US and Puerto Rican statutes and the Sherman Act by dividing the markets and therefore preventing himself (Soler) from shipping to Chrysler dealers in the continental United States. The District Court ordered arbitration of Mitsubishi's claims and Soler's counter-claims except the Sherman Act counter-claim because arbitration of anti-trust claims arising in international commercial disputes involving products sold in the US would unacceptably weaken US anti-trust enforcement. In *amicus curiae* briefs the American Arbitration Association and the ICC argued that the anti-trust question is capable of being decided by arbitrators in accordance with the parties agreement. (AAA brief dated December 17, 1984, ICC brief dated December 17, 1984.) This decision was overturned by the Court of Appeals but reinstated by the Supreme Court.

The arbitrator and *amiable compositeur*

Definition

The power of an *amiable compositeur* to decide a case according to equity and good conscience, *ex aequo et bono* (and similar expressions which are considered to mean the same thing) permits an arbitrator to depart from the strict application of rules of law.

The institution of *amiable compositeur* is well known in civil law systems, where it is expressly recognised (although not defined).[63] In common law systems it poses great theoretical difficulties.[64] Until recently it was considered impossible to grant to an English arbitrator the powers of *amiable compositeur* since it was deemed a matter of public policy that an arbitrator decide according to the law.[65] The arbitrator's power in common law includes the possibility of deciding a case by applying standards of equity without being named *amiable compositeur*, since such power is part of the law. The difficulty lies in defining what exactly an *amiable compositeur* may do.

When trying to define the limits of the arbitrator's powers as *amiable compositeur* the following questions emerge:

(a) If the arbitrator may deviate from rules of law in general, is he not bound by mandatory rules at the place of arbitration and/or enforcement (public policy rules)?
(b) Can the arbitrator depart from the terms of the contract and trade usages?
(c) Does the power of *amiable compositeur* authorise the arbitrator to deviate from procedural rules?
(d) Must the arbitrator give reasons in the award?

Various definitions of the term have been proposed, but there does not seem to exist a generally accepted one.[66]

63 The French Code of Civil Procedure, Article 1774 provides: 'The arbitrator shall decide the case in conformity with rules of law, unless the parties have given him the power to decide as *amiable compositeur*'.

64 Mustill and Boyd, *op cit*, at 605.

65 *Ibid*, at 246.

66 Widely used arbitral rules do not have one either; see UNCITRAL Arbitration Rules, Article 33.2, where reference to the power of *amiable compositeur* is made, and the Rules of the ICC Court of Arbitration, Article 13.4.

Eric Loquin states in *L'amiable composition en droit compare et international*, Paris 1980, at 341–2:

> 'Amiable composition has just been described as a clause permitting the privileged application of the *lex mercatoria*. This institution authorises a different approach to litigation. Arbitration by amiable composition is then a technique trying to rival the law: "it is not in the service of the law," M David has written, "it constitutes an alternative to the law". The arbitrator resolves the dispute using extra-legal criteria. The terminological assimilation of amiable composition with judgment in equity or *ex aequo et bono* reveals this reality: The duty of the amiable compositeur is no longer that of reaching the solution of the case by applying rules of law, regardless of their origin, but of re-establishing harmony in commercial dealings.
>
> This desire to heal relations is demonstrated by the parties abandoning their own subjective laws. The parties in agreeing to submit themselves to an arbitration by amiable composition, give up certain of their rights accorded under the law, in order to allow the arbitrator to provide for them the most reconciliatory solution. The stipulation of an amiable composition clause is already in itself clear and above board. The clause has a preventive function. The agreement of the parties over its choice is the sign of good faith

The power of *amiable compositeur* does not relieve the arbitrator from deciding which law applies to the contract, unless it is the parties' intention to exclude the application of a particular law. Having decided an applicable law on which to base his decision on the merits, the arbitrator attenuates its effect by applying his *amiable compositeur* powers.[67] A study of 91 disputes in East–West relations referred to the ICC Court of Arbitration in 1980–1982, reveals that the parties to a great extent waived the recourse to a particular law in their contracts, and empowered the arbitrator to decide exclusively *ex aequo et bono.*[68]

Scope of powers

Mandatory rules of law having a public policy character apply to an arbitrator acting as *amiable compositeur.*[69] This follows from the arbitrator's duty to make everything possible that the award is enforceable. If awards have been set aside at the place of arbitration they are not recognised or enforced in a country outside the country where the arbitration took place, at least where the New York Convention applies. The arbitrator's duty is to assure himself of the public policy of the *lex fori* at least, and the corresponding mandatory rules at the place of enforcement, where this place can be determined in advance.

The terms of the contract may not be modified by the arbitrator acting as *amiable compositeur.*[70] At least this seems to be the case concerning contract conditions that are part of the terms necessary for the safety of international business transactions. In Case No 3267 the arbitrators held that if it was permitted to deviate from the conditions of the contract on a domestic level it was not so in an international arbitration. The arbitrators held it to be a basic rule which any international arbitrator must apply in the interest of safety of international business, and that this principle was supported by Article 13.5 of the Rules of the ICC Court of Arbitration. In another case, however, the

---

which should permeate their future relations. It indicates that contracting parties are prepared to abandon certain of their rights to facilitate their working together.

Arbitration, in this perspective, responds differently than in a classic contentious procedure. It is characterised by a weakening of the juridical character of litigation and by the predominance of its technical, psychological and commercial aspects. The amiable composition clause gives to the arbitrator the means of reducing the influence of the law over the case in favour of other factors and allows him to extract from the facts what, in a healthy commercial environment, merits different treatment from the application of strict rules.' (*Editor's translation.*)

In one ICC case the arbitrator stated: 'Equity consists of the ability to deviate from and modify the rigour of *summum ius*, by taking into account elements, circumstances, and particular situations which are not brought into consideration which do not have any influence according to the law. This does not stop the arbitrator being able to apply the strict law when that coincides in the actual rights of the case. In effect, positive law and equity are two juridical sets of rules which coexist and sometimes coincide, the latter being the greater and includes the former.' (*Editor's translation.*)

67 Craig, Park and Paulsson, *op cit*, No 18.02.

68 Sigvard Jarvin, 'Commercial Arbitration in East–West Relations: The Experience of the ICC Arbitration Court with Regard to Choice of Law, Number of Arbitrators and Seat of Arbitration', 10 *International Trade, Law and Practice*, 117 (1984).

69 Comments to ICC Case No 3267, 107 *Clunet* 969 (1980), by Derains.

70 ICC Case No 3938, 111 *Clunet* 926 (1984).

arbitrator felt free to reduce the percentage of an agent's commission although it had been expressly defined in the disputed contract.[71]

Procedural rules may be more freely modified by the arbitrator acting as *amiable compositeur* than rules relating to the merits. However, there are also obvious limits here, such as the right to be heard, and other basic rules of defence.[72] In one case the arbitrators held that since they were not *amiable compositeurs* they could not relieve the party alleging certain facts from his duty to prove them if he wished to rely on them.[73] Would this imply that an arbitrator acting as *amiable compositeur* was freer than one acting according to the rules of law to base his decision on non-proven arguments? Probably not, but the arbitrator might be empowered to evaluate the evidence by using less strict norms than those applicable under national procedural rules, eg, by applying a lower degree of conviction when accepting facts as proven..

In ICC practice the arbitrator acting as *amiable compositeur* is not relieved from giving reasons *for the award.* This duty flows from the Court's practice applicable to all awards to be approved by it whether arbitrators are deciding strictly according to the law or not, and is based on the principle that the parties have a right to be informed of the reasons for the award. This should increase their understanding of the decision and make it more readily acceptable, and therefore contribute to an early voluntary implementation.

The *amiable compositeur* may not *adapt the contract* or act as *mediator*, without express powers of the parties.[74]

71 ICC Case No 4206, published in *Affarsratt*, No 3, 1984. Article 13.4 and 13.5 of the ICC Rules stipulates: 'The arbitrator shall assume the powers of an amiable compositeur if the parties are agreed to give him such powers. In all cases the arbitrator shall take account of the provisions of the Contract and the relevant trade usages.'

72 Comments to ICC Case No 3327, in 109 *Clunet* 976 (1982), by Derains.

73 ICC Case No 4095 (unpublished).

74 See ICC Case No 3938, 111 *Clunet* 926 (1984).

Determination of arbitrators' jurisdiction and the public policy limitations on that jurisdiction 7

Julian D M Lew*

The authority and jurisdiction of arbitrators are in every instance dependent upon two factors: the autonomy of the parties and the laws of the competent national jurisdictions. Arbitration, as an alternative forum to national courts for the determination of disputes arising out of international commercial and other relationships, can only take place if agreed to by the disputants, either in advance, ie, in an arbitration agreement (normally an arbitration clause in a contract), or by way of a submission to arbitration of a specified existing dispute. It is because arbitration will generally be resorted to only if the parties have so agreed, that it is most accurately described as a private dispute settlement mechanism.[1]

In addition to the agreement of the parties, the relevant national laws also, directly or indirectly, influence the effectiveness of an arbitration agreement. If an arbitration agreement does not cover the nature of the dispute submitted to arbitration or is in respect of a subject-matter which the law prohibits from being dealt with by arbitration, it will be ineffective: it will neither be recognised nor enforced under the laws of an interested legal system. Thus, for example, if a particular subject-matter cannot be submitted to arbitration under the law of the place of arbitration or under the law governing the contract, then the arbitration agreement will be unenforceable.[2]

In such circumstances, if the arbitrator's jurisdiction and authority are challenged he may determine that he is legally unable to undertake the arbitration, or certain parts of it, on the grounds that, eg, the subject-matter is not capable of settlement by arbitration[3] and will stop the proceedings and allow the parties to seek to determine and enforce their rights and remedies in another forum. If the arbitrator does continue with the arbitration and proceed to reach an award on the merits, he does so with the knowledge that if he did not validly have jurisdiction he runs the risk that the award will be defective

* The author acknowledges the assistance in the preparation of this paper of Adam Samuel, BA (Oxon), barrister-at-law, Calker Scholar of the Institut Suisse de Droit Comparé.

1 J Robert, *L'Arbitrage: droit interne, droit international prive*, 5th edition, Dalloz, Paris 1983, No 1 at 3; English House of Lords Judgment in *Bremer Vulkan* v *South India Shipping Corporation* [1981] AC 909, at 983.
2 New York Convention, Article II(1) and (2); UNCITRAL Model Law, Article 8(1).
3 New York Convention, Article II(1) and (2).

and either the party against whom it is made will seek to have it set aside, or the award will simply be unenforceable.[4]

Regardless of the implications of the law on an arbitration agreement, the principal issue to be determined in any case is the extent of the parties' autonomy, as this is the basis of every arbitration agreement. In the absence of the parties' express agreement there can be no arbitration, and the parties must seek their remedies before the competent national courts. The authority of arbitrators to determine specific disputes arising out of a contract or other contractual relationship is based on the parties having directly specified or impliedly indicated that particular disputes or types of dispute 'arising out of or in connection with such contract' should be resolved by arbitration. It is also for the parties to determine the form of arbitration, ie, *ad hoc* or institutional, and should they wish all other technical and procedural matters affecting the arbitration. Failure of an arbitrator to stay within the parameters of his authority as set forth in the arbitration agreement or as otherwise specified by the parties could result in the award being set aside or unenforceable.[5]

Two separate issues arise where the authority or jurisdiction of the arbitrators is in issue. First, who should determine the authority or jurisdiction of the arbitrator: he himself or a competent national court? Essentially the arbitrator's jurisdiction may be questioned either on the grounds that the arbitration agreement does not cover the issue in dispute, or because the arbitration agreement is void due, for example, to the subject-matter being one which the relevant law precludes from being submitted to arbitration. Second, some matters are precluded from being submitted to arbitration under the mandatory provisions of the applicable law or public policy (*ordre public*), irrespective of the will of the parties.

Determination of arbitrator's jurisdiction

Notwithstanding the existence of an arbitration agreement, questions may be raised in many instances as to the validity or effectiveness of an arbitration agreement. In some cases one party may, for various reasons and with hindsight, wish to avoid arbitration and prefer the dispute to be considered by national courts. This situation may manifest itself as a result of different actions taken by one of the parties.

First, one party could start court proceedings on the dispute leaving it for the other party to seek a stay of those proceedings on the basis of an existing and valid arbitration agreement. Whether such a stay is granted would be a question to be determined by the national courts. Essentially it would depend on the validity of the arbitration agreement, the attitude of the court to arbitration, and the balance of convenience. As a general rule most national courts will defer to arbitration proceedings provided the arbitration is 'in respect of a defined legal relationship, whether contractual or not, concerning a subject-matter capable of settlement by arbitration'[6] and 'unless it finds that

4 New York Convention, Article V(1)(a), (c) and (2): UNCITRAL Model Law, Article 36(1)(a)(i) and (iv) and (b).

5 New York Convention, Article V(1)(a) and (c); UNCITRAL Model Law, Article 36(1)(iii) and (iv).

6 New York Convention, Article II(1).

the agreement is null and void, inoperative or incapable of being performed'.[7]

Second, it may be possible for a party to petition the court for a declaration that the arbitration agreement is void or, in the particular circumstances, should have no effect.[8] Such a declaration may be sought for various reasons: to clarify various differences between the parties, or to open the way to seek the setting aside of an award in another country, or as a prelude to defending an action to enforce an award. The obtaining of such a declaration would depend on criteria of national law, whether the arbitration agreement concerns a subject-matter that can be settled by arbitration, 'is null and void, inoperative or incapable of being performed', and national and international public policy.[9]

The third situation is, I believe, the most common: it is where one of the parties challenges the arbitrator's authority and jurisdiction in front of the arbitrator. The challenge may be raised as soon as the arbitrator gives notice of his appointment, requires the parties to appear before him, makes an order as to procedure, time-table or discovery, or at any later stage.[10] The party challenging the arbitrator's jurisdiction will present his arguments either on a general basis, that the arbitration agreement is null and void, inoperative, incapable of being performed, etc, or on some specific ground, that the dispute does not fall within the scope of the arbitration agreement, or the subject-matter is one that cannot under its proper law or for some other reason be submitted to arbitration. In some circumstances, the challenging party may reserve his position so that his challenge to the arbitrators cannot be construed as an acceptance of the arbitrators jurisdiction. In this situation, in the event that the arbitrator should decide that he does have jurisdiction to hear and make an award on the merits, the challenging party will have to decide whether to participate in the arbitration and present his case on its merits, or to stand back and allow the arbitrator to make his award on the basis of the evidence presented by the claimant only, and then to seek either to have the award set aside in the courts or to challenge it when the claimant looks to enforce the award.[11]

The principal question which has long been a source of confusion is whether the arbitrator has the right to determine his own jurisdiction. The reasons for

7 New York Convention, Article II(3); UNCITRAL Model Law, Article 16(1).

8 This possibility exists particularly in England; see Mustill and Boyd, *The Law and Practice of Commercial Arbitration in England*, Butterworths, 1983, at 514–15.

9 By corollary, in the United States a party can seek an order of a court that the other party submit to arbitration in respect of a specified matter: Arbitration Act 1925, Section 4.

10 With specific reference to the issue of the arbitrator's jurisdiction, to obviate situations of one party raising the matter late on in the proceedings when he anticipates the award may not be in favour and he wishes to prepare the ground for a possible application for the award to be annulled or as a defence against enforcement, the UNCITRAL Model Law has expressly provided: 'A plea that the arbitral tribunal does not have jurisdiction shall be raised not later than in the statement of defence' – Article 16(2). See also, *European Convention on International Commercial Arbitration*, Geneva, 1961 Article V(1).

11 In some jurisdictions a party who makes it clear that his participation is without prejudice to his subsequent right to challenge the award, does not waive that right. See, with respect to England, Mustill and Boyd, *op cit* 519–20. In other legal systems, the parties may be better off arguing the issue of the arbitrator's authority and withdrawing from the arbitration and challenging the arbitrators authority in the courts if his challenge does not succeed: eg, Switzerland, see: *Le contrat International: L'arbitrage international*, vol 1, Repertoire de droit international prive suisse, Berne, Staempfli, 1982, No 207–210.

the challenge to the arbitrator's authority or jurisdiction may be various: it may relate to the subject-matter of the dispute or the purport of the arbitration agreement; equally, it may give rise to fundamental questions as to the validity of the main contract in which the arbitration agreement is included and the arbitration agreement in itself. In this latter situation it would be argued that as the main contract is null and void, eg, induced by fraud or for an illegal purpose, so all its provisions including the arbitration clause, are void and of no effect. Accordingly, it should follow, as the arbitration provision is void *ab initio*, the arbitrator has no authority to undertake any arbitration proceedings, not even to determine the validity of the main contract and whether, in fact, the main contract is null and void (eg, was there fraud or is the purpose illegal, and is this sufficient to nullify both the main contract and the arbitration agreement?).

The main issue then is who should decide the validity of the main contract, ie, national court or arbitrators, and whether the arbitration agreement stands and falls with the main contract? Traditionally most legal systems considered that questions of the arbitrators' jurisdiction should be determined by the national courts. This was particularly the position in England where, under the old case stated method, it was possible for an arbitrator to refer the question to the court.[12]

However, in recent years, with the increase in the use of arbitration to resolve international trade issues and the development of a body of rules and practices for international commercial arbitration, the laws of many countries have altered to uphold the effect of an arbitration agreement even where the validity of the main contract is in issue or is void. This situation recognised the doctrine of 'separability' for the arbitration agreement, treating it as additional to and separate from the main contract, thus surviving the completion, termination or voiding of the main contract.[13]

Thus in the *Gosset* case[14] the French Cour de Cassation declared that the arbitration clause was separate from the contract, and if the main contract was void the arbitration agreement only became void if the reason for the nullity of the main contract also affected the arbitration agreement. The same concept was endorsed by the United States Supreme Court in *Prima Paint* v *Flood & Conklin*[15] where it was alleged that the contract had been induced by fraud. The court held:

> 'Except where the parties otherwise intend arbitration clauses as a matter of federal law are separable from the contracts in which they are embedded, and where no claim is made that fraud was directed to the arbitration clause itself, a broad arbitration clause will be held to encompass arbitration of the claim that the contract itself was induced by fraud.'[16]

English law still appears not to have adopted the separability doctrine as fully as other countries.[17] It would appear that where a contract is illegal and therefore void *ab initio*, an agreement to arbitrate contained therein is also

12 Section 21, Arbitration Act 1950, repealed by Section 1 Arbitration Act 1979.
13 See, eg, Article 8, Concordat suisse; French Code of Civil Procedure, Article 1466.
14 Cass Civ, May 7, 1963.
15 388 US 395 (1967).
16 *Ibid*, at 402.
17 See Mustill and Boyd, *op cit*, at 78–82.

void[18] and whilst questions concerning the existence of the contract may be considered by the arbitrator, his award will not be binding and may be reconsidered by the courts.

The doctrine is today also recognised in most of the international arbitration rules. Accordingly, Article 8 of the Rules of the ICC Court of Arbitration provides:

> '3. Should one of the parties raise one or more pleas concerning the existence or validity of the agreement to arbitrate, and should the Court be satisfied of the prima facie existence of such an agreement, the Court may, without prejudice to the admissibility or merits of the plea or pleas, decide that the arbitration shall proceed. In such a case *any decision as to the arbitrator's jurisdiction shall be taken by the arbitrator himself.*
> 4. Unless otherwise provided, the arbitrator shall not cease to have jurisdiction by reason of any claim that the contract is null and void or allegation that it is inexistent provided that he upholds the validity of the agreement to arbitrate. *He shall continue to have jurisdiction, even though the contract itself may be inexistent or null and void, to determine the respective rights of the parties and to adjudicate upon their claims and pleas.*'
> (*Emphasis added*)

Similarly, Article 16 of the UNCITRAL Model Law on International Commercial Arbitration provides:

> '(1) The arbitral tribunal has the power to rule on its own jurisdiction, including any objections with respect to the existence or validity of the arbitration agreement. For that purpose, *an arbitration clause which forms part of a contract shall be treated as an agreement independant of the other terms of the contract.* A decision by the arbitral tribunal that the contract is null and void *shall not entail ipso jure the invalidity of the arbitration clause.*'
> (*Emphasis added*)

Although the provisions of some national laws may not yet have adopted the liberalism of the ICC Rules and the UNCITRAL Model Law, it would appear that today an arbitrator appointed pursuant to a valid arbitration agreement in respect of a dispute arising out of an international contract, has the widest powers and duties to consider all aspects of his authority and jurisdiction. He should not decline jurisdiction or refuse to consider and reach a decision on a particular issue, merely because one of the parties has raised an objection to his jurisdiction or indicated that he will seek to have the arbitrator's award set aside or challenge it when enforcement is sought. Rather he can and should consider the extent of his authority and his jurisdiction under the arbitration agreement, the validity of the main contract in which the arbitration agreement is included, and notwithstanding his conclusion on this matter, the rights and obligations of the parties in the prevailing situation.

Furthermore, even if he concludes that the main contract is invalid, this does not affect the arbitrator's authority under the arbitration agreement, and his award on any of these matters will generally be recognised and enforced subject to the provisions of the New York Convention.

18 *Joe Lee Ltd* v *Lord Dalmeny* [1927] 1 Ch 300.

Public policy restrictions on arbitration

Although arbitrators are free and indeed have a duty to investigate fully the extent of their jurisdiction, the questions as to their competence become even more strenuously contested where serious issues of mandatory law or public policy are involved. An award made in contradiction to or merely ignoring a mandatory law or public policy could subsequently be set aside or be unenforceable. In this regard, Article V.2 of the New York Convention provides that the court where recognition and enforcement are sought may refuse such recognition and enforcement if it finds:

> '(a) The subject-matter of the difference is not capable of settlement by arbitration under the law of that country; or
>
> (b) The recognition or enforcement of the award would be contrary to the public policy of that country.'

These same conditions are equally grounds for a court to set aside the award. Thus an arbitrator should always be mindful of his fundamental duty to reach a just and fair award which is valid and enforceable: if it is not, the whole arbitration will have been for nothing.

There are certain subject-matters which have a 'public policy' character and immediately give rise to fundamental challenges to the arbitrator's jurisdiction. We shall deal here with two particular questions: (1) anti-trust law, and (2) bribery and corruption. It is often alleged that the existence of questions affecting either of these matters precludes the arbitrator immediately from hearing the dispute and reaching a decision on the merits.

Anti-trust law

The regulations that protect the essential fabric of the market economy system have traditionally been considered to have mandatory application and a public policy character.

The application and effect of these rules differ in the territory of application. This is perhaps most notable in the distinction between the European Economic Community and the United States anti-trust rules. In the United States there is no procedure for obtaining an administrative ruling or clearance for a particular arrangement, except in the case of a merger or acquisition. Violation of anti-trust law is a felony punishable by a fine of up to US$1 million. Furthermore, any party injured by reason of such a breach may bring a civil action which, if successful, gives rise to treble damages. In the EEC, by contrast, punitive damages *inter partes* are not recoverable; however, very high fines may be imposed by the Commission of the European Communities ('EC Commission') for contracts, practices or arrangements which are considered to affect or restrict free competition between Member States.

In the event of a dispute arising out of an international commercial contract that provides for arbitration, the question arises how the arbitrator should react in the event of an issue of anti-trust law being raised. Specifically, can an arbitrator consider the merits of a dispute that involve the determination of certain competition law questions, or should he decline jurisdiction and direct the parties either to the national courts or competent executive organs to resolve the anti-trust issue before he considers the merits of the dispute.

In both the EEC and the United States the law and attitude on this matter is in a state of evolution. We shall consider briefly the rules of both systems and the position that arbitrators should and do generally take where their jurisdiction is challenged because of anti-trust implications.

The EEC

Article 85(1) of the Treaty of Rome 1957 prohibits as incompatible with the common market all agreements, decisions and concerted practices 'which may affect trade between Member States and which have as their object or effect the prevention, restriction or distortion of competition within the common market'. Such agreements or decisions are declared to be 'automatically void'[19] subject to express exemption being given from Article 85(1) for agreements, decisions and concerted practices which contribute

> 'to improving the production or distribution of goods or to promoting technical or economic progress, while allowing consumers a fair share of the resulting benefit, and which does not:
> (a) impose on the undertakings concerned restrictions which are not indispensable to the attainment of these objectives;
> (b) afford such undertakings the possibility of eliminating competition in respect of a substantial part of the products in question.'[20]

Only the EC Commission has the power to grant exemption from Article 85 – Council Regulation 17. However, until such time as the EC Commission shall have initiated proceedings under Regulation 17 with respect to a particular arrangement, 'the authorities of the Member States ... remain competent to apply Article 85(1)'.[21] To facilitate the granting of exemptions, under Article 85(3), the EC Commission has issued several block exemptions[22] which automatically exempt transactions that would otherwise fall within Article 85(1) – normally on terms that any arbitration award on an automatically exempted agreement be notified to the EC Commission – thus precluding the parties from the obligation to notify the agreement to the EC Commission with a request for exemption from Article 85.

There has been uncertainty as to how an arbitrator should act when faced with a question of EEC law. Clearly he is bound to apply relevant EEC law provisions as they are incorporated into the laws of Member States; and failure to do so could render an award unenforceable, particularly where the particular EEC law has mandatory effect.[23] However, arbitrators are not considered to be a 'court or tribunal of Member States' for the purposes of a reference under Article 177 of the Treaty of Rome.[24] In the circumstances

19 Article 85(2).
20 Article 85(3).
21 Regulation 17, Article 9(1).
22 See, eg, Regulation No 1983/83, on the Application of Article 85(3) of the Treaty to Categories of Exclusive Distribution Agreements; Regulation No 184/83, on the Application of Article 85(3) of the Treaty to Categories of Exclusive Purchase Agreements.
23 Ie, Community Regulations and Decisions are directly applicable in all Member States and have mandatory application – Article 189 Treaty of Rome.
24 European Court of Justice, Case No 102/81, March 23, 1982; *Nordsee Deutsche Hochseefischerei Nordstern GmbH* v *Reederei Mond Hochseefischerei Nordstern AG & Co*, and *Friedrich Busse Hochseefischerei Nordstern AG & Co* [1982] ECR 1095. This problem can be avoided under English law through the possibility of an appeal to the High Court, the court (rather than the arbitrators) will refer a question of EEC law to the ECJ: Section 1(2), Arbitration Act 1979; *Bulk Oil (Zug) AG* v *Sun International Ltd* [1983] 2 Lloyd's Rep 587.

then, can an arbitrator be considered 'an authority' of a Member State for the purpose of applying Article 85(1), prior to the EC Commission being involved? Or should an arbitrator decline jurisdiction immediately the relevance of Article 85(1) is raised? No definitive answers exist and the EC Commission has stayed away from the debate.[25] Nonetheless, from the earliest times, it has generally been thought that except where an issue is reserved exclusively for the jurisdiction of the EC Commission or some other Community organ, an arbitrator is not prevented by *ordre public communautaire* from determining his own jurisdiction in the light of EEC law.[26]

In reality, the attitude and action of an arbitrator faced with an EEC anti-trust issue should be influenced by pragmatism rather than principle. Whilst an arbitrator may have been appointed pursuant to a valid agreement entered into *bona fide* by the parties, he must always be mindful that his award must be enforceable: if it is not, then the arbitrator fails the parties. Practically then, if one party should challenge the arbitrator's jurisdiction on the basis that the main contract is void contrary to Article 85(1) and the arbitration agreement falls with the main contract, the arbitrator's duty, to both parties, is to investigate the facts and relevant issues to reach at least an initial opinion as to whether Article 85(1) has been infringed.[27] The generally recognised doctrine of separability must be accepted as extending to EEC anti-trust law, notwithstanding the public policy character of Article 85.

On the other hand, three fundamental limitations to this position must be recognised. First: in view of the complexity of Article 85 and the criteria that are normally taken into account by the EC Commission when determining its applicability to a particular factual situation, the arbitrator's decision can be, at best, *prima facie*. Whilst it will enable him to reject spurious and totally unjustifiable claims, which may be intended primarily to deprive the arbitrator of jurisdiction, the arbitrator's award cannot definitively resolve the fundamental issue, *viz*, whether the main contract did violate Article 85(1), due primarily to the fact that much of the economic data which the EC Commission would take into account is not available to him. However, the arbitrator's award should be considered dispositive *inter partes*: if enforcement of the award is sought, a court should generally recognise the arbitrator's award unless there is some manifest inconsistency or error. If one party remains dissatisfied and considers the arbitrator to be wrong on the basic issue, he could notify the contract to the EC Commission and request negative

25 The attitude of the EC Commission to arbitration as a dispute settlement mechanism was always – albeit not openly – slightly hostile. The early drafts of the directive on block exemption for patent licence agreements contained a provision, as have many decisions exempting specific arrangements from Article 85(1) of the Treaty, that any decision of arbitrators relating to the arrangement must be sent to the EC Commission. This is contrary to the fundamental principle of confidentiality and privacy in arbitration.

26 A resolution adopted at the second ICCA conference held in Rotterdam in 1966 stated that 'subject to the exclusive jurisdiction granted to the Community authorities, it falls to the arbitrators seized of disputes involving community law, to verify their authority and to decide on the merits of Community public policy under the control of the appropriate authorities.' [1966] *Revue de l'Arbitrage (Special)* 62. This resolution was strongly opposed by an influential group led by Maitre Jean Robert.

27 This is in fact the policy that has been followed in practice. See cases discussed in Julian DM Lew, *Applicable Law in International Commercial Arbitration*, Oceana, 1978, at paras 340–1.

clearance[28] though it is hard to imagine any circumstances where this would be in the best interests of the parties.

Second: if the arbitrator decides that the main contract does violate Article 85(1), he cannot make a decision as to the applicability of Article 85(3). This power is expressly granted to the EC Commission alone; not even a national court can do so. Thus even if the arbitrator should conclude that a contract or arrangement is void under Article 85(2), he cannot proceed to consider the merits of the dispute. The disappointed party may still, however, notify the contract to the EC Commission for exemption under Article 85(3), and if the party advises the arbitrator of his intention to do so, the arbitrator will almost certainly agree to stay the arbitration proceedings until after the decision of the EC Commission. On the other hand the arbitrator is free to decide that a contract does not violate Article 85(1) because it falls within a particular block exemption, he should not, of his own volition, refer the matter to the EC Commission for exemption under Article 85(3).

Third: if the main contract is void under Article 85(2), the arbitrator is empowered, pursuant to the doctrine of separability, to decide issues which are incidental or peripheral to the main contract, eg, to unravel the rights of the parties, order payment, repayment and restitution, and other property rights which were the subject-matter of the contract. These are matters which one would normally expect to fall within the arbitrator's jurisdiction and it is believed the parties would be able, notwithstanding the main contract being null and void *ab initio*, to enforce the arbitrator's award within these restricted confines.

The United States

Notwithstanding its pre-eminent position in world trade, the United States has not always shown the most liberal attitude towards arbitration: in fact it only adhered to the New York Convention in 1970. However, the Arbitration Act of 1925 recognises the position of arbitration as a dispute settlement mechanism in inter-state and international trade,[29] and the Supreme Court decision in *Prima Paints*,[30] recognising the separability of an arbitration agreement from the main contract, shows an approach to arbitration akin to that in Europe.

It is perhaps due to the 'primacy' accorded anti-trust law in the United States,[31] that one respected commentator has stated:

> '... nothing seems more well established than the rule that anti-trust claims are not subject to arbitration.'[32]

However, in the recent decision of the United States Supreme Court in *Mitsubishi Motors Corporation* v *Soler Chrysler-Plymouth Inc* the accepted

28 Regulation 17, Article 2.

29 *Op cit.*

30 Section 2 of the Arbitration Act provides that an arbitration clause in a maritime commercial transaction 'shall be valid, irrevocable and enforceable'.

31 Timberg, 'Anti-trust Aspects of Patent Litigation Arbitration and Settlement', in *Arbitration and the Licensing Process*, R Goldscheider and M de Hass, eds, Licensing Executive Society International, New York, 1981, at No 3–39.

32 *Mitsubishi Motors Corporation* v *Soler Chrysler-Plymouth Inc*, 24 *ILM* 1064 (1985).

rule that arbitrators cannot decide questions concerning anti-trust law was held not to apply to international (as opposed to domestic) arrangements.[33]

In the *Mitsubishi Motors* case a distributorship contract between related Japanese, Puerto Rican and United States parties contained a provision that all 'disputes, controversies or differences which may arise between [Mitsubishi and Soler] . . . shall be finally settled by arbitration in Japan in accordance with the rules and regulations of the Japan Commercial Arbitration Association'. The dispute arose when Soler failed to meet its obligations under the distributorship agreement, and Mitsubishi petitioned for an order compelling Soler to submit to arbitration. Soler denied Mitsubishi's claims and counter-claimed, *inter alia*, that the agreement could not be referred to arbitration as certain of its provisions had the effect of dividing the United States market and were therefore in violation of the Sherman Act. The United States Court of Appeals, First Circuit Court had held[34] that the anti-trust rules of the United States were of such importance that by allowing them to affect the arbitrability of an issue could not be considered parochial.[35] This decision was further explained on the grounds that due to the public policy character[36] of the Sherman Act, the arbitration agreement did not concern 'a subject-matter capable of settlement by arbitration' as required in Article II(1) of the New York Convention and could therefore not be enforced by virtue of Article V(2)(a) of the New York Convention. However, the decision was reversed by the United States Supreme Court, which held that in international transactions it was open to arbitrators to rule on an allegation that the transaction violated United States antitrust laws.[37]

Bribery and corruption

The meaning of public policy has been for many years, and remains, the subject of debate and diverging views. Initially a national doctrine, public policy has expanded to have effect beyond ordinary national territorial jurisdiction. Although certain basic concepts have become recognised as reflecting public policy, there still remains uncertainty, in the absence of an applicable mandatory law considered to have a public policy character as to what arrangements or actions are contrary to public policy. It is often difficult to define public policy, but courts are generally able to identify when a specific issue does not accord with public policy.

Most national laws recognise two levels of public policy: that applicable to purely domestic situations and that which applies where there is some international element. It is the latter type of public policy, 'international public policy' (*ordre public international*), which is relevant in the context of

33 Reversing the decision of the United States Court of Appeals, First Circuit.

34 723 F 2d 155 (1983).

35 In this respect the Court had in mind the Supreme Court decision in *Bremen* v *Zapata Off-Shore Co*, 497 US 1, at 9.

36 It is noteworthy that the Court classified the Sherman Act as of such importance that it applied in an international arrangement which extended beyond the territory of the United States, distinguishing *Scherk* v *Alberto-Culver Co*, 417 US 506 (1974) where the securities legislation was held to only have mandatory effect, excluding a reference to arbitration, in such situations which involve United States residents.

37 See *supra*, Introduction at 3–4.

international arbitration. Thus a national court having to determine whether to enforce a foreign arbitral award would only refuse to do so if its content violates the international public policy of the forum.

An international arbitrator must be mindful of two types of public policy: the national international public policy of the country or countries in which the award may need to be enforced, and truly international[38] or transnational public policy.[39] This international public policy is not concerned with any national influences – albeit internationally orientated, but rather reflects only the fundamental standards of the international community, covering both trading standards and other humanitarian criteria, and is developed from common standards of national policies, as well as fundamental concepts which have been embodied in international conventions or other international instruments. Examples of international public policy of this type would include the maintenance of the basic human rights as set out in the United Nations Declaration, preventing terrorism, avoiding abuses by multi-national companies and eliminating bribery and corruption.

On a practical level how does international public policy affect the jurisdiction of an arbitrator? Essentially one party could challenge the arbitrator's jurisdiction on the ground that the base contract is void *ab initio* due to being contrary to international public policy, thus rendering the arbitration agreement void as well. In circumstances where international public policy is alleged to deprive the arbitrator of jurisdiction, as in all other cases where his jurisdiction is challenged, it is considered to be incumbent upon him to verify the facts and determine whether the contract is, in fact, contrary to some principle of supra-national public policy. The fact that the main contract is unenforceable due to its being for a purpose that violates supra-national public policy should not leave the arbitration clause without effect.

One recent award[40] in which arbitrators sought to uphold international public policy concerned several inter-related contracts between two Yugoslav entities, and Dutch and Swiss entities. One of these contracts was fictitious with the sole object of getting round the restrictions of Yugoslav foreign exchange controls. The arbitrators held:

> 'These fictitious operations, giving rise to a credit which is itself fictitious, are contrary not only to Yugoslav legislation, but also to ethical and moral standards.
>
> In general, any contract having an object contrary to the imperative laws or public policy, to ethics and moral standards is null and void absolutely. It is so according to the Austrian General Civil Code, Article 879, in force in Croatia and Slovenia in 1974, and according to the Yugoslav law on contractual obligations which came into force in 1978.
>
> This principle is admitted in every country and all laws. It constitutes an international rule, an element of common law of contract in the international domain.'[41]

38 See Lew, *op cit*, at paras 407, 413.

39 Matray, 'Arbitrage et ordre public transnational' in *The Art of Arbitration: Essays on International Arbitration Liber Amicorum Pieter Sanders*, eds J C Schultsz and A J van den Berg, Kluwer, 1982, at 241.

40 ICC Case No 2730/1982. *Translation by the author.*

41 *Op cit*, at 917–8.

The arbitrators accordingly held all the related contracts to be affected by the invalidity of the fictitious contract and to be void and rendered an award accordingly.[42]

Most of the situations which appear to be contrary to international public policy, eg, contracts for bribing or corrupting Government officials,[43] smuggling, drug trafficking, fighting as a mercenary or terrorist action, kidnapping or murder, are unlikely even to come to arbitration. However, in recent years arbitrators have on several occasions been faced with issues which violate international public policy. In this context, two specific issues exist. First, should the arbitrator raise the issue of international public policy if the parties do not argue the point and wish the matter to be considered on its merits? Second, if the arbitrator finds the contract to violate international public policy should he stay his jurisdiction or reach an award on the merits.

The issue of international public policy in a particular transaction may become apparent because the arbitrator identifies it as a major influence on or the object of the contract, or because one of the parties specifically raises the issue in the arbitration.[44] The first situation arose in the now well-known Argentine bribery case[45] where the arbitrator was asked to determine entitlement to commission due to a contract having been obtained as a result of the agent's 'activities' on behalf of the tendering company. Notwithstanding that neither party raised the issue of public policy and that they both wanted the matter considered on its merits, the Swedish arbitrator, Judge Gunnar Lagergren, held the object of the contract which he found was bribery, to be contrary to the public policy of all the systems of law involved and to be void: he therefore refused to make an award on the merits.

International public policy was brought into issue by one of the parties in a recent ICC case[46] in which the Iranian plaintiff sought commissions for obtaining contracts for the Greek defendant with the Iranian Government. The defendant claimed that the plaintiff's efforts had not been dispositive in leading to the contract being awarded, and, moreover, that the agreement was void as the plaintiff's function had been to influence Iranian Government officials through secret payments and commissions. Although there was no evidence to prove conclusively that the plaintiff attempted to or did bribe Iranian Government officials, the Austrian arbitrator took cognisance of the endemic corruption of the previous Iranian regime and the success of the plaintiff's efforts on behalf of the defendant. Referring to the Argentine bribery case, the arbitrator held the base agreement to be void and rendered his award accordingly refusing to order commission payments for the plaintiff.[47]

42 This award appears to give national imperative laws an international or supra-national effect which is akin to the United Kingdom doctrine not to enforce a contract contrary to the law of a foreign and friendly state: *Foster* v *Driscoll* [1929] 1 KB 470; *Regazonni* v *K C Sethia (1944) Ltd* [1958] AC 301. As a general rule, the principle may be too widely construed.

43 El Kosheri and Leboulanger, 'L'arbitrage face a la corruption et aux trafics d'influence' [1984] *Revue de l'Arbitrage* 3.

44 El Kosheri and Leboulanger, *op cit*, at 6, suggest bribery will be raised before arbitrators by a plaintiff who was to have benefited from the bribery had it been successful and is now seeking to recover money paid, or by a defendant when a plaintiff claims commissions to which he is entitled under an 'agency' contract and the defendant alleges that the contract, even if successful, was for bribery and therefore illegal.

45 ICC Case No 1110/1963, reported in Lew, *op cit*, at para 423.

46 ICC Case No 3916/1982, 111 *Clunet* 930 (1984).

47 See also, ICC Case No 3916/1981, reported in a comment in 111 *Clunet* 920–921 (1984).

These two awards reflect the obligations of arbitrators, accepted as private guardians of international commercial transactions and the developers of the *lex mercatoria*, to uphold the fundamental and accepted standards of international trade and not to fall into the role of enforcing international practices regardless of whether they concur with prevailing applicable law and accepted international commercial standards. In this capacity, there is justification for the arbitrator to react to a manifest violation of international public policy, even though the issue has not been raised by either party.

This commitment ties in to the requirement that an arbitrator should ensure the award is ultimately enforceable in a national court as is well illustrated in the recent decision in *Northrop Corporation* v *Triad Financial Establishment*.[48] A contract had been made which involved the payment of 'commissions' to an agent in respect of arms sales to Saudi Arabia. The payment of commissions in this case was contrary to the United States Foreign Corrupt Practices Act and the Saudi Arabian Decree No 1275, of September 17, 1975. The arbitrators held that commission was payable to the agent under the contract, but the California Federal District Court refused to enforce the award on the grounds that the base contract was illegal under both United States and Saudi law and was therefore unenforceable. Although the court's decision was based on the legality of the commission arrangement and the United States' international public policy, contracts for the corruption of government employees are now generally recognised as contrary to supra-national public policy, which is perhaps the correct basis upon which the arbitrators should have refused to make an award in favour of the commission being payable.[49]

48 593 F Supp 928 (1984).
49 This case is being appealed and the result is awaited with interest.

8 The sources and limits of the arbitrator's powers in England

Kenneth S Rokison

Introduction

The sources, extent and limits of the powers of an arbitrator can be considered under three heads, namely:

1 jurisdiction;
2 procedural and interlocutory powers; and
3 powers in relation to the award.

Preliminary observations on the English approach to some fundamental issues in arbitration law

Before considering these three heads, some preliminary observations may be appropriate as to the English approach to the important conceptual questions to which these topics give rise.

Many of these issues have only recently been considered by the courts in England. First, to what extent is an arbitrator, in the exercise of his powers, to be equated with a judge? Second, to what extent should arbitrations be conducted in accordance with the rules and practices of the courts? Third, an associated question, to what extent should the powers of an arbitrator be subject to the general supervision and control of the courts? Two recent developments in England throw light on these general questions.

The Arbitration Act 1979

First and foremost, there is the Arbitration Act 1979 and the subsequent decisions of the courts, notably the House of Lords, as to its interpretation and application. This Act, as is well known, considerably reduced the extent of the English court's powers of judicial review on the merits over arbitrations in England. The abolition of the Special Case procedure, whereby arbitrators were entitled, and in cases involving a discernible point of law (which included questions of construction) could be required, to make their awards dependent upon the decision of the courts on that point of law, has meant that arbitration is no longer simply a preliminary step on the way to the final resolution of the dispute by the courts. This all-important limit on the powers of an arbitrator to make a final award has now been eliminated. The right of appeal on a point of law given by Section 1 of the 1979 Act, which replaced the Special Case procedure, has been held by the House of Lords to be very limited indeed.[1] Leave to appeal, necessary in the absence of all the parties' consent, will only be given in a dispute involving a 'one off' point of law or 'one-off facts', if the arbitrator was in the judge's view so obviously wrong as to preclude the possibility that he might be right.[2] Where the dispute concerns a contract term or event of common occurrence, a strong *prima facie* case must be made out that the arbitrator was wrong, for leave to be given.[3]

Similarly, the abolition by the 1979 Act of the court's power to set an arbitrator's award aside for an error of law appearing on its face[4] has eliminated a powerful incentive not to make reasoned or motivated awards for fear of giving grounds for the award to be set aside. The 1979 Act encourages reasoned awards[5] and has resulted in a transformation of the practice of arbitrators in England. The non-speaking award, with its inherent problems of enforcement, will soon, hopefully, be a thing of the past.

The Bremer Vulkan *case*

The second important recent development has come not from Parliament, but from the courts themselves. In 1981 in *Bremer Vulkan Schiffbau und Maschinenfabrik* v *South India Shipping Corporation*[6] the House of Lords upheld the decision of the Court of Appeal to the effect that an arbitrator has no power parallel to that of a Court to dismiss a claim for want of prosecution. This part of the decision was not controversial. However, their Lordships also held, by a majority of 3 to 2, reversing the unanimous decision of the Court of Appeal (which included Roskill LJ as he then was), and the decision of the Commercial Court Judge, Donaldson J (as he then was) that the court had no power to intervene to restrain a dilatory claimant from proceeding with the arbitration, even where the delay was such that a fair hearing was no longer possible.[7] This aspect of the decision has been subject to a great deal of criticism, but it does emphasise that the current climate in England is towards non-intervention by the courts in arbitrations even where injustice might otherwise result.

Quite apart from the decision, the speeches in the House of Lords, and in particular that of Lord Diplock, are illuminating on the wider question of the nature of arbitration itself. Lord Diplock pointed out that arbitration was fundamentally different to proceedings in court. Whereas litigation was essentially adversarial, the duty being on the plaintiff to pursue his claim with reasonable despatch, arbitration was essentially consensual, and each party was under an equal obligation to do whatever was necessary to achieve a timely resolution of the dispute.[8] It was for this reason that the court declined to

1 *Pioneer Shipping Ltd* v *BTP Tioxide* [1982] AC 724; *Antaios Compania Naviera SA* v *Salen Rederierna AB* [1985] AC 191.
2 *Antaios Compania Naviera SA* v *Salen Rederierna AB* [1985] AC 191, at 206.
3 *Ibid*, at 203.
4 Arbitration Act 1979, s1(1).
5 *Ibid*, s1(5).
6 [1981] AC 909.
7 *Ibid*, at 987.
8 *Ibid*, at 983–4.

intervene at the respondents' behest to extricate them from a situation which had developed from their own as well as the claimants' fault.

In 1910, in *Re Crighton and Law Car and General Insurance Corporation Limited*[9] Scrutton J described an arbitrator as 'a judicial officer' exercising powers analogous to those of a judge. In 1951, in *Chandris* v *Isbrandtsen-Motor Co Inc*[10] Tucker LJ said that an arbitrator not only must decide the dispute according to the law, but that 'every right and discretionary remedy given to a Court of Law may be exercised by him'.[11] By contrast, Goddard LJ in *R* v *National Joint Council for the Craft of Dental Technicians* said:

> '... although the arbitrator is going to settle the dispute between the parties, in one sense he is the antithesis of a court. A person goes to arbitration because he does not want to go to court. Therefore he sets up his own private judge to decide the case but the arbitrator is not deciding it as a judge, he is deciding it as an arbitrator, and procedural rights and all matters relating to procedure are to be found in the Arbitration Act, 1950'.[12]

It was the latter view which commended itself to the majority of the House of Lords in the *Bremer Vulkan* case. Lord Diplock said:

> '... the parties make the arbitrator the master of the procedure to be followed in the arbitration. Apart from a few statutory requirements under the Arbitration Act 1950 ... he has a complete discretion to determine how the arbitration is to be conducted from the time of his appointment to the time of his Award, so long as the procedure he adopts does not offend the rules of natural justice'.[13]

The fragmentary nature of the subject-matter

In discussing the question of the procedural powers and duties of an arbitrator, Mustill and Boyd comment[14] that no comprehensive statement of an arbitrator's powers is to be found in statute, and that:

> 'The law on the conduct of the reference is, in effect, the law of misconduct transformed from the negative into the affirmative, and it is difficult to make a reliable synthesis from this fragmentary material.'[15]

A further note of caution was sounded by that experienced post-war commercial judge, Sir Alan Mocatta, in *Star International Hong Kong (UK) Limited* v *Bergbau-Handel GmbH* when he said:

> '... there are few subjects on which it is more difficult to make an accurate generalisation than arbitration, or at least that is my experience.'[16]

9 [1910] 2 KB 738, at 745.
10 [1951] 1 KB 240.
11 *Ibid*, at 262.
12 [1953] 1 QB 704, at 708.
13 [1981] AC 909, at 985.
14 *The Law and Practice of Commercial Arbitration in England* (1982 Butterworths), at 241.
15 *Ibid.*
16 [1966] 2 Lloyd's Rep 16, at 18.

The sources of the arbitrator's powers

With this warning in mind, it is convenient to look first at the sources of the arbitrators' powers, namely:

1 the agreement of the parties;
2 the law.

The agreement of the parties

The agreement of the parties may of course involve not only their agreement as specifically expressed in the contract, whether it is a contract containing an arbitration clause, or a specific agreement to refer to arbitration, but also any arbitration rules which they may have incorporated by reference. These may be the rules of some trade association such as the Grain and Feed Trade Association, the London Metal Exchange, or the Refined Sugar Association. Most, if not all, of the trade associations in London dealing with the sale and purchase of commodities, not only in England but world-wide, have their own standard forms of contract, invariably incorporating arbitration clauses. Many of them have their own arbitration rules which may specify the powers of the arbitration tribunal in some detail. These may be the rules of some institution which administers arbitration, such as the ICC or the LCIA. The ICC, which, although it has its headquarters in Paris, administers arbitrations in many countries, does not promulgate detailed rules concerning the procedure to be adopted at all stages of the arbitration. By contrast, the LCIA, which is concerned only with international commercial arbitrations in London, does have quite detailed rules which, nonetheless, give the arbitrator a wide discretion to tailor the procedure to the needs of the particular dispute and the wishes of the parties.

The law

In relation to the *extent* and *limits* of the arbitrator's powers, the law may be found either in statute, or in the decisions of the courts. The relevant statute law is now contained in the Arbitration Acts of 1950, 1975 and 1979. In dealing with the three heads of jurisdiction, procedural and interlocutory powers, and powers to make an Award, I shall consider some of the main statutory provisions and some of the leading cases.

Jurisdiction

As regards jurisdiction, the extent and corresponding limits of the arbitrator's powers are essentially contractual. The arbitrator has the power, and indeed the duty, to determine the issue or issues referred to him by the parties: no more and no less. All this seems very simple, but a number of problems arise.

Is there a 'dispute'?

First, although there is no one form of arbitration clause which is in universal use, most common forms refer to 'disputes' between the parties. This may raise difficult problems in cases where the claimant's demand has been met by mere silence. In these circumstances, there may be no dispute on which the arbitrator can adjudicate. What is required in order to constitute a 'dispute' is also relevant in an associated context. Under the 1950 Act, by Section 4, the English court has a discretion to stay an action commenced in court in respect of a matter which is the subject of an agreed reference to arbitration. Under the 1975 Act, by Section 1, in a non-domestic situation, ie, unless both parties are English, the court *must* stay the action unless satisfied that there is no dispute between the parties. Claimants under a contract containing an arbitration clause may commence proceedings in court and apply for judgment under Order 14 of the Rules of the Supreme Court, whereby summary judgment without trial may be obtained by a plaintiff when there is no good *arguable* defence. The courts have treated an application for summary judgment by a plaintiff and the application for a stay by a defendant as the opposite sides of the same coin, so that, if there is no arguable defence to the claim, the court may give judgment and decline to grant a stay on the basis that there is, in fact, no 'dispute'.[17]

Did the parties agree to submit the dispute to arbitration?

Even if a dispute is established, questions may arise as to whether it is a dispute of a kind which the parties have agreed to submit to arbitration. This is a question of the construction of the arbitration clause, as was pointed out by Lord Porter in *Heyman* v *Darwins*.[18] In that case, a dispute as to whether the contract had been terminated in consequence of the breach was held to be a dispute 'arising out of the contract'. The most common form of widely-drawn arbitration clause, which refers to 'any dispute arising out of or in connection with the contract', may be wide enough to cover claims framed in quasi-contract or even tort.[19] However, it is doubtful whether, even if the arbitration clause were held to be severable and *prima facie* enforceable, such a clause could be construed as having any effect if it were concluded that the contract containing the arbitration clause were otherwise void or of no legal effect. There would then be no contract upon which the arbitration clause could bite.

Can the arbitrator determine his own jurisdiction?

To what extent does an arbitrator have the power to determine his own jurisdiction? Logic and common sense dictate that an arbitrator cannot have the power to determine finally disputes which impugn the validity of the very agreement to refer under which he was purportedly appointed, whether for illegality, fraud, mistake, want of consideration, or because some necessary precondition has not been satisfied. Arbitration rules incorporated into the 'contract' by reference may purport to give the arbitrator the power to determine his jurisdiction, but such rules would themselves only be binding upon the parties by reason of their incorporation in the contract, which, if

17 See for example, *Nova (Jersey) Knit Limited* v *Kamngarn Spinnerei GmbH* [1977] 1 Lloyd's Rep 453.

18 [1942] AC 356, at 392.

19 *Astro Vencedor Compania Naviera SA* v *Mabanaft GmbH* [1971] 2 QB 588.

void, could have no binding effect. The parties may of course agree to confer a special jurisdiction upon the arbitrator to decide the point. Even if they do not, the arbitrator is entitled to enquire whether he has jurisdiction before proceeding further. It is submitted however that his conclusion cannot be final and binding upon the parties. Since whatever may be the decision of the arbitrator, it will be open to challenge, it may in most cases be preferable for such disputes to be resolved directly in the courts at an early stage.

May an arbitrator rectify a contract?

An associated problem which is partly one of jurisdiction and partly one concerning the arbitrator's powers in relation to the award, is the extent to which an arbitrator can rectify the contract containing the arbitration clause pursuant to which he was appointed, if it does not accurately reflect the real agreement between the parties. Provided the real agreement between the parties was at least accurately reflected in the arbitration clause, there seems no reason in principle why the arbitrator should not correct some other part of the written contract. However, it is unclear if a dispute as to whether rectification should be ordered is one 'arising out of this contract'.

Is the dispute arbitrable under English law?

There are certain types of disputes which, although as a matter of construction may fall within the scope of the agreement to refer, the English courts, as a matter of policy, consider inappropriate to be adjudicated upon by an arbitration tribunal.

Thus, under Section 24 of the 1950 Act, the court has the power to revoke the authority of an arbitrator where the dispute involves a question of fraud. However, again, parties can agree to confer on an arbitrator a specific jurisdiction to determine such questions, by express agreement or the incorporation, by reference, of arbitration rules which give such a power.

Procedural and interlocutory powers

Sources

The parties' agreement

Unlike the question of jurisdiction, the parties very rarely specifically define in their agreement the manner in which the arbitration tribunal shall carry out its function. The arbitrator's procedural and interlocutory powers are therefore generally found either in arbitration rules incorporated into the contract by reference, or in the law. Quite apart from specific statutory provisions, eg, in the Arbitration Acts, the courts will as a matter of law imply into any contract, including one containing an agreement to refer a dispute or disputes to arbitration, such terms as may be necessary in order to give business efficacy to the contract.[20] They will, in addition, imply terms by custom, if proved either generally or in relation to a particular trade. Thus an arbitrator will generally have such powers as are reasonably necessary to enable him to exercise his

20 *Luxor (Eastbourne) Ltd* v *Cooper* [1941] AC 108, at 137.

jurisdiction and to adjudicate upon the issues referred to him. The court will not usually interfere with the exercise by the arbitrator of what is a wide discretion to conduct the proceedings in whatever manner seems to him to be appropriate.

The *Law Reports* tend to give a very false impression as to the conduct of arbitrations generally. This is because primarily those arbitrations which are brought before the courts tend to be those where, unusually, something has gone wrong, or at least is alleged to have gone wrong. Furthermore, those arbitrations tend to be those in which, the arbitration tribunal has adopted a procedure akin to that laid down and practised in court litigation. It is principally in such cases that the lawyers, who are mainly responsible for bringing such cases before the courts, will be involved. These cases are the exception rather than the rule. One should therefore not be misled into thinking that, arbitration procedure in England is for the most part conducted in an adversarial manner, despite what was said by the House of Lords in the *Bremer Vulkan* case. There is nothing in the English law of arbitration which prohibits an inquisitorial approach, and many arbitrations proceed quite informally, without pleadings, without discovery, without lawyers, without problems, and without anyone outside the particular trade hearing anything about them. As already pointed out, many sets of rules, such as those of the LCIA, make very detailed provisions for interlocutory powers, in some cases giving the arbitrator a very wide discretion. Where the parties expressly agree upon matters of procedure, eg, by incorporating a set of arbitration rules, the question may arise as to whether the rules so agreed and incorporated are intended to be comprehensive, thus excluding any implication which might otherwise arise, by law, custom, or some other basis. This problem arose recently in *Bank Mellat* v *Helleniki Techniki SA*[21] in which Kerr LJ (in the majority judgment) expressed the view that the ICC Rules (which were incorporated) were intended to be 'self-sufficient', and since those Rules contain detailed provisions in relation to the securing of the costs of the tribunal, but none concerning the securing of the costs of the parties, the parties must be deemed to have intended to exclude the right which the respondents might otherwise have had, to apply to the court for security for their costs. Robert Goff LJ disagreed, holding that this reasoning could only be applied if the relevant provisions of the Rules adopted by agreement were inconsistent with any term which might otherwise be implied. Nevertheless, in the exercise of the court's discretion, he agreed in the result that no security for costs should be ordered.[22]

Problems may arise if the parties purport to agree upon the manner in which the arbitration shall be conducted, but do so in vague terms such as, 'arbitration in the usual way'. In *Scrimaglio* v *Thornett and Fehr*,[23] Scrutton LJ construed this phrase to mean in accordance with the laws of England and the Arbitration Act. However, in *Naumann* v *Edward Nathan & Co, Limited*, the Court of Appeal preferred the approach that this reflected a presumed intention of the parties that the arbitration was to be conducted in the manner habitually adopted in the particular trade.[24]

21 [1984] QB 291.
22 *Ibid*, at 310–18.
23 (1924) 18 LlLR 148.
24 (1930) 37 LlLR 249.

If no procedure or interlocutory powers are agreed upon either specifically or by reference, then some implication may be necessary. In *London Export Corporation Limited* v *Jubilee Coffee Roasting Co Limited*[25] Diplock J suggested that an arbitrator's powers may be implied (i) from the language of the reference, (ii) by statute, (iii) from surrounding circumstances, and (iv) by the custom of the trade.[26]

The Arbitration Acts

The Arbitration Acts say very little about the powers of the arbitrators. Section 12(1) of the 1950 Act gives the arbitrator powers to examine witnesses on oath or affirmation, call for documents and compel the parties to do all such other things which, during the proceedings on the reference, they may require. However, even this wide power has been construed as limited to such things as may be required to assist the arbitrator in arriving at a determination of the dispute referred.

The limits on the arbitrator's powers

An arbitrator does not have vested in him all the powers which would be vested in a judge. He cannot, for example, order security for costs to be furnished by either party,[27] nor can he commit to prison or fine for contempt, grant injunctions, or bind third parties, for example, by issuing subpoenas to compel the attendance of witnesses. Nor, it seems, does an arbitrator have power to order security to be furnished in respect of the claimants' claim.[28] In court proceedings, where an application is made for summary judgment under Order 14 of the Rules of the Supreme Court, if the court concludes that there is only a very weak or shadowy defence, it may be given leave to defend only upon terms of payment into court of the sum claimed or a proportion of it.[29] Before the abolition of the Special Case procedure by the 1979 Act, where a barely arguable point of law arose, some arbitrators used to agree to state their award in the form of a Special Case only on condition that security for the claim was furnished. With the abolition of the Special Case, this practice no longer exists.

The power of the arbitrator to secure his fees

A question which may be of some importance to the arbitrator concerns what power he has to secure his own fees. The rules of the ICC and other institutions may require sizeable deposits to be paid in advance in respect of the costs of the tribunal. The practice that an arbitrator's fees are in general only payable against the taking up of the award has led to an unfortunate reluctance on the part of some arbitrators to give any indication in the course of the hearing of their preliminary views on the matters in issue, when time might be saved if

25 [1958] 1 Lloyd's Rep 197. This decision was upheld in the Court of Appeal at [1958] 1 Lloyd's Rep 367.
26 *Ibid*, at 202.
27 Mustill & Boyd, *op cit*, at 296.
28 *Ibid*, at 298, 301–2.
29 Rules of the Supreme Court, Order 14, Rule 4(3).

they did. Complex cases with long hearings can produce serious problems for arbitrators. Weeks or even months may be set aside but the dispute may be compromised at the last minute. Nevertheless in a recent decision in chambers an arbitrator who refused to set aside a period of 12 weeks for a hearing without some undertaking that some payment would be made in respect of the time set aside in any event, was said by the court to be holding the parties to ransom. I know about it only because I was the arbitrator!

The arbitrator's power to prevent delays during the arbitration

As we have seen, the arbitrator does not have the power to strike out a claim for want of prosecution, but he can require the parties to furnish pleadings, and, if necessary, particulars of them. As it seems to be accepted that an arbitrator can impose sanctions for failure to comply with his order, a strong arbitrator can do much to avoid any undue delay by either party. Some confusion arises by reason of Section 5 of the 1979 Act, under which the court may, on application, vest in the arbitrator a power to continue the reference in default of appearance or any other act by the parties in the same manner as a judge of the High Court. This suggests that without an application to the court, the arbitrator would not have such a power. Furthermore, continuing with the reference in default may not be an appropriate or helpful remedy, especially where the default is that of the claimant.

The relationship of the powers of the court in arbitrations with those of the arbitrator

Further confusion is introduced by Section 12(6) of the 1950 Act, whereby specific powers are given to the court in relation to arbitration proceedings. It might be assumed that the court is given these powers because the arbitrator does not possess them himself, but this is not necessarily the case. Although an arbitrator has no power under the general law for example, to order security for costs or for the amount in dispute, he does have the power to order discovery or interrogatories and to make preservation orders regarding the property the subject-matter of the dispute.[30]

Discovery

Of all the various powers which an arbitrator may have, the power to order discovery of documents warrants special mention, because it involves a concept which is totally alien to some systems of law. The idea of a party being obliged to disclose to the tribunal and his opponent documents which, far from supporting his case, can be fatal to it, may seem astonishing. Nevertheless, the procedural rules governing litigation in the English courts require the production by all parties of all non-privileged documents in their possession, custody or power which relate to any matters in issue, or may lead to a relevant train of enquiry. The obligation is broad, and must be complied with strictly. Contrary to popular belief, there is no such general obligation to give discovery in English arbitrations. In the absence of agreement between the parties,

30 Arbitration Act 1950, Section 12(1).

specifically or by a system of rules incorporated in the contract which requires discovery, it is for the arbitrator in his discretion, upon application if necessary, to decide what degree of discovery is necessary to enable him to perform his function properly. He may order no discovery or only limited discovery. He is the master of the procedure, and will not be regarded as having misconducted himself by not ordering the discovery of a particular document or class of document.[31]

Does the arbitrator have the power to consolidate arbitrations?

A further important topic concerning procedure must be mentioned. In the absence of agreement between the parties, an arbitrator has no power to consolidate two sets of arbitration proceedings. The reason is said to be twofold, namely (i) that each arbitration is a private proceeding and the parties are entitled to insist upon that privacy being maintained, and (ii) more important, that the parties to each arbitration proceeding are entitled to exercise a free choice as to the appointment of arbitrators. In Hong Kong, the law has recently been changed to give the courts a power to order consolidation in an appropriate case,[32] and many think that a similar power should be given to the courts in England. In the absence of an express agreement between all the parties, the only way in which consolidation may be achieved in England is if the arbitration is to be conducted in accordance with a set of rules, which themselves provide for consolidation. This will normally only be possible if the tribunal is chosen not by the parties, but by an institution, appointing authority or some third party.

Must the arbitrator apply the law in deciding the case?

Leaving aside particular powers possessed by arbitrators, there are two more fundamental questions concerning the arbitrator's powers in relation to the conduct of proceedings.

Must arbitrators reach their decisions on the basis of the strict application of some identified system of law, or may they simply decide in accordance with what appears fair in all the circumstances?

Although the differences between arbitration and legal proceedings were emphasised in the *Bremer Vulkan* case, it remains the case that arbitrators are at least *prima facie* bound to decide in accordance with the applicable law. This may not necessarily be English law, since it is open to the parties to choose a substantive law different from that of the place of arbitration. It is also open to arbitrators, where no proper law is specified, to conclude that the substantive rights of the parties are to be governed by some foreign law which will then have to be proved, if disputed, as a matter of fact. The arbitrators' conclusions of fact cannot be made the subject of an appeal under the 1979 Act.

The question arises whether it is open to an arbitrator to decide '*ex aequo et bono*' if the parties have agreed that he should. There seems no reason why the

31 *The Anangel Peace* [1981] 1 Lloyd's Rep 452.
32 Arbitration Ordinance, s6 B(1).

common will of the parties should not prevail, but the English courts have been reluctant to give full effect to the parties' agreement in this context. In *Orion Compania Espanola de Seguros* v *Belfort*[33] Megaw J said:

> '. . . arbitrators must in general apply a fixed and recognisable system of law which primarily and normally would be the law of England . . . they cannot be allowed to apply some different criterion such as the view of the individual arbitrator or umpire on abstract justice or equitable principles . . .'[34]

Lord Denning MR in *Eagle Star Insurance Co* v *Yuval*[35] suggested that an 'equity' clause does not displace the whole panoply of the law, but 'merely ousts technicalities and strict construction'.[36] Mustill and Boyd conclude that the solution to the problem of such clauses in England has yet to be worked out.[37]

Must arbitrators adhere to the rules of evidence which would apply before an English court or may they admit or decline to accept evidence at their discretion?

Agreements to refer disputes to arbitration frequently provide that the arbitrators shall not be bound by the strict rules of evidence. Arbitration rules often have similar provisions, and there is no reason in principle why such provisions would not be given effect to, subject to the rules of natural justice or fairness. However, if the parties have made no such agreement, to what extent is an arbitrator bound by the rules of evidence or free to exercise his discretion? The weight of English authority suggests that an arbitrator is *prima facie* bound to apply the strict rules of evidence but the principle is obscured by an apparent willingness in the courts to find an exception in the particular circumstances of the case.[38] Thus the court may infer an agreement to waive the strict rules of evidence on the basis that such rules are habitually disregarded in the type of arbitration under consideration. With the modern trend of non-interference in the conduct of arbitrations, it may well be that the courts would not intervene unless the breach of the rules of evidence is fundamental to the arbitrator's decision[39] or amounts to a breach of the rules of natural justice. Thus, an award would be set aside if it were based upon evidence received by the arbitrator from one side without the other side being afforded an opportunity of considering and dealing with it.[40] Conversely an arbitrator may be guilty of misconduct if he refuses to look at relevant evidence, having formed the view in advance that it would not assist him.[41]

A similar principle is applied to the case of an arbitrator using knowledge which he has gained from some other source. An arbitrator may of course use the skill and experience which he has derived from his business career. Indeed, the possession of such skill and experience is often the reason for the particular

33 [1962] 2 Lloyd's Rep 257.
34 *Ibid*, at 264.
35 [1978] 1 Lloyd's Rep 357.
36 *Ibid*, at 362.
37 Mustill & Boyd, *op cit*, at 605–17.
38 *Ibid*, at 311–12.
39 *Agroexport* v *NV Goorden Import SA* [1956] 1 Lloyd's Rep 319.
40 *The Government of Ceylon* v *Chandris* [1963] 1 Lloyd's Rep 214.
41 *Faure Fairclough* v *Premier Oil and Cake Mills Limited* [1968] 1 Lloyd's Rep 237.

arbitrator having been appointed, especially in quality arbitrators. However, it will be misconduct for an arbitrator to make use of his knowledge concerning a particular fact or state of affairs relevant to the particular case without giving the parties or their witnesses an opportunity of dealing with it.[42]

The overriding obligation of the arbitrator to observe the rules of natural justice

Finally, in relation to procedure and the conduct of the arbitration generally, it must be emphasised once again that the overriding limit on the powers of an arbitrator is that he must act fairly in accordance with the principles of natural justice. In this respect at least, an arbitrator is subject to the same or equivalent constraints as a judge, and in this respect, the Court's former power of control has not been affected by the 1979 Act.

If parties have agreed to submit their disputes to arbitration, then the courts will strive to give effect to that agreement and will not usually interfere. However, in the last resort, and indeed as a protection to the parties, an arbitrator who does not conduct the proceedings fairly may find his award set aside.

The award

The primary *source* of the arbitrator's power to make an award must be the agreement between the parties to submit a particular dispute to him. Thus, where the dispute is simply as to the parties' respective legal rights and obligations, the arbitrator's power, and indeed his duty, is to declare what those rights and obligations are. Similarly, if the claim is for a debt or damages, the successful claimant should obtain an award ordering the payment of the appropriate sum of money. A number of particular problems have arisen in relation to arbitration awards, and I shall consider some of them briefly.

'Default' powers

As has already been noted, an arbitrator has no power to dismiss a claim for want of prosecution, but he can make a peremptory interlocutory order, requiring a particular course of action, and provide that failure to comply will, for example, debar the party concerned from adducing evidence on a particular point or making an amendment to its pleadings. I have already mentioned Section 5 of the 1979 Act, but it is doubtful still to what extent an arbitrator could debar a claimant from proceeding or a respondent from defending himself against a claim, merely because of some default in furnishing a pleading, giving discovery or the like. Only time will tell.

Interim award

Section 14 of the 1950 Act gives the arbitrator power to make interim awards, but this can only be used within the scope of the reference. An interim award of

42 *Fox* v *P G Wellfair* [1981] 2 Lloyd's Rep 514.

money can therefore be made when a sum has been admitted or found to be due and owing, but an arbitrator would be guilty of misconduct if he were to make an interim award in relation to an issue on which he has not yet given the parties a full opportunity to be heard.

Specific performance and injunctions

By Section 15 of the 1950 Act, an arbitrator can order specific performance of a contract other than one relating to land. There are *dicta* suggesting that injunctive relief is the exclusive prerogative of the courts[43] but there seems no reason in principle why an arbitrator should not be given power to grant an injunction. Arbitrators certainly make interlocutory orders which require something to be done by one of the parties. It is said that the reason why an arbitrator cannot grant an injunction is that he does not possess the coercive committal powers of the courts, but the same argument would hold good in respect of an order for specific performance.

The currency of the award

Even before the rule that the English courts had to make money awards in sterling was changed by the House of Lords in *Miliangos* v *George Frank Textiles Ltd*[44] arbitrators in London were commonly making awards in foreign currencies where they considered it appropriate. Indeed, this practice was recognised and approved in *Jugoslavenska Oceanska Plovidba* v *Castle Investment Co Inc*[45] and the case was relied upon in the *Miliangos* case as reflecting a change in commercial needs and practice. The reasoning in the *Jugoslavenska* case is instructive. Lord Denning MR dismissed arguments based on doubts as to enforceability by saying:

> '... when commercial men are in dispute and go to arbitration they wish to have the dispute resolved. They want a decision one way or the other. Once given, they abide by it ... There is rarely any need to call in the sheriff or his officer to enforce the Award ... But when a plaintiff goes to a court of law, it is, as often as not, because the defendant cannot pay or will not pay. The plaintiff wants to get judgment against him and, if need be, levy execution upon his effects'.[46]

This argument is consistent with the *dicta* in the *Bremer Vulkan* case which distinguished between the aims of parties in arbitration and litigation. It also undermines the possibility of limitations being placed on an arbitrator's powers on the basis that his interlocutory or final decisions must be capable of judicial enforcement.

Interest

Section 19A of the 1950 Act (inserted by Schedule I Part IV of the

43 *Chandris* v *Isbrandtsen-Moller* [1951] 1 KB 240 at 262, *per* Tucker LJ.
44 [1976] AC 443.
45 [1974] QB 292.
46 *Ibid*, at 299.

Administration of Justice Act, 1982) confers statutory powers on an arbitrator to award simple interest on:

1 a debt paid late after proceedings for its recovery have begun, but before they have been concluded, and
2 a debt remaining unpaid until a money judgment is given as a result of the conclusion of proceedings brought for its recovery.

However, arbitrators do *not* have power to award either (i) interest on a debt paid late before proceedings for its recovery have begun, or (ii) compound interest.

These propositions derive from the judgments of the House of Lords in *President of India* v *La Pintada Compania.*[47] In the course of his speech, Lord Brandon said:

> 'Where parties refer a dispute between them to arbitration in England, they impliedly agree that the arbitration is to be conducted in accordance in all respects with the law of England.'[48]

To the extent to which Lord Brandon was equating the *practice* in arbitration with the *practice* laid down by statute or otherwise prevailing in the courts, there would seem to be a conflict of principle between the House of Lords in the *La Pintada* case and the speeches in the *Bremer Vulkan* case.

Costs

Section 18(1) of the 1950 Act gives an arbitrator discretion as to the award of costs, subject to an expression of a contrary intention. Section 18(3) curiously limits the parties' freedom to decide that each party shall, in any event, pay its own costs, but only in respect of an arbitration agreement to submit future (not existing) disputes. In this area of the exercise of arbitral power, the courts have consistently emphasised the similarities between an arbitrator and a judge. An arbitrator must, it appears, exercise his discretion in the same way as a judge,[49] so that, as a matter of general principle, a party who is successful ought to be awarded his costs, to be taxed, if not agreed.

The form of the award

As a general rule, there is no mandatory form for an arbitration award. An arbitrator is not bound to give the reasons for his decision, although under Section 1(5) of the 1979 Act, the court has the power to order an arbitrator or umpire to state his reasons or further reasons, if either party asked for a reasoned award, or there is some other special circumstance. However the need to give reasons should not give rise to any concern. They do not need to be couched in any formal legal language. With the fear of an award being set aside for error of law on its fact having been removed by the 1979 Act, it may be hoped that the growing trend for arbitrators to give their reasons, however informally, may be continued. If an arbitrator is capable of reaching a decision, he ought to be able to tell the parties why he has done so.

47 [1985] AC 104.
48 *Ibid*, at 119.
49 *Matheson & Co* v *A Tabah & Sons* [1963] 2 Lloyd's Rep 270.

Supplementary powers

Once an arbitrator has made his final award, he is *prima facie functus officio*, subject to any remission by the court. His powers and duties are thereupon terminated. But he does retain a residual power to correct any clerical mistake or error arising from an accidental slip or omission,[50] and he may, on application by one of the parties, add to his award provisions as to costs if he did not include them in the original award.[51]

Conclusion

In this paper, I have covered a large number of topics, necessarily, some only in the barest outline. If any conclusion can be drawn, it is that however fragmentary the principles and rules of English arbitration practice may be, there is a significant discernible trend away from judicial control at all stages, and towards giving effect to the parties' presumed intentions.

50 Arbitration Act 1950, s17.
51 *Ibid*, s18(4).

The law applicable to the merits of the dispute 9

Ole Lando

This paper deals with the law applicable to the merits of an international commercial dispute. It treats the rules and practices of the arbitral tribunals of the western countries.

National and non-national arbitral tribunals

Most disputes submitted to arbitration are taken to national tribunals. The parties choose the seat of the arbitration. In many cases they agree to bring their dispute before a tribunal of an arbitration institution such as the London Court of International Arbitration or the Arbitration Institute of the Stockholm Chamber of Commerce. The institution selects the arbitrator or, if the tribunal is to be collegiate, the chairman of the tribunal. The Institution generally makes its selection from a panel of domestic arbitrators.[1] The proceedings are conducted under the arbitration rules of the institution supplemented by the rules of the domestic law of arbitration and civil procedure.[2] Parties which do not resort to institutional arbitration may establish a national arbitration *ad hoc*. They appoint the arbitrator or choose a court or another national authority which is to appoint the arbitrator or the chairman of the tribunal. Failing an agreement to the contrary the tribunal will sit in the country where the arbitrator or chairman is selected, and the proceedings will be conducted under the rules of procedure of that country.

Reference is to an increasing extent made to non-national arbitration. The parties who have neither chosen the seat of arbitration nor the arbitrator agree to entrust an international body, such as the Court of Arbitration of the International Chamber of Commerce, with the choice of the arbitrator or the chairman of the tribunal. The institution or the arbitrator selects the seat of the tribunal. The tribunal follows the arbitration rules of the institution and is not bound to apply the rules of procedure of the place of arbitration.

The parties may also decide that an arbitration *ad hoc* shall be referred to a non-national tribunal. An international institution such as The Permanent Court of Arbitration at The Hague may then be called upon to nominate or appoint the arbitrator. The arbitrator will apply the rules of procedure which

1 Stockholm Chamber of Commerce, *Arbitration in Sweden* (1984), Stockholm 1984, at 7: 'So far most arbitrators appointed by the Institute have been of Swedish nationality ...'.
2 *Ibid.*

the parties have agreed upon. They may select the Arbitration Rules of the United Nations Commission on International Trade Law (UNCITRAL).

A non-national arbitration tribunal is often chosen because the parties wish to have the case decided by a neutral tribunal. In the absence of such an agreement the plaintiff will bring an action before a court in the defendant's country. The court is expected to be impartial but the case is tried in the defendant's language and according to the procedure of his country. The defendant has the advantage of 'playing at home'. To avoid this the parties may refer their dispute to a court or the national arbitration institution of a 'neutral', third country. However, by doing so they submit to proceedings and often also to substantive rules which are alien to both of them: they often cannot frame the proceedings as they wish. Neutrality and freedom is obtained only by selecting a non-national arbitral tribunal.[3]

The situations described above are typical cases. It is for the parties to decide the character of the tribunal; they may decide that it shall have some traits of a national and some of a non-national arbitration. Many shades between the two types are seen. Sometimes the parties, though they have selected the arbitrator from a certain country and placed the seat of arbitration in that same country, have wanted him to apply an autonomous set of procedural rules. Some tribunals of the ICC have in some respects acted as national ones.

Article VII of the European Convention of 1961, and its followers

Many countries, including the United Kingdom, have no statutes dealing with the law to be applied by an arbitrator to the merits of the dispute. It is generally understood that to determine the applicable law the arbitrator will apply the choice-of-law rules of the forum country.

In Europe[4] the most prominent provision on the issue is Article VII of the European Convention on International Commercial Arbitration, which provides:

1 The parties shall be free to determine, by agreement, the law to be applied by the arbitrators to the substance of the dispute. Failing any indication by the parties as to the applicable law, the arbitrators shall apply the proper law under the rule of conflict that the arbitrators deem applicable. In both cases the arbitrators shall take account of the terms of the contract and trade usages.

2 The arbitrators shall act as *amiables compositeurs* if the parties so decide and if they may do so under the law applicable to the arbitration.

Article VII, paragraph 1, second sentence, makes every arbitrator his own legislator. He is not bound to apply the choice-of-law rules of the forum country. The European Convention has been ratified by at least 18 states in the

3 On the issue of 'the arbitration unbound', see Lalive, 'Les règles de conflit de lois appliqués au fond du litige par l'arbitre international siègeant en Suisse', [1976] *Revue de l'arbitrage* 155; Paulsson, 'Arbitration Unbound: Award Detached from the Law of its Country of Origin', 30 *ICLQ* 358 (1981); Park, 'The Lex Loci Arbitri and International Commercial Arbitration', 32 *ICLQ* 21 (1983); Paulsson, 'Delocalisation of International Commercial Arbitration: When and Why it Matters', 32 *ICLQ* 53 (1983).

4 Jayme and Hausman, eds, *Internationales Privat-und Verfahrenstrecht* (1978), 256.

East and the West. Article VII has had a considerable impact upon later texts. Article 38 of the Rules of Arbitration of the United Nations Economic Commission for Europe 1966 and Article VII(4)(a) of the Arbitration Rules for the Economic Commission for Asia and the Far East provide almost identical rules.

Article 33 of the UNCITRAL Arbitration Rules provides:

1 The arbitral tribunal shall apply the law designated by the parties as applicable to the substance of the dispute. Failing such designation by the parties, the arbitral tribunal shall apply the law determined by the conflict-of-law rules which it considers applicable.
2 The arbitral tribunal shall decide as *amiable compositeur* or *ex aequo et bono* only if the parties have expressly authorised the arbitral tribunal to do so and if the law applicable to the arbitral procedure permits such arbitration.
3 In all cases the arbitral tribunal shall decide in accordance with the terms of the contract and shall take into account the usages of the trade applicable to the transaction.

Article VII of the European Convention has also influenced the Arbitration Rules (1975) of the International Chamber of Commerce (ICC), which in Article 13(3)–(5) provides:

3 The parties shall be free to determine the law to be applied by the arbitrator on the merits of the dispute. In the absence of any indication by the parties as to the applicable law, the arbitrator shall apply the law designated as the proper law by the rule of conflict which he deems appropriate.
4 The arbitrator shall assume the powers of an *amiable compositeur* if the parties are agreed to give him such powers.
5 In all cases the arbitrator shall take account of the provisions of the contract and the relevant trade usages.

Article VII(1), second sentence, of the European Convention and Article 13(3), second sentence, of the ICC Arbitration Rules give the arbitrator much freedom in his determination of the applicable law. Arbitration is secret and the awards do not have the authority of precedents. However, how the arbitrators have decided disputes, how they have used the freedom they have been granted, is regarded as valuable knowledge. The psychological factors which lend persuasive authority to precedents also operate in the case of arbitral awards. Faced with a problem one wants to know what others in similar situations have done, and one tends to copy them.[5] So a number of awards have been published[6] and several are passed on from hand to hand.

The awards published show that the arbitrators of the western countries have made extensive use of their freedom. They have applied a variety of methods and rules when deciding which law to apply to an international contract. These methods will be described below.

5 'Chronique des sentences arbitrales', Cour d'arbitrage de la Chambre de Commerce, ('Chronique CCI'), in 109 *Clunet* 967 (1982), on the inclination of arbitrators to cite published awards.

6 See cases published in *Yearbook: Commercial Arbitration* (P Sanders ed) 1976 to-date; *Revue de l'arbitrage* (France); and reports, Chronique CCI in *Clunet* 1974 to date. Also very copious reports in Julian D M Lew, *Applicable Law in International Commercial Arbitration*, New York 1978.

Choice of law by the parties

Express choice of law

Today many contracts contain clauses which expressly submit them to the law of a certain country. The reported cases show that the arbitrators invariably apply the law selected by the parties.[7] Some do so without reference to any national private international law authorising the choice of law by the parties.[8] Other awards find an authorisation of the choice of law in the conventions or in the conflict-of-law rules of a country.[9]

No case is known in which an arbitrator has set aside the parties' express choice of law on the ground of lack of connection with the intended legal system.[10] Several awards uphold the choice of a law unconnected with the contract.[11] It appears that the parties in these cases often wanted a neutral law or a well-developed law to apply. Choice-of-law clauses which were made with an evasive intention and by which the parties committed what the French call *fraude à la loi* have not been found in the arbitration cases.[12] Nor have I found any court decision which has set aside an award on the ground that the arbitrator had given effect to a choice which was not *bona fide* and legal.

Choice of the *lex mercatoria*

A choice of the *lex mercatoria* is becoming more and more frequent in international contracts. It takes different shapes.

The parties to an international contract sometimes agree not to have their dispute governed by any national law. Instead they submit it to the customs and usages of international trade, to the rules of law which are common to all or most of the states engaged in international trade or in those states connected with the dispute. Where such common rules are not ascertainable the arbitrator applies the rule or chooses the solution which appears to him to be the most appropriate and equitable. In doing so he considers the law of several legal systems. This judicial process is partly an application of legal rules, partly a selective and creative process. The choice described here is the choice of the *lex mercatoria* as the system of law to govern the contract. A combination of the *lex mercatoria* with one legal system is also frequent. Furthermore parties often choose a combination of the *lex mercatoria* and equity (*amiable compositeur*).[13]

I shall not here deal with merits of the *lex mercatoria*. Professor Goldman has done so convincingly.[14] Let me just note that in Europe the *lex mercatoria* is a fact. Arbitrators apply it and those courts which have faced awards applying it have accepted its application.

7 ICC Award No 1512/1971, reported by Lew, *op cit*, Nos 105 and 106.
8 Eg, ICC Award Nos 3160/1978, and 3349/1978 (unreported).
9 Eg, ICC Award No 893/1955, reported by Lew *op cit*, No 106.
10 On the views of some writers see Lando, 'Contracts', in *International Encyclopedia of Comparative Law* (K Lipstein, ed), Volume III, Chapter 24.
11 Lew, *op cit*, Nos 126 and 128.
12 *Ibid*, No 128.
13 See Goldman, 'La lex mercatoria dans les contrats et l'arbitrages internationaux: réalités et perspectives', in *The Influence of the European Communities upon Private International Law of the Member States*, Brussels 1981, 211.
14 *Ibid*, and Goldman, 'Les conflicts de lois en matière d'arbitrage international de droit privé', 109 *Recueil des cours de l'Académie de droit international de la Haye*, 347 (1963).

Tacit choice of law by the parties

The cases of an implied choice of law fall into two categories. One is where the intention is demonstrated with reasonable certainty by the terms of the contract or the circumstances of the case. If, for instance, the parties had used a contract formula which was current in a country, they had chosen an arbitration institution established in that country, which was also the country of the place of performance of the contract, then it is argued there is a tacit choice of law.

The other category is where the facts of the case do not support a tacit choice of law. Formerly British, French and German cases made frequent use of the presumed intention of the parties[15]; often they found that the parties had intended the law of the forum to apply. This practice, which has caused much uncertainty, has also been found in the arbitral case law. The choice by the parties of an arbitrator of a certain nationality, an arbitral institution based in that country which is to be the seat of arbitration, has been regarded by some arbitrators as a presumed choice of the law of the nationality of the arbitrator or of the seat of arbitration.

However, the rule *qui eligit arbitrum eligit jus* does not apply generally to international arbitrations.

It does not apply to the non-national tribunals which have no forum in the ordinary sense of the word. Many, if not most, references brought to the ICC Court of Arbitration will not have any allegiance to a certain country. The ICC Court of Arbitration will ask the National Committee of the ICC in a country to which neither party belongs to nominate the arbitrator or third arbitrator (chairman). The ICC Court also chooses the place of arbitration to be in a 'neutral' country. As mentioned above the selection of a neutral arbitrator and a neutral place of arbitration has great advantages in international commercial arbitration. However, the place of arbitration and the nationality of the arbitrator have no connection with the dispute.

The same may apply to a non-national arbitration *ad hoc*. Imagine British and Polish parties who have referred their dispute to *ad hoc* arbitration under the UNCITRAL Rules. The appointing authority selected under these Rules has appointed an arbitrator from Malmö in Sweden. After his appointment the parties have agreed to conduct the reference in Copenhagen mainly because this city is convenient to reach for all persons involved. In such circumstances there is no reason why this reference should be governed by Swedish or Danish law.

In cases tried by a non-national tribunal it is not even reasonable to apply the choice-of-law rules of the seat of arbitration or the nationality of the arbitrator. See on this question *infra* at IV(1). There is then even less reason to apply the substantive law of the place of arbitration or the home country of the arbitrator. If the case is tried by a national arbitral tribunal the answer may be different. This is shown by the national court decisions which have dealt with the effect of the choice by the parties of a national tribunal upon the law governing the merits of the dispute.

English courts have held that an agreement to submit to the jursidiction of the courts or to arbitration in a particular country is evidence of an intention to

15 See Lando, *op cit*, Nos 115–17, and 126.

apply the law of that country. In most cases this has led to the application of English law.[16] In two leading cases dating from the end of the nineteenth and the beginning of this century submission to arbitration in England led the English court to uphold an arbitration clause which was valid by English law, and which would have been invalid according to Scottish and Jersey law respectively, and which would have applied respectively in the absence of an effective choice of law.[17] However, in 1970 the House of Lords held that a contract made in France between a French shipowner and a Tunisian charterer for the transport of oil from one Tunisian port to another, payment to be made in France, was governed by French law although the charterparty provided for arbitration in London. The charterparty also contained a clause that it was governed by the law of the flag. However, since the ships used for the transport of the 350,000 tons of oil were Norwegian, Swedish, French, Liberian and Bulgarian, and all were chartered by the 'shipowner', the clause was held incapable of application. Apart from the arbitration clause the contract had no other connection with England. Their Lordships agreed that even if the parties had failed to make an express choice of law the proper law of the contract was French law with which the contract had its closest connection. They also agreed that where the parties had made no express choice of law, the inclusion of an arbitration agreement is very strong evidence of an intention to apply the law of the place of arbitration, but that such an agreement '... should not be treated as giving rise to a conclusive or irresistible inference ...'.[18]

The French courts have also been induced by an arbitration or jurisdiction clause to conclude that the parties intended to submit the contract to the law of the chosen forum.[19] In one of the leading cases the court was faced with the issue whether the submission to arbitration and to the courts in England constituted a valid choice of English law with the result that the arbitration agreement was valid, while it was invalid according to French law which would have applied in the absence of a valid choice of law. The court held that the submission constituted a tacit and valid choice of English law and upheld the arbitration clause.[20]

In West Germany the courts have held over a long period of time that a clause submitting to the courts or to arbitration in a particular country

16 Jurisdiction clauses: *NV Kwik Hoo Tong Handel Maatschappij* v *James Finlay & Co Ltd*, [1972] AC 604 HL. Arbitration clause: *Hamlyn & Co* v *Talisker Distillery*, [1984] AC 202 HL; *Spurrier* v *La Cloche*, [1902] AC 446 PC; *Tzortzis* v *Monark Line A/B*, [1968] 1 WLR 406 CA. See also Dicey & Morris *The Conflict of Laws*, 9th edition, London 1980, at 735–6, 761; and Russell, on *Arbitration*, 20th edition, London 1982, at 58 *et seq*.

17 *Hamlyn* v *Talisker*, and *Spurrier* v *La Cloche*, *op cit*.

18 *Compagnie d'Armement Maritime SA* v *Compagnie Tunisienne de Navigation SA* [1971] AC 572, HL, at 596, *per* Lord Wilberforce.

19 Jurisdiction clause: Cass civ June 28, 1937, *Rev crit d.i.p.* 1938, 62; Cour Rouen February 12, 1953, *DMF* 5 (1953) 677; Cass civ July 1, 1964, *Rev crit d.i.p.* 1966, 47. See also decision cited by Batiffol & Lagarde, *Droit international prive*, 7th edition, Paris 1983, No 589. Arbitration clause: Cass civ February 19, 1930 (also a jurisdiction clause) and Cass civ January 27, 1931 (also choice of law), *S* 1933. 1.41. In a later case the Cour de Paris (October 26, 1962, *Rev crit d.i.p.* 1965, 535) said 'that the clause by which the contracting parties have agreed to submit disputes arising out of their contract to the decision by arbitrators of a certain country is one of the most significant indications that the contract, as they have conceived it, is localised in the country thus designated'.

20 Cass civ February 19, 1930, *op cit*.

constituted a tacit choice of law of that country.[21] Sometimes other connecting elements or other indications of intention were taken into account as additional evidence of a choice of law.

Scandinavian practice is mainly in accordance with that in Germany.[22] Both arbitration and jurisdiction clauses are usually regarded as indicating a tacit choice of law. As in West Germany and Switzerland other elements are often invoked together with the submission clause as proof of the intention.

Some of the published awards go, as mentioned, in the same direction.

An opposite trend is, however, discernible. The presumption does not apply when the seat of arbitration has been chosen by two parties who wished to arbitrate at a neutral place. The contrary has been held by the English Court of Appeal in the case *Tzortis* v *Monark Line AB*[23] where the choice of arbitration in London by a Greek and a Swedish party was considered to be a choice of English law. This, however, was later criticised in the House of Lords.[24] The leading textbook on international arbitration in Sweden does not even mention any presumption in favour of the *lex loci arbitri.*[25] However, together with other connecting elements, notably the habitual residence of one of the parties, their selection of the seat of arbitration may carry weight as a connecting element.[26]

Choice of law by the arbitrator

For cases where the parties have not selected the law, the European Convention and the ICC Rules have almost identical texts. The European Convention provides:

> 'Failing any indication by the parties as to the applicable law, the arbitrators shall apply the proper law under the rule of conflict which the arbitrators deem applicable.'

The ICC Rules have preferred the word 'appropriate' to the word 'applicable'. It is doubtful whether this implies any difference of meaning.

This rule gives the arbitrator a number of possibilities. A great variety of methods and solutions are found in the reported cases on the choice of law by the arbitrators. Most of the cases referred to in the following pages are cases decided by ICC arbitrators.

When giving reasons for the award the arbitrator has a double concern. As the servant of the parties he must persuade them and especially the losing party

21 BGH December 5, 1966, AWD 1967, 108 IPRspr 1966/67 No 41(b); BGH July 1, 1964, IPRspr 1964/65 No 38; KG December 6, 1955, IPRspr 1954/55 No 186; OGHBZ May 4, 1950, IPRspr 1950/51 No 18; see also G Kegel, *Internationales Privatrecht*, 4th Edition, Munich 1977, at 292.

22 DENMARK: Landsover–samt Hof og Stadsretten October 9, 1899, UfR 1899 A 995; HD October 11, 1928, UfR 1928 A 1045. NORWAY: Byrett Oslo September 22, 1949, NDS 1949, 409; HD October 17, 1896, NRt 1897, 289; HD May 26, 1934, NRt 1934, 549. SWEDEN: HD May 19, 1899, NJA 1899, 184.

23 [1968] 1 WLR 406 CA.

24 See the *Compagnie d'Armement* case, *op cit*; Russell, *op cit*, at 63; and Dicey and Morris, *op cit*, at 761.

25 *Arbitration in Sweden*, *op cit*, at 46 *et seq*.

26 See Batiffol & Lagarde, *op cit*, No 589.

of the justice of his award. Furthermore, he must make sure that the award is enforceable in the country or the countries where enforcement may be sought. This leads many arbitrators to justify their conclusions by referring not only to the law which they deem applicable to the dispute but also to other laws connected with the parties or the subject-matter of the dispute. The arbitrator will often refer to the law of the unsuccessful party to show that this law confirms his findings.

The differing reasons given by arbitrators for their determination of the applicable law, include the following:

National conflict of law rules

There are several reported cases in which the arbitrator has applied the conflict-of-law rules of a national legal system. Often the arbitrator applied the conflict rule of the country where the case was tried.[27] If the parties have referred to a national arbitration institution the arbitrator will follow the conflict rules of that institution.[28]

It is doubtful to what extent the arbitrator in other cases is bound to apply the conflict-of-law rules of the country in which he hears the case. Article VII of the European Convention, Article 33 of the UNCITRAL Rules, and Article 13(3) of the ICC Rules, all authorise the arbitrator to select his own conflict-of-law rule. It has been convincingly argued that Article VII should be followed by non-national arbitral tribunals even in countries which have not adhered to the European Convention.[29]

There are also numerous awards in which the arbitrator has made a cumulative application of identical or converging conflict-of-law rules of the countries connected with the dispute.[30] If an arbitrator who is confronted with the choice between the laws of two countries cannot show that their laws agree on the substance of the issue he can sometimes demonstrate that their conflict-of-law rules agree on the application of one of the laws.[31] In some cases the arbitrator has shown how abundantly the legal systems agree. Confronted with two legal systems A and B he first shows that the conflict-of-law rules of A and B both lead to the application of the law of A. Then he points out that the substantive laws of A and B also agree on the issue to be decided.[32]

General principles of private international law

Awards have been found where the 'general principles' of private international law have been invoked.[33] The arbitrator has alleged that there was unanimity among the private international laws of the world or at least among all the major legal systems on the issue. This has sometimes been done with some

27 See Lew, *op cit*, No 234.
28 *Arbitration in Sweden*, *op cit*, at 44.
29 *Ibid*, at 46.
30 Eg, ICC Award No 4434/1982, 110 *Clunet* 889 (1983).
31 See Derains 'L'application cumulative par l'arbitre des systèmes de conflit de lois interessées au litige', [1972] *Revue de l'arbitrage* 99; ICC Awards No 422/1966 and 1990/1972, 101 *Clunet* 884 and 897 (1974); Lew, *op cit*, No 287.
32 See ICC Award No 3235, reported in 108 *Clunet* 925, (1981).
33 Lew, *op cit*, No 238; ICC Award No 3880/1982, 110 *Clunet* 897, (1983).

audacity. In a case from 1967[34] it was stated that it was 'in conformity with the constant theory and case law concerning the conflict of laws (... that ...) preference has to be given to the law of the place where the conract has been made, and subsidiarily, to that of the place of performance'. This holds true of some legal systems but by no means of all.[35]

'International' conflict of law rules

In other cases reference has been made to international conventions on private international law. The Hague Convention on the Law Applicable to International Sale of Goods 1955 has been invoked. This has happened even where none of the states connected with the matter had adhered to the Convention.[36] Reference to this Convention has also been made by state courts of countries which were not parties to the Convention.[37] State courts have also invoked conflict of law rules in texts which do not have legally binding character, such as draft conventions and draft laws.[38] Article VII of the European Convention, Article 33 of the UNCITRAL Rules and Article 13(3) of the ICC Rules allow the arbitrator to make use of such texts.

Non-national conflict of law rule

In several cases the arbitrator has relied on a conflict-of-law rule without disclosing from which legal system or other source he has derived it.[39] The arbitrator has, for instance, stated that he chooses the law of the country in which the contract was made or was to be performed. In most cases it has been easy to find authorities which support the rule chosen by the arbitrator.

Direct choice of substantive law

In a number of cases the arbitrator has taken a short cut to the substantive law, thus avoiding the intricacies of private international law.[40]

First, in some cases the arbitrator has compared the substantive rules of the various countries connected with the dispute and has found a happy convergence. All rules led him to the same outcome.[41] In most of these cases this short cut has been justifiable. Any conceivable conflict rule would have led him to one of the converging laws. Secondly, in other cases the arbitrator has stated, without giving reasons, that he applied the substantive law of a certain country.[42] He has not revealed whether the laws of other connected countries would have led him to the same result. It is submitted that the arbitrator chose the law which he found most appropriate for the dispute.

34 ICC Award No 1404/1967, Lew, *op cit*, No 285.
35 Lando, *op cit*, Nos 107–42.
36 Eg, ICC Award No 1717/1972, 101 *Clunet* 890 (1974).
37 Lando, *op cit*, No 120 (on the Netherlands).
38 Eg, German BGH September 19, 1973, *IPRspr*, 1973 No 11.
39 ICC Award No 2735/1976, 104 *Clunet* 947 (1977); see also two cases cited at 949, and ICC Award No 2870/1978 (not reported).
40 Lew, *op cit*, No 302 *et seq*.
41 ICC Award No 2886/1977, 105 *Clunet* 996 (1978); see also Derains, *op cit*.
42 Eg, ICC Award No 1422/1966, Lew, *op cit*, No 270.

Apply international substantive law

In some cases the arbitrator, in addition to invoking a rule of national law, has supported his finding by reference to the *lex mercatoria* or to the general principles of law.[43]

(a) In most of the cases this has been the international trade usages or the prevailing practices of international trade.[44] This reference is in accordance with Article VII(1) of the European Convention, and Article 13(4) of the ICC Rules of Arbitration. In these situations the arbitrator need not search for a proper law of the contract.
(b) Other cases show that the arbitrator has relied exclusively on a non-national law. In fact more and more arbitrators rely on the general principles of law without having been expressly or tacitly authorised to do so by the parties. This is now permissible under French law[45] and probably also under Austrian law.[46] Whether the courts of other European countries will permit it is open to doubt.

An arbitrator who relies solely on 'the general principles of law' is often unable to find principles which are truly 'general' in the sense that they belong to the common core of all legal systems or even the laws connected with the dispute. He will therefore, to a large extent, have to use his creativity and act as a social engineer.

If the parties direct the arbitrator to apply the *lex mercatoria* they will know its merits and its demerits, one of which is the scarcity of 'authority' on which the arbitrator can base his decision. They will know that the arbitrator cannot make scientific investigations to ascertain the 'common core' of many legal systems and that he will often have to use his *bon sens*.

For the same reason an agreement by the parties to have the case decided by *amiable composition* will also allow the arbitrator to apply the *lex mercatoria*. Whereas a selection of the *lex mercatoria* cannot be regarded as an agreement on *amiable composition*, the elements of the *lex mercatoria*, ie, international usages, general principles of law, arbitral case law, are appropriate bases for the decisions of an *amiable compositeur* in an international dispute.[47]

Furthermore, a non-national arbitral tribunal is often selected in an effort to 'denationalise' the arbitration. Therefore such a tribunal should be permitted to apply the *lex mercatoria* to cases where the tribunal finds that the contents of the law applicable has not been ascertained. In these situations most national arbitral tribunals would do as the courts, and apply the *lex fori*. Non-national tribunals, however, have no real forum. Instead of applying the law of the casual seat of the tribunal it is an appropriate way out of the difficulty to apply the *lex mercatoria*.[48] Also, if in a case where the law applicable to the contract has not been selected by the parties one of them pleads the application of the *lex*

43 ICC Award No 1675/1969, 101 *Clunet*, 895 (1974).
44 Lew, *op cit*, Nos 367–72; ICC Award No 2583/1976, 104 *Clunet* 950 (1977); ICC Award No 2375/1975, 103 *Clunet* 973 (1976).
45 Code de procedure civil, Article 496.
46 Supreme Court Decision of November 18, 1982, see IPRax 1984, at 97 and 106.
47 See 107 *Clunet* 967 (1980).
48 See 108 *Clunet* 922 (1981).

mercatoria a non-national arbitral tribunal should be permitted to comply with his request.

In other cases, however, where both parties have pleaded application of a national legal system th , arbitrator will, it is submitted, act in excess of his powers if he applies the *lex mercatoria* to the contract.

Conclusion

Reading the awards one sees a multitude of approaches and ideas. International commercial arbitration is being practised by lawyers of different nationalities and attitudes. Thereby and through the open-mindedness of many arbitrators it has the freshness and inventiveness of a young science. On the other hand the reported cases show little coherence.

I believe that in many arbitrators, as in many lawyers, there are two conflicting attitudes. One wishes the law to be a perfect and stringent system of rules under which the good lawyer can always find the true and only solution. To apply the law is the same as to apply the theorems of mathematics. This will produce certainty and predictability for the citizen.

The other attitude tells the arbitrator that absolute predictability is not attainable. Each legal system has many gaps and the most provident legislator cannot close them all. Nor can he prevent new gaps from arising when social conditions change. No legal system provides certain solutions to all problems. Even the best lawyer in the most highly-developed country is often in doubt. Besides, predictability is only one of several legal values. Rules which create certainty also tend to bring about rigidity. They do not consider special circumstances and changing conditions. The legal process is not and can never be a mere syllogism. It is above all an effort to reach the most fair and appropriate decision. In this process which is often inventive the arbitrator will weigh the possible solutions against each other and make his choice.

In international arbitration the inventive attitude will probably always be more in evidence than in the courts of law. However, the law and practice of international arbitration is developing rapidly; the rich literature on the subject and the growing number of published awards indicate that it may become more coherent. Probably one day the arbitrators will coordinate their practices as regards the choice of the law applicable to the merits of the dispute.[49] It is likely – and recommendable – that the arbitrator will then follow the trend of the modern legislations[50] which converge with the case law of several countries.[51] It has the following characteristics:

49 See on this question Lando, 'Conflict of Law Rules for Arbitrators', *Festschrift fur Konrad Zweigert*, Munchen 1981, 156.

50 See Convention on the Law Applicable to Contractual Obligations, opened for signature in Rome on June 19, 1980, *Official Journal of the European Communities*, L 266, October 9, 1980 ('EEC Convention'). The Convention entered into force in Denmark on July 1, 1984. Austrian Federal Law of June 15, 1978 on Private International Law (BGBI 1978 No 304) (hereinafter 'AuFL'). Swiss Federal Law on Private International Law (Draft), published on November 10, 1982 as 'Message concernant une loi fédérale sur le droit international privé', by the Swiss Federal Council (hereinafter 'SwDL'). American Law Institute, Restatement of the Law Second, Conflict of Laws, St Paul, Minnesota, 1981. Vol I–III (hereinafter 'R2d').

51 See Lando, *op cit*, Nos 115–42.

1 The law chosen by the parties governs the contract.[52] Only a choice which appears clearly from indications in the contract or from the behaviour of the parties counts as a choice of law. The presumed intention is not considered.[53]
2 In the absence of a choice of law by the parties the law with which the contract has its most significant connection will govern.[54] This connection is based upon the relevant contacts notably the place of business or the habitual residence of the parties, and the place of performance.[55] The parties' choice of the place of arbitration or the nationality of the arbitrator may also carry weight.
3 It is to be presumed that the contract has its most significant connection with the country where the party who is to effect the performance which is characteristic of the contract has his place of business.[56] Thus sales of movables are presumed to be governed by the law of the seller's place of business, license contracts with the law of the licensor's place of business, and agency and distributorship contracts with the law of the agent's and the distributor's place of business.

However, employment contracts are presumed to be governed by the law of the place of work[57] and contracts the subject-matter of which are immovables, by the law of the place where the immovable is situated.[58] Other special presumptions for specific contracts exist or may come into existance.

These rules are as mentioned presumptions which means that they do not apply if it appears from the circumstances of the case that the contract has its most significant connection with the law of another country.

52 Dicey & Morris, *op cit*, Rule 145; R2d, No 187; EEC Convention, Article 3; AuFL No 35; SwDL Article 113.
53 Dicey & Morris, *op cit*, Rule 145, Sub-rules 1 & 2; R2d No 187, Comment (a); EEC Convention, Article 3(1); AuFL No 35(1); SwDL Article 113(2).
54 Dicey & Morris, *op cit*, Rule 145, Sub-rule 3; R2d No 188; EEC Convention, Article 4(1); SwDL, Article 114.
55 Dicey & Morris, *op cit*, at 769 *et seq*; R2d No 188(2).
56 EEC Convention, Article 4(2); AuFL No 36; SwDL Article 114.
57 Dicey & Morris, *op cit*, Rule 161; R2d No 196; EEC Convention, Article 6; AuFL No 44; SwDL, Article 118.
58 Dicey & Morris, *op cit*, Rule 153; R2d Nos 189 & 190; EEC Convention, Article 4(3); AuFL No 42; SwDL Article 116.

The applicable law: general principles of law – the *lex mercatoria* 10

Berthold Goldman

In the Programme of this Conference, the wording of my contribution's heading is: 'General Principles of International Commercial Law (*Lex Mercatoria*)'. Such wording seems to imply that 'General Principles . . . and *lex mercatoria*' are synonymous. However, this is a controversial issue, as is even the mere inclusion of general principles of law in the *lex mercatoria*, along with customary rules of international trade, which would be its second and different component.

This controversy goes beyond a mere matter of definition; it bears on the constituent elements of the *lex mercatoria*. I shall therefore consider it as a preliminary matter.

In a second set of observations, I shall try to show how parties to international contracts do refer to the *lex mercatoria*, and to examine whether there are applications and 'reception' of *lex mercatoria* as a source of law in international arbitration, by international Conventions, municipal statutes and case law. In other words, whether *lex mercatoria* may be viewed as a set of legal rules.

I shall then select some examples of the application of the *lex mercatoria* to decide upon several issues encountered in international arbitration, and in particular, on the issues of the substantive dispute, arbitrability of the dispute and conduct of the arbitration.

Definition and components of the *lex mercatoria*

There is a wide conception of the *lex mercatoria*, according to which it might be defined by the *object* of its constituent sources. *Lex mercatoria* would thus, irrespective of the origin and the nature of these sources, be the *law proper to international economic relations*. One would encompass not only transnational customary law, whether it is codified or not (and in the latter case revealed and clarified by arbitral awards), but also law of an interstate, or indeed state, which relates to international trade. Thus, for example, the successive Hague (1954) and Vienna (1980) Conventions Establishing Uniform Laws for the International Sale of Goods would be part of *lex mercatoria*. This would also be the case with respect to national legislation whose specific and exclusive object is international trade, such as that of the German Democratic Republic. The same applies to rules specific to international trade established by national case law, such as, for example, the French notions of the autonomy of the parties, the general validity of international arbitration agreements, and the capacity of the state and of public entities to bind themselves by such agreements. All this is considered as being well established by the 1981 French Law on International Arbitration, although the Law did not expressly incorporate these notions so as not to constrain the evolution of the case law.

This wide view has always been that of Clive Schmitthoff, and it may be compared to that of Philip Jessup in his classical work on 'Transnational Law'. I will state at once that I do not share it. For it is obvious that the specific problems of transnational commercial custom (ie, is it a rule of law? does it constitute a transnational legal order, distinct from national legal systems as well as from the international legal order *stricto sensu*?), do not arise with respect to rules of inter-state or state origin. No one contests that the latter are rules of law, nor that they are part of the legal order of the states having adopted them. I note in this respect that this is clearly so even when the origin of these rules is solely to be found in case law, as is the case with the French rules I cited as examples. The criterion for determining the ambit of *lex mercatoria* that I would follow thus does not solely reside in the *object* of its constituent elements, but also in its *origin* and its *customary*, and thus *spontaneous* nature.

It should be noted, however, that like many boundaries, the one thus drawn does not escape controversy, or if I may say, 'transboundary hypotheses'. Thus, the General Conditions of the United Nations Economic Commission for Europe (UNECE) – which are, in fact, Standard Contracts – have a transnational object, but were established under the auspices of an international organisation. Should they, for this latter reason, be eliminated from the domain of the *lex mercatoria*? One may oppose this, because they were prepared by the representatives of the concerned business sectors, whom the UNECE simply provided with logistical assistance and legal expertise, so that they are actually of professional and customary origin. Do they, however, have the status of customary law? It should be contended that the businessmen elevate them to this status only insofar as they refer to the standard contracts with such a degree of frequency that it might finally be concluded that such a reference is implicit. In fact, one meets this issue in more than one instance of the forming *lex mercatoria*.

A second 'transboundary', or at least open to discussion, hypothesis is the one where a specific rule of international trade, and in particular of international arbitration, is affirmed by a state court, without any reference to an international convention, or to a domestic statute, one may wonder whether such judicial decisions embody a rule pertaining merely to the legal system of the particular court, or rather a transnational unwritten principle or rule which the state court wishes to affirm and to apply.

At least provisionally, I would here conclude that the *lex mercatoria* comprises rules the *object* of which is mainly, if not exclusively, transnational, and the *origin* is customary and thus spontaneous, notwithstanding the possible intervention of interstate or state authorities in their elaboration and/or implementation.

Does the *lex mercatoria*, as tentatively defined according to its origin and nature, comprise both the usages of international trade which become customary rules, and *general principles of transnational law*? Furthermore, is it possible to draw a clear distinction between customary rules and general principles?

This is a difficult issue, if only because the general principles of law are themselves of double origin. There are, firstly, principles common to all, or to a large majority of national legal systems (such are the general principles mentioned as a source of international law by Article 36 of the Statute of the International Court of Justice); *pacta sunt servanda* is here the simplest, but not the only, example. Secondly, there are rules that are specific to international trade, insofar as they are not embodied in the majority of the national legal systems; an example could be here the obligation for the creditor to *minimise the prejudice* due to the non-performance by the debtor of his obligations. Indeed, while generally admitted in Common Law – as far as I know – such obligation is not clearly embodied in civil law (except, possibly, as implied in the general requirement of good faith).

Does this mean, at least, that the general principles of the first category are generated by the international *societas mercatorum*, or are specific to the international *societas mercatorum*. I do not think this first objection is decisive. Indeed (to take the example already mentioned), where a transnational contract is governed by the *lex mercatoria*, *pacta sunt servanda* is not referred to by the parties, nor by the arbitrators, as a principle taken from a particular national law, but as a principle dominating transnational law. The practical consequence is that the interpretation of this principle and its possible limitations (for instance, *force majeure*), which may differ from one national system to another, are themselves elaborated in the framework of the transnational law.

It might be more difficult to draw a clear distinction, in the framework of the *lex mercatoria*, between general principles and transnational customary rules. A good example is here the one of *minimisation of damages*: is the creditor's obligation to minimise his loss based on a general principle of law, or on a transnational customary rule? I would personally be inclined to choose the second solution. Indeed, a general principle is not purported to govern just one particular situation; it is the source of more than one rule of law, applicable to several sets of facts. Thus, *pacta sunt servanda* generates not only the obligation of each party to a contract to fulfil its promises, but also the obligation to perform them in good faith, to compensate for the damage caused to the other party by their non-fulfilment, and not to terminate the contract unilaterally where such termination is not contractually or legally provided for. One could say that a general principle of law is engendering rules of law and dominates their interpretation, while a transnational customary rule (like any other rule of law) governs a specific situation of fact; and one could think that according to this distinction the obligation to minimise the prejudice is a customary rule, rather than a general principle.

It remains to be seen whether the distinction, if so drawn, is of some practical interest. The same could be found in the mandatory and even the *public policy* character of the general principles, or at least of some of them, as opposed to the 'suppletory' character of the customary rules (which would mean that the parties could depart from the latter, but not from the general principles). Such a distinction implies that there is a 'public policy of the *lex mercatoria*', which one author has recently denied,[1] but which arbitral awards

1 A Kassis, *Théorie genérale des usages du commerce*, Paris 1984, at 473.

have effectively applied, in respect of the state's capacity to conclude arbitral agreements[2] or in cases of bribery.[3]

Whatever the case, the reading of court decisions or arbitral awards shows that when referring to transnational law, judges and arbitrators mention general principles as well as general usages of international trade, not taking very much care to distinguish clearly between them, as being two components of the *lex mercatoria*. Consequently, I shall here conclude that *lex mercatoria* is, at the least, *a set of general principles and customary rules spontaneously referred to or elaborated in the framework of international trade, without reference to a particular national system of law.*

This definition should now be substantiated; in other words, it remains to be seen whether *lex mercatoria* is a set of *legal* rules and principles.

Lex mercatoria as a set of legal principles and rules

Reference to *lex mercatoria*

The applicability of *lex mercatoria* may result from (a) clauses in *international contracts*, and (b) rules effectively applied by *international awards*.

Clauses in international contracts

One may meet clauses that expressly exclude the application of every municipal law, and provide for the exclusive application of general principles and usages of international trade.[4] In reality, such clauses cannot prevent the arbitrator (and possibly the judge) from referring, in some instances, to a municipal law: for example, where the validity of the consent to the contract or the personal capacity of one of the parties are challenged. Indeed, the *lex mercatoria* does not offer transnational customary rules to settle such issues, so that the answer should be taken from the municipal law applicable according to the choice-of-law rule the arbitrator will decide to apply (practically, the *lex personalis* or the *lex contractus*). However, such issues appear exceptionally in international arbitration with respect to natural persons.

As to legal persons, in particular companies, it is the law governing them which determines the officers or the body who are empowered to execute agreements on their behalf; however, *lex mercatoria* may play a rule, in respect of international contracts, by imposing the principle of *good faith*, which may make a contract binding for the company where an appearance of validity has been wrongly created. In addition, the more practical issue is here the ability of a state or a public body to execute an arbitral convention: the *lex mercatoria* considers that this ability is to be recognised, notwithstanding the provisions of the state's law denying it.[5]

2 See, eg, ICC Award, Case No 1939/71, cited by Derains, [1973] *Revue de l'arbitrage* 145.

3 ICC Award, Case No 1110/1963, cited by Julian D M Lew, *Applicable Law in International Commercial Arbitration*, New York 1978, at 553; El-Kosheri and Leboulanger, 'L'arbitrage face à la corruption et aux trafics d'influence,' [1984] *Revue de l'arbitrage* 3.

4 See, eg, ICC Award, Case No 1569/70, cited by Derains, 'Le statut des usages du commerce international devant les jurisdictions arbitrales', [1973] *Revue de l'arbitrage* 122, at 122, 135; and the awards cited by Derains, 105 *Clunet*, 997 (1978).

5 See however the objections of A Kassis, *Théorie genérale des usages du commerce*, Paris 1984, at 768.

Other contractual clauses do not exclude the applicability of a municipal law, but call for its combination with the *lex mercatoria*, referring either to general principles of law and of international law, or to the usages of the international trade, or to both. There are examples of such clauses in contracts containing an ICC arbitral clause; a famous example in contracts providing for an international *ad hoc* arbitration is found in the Libyan Oil Concession Agreements, where the applicable-law clause refers to the principles of Libyan Law insofar as they are in accord with the principles of international law, and lacking such conformity, to the general principles of law.[6] Now, to the extent to which general principles of law are viewed as a component of the *lex mercatoria*, such a clause is to be viewed as referring to the *lex mercatoria* and as combining it with the principles (if not with the detailed provisions) of a municipal law.[7]

Finally, certain contractual clauses may be construed as *implying* a reference to the *lex mercatoria*, for example, the *amiable composition* clause, which empowers the arbitrator to decide *ex aequo et bono*. In my opinion the *lex mercatoria* is not just 'equity' (in the civil law sense) since it is, on the contrary, a set of rules of law. However, while being authorised to decide without applying such rules, the *amiable compositeur* is of course not prevented from referring to them; and when so doing, he might rightly construe the '*amiable composition*' clause as implicitly directed to the *lex mercatoria*. Furthermore, the mere insertion of an international arbitration clause is frequently considered as an internationalisation instrument of the contract, and consequently, an implicit reference to the general principles and usages of international trade, even where the same is not expressly stipulated.

Reference to the lex mercatoria *in international awards*

International arbitral tribunals do directly apply the *lex mercatoria*, even in the absence of a contractual clause referring to the *lex mercatoria*, or in any event not relying on such a clause. For example, where the contract does not contain a choice-of-law clause, arbitral awards apply 'rules of law' (but not municipal ones) or lacking such rules, 'commercial usages'.[8] Similarly, such rules and/or usages are applied where there are no efficient connecting factors, like in cases where there are more than one place of execution and performance of the contract.[9]

As in contracts, the application of the *lex mercatoria* in international awards is in certain instances combined with the application of a municipal law. Several patterns are here followed: the *lex mercatoria* and the municipal law may be placed on the same level; or priority may be given to the general

6 See the awards in the Libyan oil cases (Liamco, BP, Texaco).

7 See, eg, ICC Award, Case No 1569/70, cited by P Sanders, 'Trends in the Field of International Arbitration', 145 *Recueil des Cours de l'Académie de droit international* 205 (1975–11), at 256.

8 ICC Awards, Case Nos 1641/69, 101 *Clunet* 888 (1974); 2291/75, 103 *Clunet* 189 (1976); 2583/76, 104 *Clunet* 950 (1977).

9 ICC Awards, Case Nos 1375/65, cited by Derains, [1973] *Revue de l'arbitrage*, at 131; 1859/73, *ibid.*

principles; or the arbitrator to municipal law only to confirm the solutions drawn from the general usages.[10]

Does the application of the *lex mercatoria* depend, like that of any other set of rules of law (including municipal ones), on a preliminary or even a double characterisation of the issue in dispute as of a contractual nature, and of the contract as international? Theoretically, the question is to be answered in the affirmative. However, such answer does not mean that the whole mechanism of conflict of law rules determines where the *lex mercatoria* is applied, like when it leads to the application of municipal laws. In fact, the contractual character of the issue in dispute is only rarely denied in international arbitrations; and so is the international character of the contract. Consequently, the *lex mercatoria* is almost always directly applied, without any discussion as to the contractual and international character of the legal relationship in dispute.

The 'reception' of *lex mercatoria* by state or interstate laws

By the 'reception' of *lex mercatoria*, I understand that municipal lawmakers or judges, or governments when concluding international treaties, or international bodies when setting up rules for international arbitrations, take account of it as being comprised of rules of law, applicable in the same manner as rules whose source is to be found in national legislation or case law.

Reception by municipal legislation

I will not speak here of adoption by lawmakers of rules that consecrate previously existing usages. The examples of this are numerous and one may doubtless say that they enable the *lex mercatoria* to penetrate national law. However, in so doing, municipal law loses its specific nature, because this mechanism changes it from a formal source of law, distinct from national law, into a mere substantive source of national law.

There is, on the other hand, a remarkable (albeit tacit) example of the lawmaker's acceptance of the *lex mercatoria* as an autonomous source of law. It is to be found in Article 1496(1) of the French Code of Civil Procedure promulgated by the Decree of May 12, 1981, which provides that in international arbitration

> 'the arbitrator shall settle the dispute in accordance with the rules of law which the parties have chosen, and in the absence of such a choice, in accordance with those rules of law which he considers to be appropriate'.

In analysing this text, one notes first of all that although it acknowledges the freedom of the parties to choose the applicable law, it does not oblige international arbitrators to refer to a system of conflict of laws to designate the applicable rules of law in the absence of such a choice by the parties.

This is the method of 'direct' choice of law, which is exactly the one arbitral tribunals employ when they decide to apply the *lex mercatoria*. However, one must emphasise especially that in the unanimous view of commentators,

10 ICC Award, Case Nos 1675/69 101 *Clunet* 895 (1974); 1512/71, 101 *Clunet* 904 (1974); 2745 and 2762/77, 105 *Clunet* 990 (1978); 1434/75, 103 *Clunet* 978 (1976); 2708/76, 104 *Clunet* 943 (1977).

several of whom participated in the drafting of Article 1496, (4) the lawmaker, in using the expression 'rules of law', meant to refer to customary rules as well as to legislative ones, and thus open the door for arbitrators, whether or not *amiables compositeurs*, to decide disputes by applying the *lex mercatoria*.

Reception in case law

This type of reception has taken place in two ways: (i) through the application of codified usages to which the parties had not made express reference; and (ii) by the recognition of the validity of awards based on the *lex mercatoria* by arbitrators who were not *amiables compositeurs*.

Application of codified usages Two decisions by the highest court of two countries should be mentioned in this connection.

First, the German Bundesgerichtshof decision on June 18, 1975, which held that if parties agree that goods should be delivered FOB, the Incoterms interpretation of such a clause is applicable even if the parties did not expressly refer to the Incoterms.

Second is a decision of the French *Cour de Cassation* of October 14, 1981.[11] A buyer of imported goods, which were to be paid for by documentary credit, had obtained by conservatory attachment the seizure of funds at the intermediary bank which were intended for payment to the seller, on the grounds that the goods delivered did not conform to specifications. The Court of Appeal upheld the attachment, but its decision was reversed because it was held by the Supreme Court to have constituted a violation of Article 1134 of the Civil Code and Article 3 of the *Uniform Customs and Practice for Documentary Credits*. Nothing in the decision gives the impression that in the case at hand, the parties had expressly referred to the 'Uniform Customs'. One might certainly think that by also citing Article 1134 of the Civil Code, which affirms the principle that contracts have binding force, the *Cour de Cassation* acknowledged that the parties had implicitly referred to the 'Uniform Customs'. However, the fact that the Court acknowledged this implicit reference without noting any particular element of fact that would tend to support such a finding, and that Article 3 of the *Uniform Customs* is mentioned among the provisions referred to in the initial part of the decision (the 'visas'), as well as in the *ratio decidendi* on the same plane as Article 1134 of the Civil Code, clearly means that the *Uniform Customs* were given at least the status of a suppletive law.

Recognition of the validity of awards at law and in which lex mercatoria *is applied* The case law now to be examined is of a much greater general importance.

Fougerolle v *Banque de Proche Orient* involved an arbitral award in favour of an intermediary which had undertaken to negotiate a contract, but whose agency had been terminated by the principal before completion of its mission. The intermediary was granted partial remuneration based on the services which he had in fact performed. The arbitral tribunal, which did not have *amiable compositeur* powers, based its decision on 'general principles of

11 *SA Discount Bank* v *Teboul*, *Recueil Dalloz*, 1982, 381.

obligation generally applicable in international trade'. The losing party resisted the attempt to enforce this award, relying on Article 1028-1 of the *Ancien Code de Procédure Civile*, under which awards could be invalidated if they were rendered 'beyond the scope of the submission'; the tribunal, it was argued, had 'usurped the powers of *amiables compositeurs*' in deciding as it had.

The challenge to the award was rejected by the judge of first instance, whose decision was confirmed by the Court of Appeal[12] which declared 'that it follows from the reasoning of the award that (the arbitrators) implicitly but necessarily referred to a usage of international trade that has evident force' and 'that thus based on *rules of law*, the arbitrators' decision was within the scope of the submission'. (Emphasis added.)

Deciding a final appeal against this decision, the Second Civil Chamber of the *Cour de Cassation*[13] in turn held 'that in referring to "general principles of obligation generally applicable in international trade" the arbitrators only conformed to the duty imposed upon them by Article 8 of the Terms of Reference to define the law applicable to the agreement'. Thus, the general principles applicable in international commerce are part of the law; to conclude that this decision signifies that the *lex mercatoria* also is law, one need only recognise that the *lex mercatoria* encompasses these general principles. The commentators consider unanimously that these decisions conferred upon *lex mercatoria* the status of a source of the law of international trade.

Norsolor v *Pabalk* engendered a veritable battle in the courts of France and Austria, from which *lex mercatoria* emerged victorious. I have already mentioned the award rendered in this case on October 26, 1979.

With respect to the most important element of the monetary award, namely the damages arising from the breach of the agency agreement, the arbitral tribunal, 'faced with the difficulty of choosing a national law' (to govern the contract) 'which would have a sufficiently strong claim to apply' (and which the arbitrators had started to search for by referring to comparative rules of conflict of laws), held that 'it was appropriate, given the international character of the contract, to avoid any constraining application of a specific body of national laws, whether Turkish or French, and to apply the international *lex mercatoria*'.

In point of fact, the tribunal found that 'one of the principles that inspires the *lex mercatoria* is the good faith that should reign when parties negotiate and perform contracts'. Applying this principle, the tribunal 'sought to determine whether ... the breach of the agency agreement was attributable to one of the parties and if it had caused the other party a loss which would thus be unjustified, and which equity requires be compensated'. Finding that the actions of UGINOR/NORSOLOR had not been compatible with the maintenance of good commercial relations, the arbitrators decided that it should 'be held liable for the breach of the agency', and, holding that this breach had caused PABALK damage, 'assessed in equity a global lump sum of 800,000 French francs as the amount of the reparation owed to PABALK'.

The President of the *Tribunal de grande instance* of Paris granted *exequatur* of this award by an *Ordonnance* dated February 5, 1980. NORSOLOR sought to

12 Decision of June 12, 1980, 109 *Clunet* 231 (1982), 2nd Case, comments by B Oppetit.

13 Decision of December 9, 1981, [1982] *Revue de l'arbitrage* 183, 2nd case, Comments by G Couchez. 109 *Clunet* 931 [1982], 3rd case, comments by B Oppetit.

have the *exequatur* set aside under Article 1028 of the *Ancien Code de Procédure Civile*, invoking the argument that the arbitrators, in spite of the fact that they did not have the power of *amiables compositeurs*, based their decision 'on equity alone' – characterised as the essence of *amiable composition* – instead of applying the rules of law applicable to the dispute'. It was argued that 'equity alone' had in this manner determined both the issue of liability in principle, which the arbitrators had deduced from the 'principle of good faith inspired by the international *lex mercatoria*', and the calculation of the damages.

This challenge was rejected by a March 4, 1981 decision of the *Tribunal de grande instance* of Paris[14] in which the court stated:

> 'In conformity with Article 13 of the Rules (of Arbitration of the ICC), the arbitrators applied the law designated by the rule of conflict of laws they deemed to be applicable to the case at hand, that is to say the general principles of obligations generally applicable in international commerce ... Accordingly, the arbitrators did not decide as *amiables compositeurs*, whether *de facto* or *de jure* ...; their decision was thus well within the scope of the submission.'

Simultaneously with these French court proceedings, NORSOLOR had brought another court case in Austria, where the award had been rendered. It asked the Commercial Court of Vienna to rule that the arbitral award was invalid, on the grounds that procedural errors had been committed and that the award, in its reasoning as well as in its amount, was rendered in equity and not by reference to a legal order. Specifically, NORSOLOR criticised the arbitral tribunal because it had failed to indicate which law it applied with respect to its order that certain agency commissions be paid. As for the damages for breach for contract, NORSOLOR argued that the arbitral tribunal had explicitly based its award on the *lex mercatoria* and on equity, whereas 'there exists no *lex mercatoria* equivalent of a legal system, and one may refer to general principles of commerce and of good faith only if the specific rules of the law applicable to the relevant agency agreement, which take precedence over general rules do not exclude such reference'.

The action was dismissed by a decision of June 29, 1981.[15] The Viennese judge declared that

> 'it is obvious ... that notwithstanding the twice-repeated word "equity", the arbitrators started from juridical considerations'.

This was particularly held to be the case with respect to the damages caused by the breach, because

> 'the principle of good faith and loyalty, applied by the arbitral tribunal in conformity with a *lex mercatoria* ... constitutes a general principle of law; a decision based on such a principle does not constitute a decision in equity'.

However, on January 29, 1982[16] the Court of Appeal in Vienna partially upheld an appeal brought by NORSOLOR against the lower-court decision, ruling that the award should be 'reversed' with respect to its points III

14 108 *Clunet* 386 (1981), comments by Ph Kahn.
15 [1984] *Revue de l'arbitrage* 513, 1st case.
16 [1984] *Revue de l'arbitrage* 513, 2nd case.

(damages of 800,000 francs) and IV (costs). To reach this result, the Court of Appeal declared, as for point III, that the arbitrators:

> 'violated Article 13(3) of the ICC Rules of Arbitration ... in failing to determine the applicable law according to the rules of conflict of laws that (they) considered appropriate but ... rather referring to a *lex mercatoria*, a worldwide law of uncertain validity, and thus refusing any connection with a national legal order, based their decision only on the principle of loyalty and good faith'.

On appeal to the Austrian Supreme Court, the decision of the Court of Appeal was reversed on November 18, 1982.[17] Essentially, the Supreme Court reasoned that in granting damages for breach of contract, the arbitrators had

> 'applied a principle of private law, which neither contradicts nor violates any of the imperative rules to be found in the laws in vigor in either of the two concerned States. ... The arbitrators' application of the principle of equity without prior authorisation by the parties did not constitute a transgression of the limits of their jurisdiction.'

Thus, the *lex mercatoria's* status as a body of rules of law has been recognised in both French and Austrian case law.

Reception by international conventions and rules of arbitration established by international bodies

I am referring here to international conventions and rules that utilise, to determine the law applicable to the substance of the case, a terminology which may reasonably be construed as comprising the *lex mercatoria.*

For example, Article 42(1) of the Washington Convention provides as follows:

> 'The Tribunal shall decide a dispute in accordance with such *rules of law* as may be agreed by the parties. In the absence of such agreement, the Tribunal shall apply the law of the Contracting State party to the dispute (including its rules on the conflict of laws), and such rules of *international law as may be applicable.*'
> (*Emphasis provided*)

The phrase 'rules of law' covers, or at least may cover, in my view, not only legal provisions of municipal laws and international conventions, but transnational customary rules as well; likewise, 'rules of international law' are in fact precise rules embodied in international conventions, as well as general principles of international law. Therefore, the provision means that the parties to an investment contract may refer to the *lex mercatoria* (whatever the wording of such reference), and that the arbitral tribunal may apply general principles and usages of transnational economic relations.[18]

In addition, Article 42(3) of the Washington Convention provides that

17 IX *Yearbook: Commercial Arbitration* 159 (1984).

18 Such was the decision of an ICSID arbitral tribunal, in the case *AMCO ASIA and others* v *Republic of Indonesia*, to be published.

'(t)he provisions of paragraphs (1) and (2) shall not prejudice the power of the Tribunal to decide a dispute *ex aequo et bono*, if the parties so agree'.

Thus, the *amiable composition* clause is lawful and has effect in the framework of the convention; now, I already said that such a clause may easily lead the arbitrators to apply the *lex mercatoria.*

The interpretation of Article VII of the European Convention on International Commercial Arbitration 1961 is more difficult. It provides as follows (with relevant French text in brackets):

'(1) The parties shall be free to determine, by agreement, the law (le droit) to be applied by the arbitrators to the substance of the dispute. Failing any indication by the parties as to the applicable law, the arbitrators shall apply the proper law (le loi) under the rule of conflict that the arbitrators deem applicable. In both cases the arbitrators shall take account of the terms of the contract and *trade usages*.' (*Emphasis added*)

'(2) The arbitrators shall act as *amiables compositeurs* if the parties so decide and if they may do so under the law applicable to the arbitration'.

It seems that 'law' (*droit*) in the first paragraph may include the *lex mercatoria.* However, where the parties did not indicate the *law* (in this sense), the arbitrators are called to apply a *loi* (statute) designated by a conflict rule, which could be construed as excluding the *lex mercatoria.* But in any event, they have to apply the usages of trade, which are a component of the *lex mercatoria.*

Finally, one should point out that both Article 33(3) of the UNCITRAL Arbitration Rules and Article 13(5) of the ICC Arbitration Rules prescribe to the arbitrator to take account of the relevant trade usages. Clearly, these rules are not international conventions, nor mandatory legal provisions. However, they are effectively applied in a large number of international arbitrations; consequently, the trade usages are, by their effect, an important source of settlement of international disputes.

Contents of the *lex mercatoria* – examples

I shall take here some examples of solutions found in international arbitral awards, which are based on the *lex mercatoria.* They concern arbitrability, conduct of the procedure and substance of the case.

Arbitrability

One meets here a first issue, which while being closely connected might be distinguished from the arbitrability strictly speaking: the issue of the capacity of the state and of public entities to conclude an arbitral convention. I say it is closely connected with arbitrability since if it would be admitted that the state has no such capacity, the result would be that disputes where the state is involved would not be arbitrable.

Now, it is well known that the national legislations are not identical in this respect. Thus, in French law, cases concerning the state or public entities can not be referred to arbitration[19] *except* according to well-established case law, where the arbitration clause is inserted in a contract affecting international trade.[20] In other countries, like Belgium for example, the exclusion is general, and in some others distinctions are to be made in respect of the public entity that is involved. But these exclusions and distinctions are not applied in international arbitrations, where it is now generally accepted that once the state (or a public entity) has agreed to an arbitral clause, it cannot deny the arbitrator's jurisdiction by invoking its lack of capacity.[21]

A controversial issue has arisen as to the arbitrability of disputes involving the application of competition law, since such disputes concern a public policy matter. International arbitral tribunals have adopted several solutions: admission of jurisdiction; examination of the contract by the arbitrators for the mere purpose to decide whether it infringes the applicable legal rules on competition, in which case they have denied their jurisdiction; jurisdiction retained on a defence claiming the nullity of the agreement, but not on a claim purported to obtain a decision declaring it null and void.[22]

Be that as it may, the fact is that these several decisions are not based on provisions of municipal anti-trust legislations, nor on EEC law; they tend to elaborate and to construe a general customary rule of international trade.

Conduct of procedure

National legislations, like for instance the new French Code of Civil Procedure,[23] and rules on international arbitration,[24] allow the arbitrator to apply such rules of procedure he chooses, without any reference to a municipal procedural law.

This power could lead to the setting up of an international customary procedure. It is difficult to say that such a procedure has already come into being. However, one may notice that in particular in international arbitrations entrusted to European continental arbitrators, the general trend is to follow a procedure which combines the main features of Common and Civil Law practices. Thus, oral and written evidence are both and simultaneously utilised, but oral evidence plays a greater role than it usually does in purely continental procedures; likewise, some kind of examination and cross-examination are performed, however, not strictly applying the English or American rules on evidence.

19 French Code Civil, Article 2060.

20 The more characteristic decision is: *Cour de Cassation*, lere chambre civile, May 2, 1966, *Galakis*, *Dalloz* 1964. 637, comments by J Robert, 93 *Clunet* 648 (1966), comments by P Level, 56, *Revue critique de droit international privé* 553 (1967), comments by B Goldman.

21 ICC Award, Case No 1939/71, cited by Derains, [1973] *Revue de l'arbitrage* 145; a recent unpublished award has again adopted this solution in a case where Belgium was one of the parties.

22 See the awards cited by Kovar, 'Droit communautaire de la concurrence et arbitrage', in *Le droit des relations economiques internationales*, Paris 1982, 110; B Goldman, 'L'action complementaire des juges et des arbitres', in *60 Years of ICC Arbitration*, Paris 1984, 271.

23 French Code de Procédure Civil, Article 1494.

24 Eg, ICC Rules, Article 11.

Substance of the case

The main issue here is the choice to be made between the strict application of *pacta sunt servanda* and the possible application of the *clausula rebus sic stantibus*.

No doubt international arbitrators stick, in principle, to *pacta*, and one could contend that this has nothing to do with *lex mercatoria*, since this principle is embodied in practically all municipal legislations (however, not without differences as to its strength, and consequently as to its effects). It is to be noted, nevertheless, that very frequently, when they apply *pacta sunt servanda* arbitrators do not refer to a particular municipal legislation; they see the principle as a general one, which means that it is applied as an element of the *lex mercatoria*, and therefore, that its actual consequences are not to be taken from any municipal law whatsoever.

This trend explains that certain awards have admitted, albeit in exceptional cases, the application of *rebus sic stantibus*. Thus, an international award, while referring to Swiss law, which admits under severe conditions the revision of contracts, decided that these conditions were to be applied in a more flexible manner in respect of international contracts.[25] Another previous award did not exclude the principle of *rebus sic stantibus*, however, stating that its application should be limited to cases where constraining reasons justify it, taking into account not only the fundamental character of the changes in circumstances which are invoked, but equally the particular type of contract involved, the requirements of fairness and all the circumstances of the case.

My last example will be the obligation for a creditor *to minimise the damage* he suffers because of the non-fulfilment by the debtor of his own commitments. This obligation, generally admitted, as far as I know, in Common Law, is not so largely and clearly consecrated in Civil Law.

Now, a number of international awards have applied it as a general principle of international trade, not referring in particular to a Common Law system.[26] Moreover, the principle may be combined with the obligation to renegotiate the contract in good faith.[27]

The examples so far mentioned are taken from arbitral procedures and awards, to which I had to limit myself, given the framework of this Conference. I would nevertheless add that the impact of *lex mercatoria* on international trade is much larger than the one it has in international arbitration. Indeed, new clauses and new types of contracts are set up by international practice, which are not based on municipal legislation, and which are in fact unknown by them: for example, the *hardship clause* and *turnkey contracts*.

Now, law is not only made of and for matters in dispute. It governs, independently of any dispute, the functioning of human society that engenders it and effectively applies it. In respect of the international economic community, I believe the *lex mercatoria* is such a law: but this is another topic.

25 ICC Award, Case No 1512/71, 101 *Clunet* 902 (1974); 2748/74, 102 *Clunet* 905 (1974).
26 ICC Award, Case Nos 2103/72, 101 *Clunet* 902 (1974); 2748/74, 102 *Clunet* 905 (1975); 2291/75, 103 *Clunet* 989 (1976); 2520/75, 103 *Clunet* 992 (1976).
27 ICC Award, Case No 2748/74, 102 *Clunet* 905 (1975).

11 The law governing the agreement and procedure in international arbitration in England

Lawrence Collins

The purpose of this paper is to consider, in the context of one specific legal system, the practical and theoretical implications of the governing law of an arbitration agreement and of the procedural law of an arbitration. Despite their fundamental character these questions have not been given the attention in England which they deserve.[1] The answer to these questions may also go some way to determining whether English law will recognise transnational or delocalised arbitrations.

Recent years have seen a large growth in arbitration with a foreign element, or international commercial arbitration as it is frequently called. Certain types of contract in use in international trade customarily provide for arbitration (very often in London). Thus contracts for the sale of commodities often provide for arbitration by a trade association, such as the Grain and Feed Trade Association (GAFTA). In other cases, parties may wish to provide for the resolution of disputes by an independent tribunal, and where they are of equal bargaining power, each may be reluctant to submit disputes to the courts of the other party, or of a third country, but may be prepared to provide for arbitration. Sometimes the arbitration will be an *ad hoc* one, sometimes it will be under the auspices of institutional arbitration, such as the London Court of International Arbitration or the International Chamber of Commerce. The arbitration clause sometimes designates the place where the arbitration is to be held or (as is sometimes said) to have its seat; sometimes it leaves the identity of the arbitrator or arbitrators and the place of the arbitration to be chosen by, eg the President of a Chamber of Commerce or of a trade or professional association or through the machinery of institutional arbitration. Questions may arise before, during and after the arbitration as to the validity of the submission to arbitration, the procedure to be applied in the arbitration, and the scope of the court's power of supervision. Or one party may, in breach of the arbitration agreement, bring proceedings in a court, and the other party may seek to enforce the arbitration agreement by applying for a stay. Where arbitration takes place in a country in which neither party has its place of business, the losing party may be dissatisfied with the award, and refuse to comply with it. The successful party may therefore need to enforce the award

1 Dicey & Morris, *Conflict of Laws* (10th ed 1980), 1122–28; Cheshire & North, *Private International Law* (10th ed 1979), 680–8; Mustill & Boyd, *The Law and Practice of Commercial Arbitration in England* (1982), chap 4; Russell on *Arbitration* (20th ed 1982), 58–63.

in other countries. This paper deals with three questions which may have an impact on these situations: (I) the law governing the arbitration agreement; (II) the procedural law of the arbitration; (III) the status of international institutional arbitration in England and the attitude of English law to 'delocalised' arbitration.

The proper law of an arbitration agreement

According to English notions an arbitration clause in a contract constitutes a self-contained contract collateral or ancillary to the main contract of which it forms a part.[2] Questions relating to the governing law of an arbitration agreement arise in a variety of contexts. A respondent may seek to restrain the continuance of an arbitration, or may resist enforcement of a foreign award, on the ground that the agreement to arbitrate, or the contract of which it forms a part, was invalid. Or a question may arise as to the jurisdiction of the arbitrator to decide a particular issue between the parties, or as to whether the arbitration agreement has been frustrated. These, and related issues, fall to be determined by the proper law of the arbitration agreement.[3]

The first question which arises is how the proper law of the arbitration agreement is determined. The proper law of the arbitration agreement is normally the same as the proper law of the contract of which it forms a part, but there may be exceptional cases where the arbitration agreement will be governed by a different law.[4] If there is an express choice of the proper law of the contract as a whole, the arbitration agreement will usually be governed by that law.[5] If there is no express choice of the law to govern the contract as a whole, or the arbitration agreement in particular, there is a very strong presumption that the proper law of contract (including the arbitration clause) is the law of the country in which the arbitration is to be held.[6] But this

2 *Heyman* v *Darwins Ltd* [1942] AC 356; *Bremer Vulkan Schiffbau und Maschinenfabrik* v *South India Shipping Corporation Ltd* [1981] AC 909. See also *Dalmia Dairy Industries Ltd* v *National Bank of Pakistan* [1978] 2 Lloyd's Rep 223, 287 (CA); *Black-Clawson International Ltd* v *Papierwerke Waldhof-Aschaffenburg* [1981] 2 Lloyd's Rep 446 at 452; Mustill & Boyd, *op cit*, 78–82.

3 *Hamlyn & Co* v *Talisker Distillery* [1894] AC 202; *Norske Atlas Insurance Co Ltd* v *London General Insurance Co Ltd* (1927) 28 LlLR 104; *Kianta Osakeyhtio* v *Britain and Overseas Trading Co Ltd* [1953] 2 Lloyd's Rep 569; *The Elizabeth H* [1962] 1 Lloyd's Rep 172; *Dalmia Dairy Industries Ltd* v *National Bank of Pakistan* [1978] 2 Lloyd's Rep 223 (CA); *International Tank & Pipe SAK* v *Kuwait Aviation Fuelling Co KSC* [1975] QB 224 (CA); *Nova (Jersey) Knit Ltd* v *Kammgarn Spinnerei* [1977] 1 WLR 713, at 718, 730 (HL); *Black-Clawson International Ltd* v *Papierwerke Waldhof-Aschaffenburg AG* [1981] 2 Lloyd's Rep 446; *Qatar Petroleum* v *Shell International Petroleum* [1983] 2 Lloyd's Rep 35 at 43 (CA); *The Marques de Bolarque* [1984] 1 Lloyd's Rep 652.

4 See *Black-Clawson International Ltd* v *Papierwerke Waldhof-Aschaffenburg AG* [1981] 2 Lloyd's Rep 446, at 455.

5 As Mustill and Boyd, *op cit*, at 89, points out, it would be an unusual case for the parties to choose only the law governing the arbitration clause.

6 *Hamlyn* v *Talisker Distillery* [1894] AC 202; *Spurrier* v *La Cloche* [1902] AC 446 (PC); *NV Kwik Hoo Tong Handel Maatschappij* v *James Finlay & Co* [1927] AC 604, at 608, 609; *Norske Atlas Insurance Co Ltd* v *London General Insurance Co Ltd* (1927) 28 LlLR 104; *Maritime Insurance Co Ltd* v *Assekuranz Union von 1865* (1935) 53 LlLR 16; *The Njegos* [1936] P 90, at 100; *NV Handels-en-Transport Maatschappij 'Vulcan'* v *ASJ Ludwig Mowinckels Rederi* [1938] 2 All ER 152, at 156; *Tzortzis* v *Monark Line A/B* [1968] 1 WLR 406 (CA).

presumption, though strong, can be rebutted, for the House of Lords has emphasised that an arbitration clause is only one of several circumstances to be considered in determining the proper law of a contract.[7]

The presumption cannot operate if no place of arbitration is agreed in the original contract, or if the place of arbitration is left to be chosen by the arbitrators or by an outside body. In such cases the proper law of the contract (including the arbitration clause) would be determined in accordance with the normal principles.

The development of these principles began towards the end of the nineteenth century. *Hamlyn & Co* v *Talisker Distillery*[8] was an appeal to the House of Lords from the Court of Session in Scotland. English merchants entered into a contract with a Scottish distillery, whereby the former agreed to supply to the distillery, and erect, a patent drying machine and to buy grain from the distillery. The contract was signed in London and provided for arbitration in London. The issue was whether a Scots action by the distillery against the merchants was to be stayed because of the arbitration clause. At that time Scots law required that, for an arbitration clause to be valid, it had to identify the arbitrators. English law had no such requirement. It was argued on behalf of the Scottish distillery, *inter alia*, that the question was a matter of procedure governed by Scots law irrespective of the governing law of the contract as a whole or the arbitration agreement in particular. It was held that the issue was not a question of procedure governed by Scots law, but a preliminary question relating to the validity of the arbitration agreement. English law was held to govern, and since the arbitration clause was valid under English law, the Scots proceedings were stayed.

Lord Herschell said that 'the language of the arbitration clause indicates very clearly that the parties intended that the rights under that clause should be determined according to the law of England,'[9] and Lord Watson said that 'the clause of reference is expressed in terms which clearly indicate that the parties had in contemplation and agreed that it should be interpreted according to the rules of English law.'[10] This decision indicates an early acceptance of the distinction between the law governing the arbitration agreement and the law governing the contract of which it forms a part. The distinction is sometimes overlooked.

In *Norske Atlas Insurance Co Ltd* v *London General Insurance Co Ltd*[11] the issue was whether successful claimants could enforce a Norwegian award in England at common law. For a foreign award to be enforceable in England, it must (*inter alia*) have been made in accordance with an agreement to arbitrate valid by its proper law. In that case Norwegian reinsurers made claims against an English company which had ceded reinsurance to the former. The

7 *Compagnie Tunisienne de Navigation SA* v *Compagnie d'Armement Maritime SA* [1971] AC 572 applied in *Atlantic Underwriting Agencies Ltd* v *Compagnia di Assicurazione di Milano* [1979] 2 Lloyd's Rep 240, at 245; *The SLS Everest* [1981] 2 Lloyd's Rep 389 (CA); *The Parouth* [1982] 2 Lloyd's Rep 351 (CA); *The Mariannina* [1983] 1 Lloyd's Rep 12 (CA); *Steel Authority of India Ltd* v *Hind Metals Inc* [1984] 1 Lloyd's Rep 405.

8 [1894] AC 202. See on this case *Compagnie Tunisienne de Navigation SA* v *Compagnie d'Armement Maritime SA* [1971] AC 572, at 596.

9 [1894] AC 202, at 208.

10 *Ibid*, at 212. But the context suggests that by 'it' he may have been referring to the contract as a whole rather than the arbitration clause. See also Lord Shand, at 216.

11 (1927) 28 LlLR 104.

reinsurance treaty provided for arbitration in Norway. In the proceedings to enforce the award arising out of an arbitration in which the English company had taken no part, the English company pleaded that the award could not be enforced since the reinsurance treaty was invalid under English law because it was not expressed in a policy and had not been properly stamped. It was held that the contract as a whole was governed by Norwegian law because the Norwegian arbitration clause pointed to the parties' intention that the contract was governed by Norwegian law, and that under Norwegian law the contract, and therefore the submission to arbitration, was valid.

The law governing the arbitration agreement determines the scope of the arbitrator's jurisdiction. Thus it will determine the question whether an arbitration clause in a contract of sale applies to claims on bills of exchange issued pursuant to them[12]; or whether an arbitration clause in a contract extends to delictual claims.[13] It will determine whether an arbitration clause in an earlier contract is imported by implication into a later one,[14] or whether an arbitration clause in a charterparty is incorporated in a bill of lading.[15] It will also govern the question whether the arbitrator is able effectively to determine his own jurisdiction.[16]

In *Black Clawson International Ltd* v *Papierwerke Waldhof-Aschaffenburg*[17] Mustill J undertook a very sophisticated analysis of the determination and scope of the governing law of the arbitration agreement. In that case the contract of sale between the parties provided for arbitration in Zurich under ICC Rules, and that any question as to the construction or effect of the contract should be decided by English law if the reference to arbitration were made by the German buyers, and according to German law if the reference were made by the English sellers. The arbitration clause also stated that the reference to arbitration was to 'be deemed to be submission to arbitration within the meaning of the Arbitration Act ... 1950'. Notice of arbitration was given in 1965, and an arbitration was held in Zurich but, for a variety of reasons into which it is unnecessary to go, an award in favour of the buyers was not rendered until 1979, and subsequently the Swiss court set aside the award and remitted it to the arbitrators. The sellers then sought an injunction in England to restrain the buyers from proceeding with the arbitration in Zurich on the ground that the arbitration agreement had come to an end as a result of frustration or repudiation or inordinate delay. The sole basis on which the sellers founded the jurisdiction of the English court was that the arbitration agreement was governed by English law. It was held (*inter alia*) that the English court did not have jurisdiction because the agreement to refer the dispute was not governed by English law, but by Zurich law. Mustill J said:

> '... there are not one, but two, sets of contractual relations which govern the arbitration of disputes under a substantive contract.'

First, there is the contract to submit future disputes to arbitration. This comes

12 *Nova (Jersey) Knit Ltd* v *Kammgarn Spinnerei* [1977] 1 WLR 713, at 718, 730 (HL).
13 *Qatar Petroleum* v *Shell International Petroleum* [1983] 2 Lloyd's Rep 35, at 43 (CA).
14 *Kianta Osakeyhtio* v *Britain & Overseas Trading Co Ltd* [1953] 2 Lloyd's Rep 569.
15 *The Elizabeth H* [1962] 1 Lloyd's Rep 172.
16 *Dalmia Dairy Industries Ltd* v *National Bank of Pakistan* [1978] 2 Lloyd's Rep 223 (Kerr J and CA).
17 [1981] 2 Lloyd's Rep 446.

into existence at the same time as the substantive agreement of which it forms part. *Prima facie* it will run for the full duration of the substantive agreement, and will then survive for as long as any disputes remain unresolved. Second, there are one or more individual sets of bilateral contractual obligations which are called into existence as and when one party asserts against the other a claim falling within the scope of the initial promise to arbitrate, which they have not been able to settle. For brevity I refer to these sets of relationships as the 'continuous agreement' and the 'individual agreements'.

> '... it must follow that at least in theory the two sets of contractual relations may be governed by different laws. It may be objected that this piles up the proper laws absurdly high: we already have the substantive proper law, and the lex fori; to these we must now add the proper law of the continuous agreement and the proper law of the individual contract to refer. In practice, this objection is unlikely ever to arise. In the great majority of the cases, the same law governs all aspects of the matter. Where the laws diverge at all, one will find in most instances that the law governing the continuous agreement is the same as the substantive law of the contract in which it is embodied and that the law of the reference is the same as the lex fori. But that the two aspects of the arbitration agreement may on occasion be governed by different laws, is in my judgment an inevitable result of the reasoning adopted by the majority in [*Bremer Vulkan Schiffbau und Maschinenfabrik* v *South India Shipping Corporation Ltd* [1981] AC 909].'

There may be issues which are on the borderline between issues of substance governed by the proper law of the arbitration agreement and issues of procedure governed by the procedural law of the arbitration. Thus in *International Tank & Pipe SAK* v *Kuwait Aviation Fuelling Co KSC*[18] a contract expressed to be governed by English law contained an arbitration clause which did not designate the place of arbitration and which provided that any dispute had to be referred to arbitration within a 90-day period. After the 90-day period had expired the intending claimant applied to the English court for an order under Section 27 of the Arbitration Act extending the time for arbitration on the ground that 'undue hardship would otherwise be caused'. It was held that the court did have the power to extend the time, notwithstanding that the ensuing arbitration might be held in some foreign country selected in accordance with the arbitration rules of the International Chamber of Commerce. The basis of the court's jurisdiction was said to be that Section 27 of the Arbitration Act 1950 was, in effect, a statutory term implied in an arbitration clause which was governed by English law, and the power to extend the time depended on the proper law of the arbitration agreement and not on the procedural law of some as yet undetermined country. It seems to follow from the reasoning in this decision that if a contract governed by foreign law provides for arbitration in England, the court would not be able to extend the time.[19] This unfortunate result could be avoided by recognising that Section

18 [1975] QB 224 (CA).

19 See *CM van Stillevoldt BV* v *El Carriers Inc*, *The Times*, July 8, 1982. It would seem to make no difference if the foreign law has a similar rule to s27, because the basis of these decisions appears to be that s27 only applies to arbitration agreements governed by English Law.

27 has both a substantive and procedural character, and applies equally to arbitration agreements governed by English law and, irrespective of the proper law, to arbitrations to be conducted in England.

The procedural law of an arbitration

There can be no doubt that certain procedural issues may depend on a law different from the law governing the contract or the arbitration agreement. These issues depend on the procedural law of the arbitration. For example the question may arise (even in enforcement proceedings) whether an arbitrator was bound to call witnesses on a disputed issue. In *Dalmia Dairy Industries Ltd* v *National Bank of Pakistan*[20] successful claimants sought to enforce a Swiss award in England. The arbitration clause provided for arbitration in Lebanon or Switzerland, and that all questions relating to the contract and the arbitration should be decided by reference to Indian law, and that the courts in India alone should have jurisdiction in all matters arising from or connected with the contract and the arbitration. It was conceded that the law governing the arbitration agreement was Indian law. That law determined the validity of the arbitration agreement and the scope of the arbitrator's authority to decide on his own jurisdiction. The arbitration was held in Geneva. It was held that the procedural law was the law of Geneva because the arbitration clause incorporated the ICC Rules, which provide that in the absence of choice of some other procedural law, procedure is governed by the law of the place of arbitration. That law determined whether the arbitrator was under a duty to call witnesses.

In that case the arbitration clause provided that the arbitration could be conducted in the Lebanon or in Switzerland at the discretion of the arbitrator. The arbitrator, Professor Lalive, sat in Geneva, and there was no purported choice of any procedural law other than that of Geneva law.[21] The ICC Rules provide for such a choice. What would be the effect of a choice of some other law? The starting point for any discussion of this subject in English law must be the decision of the House of Lords in *Whitworth Street Estates (Manchester) Ltd* v *James Miller & Partners Ltd*,[22] where it was held that the English courts had no jurisdiction to exercise their supervisory powers over an arbitration being conducted in Scotland even though it was held (by a majority) that the proper law of the contract and of the arbitration agreement was English law. This was because the parties had evinced an agreement that the arbitration should be governed by Scots law, in that the seat of the arbitration was in Scotland as a result of the conduct of the arbitrator and of the parties.

As a result of the decision, and those that follow it,[23] the primary principle in

20 [1978] 2 Lloyd's Rep 223.

21 The argument that references to Indian law in the arbitration clause related to the procedural law of the arbitration as distinct from the proper law of the arbitration agreement were rejected.

22 [1970] AC 583.

23 *Compagnie Tunisienne de Navigation SA* v *Compagnie d'Armement Maritime SA* [1971] AC 572, at 604; *Dalmia Dairy Industries Ltd* v *National Bank of Pakistan* [1978] 2 Lloyd's Rep 223, at 270; *International Tank & Pipe SAK* v *Kuwait Aviation Fuelling Co KSC* [1975] QB 224, at 232 (CA); *Bank Mellat* v *Helleniki Techniki SA* [1984] QB 291, at 301 (CA); *President of India* v *La Pintada Compania Navigacion* [1985] AC 104 at 119.

English law must be taken to be that the parties may choose the law to govern the procedure of the arbitration[24]; in the normal case this means that the parties may choose the place or seat of the arbitration and thereby choose the procedure prevailing in that place.[25] But in theory at any rate the parties may choose a procedural law other than that of the place of arbitration. The speeches in *Whitworth Street Estates (Manchester) Ltd* v *James Miller & Partners* do not, with one exception, make this explicit. The speeches of Lords Reid, Hodson, Guest and Dilhorne can each be read as saying little more than that by agreeing to an arbitration in Scotland the parties had agreed to Scottish procedural law being applicable. Only Lord Wilberforce went further and made it clear that in his view the procedural law might not be that of the place of arbitration. He said[26]:

> 'What law, then, should be taken to apply to the procedure here? The arbitration clause itself is silent, and I would agree that in the normal case, where the contract itself is governed by English law, any arbitration would be held under English procedure. Moreover, the mere fact that the arbitrator was to sit either partly or exclusively in another part of the United Kingdom, or, for that matter, abroad, would not lead to a different result: the place might be chosen for many reasons of convenience or be purely accidental; a choice so made should not affect the parties' rights.'

In the absence of express provision to the contrary the place of the arbitration provides the procedure. As Kerr LJ put it in *Bank Mellat* v *Helleniki Techniki*,[27] 'the fundamental principle ... is that under our rules of private international law, in the absence of any contractual provision to the contrary, the procedural (or curial) law governing arbitrations is that of the forum of the arbitration, whether this be England, Scotland or some foreign country, since this is the system of law with which the agreement to arbitrate in the particular forum will have its closest connections.'

It must be seldom that an agreement to refer disputes to arbitration in England would provide for the procedure to be governed by another law.[28] There appears to be no reported cases in which the parties to an arbitration to be conducted in England have submitted themselves to foreign procedure and excluded English procedure, or where the parties to an arbitration to be conducted abroad have submitted themselves to English procedure and excluded the foreign procedure. Although most systems of arbitration allow the parties considerable procedural freedom (eg, to stipulate the extent of discovery or the admission of oral evidence), it does not follow that the parties can for all purposes[29] contract out of the mandatory procedural rules of the

24 Similarly with the enforcement provisions of the Arbitration Act 1975 and the New York Convention of 1958. The Geneva Protocol on Arbitration Clauses 1923 provided that the arbitration procedure was to be governed by the agreement of the parties *and* by the law of the place of arbitration and the Geneva Convention on the Recognition of Foreign Arbitral Awards 1927 requires the award to have been made in conformity with that law.

25 *Cf* Thomas [1984] *Lloyd's Maritime and Comparative Law Quarterly* 491; Mustill & Boyd, *op cit*, 68–70.

26 [1970] AC at 616.

27 [1984] QB 291, at 301.

28 *President of India* v *La Pintada Compania Navigacion SA op cit* at 119.

29 But where a Convention award falls to be enforced under the Arbitration Act 1975 it is sufficient that it is in accordance with the law agreed on by the parties even if that is different from the law of the place of arbitration.

place where the arbitration is being conducted, except to the extent that those rules allow.[30] Thus where there are rules of English procedure which the parties cannot validly exclude by express agreement, a choice of foreign procedural law would not prevent those English rules being applicable to an arbitration in England, but, as Mustill and Boyd point out,[31] the occasions in which English law treats procedural rules relating to arbitration as mandatory are rare. It is very doubtful whether the parties could, merely by choosing a foreign procedural law, contract out of the supervisory role of the English court in relation to an arbitration being conducted in England.[32] Similarly, it might well bring an English court into conflict with a foreign court where, merely by virtue of a choice of English procedural law, the English court were to exercise its supervisory jurisdiction over an arbitration being conducted in a foreign country.[33]

The procedural law of the arbitration will determine how the arbitrators are to be appointed, in so far as this is not regulated in the arbitration agreement; the effect of one party's failure to appoint an arbitrator, eg whether an arbitrator may be appointed by a court,[34] or whether the arbitration can proceed before the sole arbitrator appointed by the other party,[35] and whether the authority of an arbitrator can be revoked. That law will also determine what law the arbitrators are to apply,[36] and whether they are expected or allowed to decide *ex aequo et bono* or as *amiables compositeurs*,[37] and if not whether the parties can give them this power or impose on them this duty. That law will also determine the procedural powers and duties of the arbitrators, eg, whether they must hear oral evidence[38] (but not their

30 *Cf* Mann, 'Lex Facit Arbitrum', in *International Arbitration: Liber Amicorum for Martin Domke* (ed P Sanders, 1967) at p 165. In *The Marques de Bolarque* [1984] 1 Lloyd's Rep 652, at 655, a charterparty between Spanish shipowners and Spanish charterers provided that it was to be governed by Spanish law and that disputes were to be settled by arbitration in London. When a dispute arose the Spanish owners sought to restrain an arbitration in London on the ground that the arbitration clause was invalid. On the evidence of Spanish law it was held that an agreement by a Spanish company to arbitrate in London was not contrary to Spanish law. In argument it was suggested that it might be possible for the arbitration in London to be subject to Spanish law, and Hobhouse J seems to have thought that although it might be 'conceptually possible ... it would, for practical purposes, be impossible'.

31 P 67.

32 For a tentative view to the contrary see Mustill and Boyd, *op cit*, 68.

33 *Ibid*, at 70. But it does seem from the *Whitworth Street Estates* case that the House of Lords did not exclude the possibility that an arbitration in Scotland could be subject to the supervisory role of the English court.

34 But *cf The Mariannina* [1983] 1 Lloyd's Rep 12 (CA), where it seems to have been assumed that the power to appoint an arbitrator under the Arbitration Act 1950, s10, depended on whether English law was the proper law of the arbitration agreement. But in that case English law was also the procedural law.

35 *Bankers and Shippers Insurance Co of New York* v *Liverpool Marine and General Insurance Co Ltd* (1926) 24 LlLR 85 (HL); *Norske Atlas Insurance Co Ltd* v *London General Insurance Co Ltd* (1927) 28 LlLR 104.

36 *Cf Orion Compania Espanola de Seguros* v *Belfort* [1962] 2 Lloyd's Rep 257, at 264. See also Lorenzen, *Selected Articles on the Conflict of Laws* (1947), 465–6; Mezger, in Domke, *International Trade Arbitration* (1958), 229, at 239–43.

37 As in *Norske Atlas Insurance Co Ltd* v *London General Insurance Co Ltd*, *supra*; *Union Nationale des Cooperatives Agricoles* v *Catterall* [1959] 2 QB 44 (CA). *Cf* for English law *Orion Compania Espanola de Seguros* v *Belfort* [1962] 2 Lloyd's Rep 257; *Eagle Star Insurance* v *Yuval Insurance* [1978] 1 Lloyd's Rep, 357; Mann (1978) 94 *LQR* 486.

38 *Dalmia Dairy Industries Ltd* v *National Bank of Pakistan* [1978] 2 Lloyd's Rep 223, at 270.

jurisdiction to decide the dispute, which is governed by the arbitration agreement and the law applicable to it). It will also determine what remedies are available to a party who wishes to apply for security for costs[39] or who wishes to challenge the award when it has been rendered and before it is sought to enforce it abroad,[40] and the circumstances in which the remedies may be excluded.[41]

International institutional arbitration and delocalised arbitration in English law

Where England is the seat of an arbitration (provided at any rate that the parties have not chosen another procedural law), English procedural law applies. For this purpose it does not matter that the arbitration is under the auspices of the same international institutional system as that of the ICC. This point was confirmed by the decision of the Court of Appeal in *Bremer Vulkan* v *South India Shipping Corporation.*[42] The decision of the Court of Appeal was reversed by the House of Lords, which held that the court had no inherent jurisdiction to prevent an arbitration continuing on the ground that there had been inordinate delay in the conduct of the arbitration. But for present purposes the importance of the decision is that there were two cases before the court, one of which involved an ICC arbitration. That case did not go on appeal to the House of Lords, but there is no reason to believe that its analysis of the point discussed here was incorrect. In that case the contract originally provided that the arbitration was to be held 'in Geneva, Switzerland, under the rules then prevailing of the International Chamber of Commerce'. By agreement London was substituted for Geneva. Accordingly, the Court of Appeal took the view that the procedure was governed by the law of England. It was argued on behalf of the party wishing to continue the arbitration that the 'Court of Arbitration' in Paris which exercised supervision over the arbitration proceedings was the proper authority in matters of procedure and that, if one of the parties was guilty of unreasonable delay, the remedy was to apply to the Court of Arbitration in Paris, and not to the English courts. Lord Denning said that he did not propose to go into the ICC Rules in any detail, and went on:

> 'Suffice it to say that I do not find in them any power in the Court of Arbitration in Paris to inflict sanctions on a party, or to dismiss a claim for want of prosecution . . . I regard the arbitration in London under ICC Rules as virtually equivalent to an ordinary English arbitration. The Court of Arbitration in Paris is a body with administrative functions only. It has no power to interfere in the judicial process of arbitrators. If there is inordinate and inexcusable delay, the courts in England can take a hand but no one else.'[43]

39 *Bank Mellat* v *Helleniki Techniki SA* [1984] QB 291 (CA).

40 *Whitworth Street Estates (Manchester) Ltd* v *James Miller & Partners Ltd* [1970] AC 583 (English special case procedure not available in Scots arbitration).

41 *Cf Marine Contractors Inc* v *Shell Petroleum Development Co of Nigeria Ltd* [1984] 2 Lloyd's Rep 77 (CA). (English remedies validly excluded in English arbitration under Nigerian law contract.)

42 [1981] AC 909.

43 *Ibid*, at 940–1.

Roskill LJ said of the argument based on a distinction between 'institutional' and 'non-institutional' arbitration[44]:

> 'No doubt institutions concerned with furthering arbitration as a means of disposal of disputes seek emancipation from control of the courts of the countries where such arbitrations take place, perhaps in the belief that such freedom facilitates expedition of decision ... for my part, I am unable to accept that there can be any logical distinction between arbitrations of one kind and the other according to whether some labels such as "institutional" can be attached. In each case the relevant question is – on what terms and conditions have the parties agreed to go to arbitration?'

Although the decision in this case relating to the power of the courts to interfere with the conduct of arbitration may no longer stand, it proceeds correctly on the basis that it is English law as the law governing the arbitration which decides whether the courts have that power. It shows that the English courts will not draw a distinction between institutional and non-institutional arbitration, and once the seat of the arbitration has been decided they will take the view that the law applicable at the seat of the arbitration is the *lex fori*.

It does not follow, however, that the fact that an arbitration is being conducted under ICC Rules is completely irrelevant in England. Thus those rules may themselves indicate what procedural law is to apply, as they were held to do in *Dalmia Dairy Industries Ltd* v *National Bank of Pakistan.*[45] The rules of procedure agreed on by the parties as a result of the adoption of ICC Rules may have very important consequences. In *Marine Contractors Inc* v *Shell Petroleum Development Co of Nigeria*[46] a contract for the laying of a pipe-line between an American company and a Nigerian company, governed by Nigerian law, provided for arbitration in London under ICC Rules. It was held that the provision in the ICC Rules that the parties waive their right to any form of appeal constituted an exclusion agreement within the meaning of the Arbitration Act 1979 so as to exclude the ability of the English court to exercise its power of review. Ackner LJ said[47] that

> 'when parties agree to arbitration by the ICC they deliberately accept an alternative tribunal to the Courts because the ICC Rules prohibit resort to municipal courts, so far as such prohibition may be lawful.'

In *Bank Mellat* v *Helliniki Techniki SA*[48] a joint venture between an Iranian Bank, a Greek company and a Danish company, for the development of land near Tehran contained an arbitration clause providing for arbitration in London under ICC Rules. None of the parties had any connection with England. The Greek company commenced an arbitration in England against the successor to the Iranian bank. The Iranian bank applied to the English court for security for costs for the arbitration on the basis that the Greek

44 *Ibid*, at 949.

45 [1978] 2 Lloyd's Rep 332, at 270, *per* Kerr J.

46 [1984] 2 Lloyd's Rep 77 (CA). See also *Arab African Energy Corp* v *Olieprodukten Nederland BV* [1983] 2 Lloyd's Rep 419.

47 [1984] 2 Lloyd's Rep, at 82. But the court would still have power to remove an arbitrator for misconduct, even if the arbitration were under ICC Rules: see *Bank Mellat* v *Helleniki Techniki SA* [1984] QB 291, at 305.

48 [1984] QB 291.

company was ordinarily resident outside England and that in addition there was reason to believe that it would not be able to pay the bank's costs if the bank were successful in the arbitration. It was held that English law, as the law governing the procedure of an arbitration, determined whether the court could order security for costs, and that the court had a discretion to order security. But the Court of Appeal went on to hold that the English court should be slow to order security in international arbitrations unless there is some more specific connection with England than that the parties have agreed that any arbitration is to take place there. In particular the ICC Rules deal in detail with security for costs of the arbitrators (and of the ICC, although not the costs of the parties) and for the English court to award security was inconsistent with the scheme and spirit of the ICC Rules.

This decision recognises that a type of 'international arbitration' may be subject to rules different from that of ordinary domestic arbitrations. But all it shows is that English law, like other systems of law, is prepared to allow international arbitrations (however defined) to operate in a way which properly takes account of the fact that the forum may be chosen by the parties who have no connection with it and choose it purely as a neutral forum. As Robert Goff LJ put it,[49]

> 'Parties to such an arbitration may well choose London as a convenient neutral forum. There are now excellent and rapidly developing services available in London for the conduct of such arbitrations. The English language is frequently a language familiar to both parties, and often too the language of the contract; for that reason too, London may be a suitable forum. The services of very experienced solicitors, counsel, experts and arbitrators are readily available here. So London may be chosen as a convenient neutral forum; or it may be nominated as such by a body such as the ICC'.

It does not follow that English law recognises the theory of 'delocalised' (or 'floating' or 'denationalised') arbitration.[50]

According to this theory it serves the aims and interests of party autonomy in international contracts for the parties to be able to stipulate in their contract for arbitration which is not to be subject to the procedural rules of any particular country, or to the rules of the conflict of laws of any particular country, or to

49 *Ibid*, at 315. See also *Pagnan and Fratelli* v *Corbisa Industrial Agropacuaria Ltda* [1971] 1 All ER 165, at 166, *per* Salmon LJ.

50 The literature is very considerable. See especially for material in favour of delocalised arbitration Goldman, 'Les conflits de lois dans l'arbitrage international de droit privé', *Recueil des Cours de l'Academie de Droit International*, 347 (1963); Fragistas, 'Arbitrage étranger et arbitrage international en droit privé', *Révue critique de droit international privé* 1 (1960); Lalive, 'Problèmes rélatifs à l'arbitrage international commercial', *Recueil des Cours de l'Académie de Droit International*, 571 (1967); Schmitthoff (ed) *Sources of the Law of International Trade*, (London 1964); Lew, *Applicable Law in International Commercial Arbitration*, New York 1978; Fouchard, *L'Arbitrage Commercial International* (1965) Vol II, 401 *et seq*; Paulsson (1981) 30 *ICLQ* 358, (1983) 32 *ICLQ* 53. For criticism see Mann, *op cit supra* n30; Wetter, *International Arbitral Process* New York 1979, Vol 2, pp 403–4, 526–31; Park (1983) 32 *ICLQ* 21. See also Hirsch 34 *Arbitration Journal* 43 (1979); Collins, in *Basle Symposium on the Law Governing Contractural Obligations* (eds Klein and Vischer 1983), 70–9.

the substantive rules of any particular legal system.[51] Instead the arbitration will be subject to the procedural rules chosen by the parties (but not to the mandatory procedural rules of the place of arbitration); the arbitrators will be entitled to apply the rules of conflict of laws, not those of the seat of arbitration, but those which they 'deem appropriate'[52] and they may apply, not the substantive rules of any particular legal system, but the general principles of law or *lex mercatoria*.

This theory finds no support in English law. An arbitrator in England is subject to the mandatory rules of English law relating to arbitral procedure, and an arbitration in England[53] is subject to the review procedures of the Arbitration Act 1979 except to the extent that they have been validly excluded in accordance with that Act. As has been seen, this applies even if the arbitration is under the auspices of international institutional arbitration. By English law a foreign arbitration is subject to the procedure of the foreign seat[54] and a foreign award which has not been made in conformity with the law governing the arbitration procedure may be refused recognition and enforcement.[55] Nor can an English arbitrator apply any conflict of laws rules other than English rules, nor can he apply any substantive law other than that of a fixed and recognisable system. It has been the policy of English law that arbitrators subject to English law must apply the law. Megaw, J, an eminent commercial judge, said[56]:

> '... it is the policy of the law of this country that, in the conduct of arbitrations, arbitrators must in general apply a fixed and recognisable system of law, which primarily and normally would be the law of England, and that they cannot be allowed to apply some different criterion such as the view of the individual arbitrator or umpire on abstract justice or equitable principles, which, of course, does not mean "equity" in the legal sense of the word at all.'

Some of the most important cases in England on the conflict of laws have been decided by the courts by way of review of arbitration awards, or in answer to questions of law posed by arbitrators.[57] The reason is that arbitrators in an

51 Arbitrations between states and private parties raise special problems: in several such cases arbitrators have applied the procedural law of the place of arbitration, but not its conflict of law rules: see, eg, *Sapphire International Petroleum Ltd* v *National Iranian Oil Co* 34 *International Law Reports* 136 (1967); *BP* v *Libya* 53 *International Law Reports* 297 (1979). But *cf Saudi Arabia* v *Armaco*, 27 *International Law Reports* 117 (1963); *Texaco Overseas Petroleum Co Ltd* v *Libya* 53 *International Law Reports* 389 (1979); *LIAMCO* v *Libya* 62 *International Law Reports* 140 (1982); *Kuwait* v *Aminoil* 66 *International Law Reports* 518 (1984).

52 The phrase in a number of institutional procedural rules (UNCITRAL, UN Economic Commission for Europe, International Chamber of Commerce) influenced by the European Convention on International Commercial Arbitration 1961 (not ratified by the United Kingdom).

53 Subject to the possibility of a choice of a different procedural law, discussed *supra*.

54 *Whitworth Street Estates (Manchester) Ltd* v *James Miller & Partners Ltd* [1970] AC 583.

55 On enforcement of 'de-localised' awards, see Van den Berg, *The New York Arbitration Convention of 1958* Kluwer (Deventer 1981), 34–43.

56 *Orion Compania Espanola de Seguros* v *Belfort* [1962] 2 Lloyd's Rep 257 (including, perhaps, public international law).

57 Eg *Compagnie Tunisienne de Navigation SA* v *Compagnie d'Armement Maritime SA* [1971] AC 572. *Cf The Hollandia* [1983] 1 AC 565, 576.

English arbitration must apply the law,[58] and that in English law a contract is governed either by English law or by some specific foreign law. Thus in *Amin Rasheed Shipping Corporation* v *Kuwait Insurance Co*[59] Lord Diplock pointed out that contracts are incapable of existing in a legal vacuum, and are mere pieces of paper devoid of all legal effect unless made by reference to some system of private law. Thus whilst English arbitration law makes a special provision for arbitrations with international elements (as do many other systems of law), Kerr LJ has pointed out[60]:

> 'Despite suggestions to the contrary by some learned writers under other systems, our jurisprudence does not recognise the concept of arbitral procedures floating in the transnational firmament, unconnected with any municipal system of law.'

But, it must be stressed, it does not follow that English law is deficient in dealing with international arbitrations. As has been seen, in the same case Robert Goff LJ drew attention to the advantages of London as a neutral forum in international arbitration, and the provisions in the Arbitration Act 1979 for agreements excluding the supervisory jurisdiction of the English court have removed what was once perceived as the main disadvantage of arbitration in England.

58 'There must be no Alsatia in England where the King's writ does not run', *Czarnikow* v *Roth Schmidt & Co* [1922] 2 KB 478, at 488 (CA), *per* Scrutton LJ. But the effect of an exclusion agreement under the Arbitration Act 1979 may be to make this duty unenforceable, at least where the parties have agreed that the arbitrator need not apply the law.

59 [1984] AC 50 at 65; see also Mann, 'England Rejects "Delocalised" Contracts and Arbitration', 33 *ICLQ* 193 (1984).

60 *Bank Mellat* v *Hellniki Techniki SA* [1984] QB 291, at 301, referring to the views of Dr F A Man, *op cit supra* n30.

Part 3

International arbitration procedure

The extent of independence of international arbitration from the law of the *situs* 12

Jan Paulsson

'It would be very bizarre formalism to require that an essentially intellectual activity such as the preparation of an award to be carried out in a particular location . . . To speak of the seat *of an arbitral tribunal is, in a sense, an abuse of language, artificially transposing to the domain of arbitration a term adapted to the needs of judicial administration . . .*

When the legislator confers upon a court a given territorial jurisdiction, it is useful also to give it a seat within this territory, so that citizens know there is a judge in the neighbourhood. An arbitral tribunal manifestly has no territorial jurisdiction. Its jurisdiction is strictly personal, since it is consensual. A "seat" may thus at the most be justified by the convenience of the parties. In any event, it is by no means indispensable . . .'[1]

Introduction

Is there still any life in the once-hot debate over the concept of arbitral awards detached from the legal system of the country where they were rendered? I am one who believed that such awards may exist, and I still believe it. In fact, I have yet to hear an argument that overcomes the simple observation that the European Convention of 1961 *requires* a national court to enforce awards rendered abroad unless it is flawed under restrictive criteria exhaustively defined by the Convention – and without regard to the question whether they have been set aside by the courts of their country of origin. Still, as a practical matter I am quite willing to allow that the delocalisation of the international arbitral process is not the wave of the future. The need to delocalise is felt in few cases, and, happily, it may reasonably be predicted that those instances will become even rarer in the future.

When one speaks of delocalising the arbitral proceedings, one refers to removing the functioning of the arbitral tribunal from the supervisory authority of local courts. To delocalise awards, on the other hand, means to remove the power of the courts at the place of arbitration to make an internationally effective declaration of the award's nullity.

Broadly speaking, the purpose of delocalising arbitrations and awards is to recognise the special status of arbitration arising out of international trade, and in so doing, eliminate or reduce unintended effects of unforeseen peculiarities

1 Aubert, Case Note, 37 *Revue critique de droit international privé* 372 (1958).

of the municipal law of the place where a dispute happens to be heard. For fear of repeating myself I would not dare to add anything now to what I have already had the occasion to write on this topic.[2] On the other hand, there have been some recent developments with respect to the manner in which delocalisation might occur.

I would suggest that one must look at the matter of delocalisation from two separate perspectives: that of the judge called upon to enforce the award, and that of the judge at the place of arbitration.

Delocalisation from the perspective of the judge called upon to enforce the award

When faced with an award rendered abroad, whose enforcement in his jurisdiction is resisted on the grounds that the award has been invalidated in the country where it was rendered, may a national judge nevertheless order that it be enforced?

The New York Convention provides in Article V(1)(e) that recognition and enforcement of a foreign award *may* be refused if it

> 'has been set aside or suspended by a competent authority of the country in which, or under the law of which, that award was made.'

One notes that the Convention does not say that the award *must* be refused enforcement under such circumstances. A decision rendered on November 13, 1984 by the Court of Appeal in Rouen, France (unpublished) illustrates how a foreign award might be enforced even though it is detached from its country of origin.

The case involved a famous arbitral award rendered in Lausanne no less than three decades ago. A French company, SEEE – or rather its liquidator, as it has gone out of business – was seeking to have the award recognised in France. Three parties resisted these efforts and appeared as appellees: the Republic of Yugoslavia, which had lost the award, the French State, which supported the Yugoslav position; and the World Bank, which at one point in the long history of this litigation had become implicated as a garnishee in whose hands SEEE had attached Yugoslavian funds. In a word, this is a case with a high profile – although, in view of the purpose of the international arbitral process to resolve rather than prolong disputes, one might admit, irrespective of one's view of its merits, that this litigation has gone on for an embarrassingly long time.

For present purposes, the following elements of the dispute might be recalled:

- In 1932, a contract was entered into between Yugoslavia and a French company, later replaced by SEEE, for the construction of a railroad by the latter.
- The contract price was reflected in a series of bonds payable within 12 years.
- The railroad was built, but payments were halted in 1941, and never resumed after World War II.

2 My last word on the subject, see: 'Delocalisation of International Commercial Arbitration: When and Why it Matters', 32 *ICLQ* 53 (1983).

- In 1950, the French Government negotiated a settlement with Yugoslavia under which a lump sum was paid to SEEE on account of the bonds.
- On the grounds that the payment on account of the bonds was not in full satisfaction of its contractual rights, SEEE brought an arbitration in Lausanne under the arbitration clause contained in the 1932 contract. SEEE appointed an arbitrator, but Yugoslavia defaulted, leading to an appointment in its stead by the President of the local court. Under the system of arbitration defined in the contract, no third arbitrator was named. The two arbitrators rendered an award in 1956,[3] holding that Yugoslavia had an independent contractual debt to SEEE which had not been extinguished by the state-to-state settlement, and ordered Yugoslavia to pay SEEE approximately 62 million French francs.[4]

Many things have happened in many jurisdictions in the aftermath of this award. For present purposes, we shall concentrate on the French courts.

In 1969, the President of the *Tribunal de Grande Instance* of Paris declared by *ordonnance* the 1956 award to have executory force in France. This *ordonnance* has been the focus of still continuing French litigation. The highest French court, the *Cour de cassation*, twice reversed courts of appeal for having invalidated the 1969 *ordonnance.* In 1977, the *Cour de cassation* held that the Court of Appeal of Paris had erred in rejecting the award on the grounds that the 1950 state-to-state settlement pre-empted any further action by SEEE.[5] The case was sent to the Court of Appeal of Orléans, which rejected the award on other grounds, namely that the award contained 'a manifest error affecting its very foundation'. The *Cour de cassation* held that this was not a reason under French law to reject a foreign arbitral award,[6] and remanded the case to Rouen.

This led to the decision I'd like to examine now. The Court of Appeal in Rouen, unlike the two previous courts of appeal, accepted the award, and in so doing demonstrated the potential effectiveness of a national award, detached from the law of the country where it was rendered.[7]

The arguments put to the Court of Rouen by Yugoslavia and France against SEEE focused on the contention that the award had been invalidated by the Swiss courts. This contention merits examination.

In fact, the first thing that had happened after the award was rendered in 1956 was that it was filed with the Lausanne district court. Yugoslavia next brought an action to have the award set aside by the cantonal court of appeal, which responded in a curious way.[8] First, it held that it was without jurisdiction because the parties had not intended to subject themselves to the law of the Canton of Vaud. But on the other hand, it stated that:

'the action is allowed in the sense that the document signed by Ripert and

3 Extracts in 86 *Clunet* 1074 (1959).
4 SEEE might be expected now also to argue that a substantial amount of interest has accumulated in the 29 years since the award.
5 Decision of June 14, 1977; 104 *Clunet* 864 (1977).
6 Decision of October 13, 1981; [1983] *Revue de l'Arbitrage* 63.
7 Lovers of paradox will doubtless speculate as the *SEEE* v *Yugoslavia* saga carries relentlessly on into its fourth decade, whether the *Cour de cassation,* having twice reversed courts of appeal that rejected the award, will not repudiate the grounds given by the Court of Rouen for accepting it.
8 Decision of February 12, 1957; 47 *Revue critique de droit international privé* 359 (1958).

> Panchaud does not constitute an arbitral decision as understood by Article 516 of the Code of Procedure of Vaud, and it shall be returned to the party having filed it.'[9]

Examining the decision of the *Vaudois* court, one is struck by the fact that it is strangely difficult to determine what it was about the award that disqualified it from being deemed an 'arbitral decision' under the law of the Canton. Yugoslavia had contested the legality of a two-member tribunal, but that did not become the grounds for the decision. Rather, the court seemed to reject the award because the arbitral clause had called for a decision by the arbitrators within one month, which the court apparently found unreasonably short – 'incompatible with the notion of an arbitral judgment as understood by *Vaudois* law.'[10] Be that as it may, the court doubtless disappointed both parties, in that the Yugoslavian challenge was rejected on jurisdictional grounds, while the award upon which SEEE wished to rely was denied the *imprimateur* of registry at the Swiss court. Absolving itself from the practical consequences of its decision in a manner worthy of Pontius Pilate, the court declared that it did not mean to

> 'prejudice the validity and the binding force of this decision with regard to the will of the parties or such law as may be applicable to it.'[11]

SEEE's appeal to the Swiss Federal Tribunal was rejected on the grounds that SEEE lacked standing to sue since it had not demonstrated that the *Vaudois* judgment had caused it harm; the Federal Tribunal emphasised that that judgment had not even partially set aside the award.[12]

Whatever the cantonal court may have said about not having intended to prejudice the validity of the award elsewhere, the fact remains that its decision meant that the court at the place of arbitration had refused to recognise the award as complying with the requirements of local law, and that other national courts might ascribe greater transnational significance to its decision than it wished to do itself.

Indeed, SEEE's repeated attempts to enforce the 1956 award in Holland ended in failure precisely because of the decision of the *Vaudois* court. In a judgment of November 7, 1975, the Dutch Supreme Court stated:

> 'Surely, even though the award did not qualify for annulment by the Swiss judge, because he did not regard the decision as an arbitral award within the meaning of his law and consequently did not consider that the provisions regarding arbitration of the relevant procedural law should apply, the decision by the judge – as a consequence of which the enforcement of the decision given by Mr Ripert and Mr Panchaud was denied by a competent authority of the country in which the decision was given, and the possibility

9 *Ibid*, at 366.

10 *Ibid*, at 363. It is hard to fathom why this would mean that the parties had created something that was not an arbitration; as M Jean-Francois Aubert pointed out in a contemporaneous comment, the one-month deadline could readily have been prolonged, 37 *Revue critique de droit international privé* 374 (1958).

11 37 *Revue critique de droit international privé* 359 (1958), at 364. It should be stressed that whatever confusion may be inspired by this decision it is of little concern to anyone examining the situation today in the Canton Vaud, where the familiar Swiss Intercantonal Arbitration Convention came into force in 1970.

12 Decision of September 18 1957; 37 *Revue critique de droit international privé* 366 (1958).

of enforcement in the same country was ruled out – should be considered as equivalent, in the present case, to the circumstance mentioned in Article V(1)(e) of the Convention, namely that the relevant authority made it impossible to enforce the award by setting it aside. Since it was not stated and does not appear that the decision was made under the law of any other country, the judgment by the Vaud Cantonal Tribunal had the same effect as an annulment.'[13]

We now return to last year's developments before the Court of Appeal in Rouen. It was hardly surprising that Yugoslavia and France argued, in line with the Dutch holding, that the 1956 award had in effect been denied executory or binding force by the *Vaudois* court. Indeed, according to the two states-appellant, the Swiss court decision implied that the award was 'without judicial existence'.

The issue of the delocalised award thus found itself centre-stage. The Court of Appeal turned out to be quite willing to recognise an award irrespective of its absence of connection with the law of the place of arbitration, reasoning *inter alia*:

> 'that the (Swiss) decisions did not have the effect of setting the award aside, nor of eliminating its legal existence; and that they only set forth that the award escapes the judicial sovereignty of Vaud;
>
> that according to Yugoslavia this conclusion had the effect of depriving the award of a final or binding character;
>
> that the law of the place of arbitration does not always and necessarily govern the arbitral proceedings;
>
> that the "procedural law" that governs the arbitration may equally be another national law or the agreement of the parties;
>
> that in this case the arbitration clause excludes the application of national laws of procedure since it defines its own procedure;
>
> that the arbitration clause provides that the arbitrators are exempt from any formality, that they may decide as *amiables compositeurs*, and that their decisions, or as the case may be those of the umpire, are final and binding on both parties;
>
> that according to the procedure applicable to the arbitration in question, the arbitrators' decision is therefore binding upon both parties in the meaning of the New York Convention of 1958'.

The Court of Appeal of Rouen accordingly held that by application of the New York Convention the original order of 1969 declaring the award to be executory in France should be reinstated.

In deciding that the arbitration clause had 'excluded the application of national laws of procedure,' the Rouen Court made an inference which not everyone will accept, namely that because the arbitration agreement establishes rules of procedure for the arbitration, it implies exclusion of national laws.[14] Indeed, some would point out that in most venues – including

13 Extracts in G Gaja, *International Commercial Arbitration*, New York Convention, V 35 2–3.

14 The Rouen Court appears to be on the same wavelength as the South African Supreme Court, which stated, in a 1976 case involving an award rendered by arbitrators functioning

Lausanne, since the advent of the Swiss Arbitration Convention – it is impossible to exclude such rules of procedure as the *lex loci* determines to be imperative. It might be noted that although the arbitration clause did not stipulate that Lausanne was to be the place of arbitration, reference was made to the cantonal court of Vaud for appointment of arbitrators. This factor was not, however, deemed to connect the award with the law of the venue of the arbitration.

Delocalisation from the perspective of the judge at the place of arbitration

In approving the cantonal court's decision in *SEEE* v *Yugoslavia*, the Swiss Federal Tribunal noted that SEEE 'did not claim that it intended to request execution of the arbitrator's decision in the Canton of Vaud' and that the cantonal court had not 'examined whether the award was binding and enforceable outside the Canton of Vaud'.[15]

This raises the question of the extent to which the courts of the place of arbitration should be concerned with the effects of awards abroad. If a foreign court were to consider the views of the court of the place of arbitration to be conclusive – as the Dutch Supreme Court did in the *SEEE* case – it would be inimical to the arbitral process for the courts of the venue to take a hands off attitude. On the other hand, if the foreign court may disregard the effect of court rulings at the place of arbitration – as the Court of Appeal of Rouen did – the position is different.

As an illustration, one may take the case of legal systems where there are no specific provisions defining the local courts' jurisdiction to hear challenges to awards concerning only foreign parties. Apart from general principles governing the exercise of jurisdiction, this situation calls into question the text and underlying policies of the New York Convention, together with conclusions about whether arbitral awards must have a 'nationality,' or whether they may 'drift' free from the constraints of the *lex loci arbitri*.

---

under the FIS Rules (full title in English: the Rules and Usages for the International Trade in Herbage Seeds):

> '... [I]n the international commercial world it has almost become a universal practice to select London as the seat for arbitration proceedings, not because parties to an international mercantile transaction necessarily have confidence in English law, but for purposes of convenience, because London is an important commercial centre and because of the expertise of London arbitrators. And if they do so they do not, unless there is an express indication in the contract or other circumstances which point in that direction, submit to the jurisdiction of the English courts ... In the present case ... [o]ther than agreeing upon an arbitral tribunal in London, there is no real or close connection with England. The parties are not domiciled there; the brokers have their offices in Canada and the United States, respectively; the purchase price was to have been paid in American currency in Japan and the purchased goods were to have been shipped from South Africa to Japan. *It seems that in the present case not even the curial law of England applied* (save to a limited extent), *because the FIS has its own procedural rules.*' (*Emphasis added*)

(The 'limited extent' related to the challenge of arbitrators.) *Benidai Trading Co Limited (Japan)* v *Gouws & Gouws (Pty) Limited*, (South Africa), 1977 *South African Law Reports*, 3, 1021; summarised in VII *Yearbook: Commercial Arbitration* 351 (1981).

15 37 *Revue critique de droit international privé* 366–7 (1958).

Thus, for example, Swedish courts have not yet pronounced themselves on their duty to decide requests for declarations of invalidity in all cases where arbitration proceedings have taken place in Sweden. In the one case in which these issues have been faced, the Stockholm *Tingsrätt* (court of the first instance) on December 14, 1983[16] held that the Republic of Uganda, which had lost an ICC arbitration in Stockholm against an Israeli contractor, could obtain local jurisdiction with respect to an action brought under Section 21 of the Swedish Arbitration Act to set the award aside on the grounds that the arbitral tribunal was not properly appointed.[17] The court reached its decision on the basis that there could be no waiver of such recourse; it did not consider whether the foreign nationalities of the parties had an effect on jurisdiction. On the other hand, the Stockholm court held that it did not have jurisdiction to entertain an action under Section 20 seeking a declaration that the award was void (on the grounds that the agreement to arbitrate had lapsed before arbitration). The court noted that as opposed to actions brought under Section 21, actions under Section 20 did not have a legally defined Swedish forum. It noted that awards deemed to be void could be resisted in any forum in which the winning party might seek to execute the award (including of course Sweden). It was unconvinced by the argument that it would be valuable in international arbitration to obtain once and for all a ruling as to whether an award is void, and that Article V I(e) of the New York Convention would suggest that the forum for such a ruling should be the place of arbitration. It rather took the view that 'there is no reason to presume that a Swedish court's declaration of voidness would be respected generally.'

A similar problem arose earlier this year before the Austrian courts. The case concerned an ICC award rendered in Vienna between two non-Austrian parties. The award was challenged before the local courts on grounds defined in Austrian law, but the court of first instance held that it had no jurisdiction to hear a challenge in a case where the parties' arbitration agreement did not expressly stipulate that Austria would be the place of arbitration. The parties had simply referred to ICC arbitration, and the ICC Court of Arbitration had in turn chosen Vienna. This decision seemed fragile, given Austrian policy to favour international arbitration. After all, one would wonder if international institutions would continue to select Austrian venues for arbitration if local courts decline to exercise any authority whatsoever to curtail abuse. And indeed, just one month ago the Court of Appeal reversed and directed the lower court judge to hear the challenge.

Is it not rather clear that enforcement judges will scrutinise a foreign award more severely if they are made aware that it was rendered in a country which provides no judicial control for fraud, excess of authority, violation of *bonus mores*?

It might be recalled that it was precisely this type of concern that was voiced by commentators in the wake of the *Götaverken* case,[18] in which the Court of Appeal of Paris declined to take jurisdiction over a challenge to an ICC rendered in Paris between Swedish and Libyan parties, on the grounds that the

16 In the matter of *Republic of Uganda et al* v *Solel Boneh International et al*; unpublished slip opinion, Stockholm Tingstratt, docket no T57/79; appeal pending.

17 Article 20 of the Swedish Arbitration Act defines void awards; Article 21 defines voidable awards.

18 [1980] *Revue de l'Arbitrage* 555; VI *Yearbook: Commercial Arbitration* 237 (1981).

award was not French. The parallel with the Swiss *SEEE* decision is striking. And whatever might be one's doctrinal or practical predisposition with respect to the degree of attachment of an international award to the legal system of the place of arbitration, the fact is that the year after the *Götaverken* decision, France passed its 1981 Decree on International Arbitration which made it clear that any award rendered in France may be challenged before French courts. Thus one of the legal systems reputed to be among the most liberal in this area has established the concept that with respect to a restricted number of grounds, a party victimised by miscarriage of the arbitral process may have the award set aside in the place where it was rendered.

Conclusions

To the extent that the grounds upon which a court at the place of arbitration will set aside an award parallel those recognised by courts elsewhere, it is most unlikely that an award annulled in its country of origin will be given life elsewhere. It really does not matter as a practical matter whether the enforcement forum refuses to recognise the award because it believes that the award has no legal existence beyond that acknowledged by its country of origin, or whether it applies its own criteria to reject the award.

With the successful extension of the New York Convention, whose grounds for rejection of foreign awards also appear to reflect a modern consensus as to the limited grounds for invalidating awards rendered within the jurisdiction but in the context of international trade, the world may be said to be becoming a safer place for international arbitration. The reasons for urging that awards might be detached from the legal systems of their countries of origin accordingly recede in importance.

In the event that the UNCITRAL Model Law becomes an international success, this tendency will become even more accentuated, because the Model Law suggests that national legislatures simply adopt the New York Convention's criteria for examining the validity of awards, whether at the challenge or enforcement stages.

A residual concern in this respect relates to arbitration in the Third World. Parties from developing countries often point out, quite rightly, that a European venue is inappropriate – and works unfair hardships on the Third World party – in the context of a contractual relationship whose centre of gravity is clearly thousands of miles away. Yet western parties are wary of the risk that local judges, whether by inexperience or because of an insufficient tradition of judicial independence, will reduce the arbitral award to a dead letter. In this light, a significant degree of delocalisation will favour developing countries in the sense that it will make venues in the Third World more readily acceptable. The way this could work is that parties would agree to arbitration in a Third World venue but explicitly subject the proceedings to other procedural laws than those of the local legal systems. The result would be that the position taken by a local judge, albeit irresistible in terms of its effect on the prospect of enforcement of the award locally, need not bar enforcement elsewhere. It is my view, illustrated by the recent decision of the Court of Appeal of Rouen, that such a result would be consonant with the New York Convention.

The role of national law and the national courts in England 13

Stewart C Boyd QC

'Despite suggestions to the contrary by some learned writers under other systems, our jurisprudence does not recognise the concept of arbitral procedures floating in the transnational firmament, unconnected with any municipal system of law'.

Introduction

I have chosen to preface my paper with this quotation from the judgment of Lord Justice Kerr in *Bank Mellat* v *Helleniki Techniki SA*[1] because it contains a statement of principle which would, I believe, be accepted unhesitatingly as correct by the overwhelming majority of English legal practitioners. Powerful academic authority for the proposition is to be found in Dr F A Mann's well-known article 'Lex Facit Arbitrum' in *International Arbitration: Liber Amicorum for Martin Domke*[2] to which Lord Justice Kerr himself refers. Yet there is, so far as I am aware, no other English case in which the possibility of what, for want of a better word, I shall call 'transnational' arbitral procedures has ever been considered. Nor indeed, was the topic strictly raised for decision even in the *Bank Mellat* case, since the curial law of the arbitration before the court was admitted to be English law.

Nevertheless, the object of this paper is not to question the correctness of Lord Justice Kerr's *dictum*, but rather to explore from the English viewpoint the extent to which it is either possible or desirable, in a theoretical and in a practical sense, to sever the relationship between the courts and arbitrations. Is there anything in the fundamental principles of English law or the present rules governing arbitration which presents an insuperable doctrinal obstacle to the concept of transnational arbitration? If not, what are the practical considerations which weigh for or against transnational arbitration in the English context? Should it be prohibited, tolerated, or encouraged?

There is, of course, no simple answer to these questions. The relationship between the courts and arbitrations does not depend on a simple link which can be severed with a single incision, but depends on a complex bundle of relationships arising out of the various statutory and common law remedies vested in the courts for the purpose of supporting and controlling the arbitral

1 [1984] QB 291 at 301.
2 P Sanders (ed), *The Hague 1967*, at 157.

process. The positive law of arbitration in England is in effect a commentary on these remedies. As so often in English law, 'substantive law has the appearance of being secreted in the interstices of procedure'.

Alternative remedies to transnational arbitration

Any systematic attempt to discuss the concept of transnational arbitration must therefore begin by identifying the remedies which the courts exercise in relation to arbitration. For the purposes of the discussion they can be grouped into three categories:

Coercive remedies

An arbitration agreement contains two promises which are generally implied rather than fully expressed: first, to resolve disputes by arbitration and not otherwise, and second, to abide by and perform the award. By 'coercive' remedies I mean those remedies which serve to give effect to these promises. In the case of the first promise they are: a stay of court proceedings in England, an injunction restraining court proceedings abroad, and (exceptionally) damages for breach of the arbitration agreement. In the case of the second promise they are: an action on the award, and proceedings for summary enforcement under Section 26 of the Arbitration Act 1950. In addition to these remedies, the court also has a range of remedies available to it for constituting or reconstituting the arbitral tribunal in a wide variety of circumstances, so as to prevent the reference from becoming abortive.

Auxiliary remedies

An arbitrator has no direct power to invoke the processes by which a court enforces compliance with its own orders, ie, committal to prison and sequestration of property. Accordingly a number of remedies which are unavailable to the arbitrator are vested in the court to be used in aid of the arbitral process, eg, interim measures such as arrest of maritime property, *Mareva* injunctions and other interim injunctions designed to preserve the subject-matter of the dispute and to maintain the *status quo* until after the award, orders for examination of witnesses by the court or for the issue of a commission or request for the examination of a witness out of the jurisdiction, etc. In addition the court has available to it a number of remedies which are or may also be available to the arbitrator but which can more readily or effectively be exercised by the court: these include power to order security for costs, discovery of documents and interrogatories, and the appointment of a receiver. The court also has power under Section 5 of the Arbitration Act 1979 to enlarge certain default powers of the arbitrator.

Corrective remedies

The category of 'corrective' remedies encompasses a wide range of powers available to the court to correct what can broadly be described as procedural mishaps and abuses. Those available after the award has been published are the power to set aside the award or to remit it to the arbitrator for reconsideration. During the course of the reference the range of remedies is wider. It includes the power to give leave to revoke the arbitrator's authority or to remove him, power to revoke the arbitration agreement, and in certain circumstances power to bring the reference to an end by injunction. The court also has remedies available to it for correcting errors of law in the award itself, exercisable on an appeal under the Arbitration Act 1979: but as this paper is concerned solely with matters of procedure I shall say nothing more about remedies which concern the substance of the award, or the extent to which they may be excluded by agreement between the parties.

A historical digression

I shall shortly turn to consider to what extent international arbitration can and should be dissociated from these three categories of remedy. Before I do so, however, I should like to make a brief historical digression. I have sometimes heard the transnational aspirations of a certain well-known arbitral institution likened to the aspirations of the medieval papacy. I have even heard it suggested that the supposed English antipathy to transnationalism has its subconscious origins in the English Protestant tradition. I do not believe there is a word of truth in this. On the contrary, the characteristic expression of the Protestant tradition in English constitutional thought has been the belief that temporal authority derives from consent and is not imposed from above. It is this same belief, as I understand it, which lies at the heart of the theory of transnational arbitration: the belief that arbitral authority has as its source, and its *only* source, the consent of the parties expressed through the medium of the arbitration agreement.

A better case could be made out for ascribing English reserve towards transnational arbitration to experience of the difficult process by which the English legal system developed into the centralised and unified form which it displays in the twentieth century. The process consisted of a long and only intermittently successful struggle to bring together into a single system the many diverse and conflicting courts administering differing rules on a local and sometimes even temporal basis, starting with the feudal courts and progressing by way of the Court of Star Chamber, the courts of equity, the Admiralty Court, and the sometimes overlapping jurisdictions of the Courts of Common Law. The battles to which these jurisdictional conflicts and jealousies gave rise finally came to an end, as we all know, in the treaty of peace embodied in the Judicature Act 1873. But one still hears echoes of them in the argument advanced in support of maintaining a right of appeal from an arbitrator's award, that 'there cannot be an Alsatia in England where the King's writ will not run', or, more colloquially, that arbitrators cannot be permitted to administer rules of mercantile law differing from the common law of England.

Yet again, I believe that the historical experience yields only a half-truth. For at the same time as the battles for jurisdictional unity were being fought, the legislature and the courts were actively encouraging and supporting arbitrations, the legislature by a series of reforming statutes, starting as early as 1694, designed to reinforce and improve the arbitral process, and the courts by an increasingly tolerant attitude to arbitral procedures which would not have been acceptable in the courts themselves. The reception of inadmissible evidence and the institution of the arbitrator-advocate spring to mind as examples which could not have survived without a benevolent attitude on the part of the courts: the latter is indeed so unorthodox as still to perplex the purists. This benevolence towards novel procedures has persisted to the present day: by way of example one may note that the Court of Appeal sanctioned the making of awards in a foreign currency some years before the same liberty was extended to the court's own judgments, first by the House of Lords and subsequently by Parliament.

The Washington Convention

So I can find nothing in the English historical experience which would justify the suggestion that the English legal tradition is fundamentally hostile to the concept of transnational arbitration. Rather the reverse. Indeed, I would point out that the arbitral institution which perhaps has the best claim to being truly transnational in character was established under the Washington Convention, which the United Kingdom has not only signed but ratified. The legislation giving effect to the Convention in the United Kingdom is contained in the Arbitration (International Investment Disputes) Act 1966, and the institution is ICSID. It is worth recalling the features of ICSID which establish its claim to be called 'transnational', since I have so far deliberately abstained from attempting a definition of that expression.

1 The Convention contains its own internal procedures for constituting and challenging the Arbitral Tribunal.[3]
2 The Tribunal is the judge of its own competence.[4]
3 The Tribunal has power to interpret its own award[5] and to revise its award after hearing fresh evidence.[6]
4 Application for annulment of the award is made to an *ad hoc* Committee constituted under the Convention and not to any national court. The grounds on which annulment may be requested are limited to those stated in the Convention.[7]
5 Contracting States recognise an award rendered pursuant to the Convention as if it were final judgment of a court in that state.

The Act of 1966 gives effect to these provisions in England by providing that the only provisions of the Arbitration Act 1950 which may apply to proceedings under the Convention are those of Section 12 (which confers procedural powers on the arbitrator and vests auxiliary remedies in the Courts regarding matters such as the attendance of witnesses, production of documents, etc) and Section 4(1), which relates to the stay of proceedings. In point of fact, a stay would now automatically be granted in relation to such proceedings under the later, and mandatory provisions of the Arbitration Act

3 Washington Convention, Articles 37–40, 50–58.
4 *Ibid*, Article 41.
5 *Ibid*, Article 50.
6 *Ibid*, Article 51.
7 *Ibid*, Articles 52 and 53.

1975. Enforcement of an award under the Convention, in contrast to the usual procedure by action or summary proceedings under Section 26 of the Arbitration Act 1950 which result in a judgment *of the Court*, is by way of registration, upon which the award becomes self-enforcing as fully as if it were a judgment of the High Court.[8] The requirements for enforcement are purely formal: there are no substantive grounds on which enforcement can be opposed, not even those applicable to enforcement under the New York Convention. For this reason, although an award emanating from ICSID would, in principle, be enforceable in England under the legislation giving effect to the New York Convention, the claimant will in practice invariably prefer to resort to the procedure of enforcement by registration.

There remains the theoretical possibility that a party might invoke those corrective remedies, few in number, which the court possesses independently of statute. But having regard to the existence of the corrective remedies laid down in the Convention itself and to the express prohibition on the use of such remedies contained in Article 53 it is inconceivable that the English court would intervene in any way in proceedings under the Convention.

Exclusion of the remedies by agreement

I have drawn attention to the Washington Convention constituting ICSID not only because it demonstrates that transnational arbitration is wholly compatible with English law and legal institutions, but also because it goes as far towards creating an arbitral institution freed from the influence of national courts as the most dedicated transnationalist would wish. Nevertheless it may be instructive to consider whether yet more radical and complete severance from the national courts is possible or desirable, and with that object in mind I now turn to consider each of the various categories of remedy which I have described earlier in this paper.

Coercive remedies

I have already indicated that the coercive remedies are of two kinds: those that enforce the agreement to arbitrate (among which it is convenient also to include the procedures for constituting and reconstituting the tribunal), and those that enforce the award. So far as the first group of remedies is concerned, it is difficult to envisage any circumstances in which parties to what is ostensibly an arbitration agreement would wish to abjure resort to those remedies which are necessary to give effect to it. The consequences of doing so would, moreover, be very odd indeed. Section 1 of the Arbitration Act 1975, which gives effect to Article II of the New York Convention, provides that 'the Court, unless satisfied that the arbitration agreement is null and void, inoperative or incapable of being performed . . ., *shall* make an order staying the proceedings.' (*Emphasis added.*) Accordingly, unless the court is satisfied of the relevant matters, it has no option but to stay the proceedings, even if the parties have attempted to exclude by agreement the court's jurisdiction to do so. There seems no room for an argument that the arbitration agreement is

8 Arbitration (International Investment Disputes) Act 1966, s2.

'inoperative or incapable of being performed' merely because the parties have agreed not to invoke a stay of proceedings. That appears to leave the court with the choice between ignoring the will of the parties and granting a stay, or else concluding that the arbitration agreement is 'null and void', with the logical consequences that if proceedings do in the event place under an agreement excluding the Court's power to stay its own proceedings, they do not amount to an arbitration and cannot result in an arbitration award. This would not necessarily mean that the 'award' could not be enforced at all, merely that it could not be enforced by the procedures available for the enforcement of an award: it might still be possible to give effect to it under ordinary principles of contract law, in mode the way that effect is given to a valuer's or expert's opinion by which the parties to a contract have agreed to be bound. But if the procedure does not amount to an arbitration it is clear that none of the auxiliary powers of the Court can be invoked in aid of it, and that none of the usual corrective powers of the Court can be invoked to control it or to view the resultant 'award'. Further, if the claimant insists on proceedings in court, and the respondent is amenable to the jurisdiction of the English court in accordance with its rules, there will be no procedural obstacle in the way of the claimant pursuing his claim to judgment, unless the purported arbitration agreement is in the *Scott* v *Avery* form.[9]

An arbitration agreement which expressly excludes the court's power to constitute the arbitration tribunal on the parties failure to do so, or to reconstitute it when casual vacancies occur (eg, through death or resignation), is unlikely to occur in practice as a result of conscious decision by the draftsman. But it may perhaps occur inadvertently, for example, if the arbitration agreement provides for appointments to be made only by a named person or institution, and for some reason that person or institution cannot or will not make an appointment necessary to get the arbitration under way. The effect under English law of a provision excluding the court's power of appointment is reasonably clear. The statutory powers of appointment[10] unlike a number of other sections in the statute, are not stated to be subject to a contrary intention expressed in the arbitration agreement, and therefore cannot be excluded by such an agreement. It follows that the court's *jurisdiction* to make default appointments cannot be excluded by express agreement. However, that is by no means the end of the matter, for all the statutory powers of appointment are expressed in terms which make it clear that they are not mandatory but discretionary, and the court will regard an agreement not to invoke its jurisdiction as a powerful and generally insuperable reason for declining to exercise the jurisdiction as a matter of *discretion*.

Last but not least of the court's coercive remedies are those designed to bring about the enforcement of the award. Once again it is difficult to conceive of circumstances in which parties to what is ostensibly an arbitration agreement would deliberately agree to exclude those powers of enforcement which would give it practical effect. Such an agreement would presumably be 'binding in honour only', to use the expression which serves to describe what is more accurately called an imperfect obligation, ie, an obligation which cannot be enforced by any legal process but nevertheless attaches to the conscience of the

9 (1856) 25 LJ Ex 308.
10 Arbitration Act 1950, ss10 and 25.

obligator. Such obligations are not without value, because they are sanctioned by the force of public opinion. So far as the courts are concerned, they are completely without force.

An agreement to refer disputes to decision by a process which will produce a legally unenforceable award is probably not an arbitration agreement at all in the eyes of English law. As already stated an arbitration agreement contains two provisions: first to refer disputes to arbitration and second to perform and abide by the award. I have also suggested that if the first promise is removed the ensuing process is no longer an arbitration. Removal of the second promise, even if the first is left intact, seems even more clearly to point to the conclusion that the ensuing process, although intended to resemble an arbitration, cannot result in an arbitration award. It is hardly worthwhile considering what name *should* be attached to such a process: it would not seem to fall into any established category of procedure. Probably it is best regarded as some form of conciliation, although intended to result in a compromise based on a judicial rather than a negotiated assessment of the merits of the dispute.

The question then arises whether the court would stay proceedings brought in breach of such an agreement. Clearly the statutory remedies could not be invoked, since they apply only where there is an arbitration agreement. But the court has an inherent jurisdiction to stay its own proceedings, and would be likely to do so if it concluded, on the true construction of the agreement, either that the agreed procedure had to be exhausted before an action could be begun, or that the agreed procedure was the only means by which the contract between the parties could be enforced. Strictly speaking, on the latter view, the court ought not merely to stay the action but to dismiss it on the grounds that not only the purported 'arbitration agreement', but also the contract to which it relates, is binding in honour only. In practice the consequences of staying or dismissing the action would be the same.

Before leaving the subject of coercive remedies it is worth noting that the Washington Convention, which I have taken as the model of transnational arbitration, does not purport to exclude either the court's power to stay proceedings or to enforce the award, with the result that these remedies remain available to give effect to an arbitration under the Convention. It is also true to say that the Convention does not exclude the powers to constitute or reconstitute the arbitral tribunal, but in practice the existence of internal procedures within ICSID itself will make resort to national procedures unnecessary.

Auxiliary remedies

The question whether resort to the auxiliary remedies available from the English court can be excluded by agreement between the parties presents fewer difficulties than in the case of the coercive remedies. It is clear that if the court has jurisdiction over the respondent in accordance with its rules, the *jurisdiction* to order auxiliary remedies cannot be excluded by agreement. However, the court's *discretion* whether or not to exercise the remedies will rarely, if ever, be exercised if the parties have agreed not to invoke it. This is certainly the case with regard to interim measures, such as a *Mareva* injunction. Not only will the court refuse to grant such relief where it is prohibited by the terms of the arbitration agreement, but it will in an appropriate case restrain a party by injunction from seeking similar relief in proceedings abroad, and if necessary compensate the other party in damages.[11] Later decisions have, however, established that the court will not resort to such measures unless it is clear that the parties have agreed to exclude resort to the court in respect of interim measures and not merely, as is more usual, in respect of measures directed solely to establishing questions of liability.

With regard to other auxiliary remedies, such as security for costs, discovery of documents, and other measures intended to reinforce the arbitral process, it is also clear that the court will not in practice grant relief where the parties have expressly agreed not to invoke it, and will rarely if ever do so even when there is no express agreement to that effect, if to do so would be contrary to an implied agreement or even simply contrary to the spirit of the arbitration agreement. Thus, the court will not order security for costs in an arbitration under the Rules of Arbitration of the ICC merely because the arbitration is held in England.[12]

Even when the court's remedies are not excluded in this way, there is a growing body of opinion (not yet reflected in any actual decision of the court) that if the arbitrator has concurrent powers, as for example in the case of the power to order discovery documents, the court should be slow to exercise its own powers until after an application has been made to the arbitrator, and that even then it should generally reinforce rather than reverse the arbitrator's decision, except perhaps where the arbitrator has made a clear mistake of principle in exercising his discretion, so as to withhold relief.

The Arbitration (International Investment Disputes) Act 1966 makes express provision for the auxiliary remedies in Section 12 of the Arbitration Act 1950 and the Foreign Tribunals Evidence Act 1856 (which was at the time the enactment relating to the taking of evidence in the United Kingdom for the purpose of proceedings before a foreign tribunal) to apply to arbitration proceedings under the Washington Convention. This was evidently in compliance with the international obligations of the United Kingdom, under Article 69 of the Convention, to 'take legislative or other measures as may be necessary for making the provisions of this Convention effective in its territories'.

Corrective remedies

It is when one turns to the subject of corrective remedies, even leaving on one side the vexed question of appeals, that one enters the most controversial area of contact between the courts and arbitrations. It is here that the terminology of 'intervention' by the court tends to be abandoned in favour of the more tendentious 'interference'. Even the apparently innocuous 'interventionist' has begun to acquire pejorative overtones, particularly when applied, as it often is, to the supposed attitude of the English court towards international commercial arbitration.

11 *Mantovani* v *Carapelli* [1980] 1 Lloyd's Rep 475.
12 *Bank Mellat*, note 1, *supra*.

Whether or not the English court is indeed 'interventionist' in an undesirable sense depends to some extent on one's point of view. Before considering the proposition in some detail, two general observations can be made. First, it is worth remembering that the English court never intervenes of its own motion to set aside or remit an award. Even in proceedings for enforcement it would only refuse enforcement of its own motion if the award were *ex facie* illegal or contrary to public policy: I can recall no case in which this has actually happened. A large part of the criticism of the English system has derived not so much from cases where the court has actually intervened, but from cases where it has been requested to intervene on grounds which have proved to be wholly specious and where it has not in fact done so. This type of abuse derives from the actions of the disappointed party and not from spontaneous interference by the court, and its existence should not lead one to the conclusion that in order to prevent the abuse it is necessary to abolish the remedies. Rather it should lead to the conclusion that the remedies should only be exercised sparingly and should be surrounded by procedural safeguards against abuse. The following are examples of the safeguards that exist:

(a) Proceedings to set aside or remit an award must be brought within 21 days of the award being published.
(b) The respondent may be required to pay the amount of the award into court as a condition of obtaining a stay of execution if it is he who is making the application.
(c) The application must be supported by affidavit evidence, in contrast to the more indulgent rule which applies to the pleadings in an action, which are unsworn.
(d) For the purpose of fixing dates for hearings, thc applications are treated as interlocutory, and thus receive priority over other proceedings.

The second general observation is that international commercial arbitration in London depends almost entirely on the services of what lawyers call 'laymen', in other words, men appointed to be arbitrators because of their experience in the commercial field or because of their technical expertise as engineers, architects, etc, rather than because they possess a legal qualification. This is considered, rightly, to strengthen rather than weaken the quality and authority of the award. But it also undoubedly increases the risk of those procedural injustices which, through inadvertence or misunderstanding, can occasionally arise even when the proceedings are conducted by the most fair-minded and experienced lawyer. If all arbitrators were Solomons we should need no corrective remedies. But they are not: and some, it must be said, are less so than others. This is a fact of life which is perhaps more characteristic of arbitration in England than of arbitration elsewhere. Those whose experience is of arbitration concerning long-term investment projects, where legal arbitrators are common, may favour less intervention. But those whose experience is of arbitration concerning everyday commercial transactions in shipping, insurance and trade, where lay arbitrators are the norm, would in general be more reluctant to abandon the safeguards provided by the corrective remedies. Seldom invoked and even more sparingly granted, they nevertheless exert a hidden but beneficial influence over the day-to-day conduct of commercial arbitration. The antipathy to the appeal procedures provided by the Arbitration Act 1950 is by no means as widespread as one might imagine. One major international petroleum company, for example, has standard forms of charter which contain express consent to an appeal from arbitration to the High Court on any question of law).

Now to the remedies themselves. To what extent can the parties validly or effectively agree to exclude them? To answer this question it is necessary to focus on the purposes for which the remedies may be invoked, rather than on the technical features of the individual remedies themselves. This is because, with the possible exception of an order giving leave to revoke the authority of the arbitrator[13] it is clear that the court's *jurisdiction* to grant the remedies does not yield to a contrary intention expressed in the arbitration agreement. As is almost always the case, the real question is whether the existence of such an agreement is a sufficient reason for refusing to grant a particular remedy as a matter of *discretion*, and that must depend almost entirely on whether the grounds on which the application for the remedy are made are sufficiently serious to warrant disregarding the agreement of the parties. It is therefore necessary to recall the principal grounds on which the court will intervene during or after the reference, namely:

(a) Fraud or corruption on the part of the arbitrator.
(b) Bias or partiality on the part of the arbitrator.
(c) Want of due process.[14]
(d) Admitted mistake by the arbitrator.[15]
(e) Discovery, after the award, of relevant evidence which was not reasonably obtainable at the hearing.

In each case the essential basis on which the court intervenes is that an injustice has occurred which can only be remedied by the court. Those who would argue that even in such cases the parties should be free to contract out of their right to complain can point to the fact that as regards errors of law in the arbitrator's decision English law has already accepted that an appeal to the court may in all cases be excluded by an agreement made after the commencement of the arbitration, and in many cases even before that time. Why, it can be argued, should the parties not be free to exclude remedies for errors of procedure to at least the same extent as they are free to exclude remedies for errors of substance?

There are in my view two answers to this line of argument. First, it raises the very difficult question whether flagrant or deliberate disregard of the substantive rules of law governing the dispute may not themselves be remediable by procedures other than appeal.[16] Second, although the concept of arbitration does not necessarily comprise the notion that the arbitrator's

13 Arbitration Act 1950, s1.

14 This is more usually termed 'misconduct', 'procedural mishap', 'breach of natural justice' or 'failure to afford a fair hearing'.

15 This ground of intervention is necessary because of the limited interpretation which the courts have until recently given to the arbitrator's own statutory power to correct errors and omissions contained in s17 of the Arbitration Act 1950. Recent cases have suggested a tendency both to extend the arbitrator's powers of correction and to limit the court's power of intervention.

16 See, M Mustill and S Biyd, *The Law and Practice of Commercial Arbitration in England*, London 1982, Chapter 37.

reasons must be beyond reproach in a legal sense, it does comprise the notion that the arbitral procedure should be beyond reproach, at least in the sense that it should correspond to fundamental concepts of impartiality as regards the arbitrator himself, and of fairness as regards the procedure which he follows. That this is so from the viewpoint of English law is almost self-evident: a procedure which involved a decision by a partial referee or by an unfair process could not and would not be recognised as an arbitration and would not attract the remedies specific to arbitration, although it might still give rise to obligations enforceable by other contractual remedies. English law is not alone in this respect. Procedures for ensuring the impartiality in the tribunal and fairness in procedure are to be found in the draft UNCITRAL Model Law Article 34 in particular provides that an award may be set aside on proof that:

> 'the party making the application was not given proper notice of the appointment of the arbitrator(s) or of the arbitral proceedings or was otherwise unable to present his case'.[17]

This ground corresponds to one of the grounds on which enforcement of an award may be refused under the New York Convention.[18] Article 52 of the Washington Convention contains a ground of annulment which is perhaps more narrowly worded but nevertheless demonstrates that the concept of arbitration is based on fundamental procedural norms. Annulment may be requested on the ground –

> 'that there has been a serious departure from a fundamental rule of procedure'.

The Washington Convention also contains provisions for annulment of the award on the grounds of 'corruption on the part of a member of the Tribunal'[19] for disqualifying a member who may not 'be relied upon to exercise independent judgment',[20] for enabling the tribunal to 'rectify any clerical, arithmetical or similar error in the award',[21] and for revision of the award 'on the ground of discovery of some fact of such a nature as decisively to affect the award, provided that when the award was rendered that fact was unknown to the Tribunal and to the applicant and that the applicant's ignorance of that fact was not due to negligence'.[22] Broadly speaking, therefore, the grounds of intervention under the Washington Convention correspond with the five grounds which I have mentioned exist under English law.

How then would the English court respond in the face of an agreement which purported to exclude its power to remedy procedural irregularities falling within one of these five grounds? First, it would have to consider whether the procedure followed has in fact constituted a serious departure from a fundamental rule of procedure. This conclusion will not be lightly drawn by the court, and will certainly not be drawn merely because the arbitral

17 See also UNCITRAL Model Law, Articles 12 and 13.
18 New York Convention, Article V(1)(b).
19 Washington Convention, Article 52(1)(c).
20 *Ibid*, Articles 14, 56–58.
21 *Ibid*, Article 49.
22 *Ibid*, Article 51.

procedure has not followed the pattern of its own proceedings. So long as the procedure has not contravened the express or implied agreement of the parties, the court will recognise as legitimate a wide range of procedures which it would not itself permit. I need mention only the hearing on documents alone, the arbitrator-advocate procedure, the admission of legally inadmissible evidence, and the fact that the tribunal may, with due notice to the parties, act on its own knowledge of the facts and rely on its own expertise instead of, or even against, the testimony of expert witnesses.

It can also confidently be said that the court will not regard the arbitration as having departed from a fundamental rule of procedure merely because the arbitration agreement provides for an inquisitorial, rather than an adversarial mode of procedure. Inquisitorial procedures are by no means unknown to English law. Inspections under Section 165 of the Companies Act 1948 are an obvious example, although their purpose is admittedly to elicit facts rather than to resolve disputes. The courts themselves administer procedures, such as interrogatories, accounts and enquiries, and taking evidence before examiners, which are essentially inquisitorial in character although in practice generally operated as if they were wholly adversarial. More to the point, Section 12(1) of the Arbitration Act 1950, which applies unless a contrary intention is expressed in the arbitration, confers powers *on the arbitrator* to examine the parties to the reference, to require documents to be produced before him, etc. In practice, commercial arbitrators exercise these essentially inquisitorial powers more often than is realised, particularly in the everyday arbitrations where the parties are not legally represented.

It can also safely be stated that the court will not regard the arbitration as having departed from a fundamental rule of procedure merely because the parties have subjected it to the procedural laws of another state. Such arbitrations are not common, but they exist and have been explicitly recognised by the courts. Whether the courts would recognise an arbitration whose internal procedures were not governed by any national procedural law, but by a transnational law of procedure drawing on its own sources of doctrine and jurisprudence, is a topic which I shall not discuss here. Nonetheless I am by no means persuaded that such a concept is irreconcilable in a doctrinal sense with any principle of English law, and I do not understand Lord Justice Kerr's dictum cited above as saying that it is. I would, moreover, suggest that the concept appears to be implicit in the Washington Convention, which forms part of English law.[23] Whether it is desirable, in a practical sense, for the parties to cut themselves off from a single known source of national procedural law, is another matter.

The real question is not whether English law recognises a self-generating body of transnational procedural law, but whether it recognises a type of arbitration which is transnational in the sense that its procedures are not subject to any corrective remedy, regardless of how seriously they depart from fundamental English concepts of impartiality and fairness. In my view the answer is that English law does not recognise such a transnational arbitration, and that not only the English court but any court would be bound to withhold recognition to an award which was made by a corrupt or partial tribunal, or by

23 Washington Convention, Article 44.

a fundamentally unfair procedure. From a theoretical point of view there are two routes by which the court could arrive at this result:

(a) By denying that the procedure is an arbitration at all or that the decision is an arbitral award.
(b) By treating that part of the agreement which contravenes a fundamental rule of procedure, or purports to prevent the court from correcting it, as being contrary to public policy and therefore void.

In most cases the court is likely to prefer the second solution as doing least violence to the wishes of the parties, particularly if the offending provision can be severed from the agreement without impairing the underlying agreement to arbitrate.

In case it should be thought that the English courts would thus be exercising a jurisdiction to strike down awards which is both exorbitant and contrary to internationally accepted jurisdictional principles, three further observations can be added. First, as has been convincingly argued by Dr Van den Berg,[24] it is difficult to accommodate into the framework of the New York Convention the concept of a transnational arbitration which is not subject to the control of any national court. Second, as is demonstrated by the same author, the jurisprudence interpreting the Convention recognises that partiality and lack of due process may in serious cases result in a refusal to enforce the award.[25] Third, the English court does not permit service abroad of proceedings to set aside or remit an award unless either the arbitration is governed by English law or has been held within England and Wales,[26] these are the grounds on which the New York Convention recognises that a national court is the competent authority to set aside or suspend an award,[27] and which have been adopted by the UNCITRAL Model Law. Even in such cases the English court will decline to exercise its jurisdiction if it is not the *forum conveniens*.

Conferring court's powers on the arbitrator

Finally, to what extent will English law permit the remedies vested in the courts to be exercised directly by an arbitrator, and with what consequences? Once again it is convenient to discuss the three categories of remedy separately.

Coercive remedies

So far as a stay of proceedings is concerned it is clear that this is a remedy which can only be exercised by the court itself. This is not just a matter of the dignity and authority of the court. There are obvious difficulties, both theoretical and practical, in entrusting the arbitrator with the decision whether, for example, a stay should be refused on the grounds that the arbitraton agreement under which he is appointed is 'null and void, inoperative or incapable of being performed'.

24 A J Van den Berg, *The New York Convention of 1958*, The Hague 1981, at 29–43.
25 *Ibid*, at 296–311.
26 Rules of the Supreme Court, Order 73, Rule 7(1).
27 New York Convention, Article V(1)(e).

Enforcement of the award by the process of execution is likewise a remedy which can only be exercised by the court, unless, as in the case of ICSID awards, there is a special statutory procedure by which awards can be made directly enforceable. However to extend such a procedure to all arbitral awards would be inconsistent with the mechanism or enforcement of foreign awards under the New York Convention.

The powers to appoint the tribunal or to fill vacancies may however be vested in an appointing authority other than the court, which will not exercise its own powers unless there is no agreed mechanism or the agreed mechanism has proved abortive.

Auxiliary remedies

Disobedience to an arbitrator's interlocutory orders is not a contempt of court: nor can an arbitrator arrest maritime property, imprison a party or a witness, or sequestrate property in order to secure compliance with his orders. There are only two exceptions to these propositions, in the case of a judge-arbitrator appointed under Section 4 of the Administration of Justice Act 1970 and (perhaps) in the case of an official referee appointed as an arbitrator under Section 11 of the Arbitration Act 1950. In each case the authority is conferred on an individual who is already endowed with judicial authority by the state. There are obvious constitutional objections to conferring such powers on an individual whose authority derives only from a private agreement, particularly where orders may affect the rights of third parties.

There would nevertheless appear to be no objection in principle to an arbitrator being given power by agreement to make orders corresponding to the auxiliary remedies, so long as they do not purport to invoke powers reserved to judicial officers of the state. (There is some authority to the contrary in the case of injunctions: but this has been doubted.) Thus, an arbitrator has a statutory implied power to make an order for specific performance of any contract other than a contract relating to real property,[28] but his order cannot be enforced by committal or sequestration without the aid of the court. Similarly, an arbitrator has power to order discovery of documents, and can treat failure by a party to comply with his order as grounds for drawing inferences averse to that party or as grounds for disallowing a claim or defence to which the order for discovery relates.

Corrective remedies

In the case of fraud, corruption, bias, partiality and want of due process, there are obvious reasons why the court's corrective powers should not be vested in the arbitral tribunal itself and the court would not regard an attempt to do so as in any way restricting its own exercise of the appropriate remedies. However it is not unusual for remedies of revision or even annulment to be vested in an appeal tribunal or other consensually constituted body or institution, and there is no reason why the English court should not recognise such remedies as legitimate and effective. Moreover, the existence of consensual procedures for revision and annulment would almost invariably result in the court

28 Arbitration Act 1950, s15.

withholding its own remedies until after the consensual procedures have been exhausted.

There is certainly no objection to the arbitration agreement conferring power to correct admitted mistakes or to admit fresh evidence on the arbitrator himself.

Conclusion

It will, I hope, be clear from the foregoing that the reason that English law does not recognise arbitral procedures unconnected with any municipal system law is not because of any fundamental antipathy between such procedures and the traditions or doctrines of English law, but rather for essentially practical reasons, specifically, that arbitration agreements and awards depend on the courts for their enforcement and that the concept of an arbitration procedure which is contrary to fundamental concepts of fairness is a contradiction in terms which no court could reasonably be expected to recognise. This has not prevented the English legal system from recognising transnational institutions such as ICSID, nor need it inhibit a full and willing recognition of other arbitral institutions which are transnational in character and outlook.

14 The role of the courts under the UNCITRAL Model Law script

Gerold Herrmann*

Apologue

It should be with trepidation, or must reflect extraordinary courage, that I dare put on paper some thoughts concerning the UNCITRAL draft model law on international commercial arbitration** after a prominent arbitrator recently revealed the calculations of his 'budding actuary that 66,000 gallons of ink have already been consumed and millions of pages written, typed or photocopied in connection with the UNCITRAL Model Law'.

Such figures are certainly heartwarming as evidence of overwhelming interest in the UNCITRAL project. Unfortunately, they exceed my own calculations by some 20,000 per cent; even more regrettably, his report about the accompanying wining and dining is beset with the same margin of irony.

Nevertheless, in an effort to limit the extent of this paper I shall sacrifice all footnotes but I am not able to offer more by keeping this paper short. Missionary zeal compels me to present in some detail the UNCITRAL draft model law's philosophy and script on the role of the courts; and the presence of so many distinguished arbitration experts induces me to solicit their critical comments and tap their wealth of knowledge by touching on controversial issues and trying out some heretical thoughts.

Some impressions from the arbitration scene

It is well known that the views and reviews of the role which national courts play or should play on the arbitration scene differ widely and, it seems, without there being hope for consensus. At one end of the spectrum you may find the view that arbitration would turn into an unacceptable theatre of the absurd or a tragedy if it is not constantly monitored, protected and assisted by a judicial director, stage-hand or, in case of emergency, *deus ex machina* (all courtesy of the local court). At the other end you may find the view that arbitration – like

* The views expressed in this paper are the personal views of the author and do not necessarily reflect the views of the UNCITRAL Secretariat where he is Legal Officer.

** Since this paper was written UNCITRAL Model Law on International Commercial Arbitration has been finally adopted at the Eighteenth Session of the Commission on International Trade Law held in Vienna in June 1985.

any good play – would suffer from outside interference and that the artistic freedom of the cast, ie, parties and arbitrators, must not be impeded by local law barriers or benches. It is no secret that a certain sympathy with the first view could be detected, for example, in the UK, while the second view seems to be prominently represented in the Paris–Geneva connection (recently extended to Djibouti).

Such strong and divergent views, admittedly overdrawn in the above picture, may be rooted in traditional legal concepts, deeply ingrained attitudes and well-established practices, often cultured by prevailing interests. This may account for the fact that, somewhat surprising to the innocent bystander, diametrically opposed views equally claim to present the most advanced state of development and, of course, to reflect best the needs of arbitration practice. Yet, a closer look at the arbitration scene and its perennial discussion of the proper role of courts may help to gain perspective as a possible basis for reconciliation.

After having 'localised' the two conflicting views, a general qualification must be made: The views of actors or theatre critics on how the appropriate stage for arbitral proceedings should look are far from being unanimous in any given place; for the benefit of lively theatre, there is within almost every jurisdiction some movement in the ongoing dispute about the art of dispute settlement.

Even if one were to look only at the actual law and its application, it is difficult to determine precisely at which point of the spectrum any particular jurisdiction would stand. One of the reasons is the following impression which is of general and practical importance on the international plane. Views on the proper role of the courts are often cast in terms of concerns or fears. Such fears about too much court interference and, less frequently, misgivings about too little judicial assistance are expressed primarily, often exclusively, with regard to foreign countries. Among the reasons for such 'xenophobic' mentality are the more technical difficulties of dealing with courts abroad and, in particular, the frequent lack of familiarity with the foreign ('strange') legal system. Even where that law is known or knowledge thereof easily obtained, fears may persist on a number of grounds. For example, a provision allowing court intervention may be taken 'at face value' as a potential threat irrespective of its – often unknown – actual application in terms of frequency and success. A more subtle ground for fear – or misconception – is the human factor, known to every comparative lawyer as a defect and source of confusion, which is to take familiar concepts of one's own system for granted and transpose them to other systems. A pertinent example in arbitration relates to the attitude of courts, which in one system is more favourable and supportive than in another one that has less sympathy with 'private hotel-room justice'.

A last point is that extreme views, if based on almost ideological conviction, can be misleading and detrimental when it comes to concrete issues – and should, therefore, despite their sweetness, be taken with a 'grain of salt'. For instance, in the well-known controversy about whether the arbitrators' ruling on their jurisdiction should be reviewed by the court immediately or only after the award on the merits is made it would be misleading simply to react on the basis of a general *pro libertate arbitri* or a *semper iudex* stance, instead of quantifying the respective advantages and disadvantages, ie, danger of delaying tactics and obstruction versus possible waste of time and money; this, in turn, might lead to the conclusion that such 'quantification' is best done in respect of each specific case by the arbitral tribunal itself which, thus, should have discretion to make its ruling in an immediately appealable award.

General approach and philosophy of the Model Law (as the national law to be of many states)

In the traditional UNCITRAL spirit of trying to understand 'foreign' positions and to reach consensus, the experts in the Working Group prepared in a comparatively short span of time a set of workable and widely acceptable rules. Fortunately, such open-mindedness increasingly characterises the many discussions all over the world which the UNCITRAL project has spurred.

Parochial fears about the imposition of unfamiliar (thus 'unworkable') systems and concepts have given way to understanding the 'foreign' features in the Model Law as a necessary and beneficial part in view of its unique international purpose. It is no longer judged by the extent to which it dares deviate from one's own beloved legal system, which itself, in some cases, has become the subject of critical examination and 'catharsis', as called (for) by Lord Justice Kerr, in his Alexander Lecture. This process of international understanding and comparative law in action may be viewed as a first contribution to reducing the earlier diagnosed 'xenophobia'.

The real therapy for treating these fears, by making foreign laws less foreign, is provided by the Model Law in two directions. The first one, at a more formal level, is the nature of the Model Law as a vehicle to achieve the widest possible acceptance and, thus, greatest possible degree of harmonisation of national laws. Uniformity, or at least essential similarity, of a large number of laws in the various legal and economic systems of the world would certainly be of considerable use in reducing the fears about the unknown and, thus, facilitate international commercial arbitration.

However, conformity as such is not an end in itself and may well lead to a negative balance, for example, where the 'lowest common denominator' is imposed as a standard for all. The Model Law, therefore, provides in its contents the substantive basis for an improved legal environment which meets the special needs of international commercial arbitration.

Let me list some essential features and principles, which reflect the Model Law's perception of its role as national law, and then take a closer look at the role of the courts under that law.

The most fundamental principle is to recognise the freedom of the parties (with minimal restrictions). Whether by reference to standard (institutional or *ad hoc*) rules or in 'one-off' agreements, the parties could effectively tailor 'the rules of the game' to their particular case and needs, unimpeded by peculiar local rules on procedure, including evidence. This guarantee would spare them frustration of their expectations by any strange foreign law.

The second and complementing principle is to grant the arbitral tribunal substantial powers and, failing agreement by the parties, wide procedural discretion. This is to ensure the effectiveness of the arbitral process and to free the conducting of the proceedings from local law restraints. Taken together with the autonomy of the parties, it goes a long way towards establishing procedural autonomy of the international arbitral process to suit the tremendous variety of needs and circumstances.

The third principle is to ensure fairness and due process in the proceedings, although, as we shall see, the relevant court control would normally be exercised only at the post-award stage. To state the main examples of this principle, the parties shall be treated with equality and each party shall be given a full opportunity of presenting his case.

The fourth 'principle' is less a separate principle than a special design or cumulative effect of the foregoing and may be described as a certain 'delocalisation of international arbitral proceedings and awards'. The Model Law, while not adopting the radical idea of 'delocalisation' or 'de-nationalisation' in its strict sense, detaches the arbitral process from the traditional domestic procedures by replacing them with a liberal framework for international cases. It recognises that the place of an international arbitration may be chosen rather fortuitously and often for reasons other than the law ruling there. By virtue of its liberal provisions ('loosening the local strings') and its expected wide acceptance in the various parts of the world, it would further reduce the relevance of that place and, thus, offer parties and arbitrators a wider choice. While the Model Law would be suitable also for any advanced system of domestic arbitration, it contains a number of features which are of particular relevance to international cases. One such 'delocalising' feature, which we shall see in the discussion on recognition and enforcement, is the uniform treatment of all international awards irrespective of their place of origin. Another such feature is, for example, to reduce the fear about the unknown foreign law by providing certainty as to the availability and involvement of the courts there. We shall see an implementation of this idea in the general provisions to be considered now.

Court functions under the Model Law

Two innovative provisions of general nature

The Model Law contains two innovative general provisions (Articles 5 and 6) which should facilitate international commercial arbitration, in particular, by assisting persons from outside the Model Law state.

Particular court for certain arbitration matters

Article 6 calls upon each state adopting the Model Law to entrust a particular 'Court' with performing certain functions of arbitration assistance and supervision, relating to appointment of arbitrators (Article 11), decision on termination of arbitrator's mandate (Articles 13, 14) and setting aside of award (Article 34). Except for the last function, the 'Court' does not necessarily have to be a full court or chamber; it may well be only the president of the court or of a chamber for those functions where speed and finality are particularly desirable. On the other hand, it need not necessarily be only one court; especially bigger countries may wish to designate one type of court, eg, all commercial courts or commercial chambers of district courts.

The expected advantages of such designation are, in short, centralisation, specialisation and acceleration. Another advantage of Article 6 may be seen in the fact that it establishes, or at least clarifies, the international competence of the court for the functions listed, irrespective of whether the case has any (otherwise required) connection with the forum state, other than the obvious condition that the arbitration is governed by the (Model) Law of this state.

Express limits to court intervention

Article 5 provides laconically (some thought 'draconically'): 'In matters governed by this Law, no court shall intervene except where so provided in this Law'. When this truly innovative provision was born, the response was rather mixed, not surprisingly often along the lines of the earlier mentioned extreme views. However, the child seems to be now widely accepted after a remarkable process of getting to know it better.

The first feature, which alleviated some of the fears, is the limitation expressed by the words 'in matters governed by this Law'. Article 5 would, thus, not exclude court intervention in any of those matters of international commercial arbitration which are not regulated in the Model Law (eg, impact of state immunity, consolidation, contractual relations between arbitrators and parties or arbitral institutions, arbitration fees or costs including security therefor).

The more important realisation was that Article 5 itself does not take a stand on what is the desirable extent of court intervention. All it does is to compel the drafters of the law to list the instances (possibly many) where judicial supervision or assistance is appropriate. In particular foreign parties and arbitrators will appreciate such exhaustive listing, which spares them from unwelcome surprises or the need of screening the laws of the land.

It is, thus, a different question, not regulated in Article 5, whether the role which the courts would play under the script of the Model Law is conceived in an appropriate and acceptable manner. The answer to this substantive and fundamental question can only be given after a short survey of the various functions entrusted to the courts by the present draft text.

Giving 'universal' effect to arbitration agreements and awards

Recognition of arbitration agreement

Article 8(1) give effect to the agreement of the parties that any dispute be settled by arbitration, ie, to the exclusion of court jurisdiction. While naturally addressed to the courts of the Model Law state only, it is intended to cover all international commercial arbitration agreements irrespective of the place of arbitration. This 'global' effect of recognition will be enhanced by wide acceptance of the Model Law, embracing the courts of many states.

The provision is closely modelled on Article II(3) of the 1958 New York Convention, with some useful clarifications added. It sets a time-limit for making the request 'to refer the parties to arbitration', ie, to decline (the exercise of) court jurisdiction, and empowers the arbitral tribunal to continue the proceedings while the issue of its jurisdiction is pending with the court (Paragraph (2)).

Yet another clarification in support of upholding arbitration agreements is contained in Article 9. Contrary to some New York court decisions in the context of the 1958 New York Convention of the same place, it provides that it is compatible with the arbitration agreement for a party to request, before or during arbitral proceedings, from a court an interim measure of protection (eg, pre-award attachment), and for a court to grant such measure. This principle of compatibility is intended to have the same universal effect as the 'recognise and refer' provision of Article 8(1).

Recognition and enforcement of award irrespective of place of origin

Article 35 grants judicial effect to the results of the agreed upon dispute settlement method by obliging the courts to recognise and enforce arbitral awards (within the limits laid down in Article 36). It sets forth certain conditions as maximum standards, which – following the lines of Article IV of the 1958 New York Convention – are, in fact, rather minimal requirements: application in writing, accompanied by the arbitration agreement and the award. It further provides that filing, registration or deposit of an award in the country of origin is not a precondition for recognition or enforcement, thus taking the philosophy of the New York Convention, not to require a 'double-exequatur', a step further.

More importantly and controversial, Article 35 takes the dividing line of the New York Convention, which covers foreign awards and excludes domestic ones, a step further by drawing the line between 'international' awards in terms of Article 1 and 'non-international' awards. Without being able to go into the various pros and cons of this step and, more generally, of covering in the Model Law recognition and enforcement at all, let me single out two important issues.

First, whether it is appropriate to treat an international award made in a Model Law state like any foreign international award. The prevailing view of the Working Group, which I wholeheartedly share, was that it is sound policy to treat in a uniform manner all international awards irrespective of their place of origin. This policy seems to be a logical consequence of the conviction that the place of arbitration is of minor importance in international cases. Although the idea may conflict with deeply ingrained thinking, 'delocalisation' of arbitration means detaching it from the 'domestic' context also when it comes to recognition and enforcement. At least for foreign parties and their counsel, who may be involved over time in arbitrations at various places, it is not necessarily comforting to learn that, as is the situation in many countries, a domestic award would be enforceable like a local court decision there, with the applicable procedures varying from country to country. Finally, as regards the rather minimal maximum standards laid down in Article 35, any remaining fears about an unjustified worsening of the present situation should be met by the accompanying footnote which 'authorises' states to retain even less onerous conditions. Admittedly, there are some concerns relating to the fact that a domestic award is subject to setting aside in the same country. These will be discussed in the context of Articles 34 and 36.

The second issue is the lack of a reciprocity clause in Article 35, which may be surprising in view of the fact that the majority of the Member States to the New York Convention have made use of the pertinent reservation and, generally speaking, the restriction of reciprocity seems to be another deeply ingrained concept found in many national arbitration laws. The Working

Group, being aware that not all states may be prepared to adopt Article 35 universally, was agreed that a state which wanted to apply Article 35 only on the basis of reciprocity should express this restriction in its legislation, specifying the basis or connecting factor and the technique used by it. However, this would be a difficult and, in my view, undesirable step. It is difficult to design a workable reciprocity mechanism in relation to national laws based on a Model Law (and not simply implementing a convention). It is undesirable to use the (still most commonly used) connecting factor, ie, the place where the award was made, since it is not in harmony with the 'delocalising' philosophy of the Model Law, namely to minimise the relevance of the place of arbitration by harmonising the laws of many places at a level acceptable and conducive to international commercial arbitration. I disrespectfully submit that the use of this traditional connecting factor is either the vestige of ancient 'eye for an eye' notions or the result of the often misleading equation of arbitration (where the place is of little importance) with court litigation (where certain local links with a party or his assets are likely to exist because of the requirements for court jurisdiction).

Judicial assistance to arbitrations

Support concerning composition of arbitral tribunal

Under the Model Law, the 'Court' specified in Article 6 would render assistance in the following three ways having to do with the composition of the arbitral tribunal. The court may be asked for help under Article 11(4) and (5), to avoid any deadlock in the process of appointing the arbitrator or arbitrators, whether such process follows any rules agreed upon by the parties or the 'suppletive' provisions of the Model Law. A less administrative and more substantive function, touching upon fairness of the proceedings, is the task of making the final decision on any unsuccessful challenge of an arbitrator (Article 13(3)). Another substantive task is, under Article 14, to decide on the termination of the mandate of an arbitrator where a controversy exists about whether he became *de jure* or *de facto* unable to perform his functions or, what may be particularly disputed, whether he 'failed to act'.

These provisions envisage a certain, though rather limited, court control over the conduct of the arbitral proceedings or, more accurately, of the individual arbitrator. It is submitted, for example, that a challenge under Article 13 would be sustained in case of apparent bias in the conduct of an arbitrator and that 'failure to act' in the terms of Article 14 would cover certain grave instances of misconduct. Admittedly, it is difficult to predict exactly the extent of court supervision under such relatively vague terms. Yet, when trying to compare this system with that of a given national law, one is often faced with a similar degree of imprecision, not only from the point of view of a 'xenophobic' foreigner, as Lord Justice Kerr explained in his Alexander Lecture with regard to the English notions of 'misconduct'. Generally speaking, it seems fair to say that the philosophy of the Model Law is to provide very limited judicial supervision over and during the conduct of the proceedings. It is only after the award is made, that 'ultimate' court control is exercised which would include measuring the conduct of the proceedings by the pertinent and fundamental principles laid down in Article 19(3). The same philosophy ('wait until the end and then oversee') is adopted in the present text on court control over the arbitral tribunal's ruling that it has jurisdiction (Article 16(3)).

Assisting with measures of enforcement

Courts may help arbitrations with their inherent powers of enforcement, although the views of practitioners differ on whether any such assistance is really necessary and appropriate. The Model Law, in Article 27, provides for such assistance in the areas of obtaining evidence, ie, compelling appearance of a witness or production of a document or access to a property. Assistance would be rendered upon request by the arbitral tribunal or by a party with the approval of the arbitral tribunal; this formula, which reflects a compromise between civil law and common law concepts, would preserve a certain control by the arbitral tribunal. Depending on the court's competence and evidence rules, the evidence would be taken by the court itself or it would be provided, by order of the court, directly to the arbitral tribunal.

Article 27 envisages court assistance to arbitral proceedings held in the state of the Model Law or under that law. While Article 27 represents the only express provision on court assistance to arbitral proceedings by giving 'the arm of enforcement', the Model Law would not preclude states from retaining or adopting provisions on this type of assistance in certain other fields. For example, as stated by the Working Group, any interim measure of protection ordered by the arbitral tribunal under Article 18 could be made enforceable (although there may be little need in view of the limited range of measures covered by Article 18 and the considerably wider range envisaged under Article 9, which, anyway, makes available direct resort to courts for enforceable measures of protection). In addition, measures of enforcement or compulsion could be offered in respect of some subject-matters not regulated in the Model Law (eg, consolidation of proceedings, fees of arbitrators or arbitral institutions).

Ultimate court control at post-award stage

Review of award in setting aside proceedings

Existing national laws often equate arbitral awards with local court decisions and provide a number of different means of recourse, not seldom with rather long time periods and extensive lists of grounds that differ widely in the various legal systems. The Model Law promises improvement by providing, in its Article 34, one exclusive type of recourse, with a time period of three months and a fairly short, exhaustive list of grounds.

These grounds, on which an award may be set aside if attacked by a party, are essentially the same as those which a party may rely on in defence against the other party's initiative of seeking recognition or enforcement of that award (Article 36(1)). Since the grounds are taken from the well-known Article V of the 1958 New York Convention, they need no introduction here. However, allow me a few words on some specific grounds in the context of the Model Law and later some remarks on the appropriateness of using the same list of grounds for both purposes, ie, judicial review in setting aside proceedings and in recognition or enforcement procedures.

Most of the grounds listed in Article 34(2)(a) should be interpreted restrictively in the light of Articles 4 and 16(2) which impliedly preclude a party who failed to raise certain objections without delay, from invoking them at the post-award stage. Article 4 could be relevant in the context of sub-paragraph (iv) in cases of alleged non-compliance with the agreement of the parties or with non-mandatory provisions of the Model Law. Article 16(2), which sets a time-limit for any plea that the arbitral tribunal lacks jurisdiction or is exceeding its authority, could be relevant in the context of sub-paragraph (i) regarding invalidity of the arbitration agreement and, possibly, sub-paragraph (iii) if there were early and clear indications that the arbitral tribunal would decide on a matter beyond the scope of the submission to arbitration. These grounds would retain their practical use for those cases where a party either raised his objections timely but without success or did not proceed with the arbitration, if he initially participated at all.

Another point worth mentioning is the divergence of views on sub-paragraph (b)(i), under which the award would be set aside if the subject-matter of the dispute is not capable of settlement by arbitration under the law of the forum state. While the requirement of arbitrability as such is not in doubt, it has been questioned whether the specified applicable law is the appropriate one. It is, indeed, not easy to understand why the law of the place of arbitration should govern this issue with global effect, by virtue of the refusal of recognition or enforcement of a set aside award under Article 36(1)(a)(v) (or Article V(1)(e) of the 1958 New York Convention). It would seem to be better not to specify the applicable law (and simply say 'under the applicable law'), unless agreement could be reached on whether to specify the applicable law along the lines of Article 34(2)(a)(i) concerning the validity of the arbitration agreement, which should be acceptable, at least, to those legal systems, which, anyway, regard arbitrability as an element of the validity of the arbitration agreement, or whether the issue of arbitrability should be governed by the law of the main contract, subject to public policy limits.

Judicial control of recognition and enforcement

The last type of court intervention in the Model Law is the control exercised in recognition of enforcement proceedings. The standards of such control are set forth in Article 36(1) which is an almost true copy of Article V of the New York Convention. This was done for the sake of harmony, although it was realised that one or the other of its provisions could be improved. Of course, Article 36 covers not only foreign awards but, as a companion to Article 35 and for the reasons stated above, all awards irrespective of their place of origin.

Parallel grounds for setting aside and refusing recognition or enforcement

The fact that the grounds for setting aside are essentially the same as those on which recognition and enforcement would be refused has led to some criticism in two directions. The first objection is the list of grounds, though appropriate for the control of recognition and enforcement of foreign awards, is far too short for the judicial review of domestic awards in setting aside proceedings. It is said, for example, that the courts of the country where the arbitration is held have a special task in controlling and supervising this arbitration and that their standards must be what is believed to be right in their territory; on the other hand these courts are not entitled to insist on any similar right of supervision or control over foreign awards for which recognition or enforcement is sought, since here the accepted standards are those of Article V of the New York Convention. This dichotomy is said not to be illogical. I agree.

I hasten to add, however, that parallelism of grounds is no less logical. It even appears to be sensible and justified in the light of the Model Law's philosophy of 'delocalising' international arbitrations and reducing the impact of the place of arbitration. The doctrine of 'territorial justice', ie, to ensure that any 'national' award is made according to the peculiar concepts of the place, is probably not easily swallowed by two foreign parties who have chosen that place for convenience's sake. Yet – if I may inject an idea here in self-contradiction and in contradiction to the pertinent conviction of the Working Group that the list of grounds in Article 34 is in substance appropriate – where a State deems it absolutely necessary to add a further ground, for example, some limited review on matters of law, it may wish to consider using the technique of 'inclusion agreement', which, at least, would require the full awareness of the parties.

Returning to the doctrine of 'territorial justice', another of its flaws is that it is not truly territorial, since it is exported by virtue of Article V(1)(e) of the New York Convention (or Article 36(1)(a)(v) of the Model Law). As is well known, this radiating and potentially global effect of a setting aside is cut off by Article IX of the 1961 European Convention in all those cases where the award was set aside for reasons other than the ones listed in Article V(1)(a)–(d). *Voilà*. The Model Law merely takes this philosophy one step further, thus avoiding 'split' or 'relative' validity of international awards, ie, awards which are void in the country of origin but valid and enforceable abroad.

Finally, it may be noted that parallelism of grounds does not necessarily mean full substantive parallelism. While under Article 34(2)(a)(iv) defects in the arbitral procedure would be determined in accordance with the Model Law, in the case of Article 36(1)(a)(iv) the relevant law would be that of the country where the arbitration took place; this may or may not be a national law based on the Model Law. I may add that wide acceptance of the Model Law, with its few restricting mandatory provisions, would help to minimise the present dilemma which stems from the predominant interpretation of Article V(1)(d) of the New York Convention. The interpretation, which I suspect will be carried over to Article 36(1)(a)(iv), is that 'failing agreement of the parties' means that a procedural stipulation prevails even if it is in conflict with a mandatory provision of the 'applicable' law. While one may share the concerns behind the internationalists' view, which should be alleviated by wide acceptance of the Model Law, one should recognise the, in my view unacceptable, dilemma: an arbitrator could either disregard such a procedural stipulation and follow the mandatory law provision, with the result that enforcement of the award may be refused under Article V(1)(d), or comply with the stipulation, with the result that the award may be set aside for violation of a mandatory local provision and, by virtue of Article V(1)(e), its enforcement abroad refused. In such (fortunately infrequent) cases, the only practical way out seems to be the not always feasible one of getting the parties to modify their agreement. Better still would be a reconsideration of the predominant interpretation of Article V(1)(d). By the way, this could have a beneficial effect in meeting the objections to Article 1(2) of the UNCITRAL Arbitration Rules, by restoring its original quality as a merely declaratory provision.

The second objection to the parallelism of grounds in Articles 34 and 36 is concerned only with 'domestic' awards, for which, it is said, the Model Law establishes an undesirable double-control. One concern is, at a more technical level, the potential of parallel proceedings, duplicating court review, and of conflicting decisions within the same country. In a short response, one may point out that the risk is minimised – if not already zero as in those cases where only one particular court is involved – through the provision of Article 36(2) which 'suggests' suspension to the enforcement judge in the (probably not too frequent) case that enforcement is sought in that country already during the short period for setting aside or while such action is still pending.

A more substantive and serious concern is that a party, who did not use the recourse under Article 34 for raising his objections, should not be allowed to invoke the very grounds, after expiration of the time-limit for such application, as a defence in recognition or enforcement procedures; as provided in some national laws, his only defence should then be violation of public policy. Although the solution of the Model Law has been attacked as confusing setting aside with enforcement proceedings, it may well be defended as not confusing strictly domestic awards with international awards made in the country where enforcement happens to be sought.

Once again, 'delocalisation' of international commercial arbitration with little relevance of the place of arbitration leads to uniform treatment of all awards. It is sound policy, as approved by the Working Group, to provide a party with an alternative mechanism, that is, with the option of either taking the initiative, within three months after receiving the award, with the aim of 'killing the award at the root' or of taking the more risky course of waiting and defending himself in any place where the other party may seek enforcement. After all, this option already exists with regard to all other countries and it is difficult to understand why it should be excluded in the case where enforcement happens to be sought in the country of origin. The place of setting aside under Article 34, ie, the Model Law state, may be as far away and inconvenient for a party as any 'foreign' place for setting aside in the many cases where enforcement is sought of a foreign award in the Model Law state and where, undisputedly, the option is retained with all the grounds on the list being available. Finally, it seems to be unjustified to put a party at a disadvantage because of his failure to ask for setting aside within three months where, for instance, it is only much later that enforcement becomes possible by reason of his moving assets into that state.

Conclusion

There cannot be any real conclusion in a question so complex and vital to arbitration as the extent of judicial control and assistance. However, as a tentative conclusion I dare submit to you, on the basis of comments received from Governments and international organisations and supported by many observations at conferences and symposia, including the ICCA-Interim Meeting at Lausanne, that the role of the courts is perceived by the

UNCITRAL draft Model Law in a balanced, appropriate and widely acceptable manner.

The Model Law contains a number of novel features, whose implications may be fully assessed only in its actual application. It certainly does not petrify today's state of the art but provides food for thought and further development, in particular, as regards its tendency of 'delocalising' international commercial arbitration and of harmonising and improving the disparate national laws of the world. I would not be surprised if and certainly hope that these concepts and ideas will become common stock-in-trade in the classrooms and halls of this new School of International Arbitration.

Annex

UNCITRAL model law on international commercial arbitration

(As adopted by the United Nations Commission on International Trade Law on June 21, 1985)

Chapter I General provisions

*Article 1 Scope of application**

1 This Law applies to international commercial** arbitration, subject to any agreement in force between this state and any other state or states.
2 The provisions of this Law, except articles 8, 9, 35 and 36, apply only if the place of arbitration is in the territory of this state.
3 An arbitration is international if:
   (a) the parties to an arbitration agreement have, at the time of the conclusion of that agreement, their places of business in different states; or
   (b) one of the following places is situated outside the state in which the parties have their places of business:
      (i) the place of arbitration if determined in, or pursuant to, the arbitration agreement;
      (ii) any place where a substantial part of the obligations of the commercial relationship is to be performed or the place with which the subject-matter of the dispute is most closely connected; or
   (c) the parties have expressly agreed that the subject-matter of the arbitration agreement relates to more than one country.
4 For the purposes of paragraph (3) of this article:
   (a) if a party had more than one place of business, the place of business is that which has the closest relationship to the arbitration agreement;
   (b) if a party does not have a place of business, reference is to be made to his habitual residence.

* Article headings are for reference purposes only and are not to be used for purposes of interpretation.

** The term 'commercial' should be given a wide interpretation so as to cover matters arising from all relationships of a commercial nature, whether contractual or not. Relationships of a commercial nature include, but are not limited to, the following transactions: any trade transaction for the supply or exchange of goods or services; distribution agreement; commercial representation or agency; factoring; leasing; construction of works; consulting; engineering; licensing; investment; financing; banking; insurance; exploitation agreement or concession; joint venture and other forms of industrial or business co-operation; carriage of goods or passengers by air, sea, rail or road.

5 This Law shall not affect any other law of this state by virtue of which certain disputes may not be submitted to arbitration or may be submitted to arbitration only according to provisions other than those of this Law.

Article 2 Definitions and rules of interpretation

For the purposes of this Law:

(a) 'arbitration' means any arbitration whether or not administered by a permanent arbitral institution;
(b) 'arbitral tribunal' means a sole arbitrator or a panel of arbitrators;
(c) 'court' means a body or organ of the judicial system of a state;
(d) where a provision of this Law, except article 28, leaves the parties free to determine a certain issue, such freedom includes the right of the parties to authorise a third party, including an institution, to make that determination;
(e) where a provision of this Law refers to the fact that the parties have agreed or that they may agree or in any other way refers to an agreement of the parties, such agreement includes any arbitration rules referred to in that agreement;
(f) where a provision of this Law, other than in articles 25(a) and 32(2)(a), refers to a claim, it also applies to a counter-claim, and where it refers to a defence, it also applies to a defence to such counter-claim.

Article 3 Receipt of written communications

1 Unless otherwise agreed by the parties:

(a) any written communication is deemed to have been received if it is delivered to the addressee personally or if it is delivered at his place of business, habitual residence or mailing address; if none of these can be found after making a reasonable inquiry, a written communication is deemed to have been received if it is sent to the addressee's last-known place of business, habitual residence or mailing address by registered letter or any other means which provides a record of the attempt to deliver it;
(b) the communication is deemed to have been received on the day it is so delivered.

2 The provisions of this article do not apply to communications in court proceedings.

Article 4 Waiver of right to object

A party who knows that any provision of this Law from which the parties may derogate or any requirement under the arbitration agreement has not been complied with and yet proceeds with the arbitration without stating his objection to such non-compliance without undue delay or, if a time-limit is provided therefor, within such period of time, shall be deemed to have waived his right to object.

Article 5 Extent of court intervention

In matters governed by this Law, no court shall intervene except where so provided in this Law.

Article 6 Court or other authority for certain functions of arbitration assistance and supervision

The functions referred to in Articles 11(3), 11(4), 13(3), 14, 16(3) and 34(2) shall be performed by ... [Each state enacting this model law specifies the court, courts or, where referred to therein, other authority competent to perform these functions.]

Chapter II Arbitration agreement

Article 7 Definition and form of arbitration agreement

1 'Arbitration agreement' is an agreement by the parties to submit to arbitration all or certain disputes which have arisen or which may arise between them in respect of a defined legal relationship, whether contractual or not. An arbitration agreement may be in the form of an arbitration clause in a contract or in the form of a separate agreement.

2 The arbitration agreement shall be in writing. An agreement is in writing if it is contained in a document signed by the parties or in an exchange of letters, telex, telegrams or other means of telecommunication which provide a record of the agreement, or in an exchange of statements of claim and defence in which the existence of an agreement is alleged by one party and not denied by another. The reference in a contract to a document containing an arbitration clause constitutes an arbitration agreement provided that the contract is in writing and the reference is such as to make that clause part of the contract.

Article 8 Arbitration agreement and substantive claim before court

1 A court before which an action is brought in a matter which is the subject of an arbitration agreement shall, if a party so requests not later than when submitting his first statement on the substance of the dispute, refer the parties to arbitration unless it finds that the agreement is null and void, inoperative or incapable of being performed.

2 Where an action referred to in paragraph (1) of this article has been brought, arbitral proceedings may nevertheless be commenced or continued, and an award may be made, while the issue is pending before the court.

Article 9 Arbitration agreement and interim measures by court

It is not incompatible with an arbitration agreement for a party to request, before or during arbitral proceedings, from a court an interim measure of protection and for a court to grant such measure.

Chapter III Composition of arbitral tribunal

Article 10 Number of arbitrators

1 The parties are free to determine the number of arbitrators
2 Failing such determination, the number of arbitrators shall be three.

Article 11 Appointment of arbitrators

1 No person shall be precluded by reason of his nationality from acting as an arbitrator, unless otherwise agreed by the parties.
2 The parties are free to agree on a procedure of appointing the arbitrator or arbitrators, subject to the provisions of paragraphs (4) and (5) of this article.
3 Failing such agreement,
(a) in an arbitration with three arbitrators, each party shall appoint one arbitrator, and the two arbitrators thus appointed shall appoint the third arbitrator; if a party fails to appoint the arbitrator within thirty days of receipt of a request to do so from the other party, or if the two arbitrators fail to agree on the third arbitrator within thirty days of their appointment, the appointment shall be made, upon request of a party, by the court or other authority specified in Article 6;
(b) in an arbitration with a sole arbitrator, if the parties are unable to agree on the arbitrator, he shall be appointed, upon request of a party, by the court or other authority specified in Article 6.
4 Where, under an appointment procedure agreed upon by the parties,
(a) a party fails to act as required under such procedure, or
(b) the parties, or two arbitrators, are unable to reach an agreement expected of them under such procedure, or
(c) a third party, including an institution, fails to perform any function entrusted to it under such procedure,
any party may request the court or other authority specified in Article 6 to take the necessary measure, unless the agreement on the appointment procedure provides other means for securing the appointment.
5 A decision on a matter entrusted by paragraph (3) or (4) of this article to the court or other authority specified in Article 6 shall be subject to no appeal. The court or other authority, in appointing an arbitrator, shall have due regard to any qualifications required of the arbitrator by the agreement of the parties and to such considerations as are likely to secure the appointment of an independent and impartial arbitrator and, in the case of a sole or third arbitrator, shall take into account as well the advisability of appointing an arbitrator of a nationality other than those of the parties.

Article 12 Grounds for challenge

1 When a person is approached in connection with his possible appointment as an arbitrator, he shall disclose any circumstances likely to give rise to justifiable doubts as to his impartiality or independence. An arbitrator, from the time of his appointment and throughout the arbitral proceedings, shall without delay disclose any such circumstances to the parties unless they have already been informed of them by him.
2 An arbitrator may be challenged only if circumstances exist that give rise to

justifiable doubts as to his impartiality or independence, or if he does not possess qualifications agreed to by the parties. A party may challenge an arbitrator appointed by him, or in whose appointment he has participated, only for reasons of which he becomes aware after the appointment has been made.

Article 13 Challenge procedure

1 The parties are free to agree on a procedure for challenging an arbitrator, subject to the provisions of paragraph (3) of this article.
2 Failing such agreement, a party who intends to challenge an arbitrator shall, within fifteen days after becoming aware of the constitution of the arbitral tribunal or after becoming aware of any circumstance referred to in Article 12(2), send a written statement of the reasons for the challenge to the arbitral tribunal. Unless the challenged arbitrator withdraws from his office or the other party agrees to the challenge, the arbitral tribunal shall decide on the challenge.
3 If a challenge under any procedure agreed upon by the parties or under the procedure of paragraph (2) of this article is not successful, the challenging party may request, within thirty days after having received notice of the decision rejecting the challenge, the court or other authority specified in Article 6 to decide on the challenge, which decision shall be subject to no appeal; while such a request is pending, the arbitral tribunal, including the challenged arbitrator, may continue the arbitral proceedings and make an award.

Article 14 Failure or impossibility to act

1 If an arbitrator becomes *de jure* or *de facto* unable to perform his functions or for other reasons fails to act without undue delay, his mandate terminates if he withdraws from his office or if the parties agree on the termination. Otherwise, if a controversy remains concerning any of these grounds, any party may request the court or other authority specified in Article 6 to decide on the termination of the mandate, which decision shall be subject to no appeal.
2 If, under this article or article 13(2), an arbitrator withdraws from his office or a party agrees to the termination of the mandate of an arbitrator, this does not imply acceptance of the validity of any ground referred to in this article or Article 12(2).

Article 15 Appointment of substitute arbitrator

Where the mandate of an arbitrator terminates under Article 13 or 14 or because of his withdrawal from office for any other reason or because of the revocation of his mandate by agreement of the parties or in any other case of termination of his mandate, a substitute arbitrator shall be appointed according to the rules that were applicable to the appointment of the arbitrator being replaced.

Chapter IV Jurisdiction of arbitral tribunal

Article 16 Competence of arbitral tribunal to rule on its jurisdiction

1 The arbitral tribunal may rule on its own jurisdiction, including any objections with respect to the existence or validity of the arbitration agreement. For that purpose, an arbitration clause which forms part of a contract shall be treated as an agreement independent of the other terms of the contract. A decision by the arbitral tribunal that the contract is null and void shall not entail *ipso jure* the invalidity of the arbitration clause.
2 A plea that the arbitral tribunal does not have jurisdiction shall be raised not later than the submission of the statement of defence. A party is not precluded from raising such a plea by the fact that he has appointed, or participated in the appointment of, an arbitrator. A plea that the arbitral tribunal is exceeding the scope of its authority shall be raised as soon as the matter alleged to be beyond the scope of its authority is raised during the arbitral proceedings. The arbitral tribunal may, in either case, admit a later plea if it considers the delay justified.
3 The arbitral tribunal may rule on a plea referred to in paragraph (2) of this article either as a preliminary question or in an award on the merits. If the arbitral tribunal rules as a preliminary question that it has jurisdiction, any party may request, within thirty days after having received notice of that ruling, the court specified in Article 6 to decide the matter, which decision shall be subject to no appeal; while such a request is pending, the arbitral tribunal may continue the arbitral proceedings and make an award.

Article 17 Power of arbitral tribunal to order interim measures

Unless otherwise agreed by the parties, the arbitral tribunal may, at the request of a party, order any party to take such interim measure of protection as the arbitral tribunal may consider necessary in respect of the subject-matter of the dispute. The arbitral tribunal may require any party to provide appropriate security in connection with such measure.

Chapter V Conduct of arbitral proceedings

Article 18 Equal treatment of parties

The parties shall be treated with equality and each party shall be given a full opportunity of presenting his case.

Article 19 Determination of rules of procedure

1 Subject to the provisions of this Law, the parties are free to agree on the procedure to be followed by the arbitral tribunal in conducting the proceedings.
2 Failing such agreement, the arbitral tribunal may, subject to the provisons of this Law, conduct the arbitration in such manner as it considers appropriate. The power conferred upon the arbitral tribunal includes the power to determine the admissibility, relevance, materiality and weight of any evidence.

Article 20 Place of arbitration

1 The parties are free to agree on the place of arbitration. Failing such agreement, the place of arbitration shall be determined by the arbitral tribunal having regard to the circumstances of the case, including the convenience of the parties.
2 Notwithstanding the provisions of paragraph (1) of this article, the arbitral tribunal may, unless otherwise agreed by the parties, meet at any place it considers appropriate for consultation among its members, for hearing witnesses, experts or the parties, or for inspection of goods, other property or documents.

Article 21 Commencement of arbitral proceedings

Unless otherwise agreed by the parties, the arbitral proceedings in respect of a particular dispute commence on the date on which a request for that dispute to be referred to arbitration is received by the respondent.

Article 22 Language

1 The parties are free to agree on the language or languages to be used in the arbitral proceedings. Failing such agreement, the arbitral tribunal shall determine the language or languages to be used in the proceedings. This agreement or determination, unless otherwise specified therein, shall apply to any written statement by a party, any hearing and any award, decision or other communication by the arbitral tribunal.
2 The arbitral tribunal may order that any documentary evidence shall be accompanied by a translation into the language or languages agreed upon by the parties or determined by the arbitral tribunal.

Article 23 Statements of claim and defence

1 Within the period of time agreed by the parties or determined by the arbitral tribunal, the claimant shall state the facts supporting his claim, the points at issue and the relief or remedy sought, and the respondent shall state his defence in respect of these particulars, unless the parties have otherwise agreed as to the required elements of such statements. The parties may submit with their statements all documents they consider to be relevant or may add a reference to the documents or other evidence they will submit.
2 Unless otherwise agreed by the parties, either party may amend or supplement his claim or defence during the course of the arbitral proceedings, unless the arbitral tribunal considers it inappropriate to allow such amendment having regard to the delay in making it.

Article 24 Hearings and written proceedings

1 Subject to any contrary agreement by the parties, the arbitral tribunal shall decide whether to hold oral hearings for the presentation of evidence or for oral argument, or whether the proceedings shall be conducted on the basis of documents and other materials. However, unless the parties have agreed

that no hearings shall be held, the arbitral tribunal shall hold such hearings at an appropriate stage of the proceedings, if so requested by a party.

2 The parties shall be given sufficient advance notice of any hearing and of any meeting of the arbitral tribunal for the purposes of inspection of goods, other property or documents.

3 All statements, documents or other information supplied to the arbitral tribunal by one party shall be communicated to the other party. Also any expert report or evidentiary document on which the arbitral tribunal may rely in making its decision shall be communicated to the parties.

Article 25 Default of a party

Unless otherwise agreed by the parties, if, without showing sufficient cause,

(a) the claimant fails to communicate his statement of claim in accordance with Article 23(1), the arbitral tribunal shall terminate the proceedings;

(b) the respondent fails to communicate his statement of defence in accordance with Article 23(1), the arbitral tribunal shall continue the proceedings without treating such failure in itself as an admission of the claimant's allegations;

(c) any party fails to appear at a hearing or to produce documentary evidence, the arbitral tribunal may continue the proceedings and make the award on the evidence before it.

Article 26 Expert appointed by arbitral tribunal

1 Unless otherwise agreed by the parties, the arbitral tribunal

(a) may appoint one or more experts to report to it on specific issues to be determined by the arbitral tribunal;

(b) may require a party to give the expert any relevant information or to produce, or to provide access to, any relevant documents, goods or other property for his inspection.

2 Unless otherwise agreed by the parties, if a party so requests or if the arbitral tribunal considers it necessary, the expert shall, after delivery of his written or oral report, participate in a hearing where the parties have the opportunity to put questions to him and to present expert witnesses in order to testify on the points at issue.

Article 27 Court assistance in taking evidence

The arbitral tribunal or a party with the approval of the arbitral tribunal may request from a competent court of this state assistance in taking evidence. The court may execute the request within its competence and according to its rules on taking evidence.

Chapter VI Making of award and termination of proceedings

Article 28 Rules applicable to substance of dispute

1 The arbitral tribunal shall decide the dispute in accordance with such rules of law as are chosen by the parties as applicable to the substance of the

dispute. Any designation of the law or legal system of a given state shall be construed, unless otherwise expressed, as directly referring to the substantive law of that state and not to its conflict of laws rules.

2 Failing any designation by the parties, the arbitral tribunal shall apply the law determined by the conflict of laws rules which it considers applicable.

3 The arbitral tribunal shall decide *ex aequo et bono* or as *amiable compositeur* only if the parties have expressly authorised it to do so.

4 In all cases, the arbitral tribunal shall decide in accordance with the terms of the contract and shall take into account the usages of the trade applicable to the transaction.

Article 29 Decision making by panel of arbitrators

In arbitral proceedings with more than one arbitrator, any decision of the arbitral tribunal shall be made, unless otherwise agreed by the parties, by a majority of all its members. However, questions of procedure may be decided by a presiding arbitrator, if so authorised by the parties or all members of the arbitral tribunal.

Article 30 Settlement

1 If, during arbitral proceedings, the parties settle the dispute, the arbitral tribunal shall terminate the proceedings and, if requested by the parties and not objected to by the arbitral tribunal, record the settlement in the form of an arbitral award on agreed terms.

2 An award on agreed terms shall be made in accordance with the provisions of Article 31 and shall state that it is an award. Such an award has the same status and effect as any other award on the merits of the case.

Article 31 Form and contents of award

1 The award shall be made in writing and shall be signed by the arbitrator or arbitrators. In arbitral proceedings with more than one arbitrator, the signatures of the majority of all members of the arbitral tribunal shall suffice, provided that the reason for any omitted signature is stated.

2 The award shall state the reasons upon which it is based, unless the parties have agreed that no reasons are to be given or the award is an award on agreed terms under Article 30.

3 The award shall state its date and the place of arbitration as determined in accordance with Article 20(1). The award shall be deemed to have been made at that place.

4 After the award is made, a copy signed by the arbitrators in accordance with paragraph (1) of this article shall be delivered to each party.

Article 32 Termination of proceedings

1 The arbitral proceedings are terminated by the final award or by an order of the arbitral tribunal in accordance with paragraph (2) of this article.

2 The arbitral tribunal shall issue an order for the termination of the arbitral proceedings when:

(a) the claimant withdraws his claim, unless the respondent objects thereto and the arbitral tribunal recognises a legitimate interest on his part in obtaining a final settlement of the dispute;
(b) the parties agree on the termination of the proceedings;
(c) the arbitral tribunal finds that the continuation of the proceedings has for any other reason become unnecessary or impossible.

3 The mandate of the arbitral tribunal terminates with the termination of the arbitral proceedings, subject to the provisions of Articles 33 and 34(4).

Article 33 Correction and interpretation of award; additional award

1 Within thirty days of receipt of the award, unless another period of time has been agreed upon by the parties:
(a) a party, with notice to the other party, may request the arbitral tribunal to correct in the award any errors in computation, any clerical or typographical errors or any errors of similar nature;
(b) if so agreed by the parties, a party, with notice to the other party, may request the arbitral tribunal to give an interpretation of a specific point or part of the award.
If the arbitral tribunal considers the request to be justified, it shall make the correction or give the interpretation within thirty days of receipt of the request. The interpretation shall form part of the award.

2 The arbitral tribunal may correct any error of the type referred to in paragraph (1)(a) of this article on its own initiative within thirty days of the date of the award.

3 Unless otherwise agreed by the parties, a party, with notice to the other party, may request, within thirty days of receipt of the award, the arbitral tribunal to make an additional award as to claims presented in the arbitral proceedings but omitted from the award. If the arbitral tribunal considers the request to be justified, it shall make the additional award within sixty days.

4 The arbitral tribunal may extend, if necessary, the period of time within which it shall make a correction, interpretation or an additional award under paragraph (1) or (3) of this article.

5 The provisions of Article 31 shall apply to a correction or interpretation of the award or to an additional award.

Chapter VII Recourse against award

Article 34 Application for setting aside as exclusive recourse against arbitral award

1 Recourse to a court against an arbitral award may be made only by an application for setting aside in accordance with paragraphs (2) and (3) of this article.

2 An arbitral award may be set aside by the court specified in Article 6 only if:
(a) the party making the application furnishes proof that:
(i) a party to the arbitration agreement referred to in Article 7 was under some incapacity; or the said agreement is not valid under the law to which the parties have subjected it or, failing any indication thereon, under the law of this state; or

(ii) the party making the application was not given proper notice of the appointment of an arbitrator or of the arbitral proceedings or was otherwise unable to present his case; or
(iii) the award deals with a dispute not contemplated by or not falling within the terms of the submission to arbitration, or contains decisions on matters beyond the scope of the submission to arbitration, provided that, if the decisions on matters submitted to arbitration can be separated from those not so submitted, only that part of the award which contains decisions on matters not submitted to arbitration may be set aside; or
(iv) the composition of the arbitral tribunal or the arbitral procedure was not in accordance with the agreement of the parties, unless such agreement was in conflict with a provision of this Law from which the parties cannot derogate, or, failing such agreement, was not in accordance with this Law; or

(b) the court finds that:
(i) the subject-matter of the dispute is not capable of settlement by arbitration under the law of this state; or
(ii) the award is in conflict with the public policy of this state.

3 An application for setting aside may not be made after three months have elapsed from the date on which the party making that application had received the award or, if a request had been made under Article 33, from the date on which that request had been disposed of by the arbitral tribunal.

4 The court, when asked to set aside an award, may, where appropriate and so requested by a party, suspend the setting aside proceedings for a period of time determined by it in order to give the arbitral tribunal an opportunity to resume the arbitral proceedings or to take such other action as in the arbitral tribunal's opinion will eliminate the ground for setting aside.

Chapter VIII Recognition and enforcement of awards

Article 35 Recognition and enforcement

1 An arbitral award, irrespective of the country in which it was made, shall be recognised as binding and, upon application in writing to the competent court, shall be enforced subject to the provisions of this article and of Article 36.

2 The party relying on an award or applying for its enforcement shall supply the duly authenticated original award or a duly certified copy thereof, and the original arbitration agreement referred to in Article 7 or a duly certified copy thereof. If the award or agreement is not made in an official language of this state, the party shall supply a duly certified translation thereof into such language.***

*** The conditions set forth in this paragraph are intended to set maximum standards. It would, thus, not be contrary to the harmonisation to be achieved by the Model Law if a state retained even less onerous conditions.

Article 36 Grounds for refusing recognition or enforcement

1 Recognition or enforcement of an arbitral award, irrespective of the country in which it was made, may be refused only:

(a) at the request of the party against whom it is invoked, if that party furnishes to the competent court where recognition or enforcement is sought proof that:

(i) a party to the arbitration agreement referred to in Article 7 was under some incapacity; or the said agreement is not valid under the law to which the parties have subjected it or, failing any indication thereon, under the law of the country where the award was made; or

(ii) the party against whom the award is invoked was not given proper notice of the appointment of an arbitrator or of the arbitral proceedings or was otherwise unable to present his case; or

(iii) the award deals with a dispute not contemplated by or not falling within the terms of the submission to arbitration, or it contains decisions on matters beyond the scope of the submission to arbitration, provided that, if the decisions on matters submitted to arbitration can be separated from those not so submitted, that part of the award which contains decisions on matters submitted to arbitration may be recognised and enforced; or

(iv) the composition of the arbitral tribunal or the arbitral procedure was not in accordance with the agreement of the parties or, failing such agreement, was not in accordance with the law of the country where the arbitration took place; or

(v) the award has not yet become binding on the parties or has been set aside or suspended by a court of the country in which, or under the law of which, that award was made; or

(b) if the court finds that:

(i) the subject-matter of the dispute is not capable of settlement by arbitration under the law of this state; or

(ii) the recognition or enforcement of the award would be contrary to the public policy of this state.

2 If an application for setting aside or suspension of an award has been made to a court referred to in paragraph (1)(a)(v) of this article, the court where recognition or enforcement is sought may, if it considers it proper, adjourn its decision and may also, on the application of the party claiming recognition or enforcement of the award, order the other party to provide appropriate security.

15 Supplementary rules governing the presentation and reception of evidence in international commercial arbitration*

David W Shenton

Introduction

On May 28, 1983, the Council of the International Bar Association (IBA) adopted by Resolution and recommendation to its members and others the Supplementary Rules Governing the Presentation and Reception of Evidence in International Commercial Arbitration (Supplementary Rules). It may be of interest to those concerned with international arbitration between parties from civil law and common law countries to know the reasons and processes whereby they came about, their scope and the philosophy behind some of their individual provisions.

Numerous efforts have, from time to time, been made to develop a uniform arbitration law and uniform rules for application in international arbitration. Both *ad hoc* and institutional rules have been drawn in order to suit, as far as possible, the various disciplines and approaches to the conduct of the dispute resolving process: Rules on Commercial Arbitration were formulated by the International Law Association in 1950; a Uniform Law on Arbitration in Respect of Relations of Private Law was developed by UNIDROIT in 1935, was revised in 1954 and amended by the Legal Committee of the Consultative Assembly of the Council of Europe in 1957; the European Convention on International Commercial Arbitration was concluded in 1961; the United Nations Economic Commission for Europe promulgated its ECE Rules for International Commercial Arbitration in 1966; in 1976, UNCITRAL adopted the most important Arbitration Rules of all for *ad hoc* arbitration and suitable for adoption by arbitral institutions.[1] These Rules,[2] that are gaining in popularity, in the opinion of the author of this explanatory note, form the best attempt yet to formulate a complete code of Arbitration Rules of universal adoption by parties involved in international arbitration.

* Reproduced by kind permission of the Editor of 'The Year Book of Commercial Arbitration' of the International Council for Commercial Arbitration.

1 The author is indebted to Dr Julian DM Lew, writing in the *Business Law Review*, June 1984, for the comprehensive list of authorities cited here.

2 Adopted by General Assembly Resolution 31/98 of December 15, 1976, as the 'UNCITRAL Arbitration Rules'. The UNCITRAL Arbitration Rules are reprinted in *Yearbook* Vol II (1977), 16 with comment by Prof Pieter Sanders, at 172. See for UNCITRAL's 'Recommendations to assist arbitral institutions and other interested bodies with regard to arbitration under the UNCITRAL Arbitration Rules', UN Doc A/CN 9/230, reprinted in *Yearbook* Vol VIII (1983), 211.

Nevertheless, these Rules and the latest draft of the proposed UNCITRAL Model Law on international commercial arbitration,[3] to a large extent, duck the difficult issues by leaving to the agreement of the parties the actual procedure to be followed and, failing such agreement, to the discretion of the arbitrators. All these Rules, in the opinion of the author, do not face up to the difficult decisions of detail that have to be made, or agreed, between those advising the parties or, failing them, the arbitrators when the parties, their advisers, and the arbitrators between them come from mixed civil law and common law jurisdictions with their different disciplines and approaches towards the conduct of the judicial process, particularly as regards the reception of evidence, both oral and written.[4]

Committee D of the IBA/Section on Business Law comprising, as it does, some 380 lawyers from most countries of the world, who are interested in dispute resolution processes, seemed a particularly useful forum in which to discuss the practical problems that arise when lawyers and arbitrators from countries with different procedural rules seek together to conduct and adjudicate upon an international arbitration.

After some general discussion, a sub-committee was formed, comprising lawyers from England, France, Germany, Italy, and the United States of America. The sub-committee included a solicitor practising in England but who had been qualified in South Africa and who was therefore trained in both the Common Law and in Roman/Dutch Law. Another member of the sub-committee held both US and German legal qualifications.

In order better to appreciate the formidable problems and obstacles, the sub-committee had available to it, not only the national reports of its members, but also the reports of a Symposium held in April of 1974 by The Institute of Arbitrators (England) (as it was then called),[5] on presenting evidence in proceedings and arbitrations in civil and common law countries. These papers contained valuable reports of discussions from leading practitioners in England, the United States of America, Switzerland, France, Italy and from certain countries of Eastern Europe.

It soon became clear to the sub-committee that it would be fruitless to make yet a further attempt at a complete set of arbitration Rules, since a variety of well known Rules exist already and are in international circulation, and are most unlikely to be replaced by yet a further set of such Rules. The Committee decided to confine itself to the real 'nitty-gritty' of the mechanics of presenting or receiving evidence in a commercial arbitration.

The Committee tried to go through the sort of negotiations that would be carried out in practice if lawyers and arbitrators from common law and civil law

3 UN Doc A/CN 9/246. The model law has since been adopted. For the text, see pp. *et seq.*

4 It must, however, be emphasised that the Rules of Conciliation and Arbitration of the International Chamber of Commerce (1975/1980), the Commercial Arbitration Rules of the American Arbitration Association (1980), the Arbitration Rules of the London Court of International Arbitration (1981), the Rules of the Arbitration Institute of the Stockholm Chamber of Commerce (1976), and many others, are intended for use and frequently are used in international arbitrations between parties of mixed procedural jurisdictions to their complete satisfaction, and the comments made are the personal opinion of the author only.

5 Now The Chartered Institute of Arbitrators, 75 Cannon Street, London EC4N 5BH, also the headquarters of the International Arbitration Centre, the seat of the London Court of International Arbitration.

systems actually had to sit down together and agree upon a procedure for an actual arbitration between parties of a civil law and of a common law country.

Conflicting approach of the civil law and common law

The first and largest problem the sub-committee butted against was of course the well-known difference between the common law adversarial approach to the laying out of a case for judicial consideration and the civil law's inquisitorial system.

Common law

It is, I think, a commonplace of the adversarial system that the burden lies with the parties, or more accurately their legal advisers, (a) to allege their case, (b) to deploy and lay out the evidence they propose to put before the arbitrators in order to prove their allegations and (c) to test and, as far as possible, to discredit the evidence called in support of the allegations of the other side by the process which common law lawyers call 'cross-examination'. The tribunal is there (a) to select between the evidence and arguments deployed on behalf of the parties, (b) to rule upon its admissibility or otherwise, (c) to decide on the weight to be attached to it, (d) to act as a kind of referee ensuring that the rules of the game are observed and played in a fair manner and, finally, (e) to decide the merits on the basis of the evidence and arguments presented by the two sides. Independent advice to the tribunal in the form of arbitrator-appointed experts on fact or law, although not expressly forbidden by this procedure, is certainly kept to a minimum. It is certainly thought in England, the birthplace of the common law system, that for this procedure to be carried out with fairness the issues between the parties must be respectively, and with some particularity, set out in pleadings, so that each side knows what issues the other party will attempt to prove at the hearing and which issues the opposing party will have to meet. The tribunal has no responsibility for the preparation and presentation of evidence; the burden lies entirely with the parties.

It is an integral part of this system that the parties shall disclose to each other in advance the documentation comprising the written part of the evidence. It is also fundamental that each party will disclose to the other side all the relevant written material, whether such material is supportive of that party's case or not. This is the procedure known as 'discovery'[6] and under the Common Law system it is regarded as of paramount importance. It is a cornerstone of the system that the basic evidence will be called in the form of verbal testimony of witnesses, including the testimony of the parties to the dispute. It is equally fundamental that such evidence will be tested by cross-examination. As Mr Robert Goff, QC (as he then was),[7] stated in his presentation at the Symposium

6 The scope, nature, history and method of discovery under English procedure is set out in the text and notes to the Rules of the Supreme Court Order 24 rr 1–17 in the *Supreme Court Practice* 1985, Vol 1.

7 Now Lord Justice Goff, one of the Lords Justices of the Court of Appeal of the Supreme Court of England and Wales and previously a Judge of the Commercial Court of the Queen's Bench Division of the High Court; at the time of the Symposium one of the leading practitioners in commercial law at the English Bar and a Queen's Counsel.

referred to above, 'It is a strong conviction of English practising lawyers that, on a contested question of fact, the most satisfactory way to get to the bottom of the matter is, if possible, to see and hear the actual witnesses and to test their evidence by cross-examination in the light of all relevant matters, including contemporary documents.' He does, however, go on to say, '... but cross-examination is only likely to happen in substantial, closely contested disputes, in which lawyers are instructed. In most arbitrations, matters do not come to that stage.' The US view was not dissimilar and the importance of cross-examination was stressed. In arbitrations, however, US practitioners do not see the necessity of elaborate pre-trial discovery of facts or documents and do not see the necessity for elaborate (or any) pleadings, holding that it is sufficient that the facts and issues be fully explained by the lawyer opening his case and before calling or deploying his testimony. As Mr Robert Coulson, President[8] of the AAA explained, 'Ordinarily, arbitrators will expect the parties to provide all testimony and evidence necessary to decide the case.' However, he did not imply that any party is under an obligation to provide testimony or evidence detrimental to his case as with English discovery procedures.

Civil law

In the civil law system, whether arbitrators are expected to apply the rules of evidence and the rules of procedure in use before their national courts, or whether they are themselves left to determine the procedure for examining and taking evidence, the approach is inquisitorial. The lawyers acting for the parties, having deployed before the arbitrators in advance their written arguments, allegations and documents, it is for the judge or the arbitrator adjudicating on the matter to determine how the testimony will be received, how matters of an evidential nature that are not clear will be investigated and where or whether verbal testimony is required. It is the tribunal that questions the witness of its own motion or, at best, at the instance of the lawyers of one or other of the parties. As Prof Roger Perrot, Deputy Director of the Institute of Legal Studies, Paris, put it, 'The technique of "direct examination" and of "cross-examination" of the parties, witnesses or experts is totally unknown in our legal systems in Continental Europe. The arbitrator is the person in charge of the investigation. It is he who conducts the hearing of witnesses, who puts questions to them and who challenges them if necessary in order to obtain further details.' He goes on to allow, however, '... if the hearing proceeds in a serene and courteous atmosphere, it is often the case, even, that each counsel directly questions the witnesses summoned by the opposing party. But this only amounts to a simple measure of tolerance to which the arbitrator can always put an end.' It seems that, not only does the arbitrator conduct the reception of evidence by himself from materials and testimony tendered by the parties, he may have new witnesses appear on his own motion, and in the case of conflicting testimony, he may order an enquiry *ex officio*. As Prof Perrot pointed out, '... Once arbitrators have the power to order that witnesses be heard *ex officio*, they can at the same time appoint any third party whom they wish to hear'.

8 A position which he continues to occupy with great distinction to this day.

It is said that the civil law system does not have 'discovery' as understood by the common law system. However, in exercising its functions, any tribunal, be it a court or arbitrators, has the power to require the parties to produce documents which are considered to be conclusive for the resolving of the dispute. In the case of a court, refusal by a party or third party to produce such documents can lead to sanctions that are not within the power of an arbitrator. However, a refusal by a party to accede to the invitation of the arbitrator would be met by the well known formula that the arbitrator may 'draw all legal consequences', ie accept submissions of fact by the opposing party which, it is suggested, could have been proved by the documents that the other party refuses to produce upon the arbitrator's order. There is, undoubtedly, a strong feeling among civilian lawyers that documentary evidence is more reliable than verbal testimony. In certain jurisdictions (eg Germany) parties to a case are not even competent to give testimony on their own behalf in court proceedings. It seems that under French law witnesses may even be heard without the presence of the parties (Article 71 of the Decree of December 17, 1973), although it seems that this would seldom be done in the case of arbitrations.[9]

The constitutional protection which is accorded to parties in order to prevent injustice in these circumstances is described as the principle of 'contradiction'. This does not amount to the right of a party to hear and test all evidence called or to see or hear all facts which may influence the arbitrator's decision (including his own technical knowledge) and address him on it, but it is the right of the party to know about any testimony, verbal or written, and to address the tribunal on it in such a way as to contradict it or explain it to that party's advantage.

It is pointed out by one civil law *rapporteur* to the Symposium that difficulties can arise when there is more than one arbitrator and when arbitrators have, and are in a position to use their own technical knowledge in deciding the issues, particularly when such technical knowledge is in the possession of one arbitrator and not the others. In such circumstances, there is a legal obligation on that arbitrator to impart that knowledge and the outcome of those investigations to his co-arbitrators. Presumably, it must also be imparted to the parties in order to give rise to the right of 'contradiction'. Prof Perrot goes on to point out that in arbitrations under civil law it is not customary to make verbatim records of statements or verbal testimony but merely to report the essential features in the form of minutes.[10]

9 The hearing of witnesses is now provided for by Arts 208 and 215 of the New French Civil Procedure Law reading as follows:

'208. Le juge entend les témoins en leur déposition séparement et dans l'ordre qu'il détermine. Les témoins sont entendus en présence des parties ou celles-ci appelées. Par exception, le juge peut, si les circonstances l'exigent, inviter une partie à se retirer sous réserve du droit pour celle-ci d'avoir immédiatement connaissance des déclarations des témoins entendus hors sa présence. Le juge peut, s'il y à risque de déperissement de la preuve, procéder sans dèlai à l'audition d'un témoin après avoir, si possible, appèle lẹs parties.

215. Le juge peut entendre à nouveau les témoins, les confronter entre eux ou avec les parties. Le cas écheant il procède à l'audition en présence d'un téchnicien'.

The author is indebted to Maitre Jean-Louis Delvolvé, Avocat a la Cour, Paris, for this authority.

10 Many other learned papers on these topics were read at the Symposium, including contributions from countries in Eastern Europe, all of which were of the greatest value. Space does not permit the author to mention or quote from them all.

The IBA supplementary rules of evidence

It is against these conflicting principles and attitudes that the IBA Supplementary Rules must be understood and evaluated.

The IBA Supplementary Rules are, accordingly, not intended to provide a complete code for the conduct of arbitrations but only for the reception of evidence and where the Supplementary Rules and the general Rules of the arbitration conflict, then the general Rules prevail as do any mandatory applicable provisions of law (see Article 1 of the Supplementary Rules).

As regards pleadings, which in the Supplementary Rules are described as 'introductory submissions', little is said which would lay down a method of pleading more familiar to one system than the other. However, Article 3 provides that the introductory submissions shall contain, *inter alia*, the means by which the facts relevant to the dispute are intended to be provided, including the names of witnesses and reference to documents. Names of witnesses are not normally referred to in an English pleading, nor in pleadings habitually filed in the courts of the USA.

There is no obligation on the party to disclose documents other than those on which he desires to rely (Article 4). However, there is a provision against surprise, requiring parties to exchange lists of documents in advance and prohibiting the producing of documents at the hearing that have not been listed in advance unless the arbitrator consents. A compromise towards the common law view of discovery is provided by Article 4.4 which permits a party to serve on the other a notice to produce a document relevant to the dispute in the circumstances mentioned there. Of course, he can only do this when he knows about the existence of that document and when it has previously passed between the parties or between a third party and the opposing party. If the notice is not complied with, production can be ordered by the arbitrator who, in the event of a failure to produce, may draw the appropriate conclusions.

Article 5 provides a somewhat novel compromise between the common law and civil law approaches. Verbal testimony is presented to the tribunal prior to the hearing in the form of a written disposition. The right of a party to cross-examine exists only on those matters that are directly in issue and in respect of which advance notice is given by means of an oral evidence notice. The arbitrator has the unfettered power to decide whether oral testimony will be heard and cross-examined, where oral testimony is permitted. The witness is first questioned by the arbitrator. He may thereafter be examined, cross-examined and re-examined by the parties in the common law manner.[11] The procedure can be stopped by the arbitrator at any stage if he considers that it is unlikely to serve any further relevant purpose. Witnesses (Article 5.12) can only be called without the prior lodgement of a witness's statement if it can be shown that the witness has refused to give one and cannot be compelled to do so but is, apparently, prepared to give oral testimony at the hearing. It is felt that such occasions are likely to be extremely rare for obvious reasons.

The Supplementary Rules give to the arbitrator wide powers similar to those

11 It is thought that the full common law procedure of examination, cross-examination and re-examination in these circumstances will seldom be used, the parties' advisers being content with cross-examination and re-examination after the questioning by the arbitral tribunal.

enjoyed by the civil law system both as regards the calling of testimony on his own motion, to appoint his own experts and to rely on his own expert knowledge. They provide the best compromise that could be arrived at between two incompatible systems after extensive discussion. It is thought that they will be found to be fair and acceptable to practitioners of the two systems when a compromise has to be made. Suitable arrangements for the revision of the Supplementary Rules have been made if a revision will appear desirable in the light of experience.[12]

12 The sub-committee which worked on these Supplementary Rules remains as a standing committee to consider revisions under the chairmanship of Avv Giovanni Ughi of Milan, Italy, who will be pleased to receive comments, particularly when made in the light of experience of use of the Supplementary Rules, either at the above address or through the International Bar Association, Section on Business Law, 2 Harewood Place, Hanover Square, London W1R 9HB, England.

Judicial assistance for the arbitrator 16

J Martin H Hunter

A number of conflicting elements are responsible for the development of the relationship between arbitration and the courts. In England, at least, until some time in the middle of the last century, there existed a certain jealousy which gave rise to actual competition. Fortunately this feature has now largely disappeared, although it is still possible to discern some traces of mutual suspicion. One occasionally hears arbitrators at seminars and conferences talking about the 'fear' of having their awards set aside; and, equally, one sees expressions of shock and horror at the possibility of the 'uncontrollable excesses of arbitrators' and the like from members of the judiciary. However, realism now prevails and arbitrators and judges no longer compete for business.

Indeed, the opposite is the case. Speaking of the relationship between judges and arbitrators, the present head of the English Court of Appeal, Sir John Donaldson, himself a former president of the Chartered Institute of Arbitrators, said:

> 'working together as partners, we seek to provide a service to the world.'[1]

Nonetheless conflicting interests still arise because businessmen (who are the ultimate customers) go to arbitration specifically in order to *avoid* having their disputes settled in court. On the other hand, since arbitrators have no executory power to compel performance of their awards, a certain degree of support from the law, and from the courts, is essential in order to give effectiveness to the arbitral process. Professor Goldman states:

> 'the national judge should be armed with the powers which he alone can possess, to carry out the necessary measures for the proper operation of the arbitral process.'[2]

Yet at the same time, the willingness of the lawmakers to provide *support* for the arbitral process, particularly in relation to enforcement, is tempered by the proviso that the court should be asked to enforce awards only if the arbitral process has been subject to a certain level of supervisory control. In other

1 Paper presented by Lord Justice Donaldson to European Arbitration Conference in October 1980 entitled: 'Relationship between the Courts and Arbitrator under the European Common Law Systems', published in 47 *Arbitration* 73 (1981).

2 Goldman, 'The Complementary Roles of Judges and Arbitrators,' in *60 Years of ICC Arbitration*, Paris 1983, 257 and 282.

words, legislators and judges shrink from permitting the powers of the sovereign state to be used to enforce the result of a quasi-judicial proceeding if it has been conducted in a way which is manifestly unfair to the losing party, or if the proceedings have been otherwise contrary to public policy. The point was emphasised by Sir Michael Kerr, in the 1984 Alexander Lecture:

> 'At first sight it might be said that the role of the courts should be limited to that of enforcement of arbitral awards. This is the ultimate desired legal consequence of arbitration. But this is clearly not enough, because arbitrations, and therefore awards can be stultified by events ... after the completion of the process, some limits must obviously be imposed on the enforceability of awards: otherwise arbitrators could subject the parties to legal consequences at the result of dishonesty, bias, incompetence, or the arbitrary or capricious use of power.'[3]

Thus, the *quid pro quo* for court support of the arbitral process is the reservation of the right to supervise the proceedings.

This paper examines the *supportive* role of the courts in relation to arbitration, which may be conveniently divided into a number of sub-headings as follows:

1 Support for the agreement to arbitrate
2 Establishment of the Tribunal
3 Interim measures of protection
4 Support during the course of the proceedings
5 Enforcement of the award

The laws of most developed nations contain provisions covering each of these topics, and are designed to enable an arbitration to be taken through to its conclusion even in the absence of cooperation on the part of the respondent. The need for such provisions is also clearly recognised in the UNCITRAL Model Law on international commercial arbitration, the text of which may fairly be taken to represent prevailing international opinion on the matters it covers.

In outlining possible features of the Model Law the Secretary General of UNCITRAL stated:

> 'It is desirable, if not imperative, to envisage a certain link between the arbitration proceedings, including the award, and a national law which would give recognition and effect to arbitration agreements and awards and would provide for adequate assistance by courts, for example, as regards orders to compel arbitration or to call witnesses or to enforce interim measures of protection or to provide ultimate resort in case of deadlock.'[4]

Different systems of law treat each of the topics listed above in different ways, and at different levels of detail and sophistication, depending on the historical development of arbitration law in the countries concerned. For example, pre-award interim conservatory measures are a relatively recent development in England, but have a long history in the legal systems of continental Europe

3 50 *Arbitration* 3 (1984), at 5.
4 United Nations Working Paper A/CN 9/207.

and in America; by contrast, court support in procedural matters appears to be more highly developed in English law than is the case in civil law countries.

This paper deals primarily with English law which, taken overall, may probably be considered to be one of the leaders in the field of court support for the arbitral process, but it also refers briefly by way of illustration to other systems where appropriate. As Sir Michael Kerr put it:

> 'The entire role played by our courts is that of an executive partner to provide greater effectiveness to the arbitral process.'[5]

Support for the agreement to arbitrate

The Geneva Protocol on Arbitration Clauses 1923 was the first specific international step in the recognition of the arbitration agreement. This was almost immediately followed by the Geneva Convention on the Execution of Foreign Awards of 1927 (promoted by the League of Nations), and subsequently by the New York Convention of 1958. Article II of the New York Convention represented a significant development in the recognition of arbitration, even going so far as to compel the courts of contracting states to grant a stay of litigation commenced in breach of an arbitration agreement.

In England this provision is to be found in the Arbitration Act 1975 ('the 1975 Act') where the court is under a mandatory duty to stay litigation where a valid agreement for a 'non-domestic' arbitration exists. Similar provisions must appear in the laws of other countries which are party to the New York Convention.

The obverse side of this coin is where the claimant gives notice of arbitration, and the respondent denies jurisdiction on the grounds of invalidity of the arbitration agreement, or because he claims it does not cover the matters referred to arbitration. Different legal systems treat the arbitrator's power to rule on his own jurisdiction (*kompetenz-kompetenz*) in different ways. For instance in Switzerland Article 8.1 of the Concordat empowers the arbitrator to rule on his own jurisdiction and in France the arbitrator's power to rule 'on the validity or the limits' of his jurisdiction is clear.[6] Further, the UNCITRAL Arbitration Rules Article 2.1.1 empowers the arbitrator to rule on objections to his jurisdiction. However, ultimately the issue may become one for the courts to decide, either as a preliminary issue or as a ground for recourse or refusal of enforcement after the award has been issued.

In England a respondent can effectively elect whether to make a question of jurisdiction a preliminary issue, for determination initially by the arbitrator with recourse to the courts if necessary, or whether to save his challenge until after the award. Where a jurisdiction question is taken as a preliminary issue it is dealt with, as are all matters relating to arbitration, by the 'Commercial Court', which is a division of the Queen's Bench Division of the High Court. With specialised judges allocated to deal with its work, the Commercial Court is designed to act speedily so as to ensure that there is no unreasonable delay, an essential feature of its support for the arbitral process.

5 50 *Arbitration* 3 (1984), at 5.
6 See generally Goldman, *op cit.*

As a general point it is clear that the English courts will, where possible, read arbitration clauses with latitude so as to make an otherwise unworkable mechanism (for instance in relation to the appointment of arbitrators) realistic and effective.[7]

The role of the courts in this context has been summarised by a distinguished Spanish commentator as follows:

> 'the task of the courts is to guarantee proper fulfilment of the wishes of the parties as expressed in the arbitration agreement'.[8]

Establishment of the tribunal

Another important way in which the supportive role of the court is seen is in its ability to complete the establishment of the tribunal where the parties have either failed to provide a mechanism for the appointment of the arbitrator, or where one of the parties has refused to carry out such a mechanism.

This is a feature of many developed arbitration systems. In England the powers of the court in this respect are both complex and detailed. The composition of the arbitral tribunal and, in particular, the appointment of an umpire or a third arbitrator, are matters which the parties generally determine in the arbitration agreement. If no other provision is made, the reference is deemed to be to a single arbitrator.[9] Where the reference is to two arbitrators, the agreement is deemed to include a provision that two arbitrators may appoint an 'umpire' at any time after they themselves are appointed, and that they should do so forthwith if they cannot agree upon their award.[10] Where an umpire is appointed, he acts as if he were sole arbitrator from the moment when the arbitrators are unable to agree.

The court also exercises its supportive role to appoint an arbitrator or umpire if an arbitrator refuses to act, becomes incapable of acting or dies.[11] This power also extends to cases where the parties are at liberty, or are required, to appoint a third arbitrator or umpire and they fail to do so.[12]

At the time of writing, a curious gap in the powers of the English courts still exists in that there is no mechanism in the Arbitration Acts for the appointment by the court of a party-nominated arbitrator, in a tribunal composed of three arbitrators where a party fails to make the appointment. This contrasts with the position in relation to the 'two arbitrators and umpire' arbitration, which is covered by Section 7 of the 1950 Act. However, even though this does not appear to have given rise to practical problems, in that most institutional Rules of arbitration cover the point, the legislature has recognised the existence of this gap and a remedying provision is in the process of implementation.[13]

7 *Finzel, Berry & Co* v *Eastcheap Dried Fruit Co* [1962] 1 Lloyd's Rep 370; affirmed [1962] 2 Lloyd's Rep 11, CA.
8 Cremades, 'Should Arbitrators Maintain Their Independence?', in 44 *Arbitration* 83 (1978), at 85.
9 Arbitration Act 1950 ('1950 Act'), s6.
10 Arbitration Act 1979 ('1979 Act'), s6(1).
11 1950 Act, s10(b).
12 *Ibid*, s10(c).
13 Clause 53 Administration of Justice Bill 1985, currently due to receive its second reading before the House of Commons.

When a court exercises its power to appoint an arbitrator under the 1950 Act it will not appoint a court official as arbitrator. The court will invite the parties to submit names and it will nominate from the lists so submitted. The power is discretionary, and the court may refuse to make an appointment; however, it would only decline to exercise its discretion where there is good reason to consider that arbitration is not a suitable method of determining the dispute.

The 1950 Act gives the courts both positive and negative powers to assist in the establishment of the tribunal. Section 7(6) provides that where the arbitration agreement requires two arbitrators to be appointed, one by each of the parties, and one party fails to do so, then the arbitrator who has been appointed can decide the case as if he were a sole arbitrator. The power of the court in this respect is a negative one in that the Act retains to the court a power to 'set aside any appointment made in pursuance of this section'.

The High Court is also given powers to appoint a sole arbitrator under Section 25(2) of the 1950 Act where the authority of an arbitrator is removed by the court. The court also has power to call upon an umpire to proceed to decide the dispute as a sole arbitrator in lieu of the existing arbitrators.[14]

Many other jurisdictions and arbitral systems contain similar provisions. For instance, in the United States if no method for appointment of an arbitrator is prescribed in the agreement, or the agreement is not complied with, then the courts will make the appointment.[15] Similar powers are given to the judicial authority of a Swiss Canton in which an arbitration is taking place.[16] In France the President of the Court of First Instance may appoint the arbitrator; and the Spanish Code of Civil Procedure relating to arbitrations in that country provides that the judge appoints the arbitrator if the parties fail to agree. As Professor Berthold Goldman has commented:

> 'there is hardly any legal system which does not provide for the appointment of the arbitrator by a judge in place of the defaulting party.'[17]

Interim measures of protection

Broadly speaking, lawyers from continental Europe and the USA have been familiar with the concept of the 'pre-trial attachment' of money or other assets to provide security for monetary claims for much longer than their counterparts in England. However, whilst the English courts have long exercised powers to grant interim injunctions to preserve property and so forth, the development of the '*Mareva* injunction' in the late 1970's, which gave birth to a more general form of pre-trial (or pre-award) attachment, broke new ground in England, and was soon made effective in the context of arbitration.

The 1950 and 1979 Acts and the law as developed by judicial precedent give to the courts jurisdiction to ensure that a successful claimant is not left with an empty victory. These powers of assistance are considerable and important but

14 1950 Act, s8(3).
15 United States Federal Arbitration Act, s5.
16 *Concordat suisse*, Article 12.
17 Goldman, *op cit*, at 275.

they do not displace the ability of the arbitrator to make orders for the preservation of the subject-matter of the dispute, or to exercise specific powers which may have been conferred on him by the arbitration agreement.

In the confines of this paper, all that can be undertaken is a necessarily 'whistle stop' review of the more significant of these powers. First, the powers of the court to restrict the transfer or disposal of assets by a respondent in an arbitration. These powers are aimed at stopping attempts by a party to hinder the arbitration by tampering with or disposing of the assets about which the parties are in dispute, and may involve the attachment of assets prior to the arbitration to prevent the frustration of any eventual award. Section 12(6) of the 1950 Act provides that the High Court has, for the purposes of an arbitration, the same powers to make orders in respect of interim preservation and in respect of issuing injunctions as it has for the purpose of and in relation to an action or matter being tried in the court. Mustill & Boyd have expressed the view that the powers in Section 12(6) are 'available not only to reinforce an order made by the arbitrator, but also by way of appeal from a refusal to make an order.'[18]

The powers and remedies available to the court are as follows:

1 the grant of an interlocutory injunction;
2 the appointment of a receiver;
3 the making of an order for the preservation, custody or sale of the property; and
4 the securing of the amount in dispute.

The *Mareva* injunction, referred to above, which is more commonly known in other jurisdictions as 'pre-trial attachment', is probably the most important remedy in modern times. Lord Brandon, when in a lower court, was the first judge to state that this remedy could apply to arbitrations when in 1979 he viewed the powers of the court under Section 12(6)(f) of the 1950 Act (which permits the court to secure the amount in dispute) and Section 12(6)(h) of the 1950 Act (which permits the court to issue interim injunctions in arbitrations) as together encompassing a power to issue *Mareva* injunctions even before the arbitration had technically commenced.[19] This remedy takes the form of an injunction acting on a specific person enjoining him from disposing of or transferring either assets generally, or specified assets, pending further order of the court, except as otherwise provided for in the order itself.

The initial proceedings are *ex parte*. However, the courts require the applicant to show a strong case, reveal all material facts, produce a form of order that is reasonable, and, if possible, agree that order with the respondent's advisers before the injunction will be granted. Any injustice that results can be speedily remedied in expedited *inter partes* proceedings. Disobedience of the order involves a committal procedure for contempt of court and potentially heavy sanctions.

The value of this remedy is great. Its availability, particularly in the context of arbitration, is limited. The arbitration must be subject to English law, probably be held in England, and the assets must be within England for this

18 *The Law and Practice of Commercial Arbitration in England*, London 1982, at 289.
19 *The Rena K* [1979] QB 377.

remedy to be available. This is even before all the grounds for making such an order are established to the satisfaction of the court.

Finally, in considering the court's basket of supportive powers in relation to interim measures, the question of the respondent's costs must not be ignored. The defence of an arbitration can be an expensive business. In England, the court may make an order that, as a condition of the arbitration being allowed to proceed, the claimant shall provide adequate security for costs which may be awarded against him if his claim fails. The arbitrator cannot himself make such an order unless the parties have given him that power by agreement, express or implied. Thus the power of the court under Section 12(6)(a) of the 1950 Act to make an order for security for costs is highly significant.

Many practitioners, particularly on the continent of Europe, consider that the power of the court to make orders in relation to security for costs provides an unwanted potential for interference by the court. Some think that this form of security should never be given at all (although it seems hard to justify the possibility of pre-trial attachment in favour of the claimant without the equivalent remedy being available to the respondent). In most international cases where an arbitral institution is involved the court will not exercise its discretion to make such orders. The ICC Rules and the LCIA Rules, for example, will be taken by the courts as representing an agreement between the parties that such matters will be left to the jurisdiction of the tribunal.[20]

Support during the course of the proceedings

The words of Sir John Donaldson reveal the attitudes of the English courts as follows:

> 'the general approach is that once an arbitrator or arbitrators have been appointed and until they have made an award, the function of the Court is to assist rather than to supervise.'[21]

It is in this field that England possibly has a more highly developed legal framework than many other countries although, interestingly, the UNCITRAL Model Law contains broadly equivalent provisions in a number of important respects, for example in relation to the taking of evidence and compelling the production of documents.[22]

In England, these powers of the court are found in Section 12 of the 1950 Act, and include the power to secure the attendance of a witness at arbitration proceedings by the issue of a subpoena through the courts; the power to make orders in relation to discovery or disclosure of documents; the power to order the examination of a witness on commission or by Letters Rogatory; the power to make Orders to permit inspection of any property or thing which is the subject of the arbitration; and the power to authorise the taking of samples or the making of experiments relating to the subject-matter of the arbitration.

Not all commentators welcome the influence of the courts in the conduct of

20 *Bank Mellat* v *Helleniki Techniki SA* [1984] QB 291.
21 *Op cit*, 47 *Arbitration*, at 73.
22 UNCITRAL Model Law, Article 27.

the proceedings. Some feel that the arbitrator should be left to deal with questions of the taking of evidence, the production of documents and the like. Even under English law the arbitrators are themselves empowered to make such orders under Section 12(1), and procedural powers are found in institutional rules, including the UNCITRAL Model Law. Speaking on the subject of arbitration law reform Sir Michael Kerr said:

> 'These matters should, in my view, be left to the discretion of the arbitral tribunal alone, without any specific power of court intervention.'[23]

In England, there exists an interesting and novel additional feature. Section 5 of the 1979 Act provides that if a party fails to comply with the arbitrator's orders then the arbitrator or a party may apply to the court which may grant to the arbitrator powers similar to those the court would itself have in a High Court action to enforce its orders. Thus, for example, a respondent who fails to file a written defence to a claim, despite being ordered to do so by the arbitrator, may find that he is deprived of the right to defend the claim; judgment may be entered against him in default. Equally, a claimant who refuses to give proper details of his claim, when ordered to do so by the arbitrator, may find that his claim is summarily dismissed. These powers prevent the abuse of excessive haste on the part of the claimant or undue tardiness and postponement on the part of the respondent. The arbitrator will have powers to continue with the reference (or discontinue it) if a party fails to comply with one of his orders.

The remedy is, of course, relatively new and it has not been used a great deal. Since an arbitrator's function is essentially to 'determine' disputes and not to make summary findings without considering the merits, the court will usually specifically limit the powers it gives to the arbitrator under this section, depending upon the situation and the abuse which the power is to be used to remedy. The practical effect of these provisions is that where an interlocutory order is made by an arbitrator or umpire in the course of a reference, and a party fails to comply with it within the time specified or, if no time is specified, within a reasonable time, the court offers a remedy. The court may make an order extending the powers of the arbitrator or umpire to enable him to continue with the reference in default of appearance, or compliance with another order, by one of the parties. Therefore the orders available to an arbitrator by virtue of Section 12(6) of the 1950 Act are given added weight and, if necessary, a practical means of enforcement, by Section 5 of the 1979 Act.

As a further illustration, the situation in the Federal Republic of Germany reveals similar powers in the hands of the Courts. Dr Johannes Trappe described the position as follows:

> 'Beside the fact that the Court appoints an arbitrator for a party who fails to do so the Court may have functions to fulfil during the proceedings. Arbitrators are entitled to hear witnesses and experts who voluntarily appear before them. They, however, cannot oblige them to appear; and likewise are not entitled to ask them to give evidence under oath. If a witness is not prepared to testify or if the tribunal considers it appropriate that a

23 *Op cit*, 50 *Arbitration* 3, (1984) at 6.

witness swears on oath, or a witness living outside the town where the arbitration is held should reasonably be heard by his own local Court, or if a public authority should give information, or if a letter should be officially handed over to somebody, it is the ordinary Court which is called upon to take the respective step'.[24]

In England, a further, and interesting, example of court support for the institution of arbitration, rather than simply for the arbitrator himself, is seen in the power of the court to review the fees and expenses demanded by the arbitrator if the parties wish to challenge them. Where the arbitrator refuses to release his award to the parties before his fees and expenses are paid, the parties (or one of them) may pay the sum demanded into court and the arbitrator is then obliged to issue the award pending review by the court.[25] The width of the range of powers given to the courts is further illustrated by the provision in Section 27 of the same Act whereby the court will allow an arbitration to take place out of time where the enforcement of a contractual time limit would be harsh. Therefore, a technicality will not be allowed to defeat a worthy claim.

So, while it is true that the court's supportive powers usually involve offering practical assistance to the arbitrator, the objective is better viewed as that of supporting the institution of arbitration and the parties who have submitted their dispute to it. In the UNCITRAL Working Paper on possible features of the Model Law, Dr Gerold Herrmann put it thus:

> 'Probably the most important principle on which the model law should be based is the freedom of the parties, in order to facilitate the proper functioning of international commercial arbitration according to *their* expectations.'[26]
> (*Emphasis added*)

Enforcement of the award

The importance of the supportive role of the courts in relation to the arbitral process is seen most clearly in relation to the enforcement of arbitral awards, since it is obvious that an award is of no commercial value if it cannot be enforced:

> 'it is at this moment that will be best revealed the qualities and defects of all that has preceded, from the time of drafting of the arbitration clause to that of the award of the arbitrators.'[27]

Much has been written about the 'persuasive' value of an arbitral award; the potential stigma if an award is not implemented; and the fact that, apparently, the majority of awards are 'voluntarily' performed. However, it is suggested that this so called 'voluntary' performance is largely illusory. Most practitioners who advise clients would confirm that, in a huge majority of cases, the losing party is thoroughly aggrieved and wants to know how he can escape from complying with the award. It may be thought that the small

24 'Links between Arbitrators and the Courts', 44 *Arbitration* 73 (1978).
25 1950 Act, s19.
26 United Nations Working Paper A/CN 9/207 (*op cit*).
27 Lalive, 'Enforcing Awards', in *60 Years of ICC Arbitration*, *op cit*, 318, at 321.

proportion of awards that are challenged (either by means of recourse, or by resisting enforcement) does not so much reflect a compliant resignation with which the losing party has greeted the award, but is rather a reflection of the high *quality* of awards and the respect with which the major arbitral institutions are viewed. These arbitral institutions have highly developed procedures and highly respected arbitrators. Their awards are thus more likely to be complied with. In other words, the standard of award-writing has improved over the years, as international arbitrators have become more experienced and proficient, and accordingly challenges have declined in proportion to the total number of awards issued.

The fact remains, however, that without the support of the powers of the state, exercised through the courts, arbitration in the sense that it leads to a 'binding' award could not exist.

For the purposes of enforcement, awards may be categorised into three general classes.

The first category is 'domestic' awards. This does not refer to 'domestic arbitration', which (in slightly over-simplified terms) is where two nationals of the same country arbitrate with each other in their own country. Rather it refers to awards in international arbitrations where enforcement is sought in the country in which the arbitration takes place. This is normally a fairly simple affair. No questions of extra-territoriality are posed. The laws of most developed nations provide for enforcement of a local award in a manner broadly similar to that which applies to the enforcement of a local judgment. Sometimes, the award itself is in fact registered with the local court so that it effectively becomes a judgment.

In England, 'domestic' awards can be enforced either by suing on the award as if it were evidence of a debt or, alternatively, under the provisions of Section 26 of the 1950 Act. In the latter case the successful party may obtain an order under which the award may be enforced as if it were a judgment and execution is levied by court officials.

The second category is that of 'foreign' awards where no treaty exists. This is the most difficult case and, in general, most states require a successful party to start a court action in which he proves the amount awarded as a debt, using the award as evidence. This of course leaves the validity of the award open to challenge by the loser, who may raise arguments in respect of formal or substantive defects in the award, and who is not limited in the arguments he may put forward in this respect. In England a 'foreign' award where no treaty relationship exists is treated as if it were a domestic award. The winning party may either sue on the award or apply for execution under Section 26 of the 1950 Act. In both eventualities the loser will have the opportunity to challenge the validity of the award.

The third, and most important, category is where a 'foreign' award is to be enforced under a treaty relationship with the state in which the arbitration took place. These may be bilaterial treaties, or countries where the Geneva Convention on the Execution of Arbitral Awards 1927 still applies. However, in modern times the most important treaty relationship arises under the New York Convention of 1958. An award made in a country which has ratified the New York Convention is known as a 'Convention Award', and may be enforced by the courts of other Convention countries according to a defined legal framework.

Following the adherence to the New York Convention of Guatemala and Panama in March and October 1984 respectively there are now 68 countries party to it. It is by far the most important element in the enforcement of international arbitration awards where enforcement has to take place in a country other than that in which the arbitration was held, partly because most practitioners advise their clients to select Convention countries as the venue for dispute resolution, and partly because they will normally look first to other Convention countries for enforcement against the loser's assets.

In the quarter of a century or so in which the Convention has been operated, it has been generally considered to be successful, although there have been problems in the lack of a uniform approach by different states, particularly in relation to the grounds for refusal of enforcement contained in Article V. Professor Lalive reflects this view of the Convention as a success and, in part, attributes that to the:

> 'new distribution . . . of the roles between the claimant and the defendant in matters of recognition, and by its more marked confirmation of the international character of awards and of the autonomy of the parties.'[28]

In England, the 1975 Act gives effect to the New York Convention. It appears that, although England was relatively late in ratifying the Convention, awards may be enforced even if they were made before the date of the Act and also where the award was made before the date on which the country in which the arbitration took place adhered to the Convention.[29]

The procedure for enforcing a Convention award in England is set out in Sections 3 and 4 of the 1975 Act. Section 3 provides that a Convention award shall be enforceable in the same ways as an English award, and Section 4 goes on to require the party seeking enforcement to produe the award (duly authenticated), the original arbitration agreement, and, if necessary, an official translation of either or both of the two requisite documents. These provisions reflect the requirements for enforcement set out in the New York Convention in Article IV.

The UNCITRAL Model Law deals with the enforcement of both 'domestic' and 'foreign' awards, and in both cases adopts the basic grounds for refusal of enforcement set out in the New York Convention. It may be hoped that this development will ultimately lead to a wider harmonisation of the ability to enforce arbitration awards against assets wherever they may be, particularly in relation to foreign awards.

Conclusion

Examination of the above topics emphasises that arbitration cannot be effective without the supportive role of the courts, backed by appropriate provisions of law. Hopefully, the existence of the relevant laws, the power of the courts, act in most cases as a deterrent, so that they never actually have to be used. Awards of good quality, professionally prepared, are usually

28 *Ibid*, at 344.
29 *Government of Kuwait* v *Snow (Sir Frederick) & Partners* [1973] 1 WLR 818.

implemented involuntarily, albeit reluctantly, by the losing party. In this way, the businessman who wants to resolve his disputes privately should usually achieve his objective.

However, it is unrealistic to think that arbitration can be 100 per cent 'autonomous' in the sense of having any existence outside the framework of the law, and the exercise of the powers of the state through the courts. The same is not true of the mediation or conciliation processes, which do not result in a binding award. The key to the reason why the powers of the state are an essential ingredient is the fact that an arbitration award is intended to be binding. This binding effect can only be achieved, ultimately, by imposing sanctions which are the prerogative of the sovereign state through the legal system and the courts.

17 The supervisory and adjunctive jurisdiction of American courts in arbitration cases

Joseph D Becker

American courts supervise arbitration proceedings in two ways. First, courts exercise supervisory power, in the literal sense, when they look down (as it were) upon a completed arbitration in order to decide whether the award should be vacated or modified. That operation has not provoked much discussion. The Federal Arbitration Act specifies four grounds for vacating an award and three grounds for modification; it is the rare petitioner who will be successful in invoking any of them.[1] Attempting to vacate an award on grounds of fraud or corruption of the arbitrator, or because of the arbitrator's refusal to hear evidence, or because he has exceeded his powers, is work cut out for incurable optimists. Modification of an award for errors in arithmetic and the like is not of general importance.

Of far greater interest, and controversy, than the direct supervision of awards by American courts is what perhaps should be called the adjunctive operations of courts in relation to arbitration, that is, the process of getting arbitrations started or stopped, and keeping them on course. In procedural terms, these operations are incidents of applications for the stay of judicial proceedings in the presence of a governing arbitration clause; or, reciprocally, applications to stay arbitrations in the presence of questions that are not arbitrable.[2] Such applications may be preceded or accompanied by motions for provisional judicial relief, particularly orders of attachment and preliminary injunctions.[3] Here the perspective and action of American courts is from the side rather than from above. In connection with these operations we are currently witnessing the slow resolution of two controversies of high interest.

1 9 USCA Nos 10, 11 (1970). The Federal Arbitration Act governs proceedings in maritime, interstate, and international commerce. State arbitration acts are omitted from consideration in this paper. Section 10 of the Federal Act permits federal courts to vacate an award (a) where the award was procured by corruption, fraud, or undue means; (b) where there was evident partiality or corruption in the arbitrators; (c) where the arbitrators were guilty of misconduct in refusing to postpone the hearing upon sufficient cause shown, or in refusing to hear pertinent evidence, or in other ways prejudicial to a party; and (d) where the arbitrators exceed their powers or so imperfectly executed them that a definite award was not made. Section 11 permits modification of an award (a) where there was an evident miscalculation or misdescription; (b) where the arbitrators awarded on a material matter not submitted to them; and (c) where the award is imperfect in form not affecting the merits.

2 9 USCA Nos 3, 4 (1970).

3 See, generally, Becker, 'Attachments in Aid of International Arbitration – The American Position', 1 *Arbitration International* 40 (1985).

The first is of particular relevance to international cases that fall under the New York Convention.[4] Article II(1) of the Convention obliges the contracting states to recognise written arbitration agreements. As a corollary of that duty the Convention provides in Article II(3) that a court of a contracting state, when seized of a dispute that is arbitrable under the Convention, must 'refer' the parties to arbitration.

In the United States, and apparently in the United States alone, we have had a curious interpretation of the obligation to refer. Of the handful of decisions on the point, most, including a decision of New York's highest state court, have held that the obligation to 'refer' divests the court of all jurisdiction save the power to direct the parties to arbitration at the place agreed.[5] This view has practically nullified the availability of provisional orders of attachment in aid of arbitration.

Whereas in domestic arbitrations it has always been possible in an appropriate case, and by carefully timed procedures, to obtain an order of attachment securing property of a party against the day when a final judgment may be executed against him,[6] in international cases falling under the Convention most courts that have touched the matter have adopted the simplistic view that a duty to 'refer' parties to arbitration means just that and only that. The court must not do anything other than send the parties away to arbitrate their dispute. This has been done in the teeth of institutional arbitration rules adopted by the parties that expressly permit recourse to courts for interim measures of protection, and in the absence of any suggestion in the meagre legislative history of the Convention of any such intention to emasculate courts.[7]

One would suppose that this interpretation of the duty to refer would also sweep away the provisional remedy of injunction. It should be understood that in the United States, orders of attachment create security interests in property with a degree of priority; injunctions do not have that effect. But the distinction should not be important in this context; the issue is whether the duty to refer prescribed by Article II strips courts of all such provisional powers or none of them. Nevertheless, a recent decision of the federal district court in Manhattan granted a preliminary injunction prohibiting the drawing down of a guarantee letter of credit during the pendency of an arbitration falling under the Convention, with full recognition by the court that the power to grant orders of attachment in international cases is doubtful.[8] The court made no effort to explain the difference between the remedy of attachment and injunction in a case falling under the Convention.

In exercising their adjunctive jurisdiction United States courts have been vexed by yet another problem. It arises from the circumstance that certain kinds of questions are, by statute or declared public policy, not arbitrable in the United States. Claims involving securities fraud[9] or anti-trust

4 21 UST 2517, reprinted following 9 USCA No 201, (1984 Supp).

5 *Cooper* v *Ateliers De La Motobecane, SA*, 57 NY 2d 208 (1982) and cases cited therein.

6 Becker, *op cit*, at 41–3.

7 *Ibid*, at 43–8.

8 *Rogers, Burgin, Shahine and Deschler Inc* v *Dongsan Construction Co Ltd*, 598 F Supp 754, 759 (SDNY 1984).

9 See, eg, *Wilko* v *Swan*, 346 US 427 (1953).

violations[10] are the prime examples. The difficulty is an incident of the inescapable fact that a demand for arbitration may allege a mixture of arbitrable and nonarbitrable claims. That is, a claim of securities fraud, or a claim of unreasonable restraint trade, may be intertwined with a contract claim that would, of itself, ordinarily be fit for arbitration.

A judicial system that affirms the value of arbitration, as does the United States Arbitration Act, must be challenged by such cases. Some of our courts resolve the clash of policies by staying the arbitration proceeding entirely and taking to themselves not only the securities (or antitrust) claims but the ordinary contract issues as well.[11] They have done this not only on grounds of efficiency but to avoid the risk that an arbitration award may decide issues with *res judicata* (collateral estoppel) effects on the subsequent trial of the securities fraud (or antitrust) case; that cannot be permitted if it is assumed that the securities fraud (or antitrust) question is for the court alone.

Other courts have given effect to the policy of the Federal Arbitration Act and ordered arbitration of the ordinary contract claims, reserving to themselves only the non-arbitrable, public policy questions.[12]

Between the two views the United States Supreme Court, on March 4, 1985, made an important choice in a dispute between a stockbroker and a customer who claimed securities fraud and breach of contract on the part of the broker.[13] The Court has come down in favour of bifurcated proceedings: the ordinary contract claims go to arbitration; the securities claim is reserved to the court, which is always in a position to control the degree of issue estoppel, if any, that will be given to the decision of the arbitrators (if the award precedes the court's judgment on the non-arbitrable claim). We will soon know whether the same view applies to anti-trust cases.[14]

In exercising jurisdiction in aid of arbitration proceedings American courts do a great many other things. They will appoint arbitrators when the parties' system of appointment proves deficient[15]; they will remove arbitrators for misconduct[16]; they will enforce certain discovery orders[17]; and, when necessary, they will consolidate several arbitrations into one.[18] American practice here contains no great surprises, and what has been said elsewhere about these matters from the English standpoint[19] may be taken, *mutatis mutandis*, to be the position in the United States.

10 See, eg, *Mitsubishi Motors Corp* v *Soler Chrysler-Plymouth, Inc* 723 F 2d 155 (1st Cir 1983), cert granted, 105 SCt 291 (1984).
11 See, eg, *Dean Witter Reynolds Inc* v *Byrd*, 726, F 2d 552 (9th Cir 1984), rev'd, 84 L Ed 2d 158, 17 BNA Sec Reg & L Rep 430 (March 8, 1985).
12 See, eg, *Dickinson* v *Heinold Securities, Inc*, 661 F 2d 638 (7th Cir 1981).
13 *Dean Witter Reynolds, Inc*, *op cit*.
14 *Mitsubishi Motors Corp*, *op cit*.
15 G Wilner, *Domke on Commercial Arbitration* 20:04 (rev ed 1984).
16 *Ibid*, No 22:03.
17 *Ibid*, No 27:01.
18 *Ibid*, No 27:02.
19 See, Hunter, 'Judicial Assistance for the Arbitrator', Chapter 16, *supra* at 198 *et seq*.

18 The conduct of ICC arbitration proceedings

Ottoarndt Glossner

Introduction

The ICC Rules of today are in essence a reflection of the practical experience of the Court of Arbitration in the years since its inception. They are open universally to any litigant from any part of the world. Consequently they are basically designed as an overall comprising procedure and, therefore, built on the smallest common denominator not without, however, having a special imprint. Thus, the major legal systems, common law, civil law and socialist law are served from a common ground.

The conduct of ICC arbitration proceedings must follow the ICC Rules and necessarily their amendments or completions either according to the wishes of the parties as far as they are free to do so or giving way to the mandatory provisions of the applicable law.

It is the task of this report to elaborate on the more controversial issues rather than to reflect on routine questions of the ICC Rules.

The arbitration agreement

The classical analytical approach is to begin with the arbitration agreement and its impact as a contractual undertaking of the parties' activities in case a dispute arises.

The recommended ICC arbitration clause reads as follows:

> 'All disputes arising in connection with the present contract shall be finally settled under the Rules of Conciliation and Arbitration of the International Chamber of Commerce by one or more arbitrators appointed in accordance with the said Rules.'

The ICC statistics show that a growing number of cases has to be dealt with – in 1983 a case load of 650 had to be handled – and that the willingness of the parties to comply as a rule with an award once rendered is almost absolutely constant: approximately 90 per cent.

This standard clause allows the broadest possible access to the arbitration procedure of the ICC and is accepted as valid by practically all laws of the world which allow arbitration in the international field. The text is self-executing insofar as the ICC Rules provide for the necessary framework to conduct orderly arbitration proceedings. However, potential parties to an arbitration wish to adopt this clause so as to ensure a greater predictability of certain issues in the event of arbitration, such as the number of the arbitrators, the law applicable and the venue. As much as such precision is desirable extreme care is to be applied when completing the text in order to avoid distortion.

Even if there is equality of rights between the partners at the negotiation stage, there are certain issues which cannot be solved to the satisfaction of the parties. In a large contract the parties will generally agree readily on three arbitrators, and if more than two parties are involved in the contract, on the nomination of all three arbitrators by the ICC Court. In small cases parties prefer a single arbitrator for economic reasons (Article 2(2)).

The issue of the applicable procedural law is often a matter of controversy between parties from different countries, because each of them is reluctant to accept the law of the other party's country in case of possibly necessary interferences of a national court. To reach out to a so-called neutral or third country venue is not without problems. It is uncertain whether such third country will accept an arbitration which has no other links to that country but the stipulation of the parties (Article 11,12).[1]

The choice of the substantive law is no less problematic. Unless the parties accept a decision under *amiable compositeur*,[2] the parties may be tempted to choose the law of a third country. Such law may not match the situation of two foreign contractual partners, particularly with respect to mandatory legal provisions in their countries, as opposed to the law in the country of the venue of the arbitration procedure (Article 13).

It is desirable that parties complete the ICC standard arbitration clause, choose the applicable law and agree the number of arbitrators. Another question is whether a derogation of certain provisions of the ICC Rules is recognised by the ICC Court of Arbitration. The court drawing its authority from an agreement of the parties will be interested to maintain the basics of the ICC Rules on the one hand and the utmost freedom of the parties on the other. Naturally, the whole structure of ICC proceedings can be reversed and distorted by additions to and deletions of the ICC Rules. It may be doubtful whether an arbitration agreement which dispenses with the necessity that the arbitrators and the parties draw up terms of reference (Article 13) or that the ICC Court supervises the form of an award (Article 21) can be accepted by the ICC Court as a procedure under the ICC Rules. It occurs that parties agree on the ICC Rules, yet have entrusted the presiding arbitrator with the functions of the ICC Court, which corresponds to an all-out ousting of the ICC Court. It can hardly be upheld that such a structure is an ICC Arbitration: at best it can be considered a simile.

As to the form of the arbitration agreement, there may be certain mandatory provisions in the national or international law applicable. Thus, for example, Article II(1) of the New York Convention requires an agreement to be in writing. In principle, a lack of form of an arbitration agreement can be cured by the parties, if they give their written declaration to the arbitrator.

1 J Robert and Th Carbonneau, *The French Law of Arbitration*, New York 1984, Chapter IX, 'Public Policy and International Arbitration'. See also award *Lybia* v *Liamco*, in VI *Yearbook: Commercial Arbitration* 165 (1981).

2 E Loquin, *L'Amiable Composition en Droit Comparé et International*, Paris, 1980.

The constitution of the arbitration tribunal

The ICC Court is an administrative body, which among other functions undertakes to nominate or to confirm the nomination of arbitrators (Article 1). It grants priority to the parties to nominate an arbitrator. The ICC Court will approve such nomination and there is no known case where the ICC Court has refused such nomination. Should the parties disagree on the nomination or should they not duly proceed with the nomination, the ICC Court will act in their stead by requesting a National Committee of the ICC from a country, other than that where the parties are domiciled, to propose a suitable person (Article 2,6). One or both parties may choose to challenge the appointment of an arbitrator, whereupon the ICC Court decides on such challenge, unless – what is the preferred result – the arbitrator resigns on his own initiative (Article 2(7)). National laws may be contrary to the power of the ICC Court to give a 'final' decision for the challenge to an arbitrator. German law, for example, leaves this authority exclusively with the state court. This means that the ICC Court's decision is subject to a national court's approval.[3]

The arbitration proceedings

Since the ICC Court of Arbitration is an administrative body it is important to know, at what exact time, the arbitration proceedings begin.[4] It is undisputed that when a request for arbitration is rightfully received by the competent arbitration authority, the statute of limitation is interrupted so that one must consider such an act as the beginning of the arbitration proceedings (Article 7,8).[5] This is so regardless of whether there remains a period of time for administrative work before the arbitration can start, or the administration of the proceedings require that the ICC Court first appraise the *prima facie* validity of the arbitration agreement, a decision which may lead to turning down a party's request for arbitration if it is obviously the wrong instance (Article 8,3). Any such decision is an administrative decision and therefore, neither appealable nor enforceable.

The actual competence of the arbitration tribunal is in the hands of such tribunal which exercises the right of *kompetenz-kompetenz*, a decision which is according to the major legal systems subject to approval or rejection by national courts if so requested by a party (Article 8). The arbitration tribunal, once duly constituted, must proceed to elaborate what is known as 'terms of reference' (Article 13). This is a unique device, born out of the spirit of the *compromis* of French law, which needs careful attention. The arbitration

3 BGH 24, 3 (1958).

4 Cohn, 'The Rules of Arbitration of the ICC', 14 *ICLQ* 165 (1965); *Bank Mellat* v *Helleniki T SA* [1984] QB 291. Glossner, 'The Rules of Conciliation and Arbitration of the ICC', in *Essays in Memoriam Eugenio Minoli*, Rome 1974, 218.

5 M Mustill & S Boyd, *The Law and Practice of Commercial Arbitration in England*, London 1983, at 164.

Paragraph 220, second paragraph. German Civil Code provides:

> 'The statute of limitation will be interrupted by the fact that the claimant proceeds with the arbitration application regardless as to whether the arbitrators are nominated or the arbitration tribunal cannot function but after fulfilment of certain conditions'.

proceedings proper are really divided into two stages: one prior to the establishment of the terms of reference, and the other, thereafter, until the end of the proceedings by withdrawal of the claim, by a settlement or by an award.

The arbitrators can establish the terms of reference and let it rotate for signature by the parties. Usually they are well advised to have a draft prepared and what Article 13 allows them to do is to have discussed it orally with the parties. This gives the participants in the arbitration a chance to meet, to get acquainted with one another, to clarify controversial issues and even – *à la rigueur* – arrive at a settlement. Whether it is more advisable to issue a tight inventory of the legal questions to be dealt with – an exclusive list – or a non-exclusive list, has always remained questionable. The former method stipulates to the knowledge of the parties the issues and does not give them a chance to add questions that may come up during the proceedings, unless they mutually agree to allow an extension, for example, to raise counter-claims. The other, the open method, grants such possibility *in se*, but may suffer from being open to claims raised later. In case of the refusal of a party to sign the terms of reference, the ICC Court will direct in its discretion that the proceedings continue. This is a unique and helpful device of ICC arbitration to avoid that undue and maybe *mala fide* acts or omissions cause serious impediments for the orderly course of the proceedings. The legal nature of the terms of reference has been a topic for debate.[6] In any case, once properly signed by the arbitrators and the parties it is an instrument corroborating an existing arbitration clause or possibly curing an invalid one.

Article 11 provides that the proceedings will be conducted in accordance with the ICC Rules and those procedural provisions which the parties or the arbitrators have decided. The previous wording in Article 16 decreed that the law of the place of the arbitration was applicable. The text of 1975 Rules was supposed to give more flexibility and granted to the parties and to the arbitrators more freedom. This meant that certainly neither parties nor the arbitrators can completely dispense with any national law. There were anational proceedings construed in more recent times.[7] The mere fact that the initiative of the ICC to create a convention for the recognition and enforcement of 'international' awards – freed from liens of national laws – has been turned down and that the New York Convention limited itself to 'foreign' awards, seems to exclude speculation, or even raise doubts that the idea of a-national proceedings is – at least as far as ICC arbitration is concerned – a *chose acquise*. Free choice of law on the contrary – is an accepted standard of international arbitration.[8] No national law allows derogation from its mandatory provisions. The *Concordat Suisse* Section 1 exemplifies that states which ratified the New York Convention exercise their prerogatives in that respect.

Article 13(5) provides that the arbitrator is to take into consideration the contract and trade usages. This does not imply that the arbitrator may dispense

6 Cohn, *op cit*, at 156, *et seq.*

7 See eg, Mann, 'England Rejects Delocalised Contracts and Arbitration,' 33 *ICLQ* 193 (1984); *Libyan General Maritime Transport Company* v *Gotaverken Arendal AB*, in VI *Yearbook: Commercial Arbitration* 221, (1981) at 237; *AKSA/Norsolor, Jeantet*, in [1981] *Revue de l'Arbitrage* 306; 'Delocalised Arbitration under the New York Convention', International Law Association, Montreal Conference (1982), British Branch Committee on the Enforcement of International Arbitral Awards, unpublished paper.

8 Mustill & Boyd, *op cit*, at 61.

with the application of any law altogether. Systematically, this provision is preceded by another, namely that the law applicable is to be determined either by the parties or in the absence of their agreement, by the arbitrator.

Some claim that the ICC arbitration is advocating a supranational law, a *lex mercatoria*, instead of following the strict systematics of national laws, applying most naturally the terms of the contract and any given trade usages, which latter in themselves are results of handling a trade or business in observance of the law. The authors of the idea of *lex mercatoria* put a question mark behind their creation and feel that there is a long way to go until by practice and common efforts the *lex mercatoria* will be recognised to replace national laws.[9]

Still in the domain of procedural provisions of national laws, the differences between legal systems in this world come into the picture of ICC arbitration. This is reflected, in particular, in the opposing systems of the common law and civil law countries, the adversial and the inquisitorial approach, which makes it difficult to draw an inventory of similarities at all. The institutions of pre-discovery and cross-examination unknown to the civil law lawyer may suffice as prominent examples.[10] The ICC Rules intentionally do not deal with and settle diverging rules of civil procedure in order not to limit their application. Experience has shown that this has been a wise choice. Arbitrators dealing with cases coming from different systems tackle successfully this problem and give way to a median way, while not strictly applying the rights of the systems they apply a reasonable combination. In a similar spirit, the International Bar Association has created additional evidence rules to bridge the hiatus between the opposing systems.[11]

The language of the arbitration proceedings must be determined by the arbitrator (Article 15(3)). The approach is generally very liberal and takes economic aspects into consideration, so that no superfluous costs arise.

The arbitration award

The arbitrators will have the tendency to end the proceedings with a settlement between the parties in the form of an award by consent (Article 17) thereby making sure that it becomes an enforceable instrument under the New York Convention which covers only arbitration awards. Should, they not arrive at such a solution, they will have to decide according to Article 19,2.

Reasons are to be added to the award in the majority of cases, particularly where according to the national law applicable this is indispensible to make it understandable and open to objection in the enforcement procedure. A dissenting opinion may be attached, where it is allowed or required by the national law applicable. Should an arbitrator refuse his signature under an

9 R David, *L'Arbitrage dans le commerce international*, Collection Etudes Juridiques Comparatives, Paris, 1982; B Goldman, *Le droit des relations economiques internationales*, Paris, 1983; A Kassis, *Theorie generale des usages du commerce, droit compare, contrats et arbitrage internationaux, lex mercatoria*, Paris, 1984.

10 Thompson, 'The Court of Arbitration of the ICC', in *Handbook Institutional Arbitration in International Trade*; Cohn, Domke, Eisemann, eds, (Amsterdam, NY, Oxford), 1977; Cohn, *op cit*, 146.

11 International Bar Association, Supplementary Rules Governing the presentation and reception of evidence in International Commercial Arbitration, May 28, 1983.

award, he must be replaced by the ICC Court of Arbitration. The question comes up whether he is liable for damages, for lack of performance of his duty, because a possible repetition of the proceedings may be a costly affair.

Controversy has surrounded the application of Article 21, which provides that an arbitration award is to be presented by the arbitrators in draft form to the ICC Court which returns the award for signature to the arbitrators when it has supervised the text as to its form. It is an accepted opinion that this request does not limit the arbitrators' freedom of decision, nor does it mean that the ICC Court exercises the rights of a quasi-tribunal or otherwise impinges on the prerogatives of the arbitrators.

The award cannot be disclosed to third parties. This is expressly forbidden by Article 23(3). The ICC Court, however, giving way to a certain reasonable desire by actual or potential parties to arbitration proceedings to learn more about the principles applied according to the ICC Rules, has published in an anonymous way the results of arbitration proceedings. Further, those results that come to the knowledge of the public anyway, when awards – which is the exception – or their enforcement become disputed in the state courts, have been used to draw certain consequences for the application of the ICC Rules.[12]

Conclusion

Adapted to the needs of trade and commerce and to the exigencies of law the ICC Rules have proven in more than 4000 cases that they serve well the conduct of arbitration.

12 Thompson, Derains, and Jarvin, 'Chroniques des sentences arbitrales', in *Clunet*, starting in 1974; 25 abstracts of awards, ICC 1979, included in the participant's Congress folder at the occasion of the 60th anniversary of the ICC Court of Arbitration in 1983; Craig, Paulsson and Park, *ICC Arbitration* (Paris 1984).

19 The conduct of arbitration proceedings under English law

John A Tackaberry

This paper is limited to a brief survey of the degree of flexibility which is available in arbitration under English law, and of some of the steps that can be taken to enhance the chances of reaching what is, it is submitted, the object of all arbitration, namely a speedy but fair result, at reasonable cost.

Autonomy of arbitrators

It is convenient to begin by acknowledging that arbitration law is presently in a state of development in England; and that the main effect of that development is to allow greater autonomy to arbitral tribunals, while maintaining the quality of decisions by enabling the parties to insist on reasoned awards. This change is best exemplified by the abolition of the various forms of case stated procedure by the Arbitration Act 1979. However, it is suggested that the attitude of the courts today is such that it is likely to allow to the arbitrator a wider autonomy during the arbitration in areas other than the investigation of points of law, with the result that there is the opportunity for arbitrators, in seeking to reach fair and speedy answers, to look for and to employ methods of saving costs which would not be available to the courts.

In this context one can usefully compare two judicial statements of recent years with those in a recent and authoritative reference book. In *Bremer Vulkan* v *South India Shipping Corporation*[1] Lord Diplock stated:

> 'There is a whole variety of procedures used in arbitrations for the resolution of disputes between the parties. Most of them do not reflect at all closely the pattern of procedure in an action in the High Court. In many there is no oral hearing or oral evidence; in some, physical inspection by the arbitrator of the subject matter of the dispute is substituted for any other kind of hearing. If the analogy between the court's jurisdiction to dismiss an action for want of prosecution and its jurisdiction to grant an injunction to restrain a claimant from proceeding with a reference under an English arbitration clause is sound in law, it must be applicable to all arbitrations under such a clause and not merely to those in which the actual dispute between the parties that is referred to arbitration is of a kind where it is likely (*although not certain, for this will lie within the arbitrator's discretion*) that

1 [1981] AC 909.

> the proceedings will follow much the same pattern as they would in an action in the High Court.'[2]
> (*Emphasis added*)

In *Carlisle Place* v *Wimpey*[3] Robert Goff J (as he then was) stated:

> '... But in many other cases the terms of the submission are totally silent. In broad terms, ... this is so in the present case. In such circumstances the arbitrator's duty is to decide the matter which has been submitted to him, and he also has a duty to act fairly as between the parties. However, generally speaking, *an arbitrator is the master of his own procedure*. The courts, in my own experience – and no authority has been cited to me otherwise – do not ordinarily attempt to control the procedure in an arbitration. They do not ordinarily give directions to arbitrators. They, of course, have power under s.12 of the Arbitration Act, which expressly confers upon the court the power to make procedural orders, in relation to arbitration. But, generally speaking, courts do not interfere with procedural orders made in the course of hearing of arbitration. It might, of course, be different if an arbitrator failed in his duty to act fairly, though normally one would expect such a matter to come before the court on the basis that there had been misconduct.'[4]
> (*Emphasis added*)

This is of course a first instance decision. I have chosen to cite this particular example of the 'Master of his own Procedure' cases because it is the first of the modern line of authority; and because it comes from a strong judge well versed in arbitration. The facts of the case are also a rather dramatic example, since the arbitrator was proposing to exclude (on the grounds of economy and the avoidance of repetition) evidence which in normal circumstances would clearly be admissible.

Subsequently the same thought has been expounded or referred to in *The Kostas Melas*,[5] the *Bremer Vulcan* case[6] and in *Paal Wilson & Co* v *Partenreederei Hannah Blumenthal.*[7]

On the other hand, in *The Law and Practice of Commercial Arbitration in England*, Mustill & Boyd state:

> 'Certain types of dispute, such as those arising out of engineering and building contracts, are commonly conducted in a manner comparable to proceedings in the High Court; and an arbitrator seized of such a dispute could not properly apply an informal procedure of the type recognised in shipping and commodity arbitrations, without first warning, and *obtaining the consent of*, the parties.'[8]
> (*Emphasis added*)

A little further on Mustill & Boyd comment:

2 *Ibid*, at 976.
3 15 *BLR* 109 (1980).
4 *Ibid*, at 116.
5 *SL Sethia Liners Ltd* v *Naviagro Maritime Corpn, The Kostas Melas* [1981] 1 Lloyd's Rep 18.
6 [1981] AC 909.
7 [1983] 1 AC 854.
8 (Butterworths, London 1982), at 249.

'(f) Relaxation of strict rules of evidence.
It is widely believed that an arbitrator, merely because he is an arbitrator, is empowered to act on evidence which would not be strictly admissible in a Court of Law. This is not so. Arbitrators are bound by the Law of England, and the rules regarding admissibility of evidence are part of that law. Thus, if an arbitrator admits evidence which is inadmissible, he commits an error of law which may be appealed against. Furthermore, if the arbitrator deliberately accepts evidence which is obviously inadmissible he commits misconduct and the award will be set aside, at any rate if the evidence is important. If, however, the misreception is due to an honest mistake, the Court will not interfere.'[9]

It is difficult to reconcile the liberal tenor of the first two quotations with the restrictive precision of the later two quotations.

It is also a little difficult to see the logic of the approach set out in the third quotation. It might be said to amount to a contention of a legally enforceable 'custom of the trade' but this is not easy to reconcile with the concept of an arbitrator who is 'master of his own procedure'. Indeed, the existence of different procedures within a single legal system may more persuasively be rationalised as a convincing example of that very mastership, as arbitrators in different fields respond in their own ways to the needs of the particular disputes before them. What is more, the example of the lengthy and formal type of arbitration dispute cited in the third quotation is not as convincing as it might be. While it is certainly true that in recent years, such disputes have tended to be resolved in lengthy and formal hearings, this has not always been the case. Thirty years ago, construction arbitrations were conducted by lay arbitrators as quickly and informally as shipping ones are today.

The insistence in the last quotation on the strict applicability of the laws of evidence in English arbitrations puts the case, it is submitted, a little too high so far as the climate that exists today is concerned. To put it another way, an attack on an arbitrator for misreception of evidence based simply upon a failure to comply strictly with the rules of evidence applicable in court would not, it is submitted, be very likely to get much sympathy in the contemporary Commercial Court. Rather, it would be necessary to mount such an attack from the broad base of unfair behaviour (see the second quotation above) before one could hope for much success.

In this context it is worth noting that the procedure in a civil action in England is derived from, and still influenced by, the peculiar requirements of trial by jury. This is particularly so as regards the law of evidence.[10]

However, this very fact may provide a rationale to support the pragmatic test of unfair behaviour suggested above, since in applying that law, it is wholly permissible for an arbitrator to take into account its derivation from the jury trial. An arbitrator who deliberately rejects wholesale the law of evidence might well be guilty of misconduct. An arbitrator who accepts that law in general terms but applies it flexibly, bearing in mind the differences between jury trial and trial by judge alone, and between trial by (inexpert) judge and

9 *Ibid*, at 311.

10 See the paper by Ronald Bernstein QC on the *Phantom Lady* delivered to the Chartered Institute of Arbitrators, Guernsey 1984.

(expert) arbitrator, can in most cases reach the desired result by wholly legitimate means.

It is also worth noting that arguments as to the admissibility of evidence are common in trial by jury. They are relatively rare, and are becoming even rarer, in trial by judge alone, notwithstanding that a judge is fully qualified to decide them. A lay arbitrator has neither the qualifications nor (usually) the inclination to decide a technical argument between lawyers as to the admissibility of evidence. A legal arbitrator, though he may have both the qualifications and the inclination, will usually also know how to elude such arguments.

In the premises, this writer starts, perhaps a little controversially, from the proposition that an arbitrator does indeed have a very considerable flexibility of operation and is both in fact and in truth the master of his own procedure.

That said, of course, it is important to enter two major caveats.

Firstly, even if the proposition is justified, sight must never be lost of the fact that arbitration is a consensual matter so far as the parties are concerned. Accordingly, if both parties to the arbitration agree, they are perfectly entitled to *insist* upon following any particular procedure even if it be wholly at odds with that which the arbitrator would wish to follow.

Secondly, and it may well be a necessary conclusion from the first proposition, it is critical that any arbitrator who is minded to embark on any course of action which may come as a surprise to either or both parties, should take especial care to ensure that both parties are apprised of what he is minded to do well in advance. Furthermore he should afford them a reasonable opportunity to express any objection they might have, either to him or, if they are so minded, to the courts. There is no difficulty about formulating a procedure to enable this to be done while protecting the arbitration against time wasting and unnecessary delay.

Areas for exercise of arbitrator's authority

With this the basic approach in mind, I have decided to take four steps which will occur in some form in the course of most arbitrations and look at how they might be approached so as to achieve the economy and speed which is, as I have suggested above, the aim of all arbitrations. I shall necessarily concentrate on the lengthy and complicated type of case. Those that are already brief and speedy need less consideration.

Rather than take the wider brief, I shall concentrate on English law, and will from time to time make particular reference to points at which an arbitrator operating under the English system can get away from 'the adversarial system' – which anyway is now seen in its purest forms, perhaps, only in the criminal courts. It should also be borne in mind, of course, that many international arbitrations are governed by English procedural law, so the points hereafter set out are relevant both in the domestic and in the international sphere.

The following four aspects of arbitration will be considered:

1 The initial formulation of the claim
2 The definition of issues

3 The choice of documents for the hearing
4 The reception of evidence

The initial formulation of the claim

The first question, it is submitted, which an arbitrator should ask himself is the format in which he wants a claim to be presented at the commencement of the arbitration. For example, he may wish to see a very brief statement of the nature of the claimant's claim formulated in a matter of two or three pages. Or he may wish to have a fully detailed statement of the claim supported either at the same time or subsequently by copious schedules and appendices. Or he may wish to have a statement of the case supported by the principal documents relied upon. Or he may prefer some other method or combination of methods. However, he must ask himself that initial question: How does he want the case presented? Of course, to answer the question intelligently he will need the assistance of the parties. This assistance can either be obtained by way of an invitation to them to let him have their comments on any proposed particular method of pleading the case, or by way of a brief meeting to discuss the point.

Having once decided upon a particular method, he should review the situation from time to time to make sure that the chosen method is indeed producing the desired result; namely, identification of the issues clearly and simply.

To put it another way, what is sought to be avoided is the obfuscation of the issues by the way in which they are formulated. I recently came across Points of Claim to which were annexed so many schedules that, in the final bundle for the hearing one did not get to the Points of Defence until one was nearly at page 5000. I am sceptical whether such a lengthy formulation can ever be in any sense helpful, and, for my own part, I usually prefer as short a statement of case as can be managed, supported by *principal* documents relied upon.

However, it is sufficient for the purposes of this discussion, if I simply emphasise the need to make a positive, and, so far as possible, informal choice on this matter; and the need to review it from time to time to see if it is working out as it should.

The definition of issues

Once the parties have completed their initial written formulation of their respective cases, it is a useful exercise to embark upon the task of defining the issues. There are various reasons for this.

Firstly, it enables one to identify those weaknesses in the pleading which genuinely require elaboration. One effective test is for the arbitrator to ask himself whether, on the basis of the material before him, he would be able to identify the issues, to identify the relevant documents and to embark upon the task of obtaining evidence. If the answer to any of these questions is in the negative, then it is likely that some form of elaboration will be necessary.

The second purpose of defining the issues is to provide an informed basis upon which to approach the formulation of the bundle for the hearing.

Accordingly, an arbitrator should be keen to press the parties to put before him a formulation of issues or to meet with him to discuss the issues with a view to their formulation, or to meet each other with a similar view. It is not, of course, suggested that the issues once formulated become a binding and rigid framework beyond which the arbitration cannot go. However, it is important to try to establish at an early stage what the issues are since that substantially enhances the prospect of keeping the costs to a minimum. It achieves this firstly, by high-lighting those areas which genuinely need evidence or documentation and those which do not; and secondly, by maximising the chance of the parties settling a part or the whole of the dispute.

The benefit which can be derived from this exercise is illustrated in quite striking form by an example culled from an international arbitration in the early 1970s. The issues having been defined with maximum particularity (in a complicated construction case) the arbitrator then invited the parties to produce in concert a list of the findings of fact each sought in connection with each issue. Such an exercise is really only an extension of the Notice to Admit procedure. Nonetheless it is an important extension since producing it in concert maximises the chances of agreement – and thus the highlighting of the real issues of factual dispute. What is more, the concerted nature of the exercise was made clear by the way the exercise was done physically.

The claimant first set out on the left hand side of the schedule a list of the findings of fact which it desired, in a proper logical order. The respondent then set out its desired findings opposite the claimant's; and interposed any additional findings it wanted. Both sides then met to discuss the result, and to see what agreement could be reached. At the end of that meeting the right hand side of the schedule was annotated to note the following, using a convenient shorthand – as for example the letters set out below.

(a) The finding of fact is agreed and its relevance is agreed.
(b) The parties contend for different findings and agree on the relevance of an appropriate finding.
(c) The parties agree on the finding of fact but disagree on its relevance.
(d) The parties disagree on the finding of fact and on its relevance.

Further distinctions can be formulated as may be needed. Highlighting can be used to identify differences of intention which are agreed to be important; and of course grouping by issue, or claim, or whatever can further refine the exercise.

The approach proved to be extremely effective; although it depends to some extent upon an appreciable amount of sensible cooperation between the parties. However, even if there is not that cooperation, the exercise will be likely to assist the arbitrator in determining at the end whether one party or the other was being unreasonable, or indeed whether both of them were – a determination which may be useful when it comes to costs.

Choice of documents for the hearing

Once the issues are defined, it is then possible to turn to the question of documents. It is helpful to begin this section by looking at the English court's approach to discovery and inspection of documents.

The principle of discovery which is enforced by the English courts is a broad one. It is described in the Rules and in the leading cases on the topic as follows:

The party is 'to make and serve . . . a list of the documents which are or have been in his possession custody or power relating to any matter in question . . .'[11] The inspecting party is not limited to documents which would be admissible in evidence[12] nor to those which would prove or disprove any matter in question; any document which, it is reasonable to suppose, 'contains information which may enable the party (applying for discovery) either to advance his own case or to damage that of his adversary, if it is a document which may fairly lead him to a train of inquiry which may have either of these two consequences' must be disclosed.[13]

However, broad though the principle is, it is limited to the matters in question – a fact which is often forgotten, or ignored.

It should also be noted that discovery essentially means listing. The exercise of looking at documents is that of inspection. The difference is substantial. The former requires the parties to list the documents which come within the relevant principles even if they are privileged from production for inspection. When one comes to inspection, however, one is only able to see those documents which are *not* privileged, unless, of course, privilege has been waived. One of the purposes of the listing exercise is to enable each party to know the general nature of the documents in respect of which privilege is being claimed, so that in an appropriate case that claim of privilege can be challenged.

Clearly, what any party is looking for, are admissions in the other party's documents which help the searching party to establish its side of any particular disputed issue. For example, in an argument about workmanship, internal reports of the other party's foreman which also complain about his men's poor workmanship, are of considerable assistance to any tribunal (and of course to the party challenging the quality of the workmanship) in determining that issue.

The process is a valuable one in assisting the English courts to resolve disputes of fact which come before them. However, there is equally no serious dispute but that the procedure does not generate the same enthusiasm or respect outside the common law systems as it does within them. Indeed, it is obvious that in a dispute between parties emanating from different legal systems a common law discovery approach is likely to be less satisfactory because of the danger of the parties from different jurisdictions approaching the exercise in a different way. One therefore must ask what the arbitrator in an international arbitration being conducted in accordance with English law should regard as the proper approach.

On the assumption that the procedural law is indeed English law, then the arbitrator's powers are determined by Section 12 of the Arbitration Act 1950, which provides in pertinent part:

> '(1) Unless a contrary intention is expressed therein, every arbitration agreement shall, where such a provision is applicable to the reference, be deemed to contain a provision that the parties to the reference, and all persons claiming through them, respectively submit to be examined by the arbitrator or umpire, an oath or affirmation, in relation to the matters in dispute, and shall, subject as aforesaid, produce before the

11 Rules of the Supreme Court, Order 24/2.

12 *Compagnie Financiere du Pacifique* v *Peruvian Guano Co* (1882) 11 QBD 55, *per* Esher, MR, at 62, 63; *O'Rourke* v *Darbishire* [1920] AC 581, at 630.

13 *Compagnie Financiere du Pacifique* v *Peruvian Guano Co*, *op cit*, at 63.

arbitrator or umpire all documents within their possession or power respectively which may be required or called for, and do all other things which during the proceedings on the reference the arbitrator or umpire may require.'

It is submitted that this gives the arbitrator a very wide discretion. The discretion, so it is submitted, enables him to direct that there should be no discovery at all, as well as going to the other extreme in directing that there should be full discovery along the lines of an English court hearing.[14] If this is so, then this is a very important discretion and, as with the formulation of the case initially, so with this part of the case, the arbitrator must think very hard about precisely how he is going to approach this problem.

In reaching his conclusion on this matter, the arbitrator should be considerably assisted by any effective formulation of the issues, since he could, if he wished, restrict discovery to different levels of intensity on particular issues. He should also take the opportunity to consider how wide ranging the documentary exercise should be. Thus, it is possible to separate the documents which are likely to be thrown up by the dispute into various categories.

The primary group of documents which one expects to find generated by the dispute are the *inter partes* documents, the letters between the parties or documents which in some other way have passed between them. For example, contracts, drawings, charterparties, general correspondence and the like. The second group of documents which one expects to find are those documents which are internal to one or other of the parties. From the point of view of advancing one's case, these are likely to be the most material and are certainly in many ways much more important than the *inter-partes* documents. It is also in this area that one begins to tread on the corns of privilege and confidentiality. The documents which are internal to one or other of the parties may well be confidential by reason of the fact that, for example, they constitute advice from an in-house lawyer. Equally, if they constitute an internal appreciation of the situation, they are likely to give rise to cries of confidentiality.

The third group of documents are those passing between a person or body that is a party to the arbitration or litigation and one that is not. The next group is of documents which are in the possession of bodies or persons that are 'related' to one of the parties to the arbitration, for example agents such as architects or engineers, dealers such as brokers, subsidiary or parent companies, etc. This is a difficult area even for the courts, although in their case the tendency is to insist, so far as they possibly can, upon the production of the relevant documents.[15]

Even this 'broad brush' categorisation of documents serves to highlight the importance of the arbitrator addressing his mind to the question of the precise formulation of the directions for discovery.

What is more, given a proper definition of issues and reasonable cooperation between the parties, such a direction can be finely tuned to an appreciably higher degree – with consequent savings of time and money.

14 *Cf* the position in quality arbitrations as exemplified by *Naumann* v *Edward Nathan* (1930) 27 LlLR 359.

15 See *Lonrho Ltd* v *Shell Petroleum Co Ltd* [1980] QB 358 (Discovery was refused because of the difficulties involved).

It should also be noted that there is a further category of documents, namely those that are solely in the possession of a person or body wholly unrelated to either of the parties to the arbitration. Examples of these are the documents generated by local or statutory authorities in the exercise of their statutory functions. Here, no question arises of either party being obliged to discover such documents, since clearly they are not in the power, possession or control of the relevant party. However, while no question of discovery of such documents can arise, an arbitrator may wish to consider suggesting to the parties whether they or one of them should seek to bring those documents before him by way of *subpoena duces tecum*.

It will be seen from the above that considerable flexibility is available to the arbitrator in identifying the body of documents from which the choice of those to go before him at the full hearing can be made. I put it this way because identification of the documents by the process which I have just described is not (contrary to what many seem to believe) the end of the matter. One then has to go on to make the selection.

This brings one to another problem. Let us suppose that the dispute arises out of some aspect of business life which has necessarily and inevitably generated a substantial amount of paper. This will generally be the case with a contract for the construction of some major work of building or civil engineering or the construction of a substantial ship. Unfortunately, people's time and certainly the time of professionally qualified people is extremely expensive. Even more unfortunately the photocopier is an immediately available and comparatively cheap tool. The union of these two misfortunes ultimately tends to give birth to a third: the failure to discriminate when documents are being assembled for the hearing. What is likely to happen is that somebody (inevitably rather junior because less expensive and also, because of lack of experience, inclined to operate on the principle that it is safer to have something in than to leave it out) will have picked out virtually every conceivable document relating to the *dispute*, and will include them in the bundle. Indeed, given two or more people of such comparative juniority representing different parties, and often the same document will appear twice or even more times in the bundle. (Such duplication may be appropriate where an important document has been annotated – but otherwise it is rarely justified.)

However assembling the bundle in this way ignores two criteria which are of the utmost importance. Firstly it ignores the need to restrict the bundle to the documents which relate to the issue actually in dispute. Secondly it fails to restrict the bundle to the *material* documents relating to these issues.

The consequence is often an agreed bundle which is produced in an enormous number of copies, which is largely irrelevant and which will end up being unused in the course of the proceedings. Indeed, as is pointed out by Mustill & Boyd, it is quite common to find the lawyers who actually conduct the hearing extracting from the 'agreed bundle' a working bundle of the documents to which they will actually be referring.[16]

In consequence, the apparent saving in the original 'screening' of the documentation is more than offset by the unnecessary cost inherent in far too

16 Mustill & Boyd, *op cit*, at 288.

large a bundle being copied and distributed and in the consequential loss of time during the actual hearing itself.

This tendency towards indiscriminate copying of documents is exacerbated where, perhaps for good reasons, preparation of the bundle is left to a late stage. Of course it must be borne in mind that one of the factors which may influence the parties or their advisers is the realisation that the substantial cost involved in making an intelligent and discriminating choice of documents well in advance of the hearing may inhibit or destroy the chances of settlement.

It is therefore clear that an arbitrator's control on this aspect of the case does not and should not be limited simply to ensuring that the exercise of identifying the documents which are or are not to be discovered is kept within bounds – although this exercise should enhance the chances of success on the second stage. That control must continue by one means or another to endeavour to ensure that a proper exercise is carried out in the choosing of documents for the hearing. For example, the arbitrator may at some suitable moment engage in a firm homily on the subject of the importance of considering carefully the documents which are to go into the agreed bundle with a view to avoiding the usual unwieldy set of lever arch files.

Further, an arbitrator who is of the view that one or other of the parties is 'going over the top' in the context of putting documents into the agreed bundles can, in my view, properly order that each document that is put into the agreed bundle be colour coded or marked in some manner, so as to enable him to see instantly whether this document was put in at the instance of both parties or of one party alone. By this means it is possible at the end of the hearing to identify with fairly rapid certainty whether an excessive number of documents has been put in by one party or the other.

Another 'control' which an arbitrator can exercise is to order that the cost of discovery be separately recorded. By either or both routes he is able at the end of the day to consider the extent to which documentation before him has been of help to him and to make an appropriate order as to costs.

Finally in this area, an arbitrator should take an interest in how the bundle is to be put together. Of course if both parties agree on the method, he should be loath to interfere. However, very often they do not; and it is important to prevent this dispute being left unresolved until a week before the start of the hearing – or even worse three weeks into it.

Among the questions to be asked are these:

(a) Is the bundling to be basically by a single chronological bundle; or is it to be by subject; or by some other criterion.
(b) How are seminal documents to be coped with – eg, the contracts, charterparties, etc.
(c) Where are documents such as minutes of meetings to go? Separately grouped but with own reference sheets in a general chronology or in the relevant subject file? Or directly into the main file? Or how?
(d) Technical documents – drawings, charts, graphs, etc.

The ultimate example of what is to be avoided (and which *can* happen) is where both parties each bundle all the documents separately and on an entirely different principle! This is a real problem because both sides advisers and particularly the advocates will have done a great deal of work on the case, using the bundle they have prepared. It is very difficult indeed to expect either side to switch (without a lengthy adjournment) to the other side's bundle (or for both to switch to a composite bundle). Notes (running to many pages) have to be reannotated, references have to be changed, documents may have to be re-highlighted, etc. The size of this task is easily underestimated (particularly by an arbitrator who has never been an advocate!) and a proper amount of time *has* to be given to it, if one party is not to be severely handicapped in the presentation of its case.

The reception of evidence

Generally

The main source of factual evidence in the courts is the oral testimony of first-hand witnesses. Anyone who is familiar with the English courts will be familiar also with the process whereby such evidence is elicited by the advocates of the relevant parties by way of examination in chief, cross-examination, and examination in reply. The first question which one therefore has to ask is the extent to which arbitration can or should depart from the rules concerning the reception of the factual evidence of witnesses which the courts have evolved for themselves.

It is suggested that the arbitrator should start from a standpoint different from that of the courts, in that he should have confidence in his own ability to weigh the material before him and to resist the undue influence of apparently prejudicial matters of little weight. He should also bear in mind particularly, it is suggested, that he is free to break from the traditional manner of eliciting oral evidence which can be seen in the High Court on any working day. Particularly where the issues are complex, he should endeavour to ensure that written statements have a greater part to play.

Accordingly it is suggested that, where possible, an arbitrator should consider seeking to ensure that the proofs of evidence or skeletons of proofs of evidence of the proposed witnesses of fact are exchanged well in advance of the commencement of the hearing. The effectiveness of this manoeuvre is dependent, *inter alia*, upon the parties having identified the issues in an effective and realistic manner; and on the parties having put together a proper working bundle. If, however, both these steps have been taken, there is no reason why in most cases such a direction should not be issued. Of course, no party should be limited simply to the evidence which is contained in the statements which are so exchanged. However, one is perhaps entitled to be sceptical if one party produces a fresh tranche of factual evidence which is not in the statements, or indicated in the skeletons, unless there is an extremely good reason for it being absent therefrom. Secondly, it is suggested that an arbitrator should consider directing the parties to indicate the order in which, subject to unforeseen circumstances, they propose to call their witnesses. Again, while one might be reluctant to enforce such an order strictly, one is entitled to ask any party seeking subsequently to follow a different route why that party thinks it necessary to change the order once it has been established.

Armed with these two approaches, it should be appreciably easier to identify the points at which it may be necessary to have full oral evidence, and to restrict that evidence in those points. The effect of this, of course, is very substantially to reduce the hearing time and therefore the cost of the proceedings. The identification of the real points of departure between the various factual witnesses may also be of assistance to the parties in their endeavour to settle the dispute. In making the directions for exchange of written proofs of evidence of fact, arbitrators should bear in mind and indeed consider with the parties the question of whether or not each party should have the right to insist that any witness whose statement has been so put in should be tendered for cross-examination or whether this should be a matter essentially for the discretion of the arbitrator.

Similarly, the arbitrator should be prepared to consider evidence which strictly would not be admissible in the courts, such as hearsay evidence. It is suggested that this follows from the contention that the arbitrator should be able to weigh up the various types of evidence which are put before him. Hearsay evidence clearly is of appreciably less weight than direct evidence, but it is, it is suggested, difficult to say that in a rational world it should have no weight at all.

Similarly, in making the order for exchange of proofs or skeletons of proofs, the arbitrator should consider with the parties the extent of the right of each party to seek to call further or different evidence. This might easily arise if a party finds, having read the evidence of the other side, that it feels that it does need other evidence or witnesses if it is properly to meet the case being put against it.

However, in order to ensure that nobody deliberately holds back evidence in the hope of obtaining a tactical advantage, any such application should be carefully scrutinised, and the reason why the evidence was not put forward in the first place ascertained. In this context, it is again worth noticing the importance of having correctly identified the issues and having produced a proper bundle. Clearly the greater the extent to which this has been done, the greater the likelihood the initial statements will be or at least should be comprehensive for most practical purposes.

Expert evidence

So far as the courts are concerned, expert evidence can be called as a general rule only with the leave of the court. Such leave is granted subject to the supply to the other side in advance of the hearing of a written report containing the gist of the proposed expert's evidence. Thus the court's approach to expert evidence corresponds with the approach which has been suggested above as that which an arbitrator might adopt to factual evidence.

When an arbitrator comes to deal with expert evidence, it is suggested that he should begin by asking himself the question whether any expert evidence is necessary at all. After all, in England arbitrators will very often have a highly relevant expertise in the context of the subject-matter of the dispute. That is why they have been appointed. Presumably therefore they are expected by the parties to use that expertise.[17] It must therefore be questionable whether an expert witness is of as much assistance to a lay arbitrator as he would be to a judge. It follows that perhaps the right course is to start from the assumption

17 See, for example, *Mediterranean and Eastern Export Co Ltd* v *Fortress (Manchester) Limited* and *Thomas Borthwick (Glasgow) Limited* v *Faure Fairclough Limited* [1968] 1 Lloyd's Rep 16.

that the parties will need the arbitrator's leave before they may call expert evidence. When that leave is sought, the arbitrator may enquire as to the need for that evidence.

Of course, if the parties agree, without reference to the arbitrator, that each is to have leave to call expert evidence, then that rather takes the ground from underneath the arbitrator's feet – but then any of the propositions discussed in this paper, may be overridden by the agreement of the parties. Arbitration is a consensual activity in the first place; and is always subject to the effect of that joint consent at any particular point along the road.

If, whether because the arbitrator thinks it is useful or because parties have so agreed, expert evidence is to be called, then there should be an exchange of reports, the governing principles being those discussed in relation to factual witnesses.

Abbreviating evidence

Arbitrators should also consider another method of endeavouring to abbreviate the process of formal evidence in full hearing, namely by having the parties' witnesses on particular topics meet to endeavour to agree:

(i) what their evidence is where they are agreed, and
(ii) the differences between their evidence where they disagree.

This is a practice which has hitherto been confined generally to expert witnesses, but it should be possible in a suitable case to extend it to factual witnesses.

If, however, such a meeting is being set up, it is important to establish that all the participants are operating on the same basis. If that is not done, it is likely to disadvantage one or other of the parties. Thus, it is necessary, when organising such a meeting, to establish whether the meeting is to be an open meeting or without prejudice; to establish whether the participants have full authority to agree or not according to their own opinion, understanding the discretion; to determine the method in which any such agreements or disagreements are to be recorded, and to determine the method by which those agreements or disagreements are brought to the attention of the tribunal. In addition, it should be determined whether the meeting is to be attended by lawyers.

By the above means, it should be possible to reduce significantly the length of time expended in taking both the evidence of fact and expert opinion evidence of witnesses. Obviously where the methods indicated above fail to resolve the particular points which are the ones of critical importance in the case, then that is the appropriate moment at which to resort to the traditional full-scale oral hearing.

By way of conclusion I turn to the point at which I began. It is suggested that the overall guiding rule which an arbitrator should bear in mind in all stages of the conduct of the arbitration is the following: he has a very wide discretion in the control of the procedure of an arbitration, and it is a discretion which it is suggested should be exercised vigorously with the view to shortening and speeding up a procedure, while being fair to both parties. It is above all important for an arbitrator to ensure that he does not surprise the parties by his approach,[18] and it follows therefore that the sort of methods which are discussed above should certainly be raised and discussed with the parties. It is essential that they should have an opportunity to consider the proposed method, particularly since some of the suggestions may be regarded as controversial. Once informed, the parties may agree that the method proposed by the arbitrator is or is not appropriate. In either case that is that. Where however they *dis*agree, it is essential that the arbitrator be aware of the objections and take them into account before a final decision is made.

The golden rule which governs the exercise of the English arbitrator's wide discretion is the avoidance of surprise. Given that, and given a result which is fair to both parties, it will be comparatively difficult for either party to challenge the arbitrator's actions in the English courts.

18 See, for example, *Fisher* v *PG Wellfair Limited* [1981] 2 Lloyd's Rep 514.

20 Finality of arbitral awards and judicial review

Clive M Schmitthoff

The problem of judicial review

Arbitration is essentially a contractual system of dispute resolution. The parties agree that their dispute, or any dispute which may arise between them in the future, shall be settled by a private judge, the arbitrator, or a private court, the arbitration tribunal. As a contractual arrangement, arbitration is, at least in theory, governed by the principle of party autonomy. According to this principle the parties are at liberty to make such arrangements as they like but, as is well known, in all legal systems the principle of party autonomy is subject to a great and growing number of qualifications. In English law, the principle of freedom of contracting is not only limited by public policy considerations but also by a host of mandatory statutory provisions, contained in enactments such as the Unfair Contract Terms Act 1977, the Consumer Credit Act 1974 and the Supply of Goods and Services Act 1982.

In the law of arbitration, the principle of party autonomy postulates that the award should be final and there should be no judicial review on its merits. This, at least, is usually the intention of the parties. Provided that the arbitration proceedings are conducted in accordance with the requirements of natural justice, the parties are normally prepared to accept that the arbitrator may err in his decision on a point of fact or law. After all, public judges may also err, and the whole appellate hierarchy of the courts is founded on this assumption and aims at eradicating any mistake which, in the opinion of the higher judges, the trial judge may have made. But this process of rectifying a judicial error is slow and costly. One of the great advantages of arbitration, in the eyes of the business community, is that it eliminates this process. The experienced or well advised businessman knows that the other advantages claimed for arbitration over litigation, namely that it is cheaper or speedier, are questionable. But parties preferring arbitration to litigation expect at least finality of the settlement of their dispute and avoidance of costly and lengthy appellate proceedings. The state, on the other hand, has another interest. The courts fear that the uniformity of the law is lost if they do not exercise some kind of review over arbitrations, at least as far as questions of law are involved. Atkin LJ (as he then was) justified the new obsolete 'case stated' procedure by saying that, if the parties were allowed to oust the jurisdiction of the courts on questions of law, 'the result might be that in time codes of law would come to be administered in various trades differing substantially from the English mercantile law',[1] and one of the most eminent – and bluntest – commercial judges of this country, Scrutton LJ, said, 'There must be no Alsatia in England where the King's writ does not run.'[2] The conflicting views on the desirability of finality and the need for judicial review are the crucial issues in the relationship between arbitration and the courts.

The two kinds of judicial review

Before this issue is examined it is necessary to define what is understood by 'judicial review'.

There are, in fact, two kinds of judicial review and it is confusing and misleading if they are not kept separate because they are entirely different in character.

The first type of judicial review concerns the question whether the requirements of natural justice were observed in the arbitration proceedings and the arbitration agreement is valid under the law to which the parties have subjected it. The second type of judicial review concerns the merits of the award and here the issue is whether the arbitrator has fallen into an error.

These two types of judicial review will have to be examined later. It will be seen that quite different considerations apply to them. A judicial review of the first type is admitted by the courts of all countries because they consider it to be within the contemplation of the parties when agreeing on arbitration. But the judicial review of the second type, namely on the merits, is, as we shall see, a more questionable affair.

Judicial review in transnational arbitrations

Before proceeding to a closer examination of these two types of judicial review, it has to be considered whether any type of judicial review should be admitted in transnational arbitrations.

This, of course, raises the question whether transnational arbitrations exist at all[3] and also the wider question: what is transnational law? I have expressed my understanding of this term in the following passage[4]:

> 'It is ... wrong to attribute the character of international or supranational law to international trade law. It acquires its autonomous character by leave and licence of all national sovereigns. In character it is very different from public international law. Ultimately it is founded on national law but has been developed by international business in an area in which all national

1 In *Czarnikow & Co* v *Roth, Schmidt & Co* [1922] 2 KB 478, 491; On the old 'case stated' procedure, see CM Schmitthoff, 'Arbitration: The Supervisory Jurisdiction of the Court' in [1967] *JBL* 318.

2 *Ibid*, at 488.

3 Delaume, 'L'arbitrage transnational et les tribunaux nationaux' 111 *Clunet* 521 (1984); Sir Michael Mustill, 'Transnational Arbitration in English Law, [1984] *Current Legal Problems* 133.

4 Clive M Schmitthoff, *Commercial Law in a Changing Economic Climate*, 2nd ed, London 1981, at 22.

> sovereigns are, in principle, disinterested. The best way to describe the peculiar character of international trade law is to refer to it as transnational law.'

My understanding of transnational law is thus that it consists of uniform rules admitted by national sovereigns and developed by international commercial custom, in modern times often given a definite form by the so-called formulating agencies, such as the ICC, UNCITRAL, Unidroit, and others. Transnational law is thus founded on a parallelism of national laws, but it is not derived from a supranational source. Thus understood, it is, in my view, futile to deny its existence. Its vitality and practical effectiveness are demonstrated by formulations like the UCP or Incoterms and by conventions like the Hague-Visby Rules and the CMR.

From this point of view, it is equally futile to deny that transnational arbitration exists. There are at present four great international arbitration centres in the world.[5] They are: the Court of Arbitration of the International Chamber of Commerce in Paris, the American Arbitration Association in New York, the International Centre for Settlement of Investment Disputes in Washington and the London Court of International Arbitration. Their rules are widely used all over the world. They deal with transnational arbitrations.

Since, according to the definition of transnational law given earlier, the transnational character of these arbitrations is nationally founded, the judicial review of transnational arbitrations does not cause any special problems. The only question may be: the court of which country shall exercise judicial review? But this is an apparent rather than a real problem. After all, transnational arbitrations are not held *in vacuo*. The arbitration tribunal must sit somewhere and, if there is a gap in the transnational rules of arbitration procedure, it has to be filled by resorting to the national law of procedure of the forum. And a transnational award has to be enforced in a national jurisdiction and can be enforced there only in accordance with the national law. Consequently, even in transnational arbitrations there is always a nexus with some national court which can exercise a judicial review.

Judicial review on questions of natural justice and legality

As already observed, the courts of all countries exercise a judicial review over arbitrations on questions of natural justice and legality because they consider it a precondition of the reference to arbitration by the parties that these requirements are observed.

International and national formulations sometimes contain lists of cases in which an arbitral award shall be refused recognition or enforcement on the ground that fundamental requirements of natural justice or legality have been disregarded. The most important of these lists is contained in Article V of the New York Convention which states:

> '1. Recognition and enforcement of the award may be refused, at the

5 See Carbonneau, 'Etude histoire et comparée de l'arbitrage: Vers un droit materiel de l'arbitrage commercial international fondé sur la motivation des sentences,' in 36 *Revue Internationale de Droit Comparé*, 727 (1984), at 758.

request of the party against whom it is invoked, only if that party furnishes to the competent authority where the recognition and enforcement is sought, proof that:

(*a*) The parties to the agreement . . . were, under the law applicable to them, under some incapacity, or the said agreement is not valid under the law to which the parties have subjected it or, failing any indication thereon, under the law of the country where the award was made; or

(*b*) The party against whom the award is invoked was not given proper notice of the appointment of the arbitrator or of the arbitration proceedings or was otherwise unable to present his case; or

(*c*) The award deals with a difference not contemplated by or not falling within the terms of the submission to arbitration, or it contains decisions on matters beyond the scope of the submission to arbitration, provided that, if the decisions on matters submitted to arbitration can be separated from those not so submitted, that part of the award which contains decisions on matters submitted to arbitration may be recognised and enforced; or

(*d*) The composition of the arbitral authority or the arbitral procedure was not in accordance with the agreement of the parties, or, failing such agreement, was not in accordance with the law of the country where the arbitration took place; or

(*e*) The award has not yet become binding on the parties, or has been set aside or suspended by a competent authority of the country in which, or under the law of which, that award was made.

2. Recognition and enforcement of an arbitral award may also be refused if the competent authority in the country where recognition and enforcement is sought finds that:

(*a*) The subject-matter of the difference is not capable of settlement by arbitration under the law of that country; or

(*b*) The recognition or enforcement of the award would be contrary to the public policy of that country.'

The importance of this reservation of judicial review will be appreciated when it is realised that on January 1, 1984 some 70 countries were parties to the New York Convention though some of them subject to declarations and reservations. Among the countries which adhered to the New York Convention is the United Kingdom. Section 5 of the Arbitration Act 1975 reproduces the list in Article V of the New York Convention in an amended form. Other lists of reservations of judicial review of what has been described here of the first type are contained in Article 36 of the Swiss Concordat of 1969 and Section 20 of the Swedish Arbitration Act 1929. The most modern formulations are to be found in the French Decree on International Trade Arbitration of 1980[6] and the UNCITRAL Model Law. They may be quoted in full.

The French Decree of 1980 deals with international trade arbitration. It provides that a decision refusing the recognition or enforcement of a foreign award is subject to appeal only in the following instances:

1 absence, nullity or expiry of the arbitration agreement;

6 Introduced into the French Code of Civil Procedure by the Decree of May 12, 1981.

2 irregular appointment of the arbitrators;
3 the arbitrator's failure to respect the terms of reference;
4 violation of the principle of fairness;
5 when it is contrary to international public policy as to recognition or enforcement.

The UNCITRAL Model Law provides in Article 34(2)[7] that an arbitral award may be set aside by a competent court only if

'(a) the party making the application furnishes proof that:
(i) a party to the arbitration agreement referred to in Article 7 was under some incapacity, *or the said agreement is not valid under the law to which the parties have subjected it* or, failing any indication thereon, under the law of this state; or
(ii) the party making the application was not given proper notice of the appointment of an arbitrator or of the arbitral proceedings or was otherwise unable to present his case; or
(iii) the award *deals with a dispute not contemplated* by or not falling within the terms of the submission to arbitration, or contains decisions on matters beyond the scope of the submission to arbitration, provided that, if the decisions on matters submitted to arbitration can be separated from those not so submitted, only that part of the award which contains decisions on matters not submitted to arbitration may be set aside; or
(iv) the composition of the arbitral tribunal or the arbitral procedure was not in accordance with the agreement of the parties, unless such agreement was in conflict with a provision of this Law from which the parties cannot derogate, or, failing such agreement, was not in accordance with this Law; or
(b) the Court finds that:
(i) the subject-matter of the dispute is not capable of settlement by arbitration under the law of this state; or
(ii) the award or any decision contained therein is in conflict with the public policy of this state.' (Emphasis added.)

These provisions sound simple but their practical application may, on occasion, cause difficulty. Two illustrations will show this. The first concerns the allegation that the arbitrator was biased, the second the allegation that the arbitration is against public policy. The first illustration refers to English court proceedings and the second to American court proceedings. In English law a party need not prove actual bias on the part of the arbitrator. It is sufficient that he proves so-called imputed bias, ie, in the circumstances of the case a reasonable man in his position would have inferred from the arbitrator's conduct that there is a real likelihood that the arbitrator was not impartial. The test is an objective one: what would a reasonable man have concluded from the behaviour of the arbitrator? There have been recently a number of cases in the English courts in which this test has been applied[8] and in one[9] of them the

7 For the full text of the Model Law, see *supra*, 176 *et seq*.
8 *The Elissar*, [1984] 2 Lloyd's Rep 84, at 89; *Bremer Handelsgesellschaft mbH* v *ETS Soules et Cie* [1985] 1 Lloyd's Rep 160; *Tracomin SA* v *Gibbs Nathaniel (Canada) Ltd*, [1985] 1 Lloyd's Rep 586.
9 *Tracomin SA* v *Gibbs Nathaniel (Canada) Ltd*, *op cit*.

court found imputed bias established and removed the arbitrator. The second illustration, taken from a New York litigation, raises a question of public policy as a bar to arbitration. The question is whether an anti-trust claim founded on an alleged infringement of the Sherman Act is capable of settlement by ICC arbitration. The United States Court of Appeals for the First Circuit denied this question, but its decision was reversed by the Supreme Court, which held that an arbitrator is not delivered from hearing anti-trust claims in international commercial contracts.[10]

Judicial review on the merits

We turn now to the second type of judicial review, the review on the merits. Such review is, whatever euphemistic phraseology is used, in reality an appeal from the decision of the arbitrator or arbitration tribunal. This raises a general question of principle: has a person involved in a legal dispute a fundamental right to a second shot if the first shot has misfired? And even if this right is accorded to a litigant, as most national legal systems do, shall it be extended to a person who has agreed to arbitration? Some lawyers, conscious of the fallibility of human judgment, would be inclined to answer this question in the affirmative, but, speaking generally, the international business community is firmly in favour of finality of the award, although some commodity associations with sophisticated arbitration structures admit the second shot by providing an Arbitration Appeal Committee.

However, the question to be considered here is not an appeal procedure within the framework of an arbitral institution but an appeal, by way of judicial review, from the arbitration tribunal to the court. The admission of judicial review on the merits is, of course, a subordination of arbitral proceedings to court proceedings and an interference with the finality of the arbitral process. The question may justly be asked whether such an interference is compatible with the declared intention of the parties to have their dispute settled by private judges chosen by them, ie, the arbitrators.

When we examine the attitude of the various national systems to this problem, we find that it is highly controversial. Some legal regulations deny a judicial review of the merits of the award. This is, for example, the attitude of American law, the recent French law on international trade arbitration and Swedish law. The UNCITRAL Model Law likewise does not admit judicial review of the award on the merits. On the other hand, the Swiss Concordat, which incidentally does not apply to the Canton of Zurich,[11] allows judicial review; it provides in Article 36(f) that an action for annulment of the arbitral award may be brought before the competent judicial authority where it is alleged

> 'that the arbitral award is arbitrary in that it was based on findings which

10 *Mitsubishi Motors Corporation* v *Soler Chrysler-Plymouth Inc*, 24 *ILM* 1064 (1985).

11 For the Zurich regulation, see Article 255 of the Zurich Civil Procedure Rules of June 13, 1976. These rules are reproduced in Clive M Schmitthoff, *International Commercial Arbitration*, Doc IV B (g)1, p 167. After this paper was written it became known that the Canton of Zurich had joined the Swiss Concordat.

were manifestly contrary to the facts appearing on the file, or in that it constitutes a clear violation of law or equity.'

It should be noted that this Swiss regulation admits judicial review both on questions of fact and of law. The English solution contained in the Arbitration Act 1979 represents a compromise. First, English law distinguishes between questions of fact and questions of law. Findings of the arbitrators on the facts are conclusive and final but their rulings on the law may be subject to judicial review. The distinction between fact and law is not always clear cut. The courts had to admit questions of law and fact mixed[12] and it was not until the judgment of Kerr J in *The Angelia*[13] that it was clear that the decision what length of time constituted a 'frustrating time' within a charterparty clause raised a question of law and not of fact. It should perhaps be mentioned that the construction of a contract is a question of law in English law but a question of fact in French law.[14] The second feature of compromise in the English solution of 1979 is that, while admitting judicial review on a question of law in principle, it admits in a wide area of international arbitration advance exclusion clauses and thus recognises the finality of the award. The only cases in which advance exclusion clauses are not admitted are, for the time being, disputes falling within the Admiralty jurisdiction, arising out of an insurance contract, or arising from certain specified commodity contracts, but even in these cases an advance exclusion clause is admitted if the contract is governed by foreign law. Of course, exclusion clauses after the commencement of arbitration are always admitted. It is fortunate that the English courts interpret the provisions relating to advance exclusion clauses widely. Thus, they held that an ICC arbitration clause in a contract qualified as an advance exclusion clause.[15] It should further be mentioned that an English judge would not admit judicial review of an award if he only disagreed with the arbitrator on the interpretation of a difficult point of law; he must be satisfied that the arbitrator was wrong in law and that the rights of a party were substantially affected by the mistake. In the result, the English compromise of 1979 has in fact admitted the finality of the arbitration award in a very wide area of international commercial arbitration, if the parties have agreed on such finality. It has retained judicial review on points of law, apart from Admiralty and insurance arbitrations, essentially only for the interpretation of standard contract forms, and it has done so because in these cases many traders not involved in the dispute want to obtain certainty on the meeting of the contract clauses. This avoids further disputes. This regulation has the approval of the interested trade circles.[16] On the whole, the 1979 compromise has worked well in practice, although the House of Lords on occasion had to remind the Commercial Court that it should not be too generous in allowing judicial review[17] and that English law is now definitely committed, at least in principle, to treat international commercial arbitration awards as final.

12 *The Effy* [1972] 1 Lloyd's Rep 18, at 34.
13 *The Angelia* [1972] 2 Lloyd's Rep 154, at 163.
14 B Nicholas, *French Law of Contract*, London 1982, at 46–7.
15 *Arab African Energy Corporation Ltd* v *Olieprodukten Nederland BV* [1983] 2 Lloyd's Rep 419; *Marine Contractors Inc* v *Shell Petroleum Development Co of Nigeria Ltd* [1984] 2 Lloyd's Rep 77.
16 See the Commercial Court Users Report, 1961, Cmnd 1616.
17 *Pioneer Shipping Ltd* v *BTP Tioxide Ltd, The Nema* [1982] AC 724; *Antaios Compania Naviera SA* v *Salen Redereierna AB* [1985] AC 191.

What of the future?

The preceding observations enable us to cast a glimpse at the future relationship of international arbitration bodies to the national court. Here again, as throughout this paper, it is necessary to distinguish between the two types of judicial review identified earlier.

As regards the first type, ie, that relating to the observance of the requirements of natural justice and to the legality of the arbitration agreement, there is unanimity that judicial control shall be maintained. But when the list of reviewable cases in Article V of the New York Convention is compared with the French Law of 1980 and the UNCITRAL Model Law, it is obvious that the list of the 1958 Convention is antiquated. It should be simplified, reduced in ambit and rendered more precise by an amendment to the New York Convention. The French formulation of 1980 should be taken as a model for the amendment of the New York Convention.

As regards the second type of judicial review, namely the review on the merits, international commercial opinion clearly favours the finality of the award. This, however, does not mean that the judicial review on the merits should be excluded in all circumstances. The decisive consideration should be, as indicated at the beginning of this paper, that arbitration is a contractual arrangement and that the fundamental principle in the law of contract is that of party autonomy. It follows that it should be left to the parties to determine whether they do or do not want judicial review on the merits. The only question is that of the balance of legal regulation. The English Arbitration Act 1979 places the balance in favour of judicial review but allows the parties far-reaching discretion to contract out by means of exclusion clauses. This suits the English position and no complaint is made about this arrangement by trading interests in the United Kingdom.[18] But the aim should be to achieve a regulation which is internationally acceptable, particularly in transnational arbitrations. Here the English solution, suitable as it is for the requirements of trading interests connected with this country, cannot serve as a model. From an international point of view, the balance should be reversed. An international regulation should provide that the award is always final and conclusive unless the parties otherwise agree. Such an agreement may be in express terms or by adopting a standard contract form containing a suitably worded arbitration clause or it may be implied from a trade practice of which a party has knowledge or which, acting as a reasonable person, he ought to know. If a formulation on these lines is adopted, the general tendency in favour of finality of the award and the present English regulation under the Arbitration Act 1979 can be reconciled.

18 See the Working Paper of February 1, 1985, of the Sub-Committee on Arbitration of the Commercial Court Committee.

Part 4

International arbitration involving states and state entities

21 The strengths and weaknesses of international arbitration involving a state as a party

Philippe Cahier

Arbitration between states and companies basically protects companies by enabling them to initiate arbitration proceedings against states. To appreciate the scope of such protection, it is first necessary to assess the situation in the absence of an arbitration clause in an international contract.

If a dispute arises, one of two courses can be followed. One is to file suit in the local courts. The result is uncertain because the local courts will enforce local law, which may have changed since the contract was made. The state immunity to suit may also make the court proceeding stillborn. The second course is to claim the diplomatic protection of the state under whose laws the company is incorporated. This is no more satisfactory than the first alternative, since it may leave the company unprotected in certain cases.

Under international law, diplomatic approaches are productive only if a state was guilty of an internationally unlawful act against a foreign national. But a dispute may arise between a state and a foreign company without unlawful action being involved. International investment contracts are long in term and entail a degree of cooperation between governmental agencies and the company's executives and even renegotiation in some cases. So it is not surprising that they may give rise to difficulties in performance and divergencies of interpretation, with each party defending its interests in good faith. This is illustrated by two cases. The first is *Grands Moulins de Dakar* v *The Malagasy Republic.*[1]

The parties had signed a preliminary agreement for establishment of a lumber venture and a flour industry. In consideration of preliminary work, the Government granted the company certain privileges. The project soon turned out to be more complicated than expected, and many physical difficulties emerged. In the discussions looking to the definitive agreements, Grands Moulins de Dakar increased its demands in order to ensure the profitability of the project. The Government declined to meet the increased demands and the negotiations were broken off. The arbitrators found that the tentative agreement had not been breached, that the negotiations had been conducted in good faith and that the parties had no obligation to reach an agreement. The award to the company was only for reimbursement of certain expenses and on the basis of equity.

The upshot of the *Kuwait–Aminoil* case[2] was similar, the company was allowed compensation for a nationalisation which was lawful.

1 Unpublished award of May 1, 1972.
2 Award of March 24, 1982, 21 *ILM* 976 (1982).

But a company may be left unprotected for other reasons. First, no government is obligated to protect its nationals diplomatically. It may decline to do so on grounds of expediency. Further, a state can protect only its nationals. This was reaffirmed by the International Court of Justice (ICJ) in the *Barcelona Traction* case in 1970.[3] But one of the conditions of an investment agreement may be the incorporation of a local company which will import the capital. The nationality of the company may also differ from the nationality of the shareholders. If so, the state under whose laws the company is incorporated may consider that it has no reason to act on the company's behalf (that may be why Canada took no action after 1955 in the *Barcelona Traction* case), and even if it does not take action, the company's petition may run foul of the lack of any genuine tie of nationality.

Finally, and above all, the frequent lack of a forum between the defendant and plaintiff states may make diplomatic protection unavailing. The United States and the United Kingdom protested the Libyan nationalisations, but their protests had no effect and the oil companies would have been unprotected had they not included an arbitration clause in their contracts. The great strength of arbitration between a state and an individual thus lies simply in the fact that that remedy exists.

Does this mean that the government makes all of the concessions in such a case? Not at all. Countries importing capital know that without certain guarantees they cannot procure the investments their economies need to develop. In a sense, the inclusion of an arbitration clause forms part of the contractual equilibrium, as evidenced by the ratification and accession by a large number of Third World countries of the 1965 Washington Convention, establishing ICSID.

It would be unfair to arbitrators to assume that they make their awards without taking the countries' points of view and legitimate interests into consideration. It suffices to read the *Kuwait–Aminoil* award to appreciate the extent to which the arbitrators took account of and understood the reasons why the Government nationalised the company.

In *Benvenuti and Bonfant* v *People's Republic of the Congo*[4] the Congolese Government had shown no great alacrity in participating in the proceeding. The arbitrators not only denied the company's demand for a default award but, in view of special circumstances of a domestic political nature, allowed a Counter Memorial to be filed long after the deadline.

Mention can also be made of one case[5] in which the arbitrators dismissed an American corporation's claims and awarded Ethiopia over $700,000 on its counterclaim. In *Klöckner* v *Cameroon*, the arbitrators also found for the Cameroon Government against the company.[6]

Arbitration, a guarantee for the company, is also beneficial to the state. Its success depends not only on a sound assessment of the parties' legal positions, but on recognition of the fact that the state may have been prompted to take action in defence of the public interest. It is beyond the scope of this introductory study to discuss all of the aspects of this type of arbitration some

3 *Barcelona Traction* case, ICJ Report 1970, p 4.
4 Award of August 8, 1980, 21 *ILM* 740 (1982).
5 See J F Lalive, in 104 *Clunet* 329 (1977), at note 13.
6 Award of October 21, 1983, [1984] *Revue de l'arbitrage* 19. This award has since been overturned on appeal.

of which, such as the applicable law and the enforcement of the award, are covered by other reports. Here I propose to examine only, in light of recent cases, the necessity for consent, a few procedural problems and solutions for certain substantive problems.

The necessity for consent

The necessity for the parties' consent to arbitration is a general legal principle. Such consent must clearly appear from the arbitration clause in the contract or in a 'compromis'. For ICSID arbitration, ratification of the 1965 Washington Convention by the state in which the investment was made and by the state under whose laws the company is incorporated is also required.

The *Holiday Inns* case stands for the rule that the Washington Convention need not have been ratified before the contract was entered into.[7] It is uniformly held that the arbitration clause is independent of the remainder of the contract in the sense that an allegation of inexistence or invalidity of the contract has no effect on the validity of the arbitration clause.[8]

In principle, only the parties to the contract containing the arbitration clause are bound by that clause. Two recent cases are indicative of a trend by arbitrators to extend their jurisdiction to parties not formally privy to the contract. The first is *Southern Pacific Properties Limited* v *The Arab Republic of Egypt and the Egyptian General Company for Tourism and Hotels.*[9] Two contracts had been signed for construction of a tourist complex in Egypt, one by the three parties and the other, containing the arbitration clause, between Southern Pacific and the Egyptian Company for Tourism. At the end of the second contract were the words: 'approved, agreed and ratified' by the Minister of Tourism. The arbitrators held that that clause and other circumstances showed that the Egyptian Government was guaranteeing to the investor its continuing agreement and support of the project and that the Government must accordingly be considered a party to the arbitration clause. That award was set aside by the Court of Appeal of Paris on July 12, 1984[10] on the ground that the contract was ratified by the Egyptian Minister of Tourism only in his capacity as the supervisory authority of the Egyptian General Company for Tourism and that the Government was therefore not bound by the arbitration agreement.

The same fate may lie in store for an award of March 5, 1984.[11] In 1975, the United Arab Emirates, Saudi Arabia, Qatar and the Arab Republic of Egypt organised the Arab Organisation for Industrialisation (AOI), which the arbitrators styled supranational but which strikes us as being merely international. That organisation entered into a contract with Westland Helicopters for incorporation of a joint stock company named The Arab British Helicopter Company (ABH) to manufacture helicopters.

7 See P Lalive, 'The First World Bank Arbitration: Some Legal Problems', in 51 *British Yearbook of International Law* 146 (1980).

8 *Texaco–Libya* case, award of November 21, 1975, 18 *ILM* 389 (1979).

9 Award of March 11, 1983, 22 *ILM* 752 (1983).

10 23 *ILM* 1048 (1984).

11 *Westland Helicopters Limited* v *Arab Organisation for Industrialisation, and United Arab Emirates, and Kingdom of Saudi Arabia, and State of Qatar, and Arab Republic of Egypt, and Arab British Helicopter Company* 23 *ILM* 1071 (1984).

That contract, like the contracts between Westland and ABH, contained an arbitration clause. After Egypt recognised Israel, the three other Arab countries decided to dissolve the organisation, but Egypt promulgated a decree to the effect that AOI was still in existence as a legal entity. Westland referred the dispute to arbitration, pleading the arbitration clause against not only AOI and ABH but the four states which were not party to the contracts. The arbitrators found that AOI was a legal entity distinct from the member countries, but added that under municipal law the members of certain types of companies (general partnership) could be held liable for the company's acts. In sustaining their jurisdiction over the countries, the arbitrators held that:

> 'In the absence of any rule of applicable law, what is to be deduced from the silence of the founding documents of the AOI as to the liability of the four States? In the absence of any provision expressly or impliedly excluding the liability of the four States, this liability subsists since, as a general rule, those who engage in transactions of an economic nature are deemed liable for the obligations which flow therefrom. In default by the four States of formal exclusion of their liability, third parties which have contracted with the AOI could legitimately count on their liability.'[12]

This reasoning is curious and takes no account of the law of international organisations. In fact, the converse is true. The member countries are not liable for such organisations' actions. Such liability can be based only on an express clause in the 'founding documents'.

In making such awards, the arbitrators considered that the investments formed a whole, even though the obligations were contained in different contracts. Since the arbitration clause is intended to guarantee the investment, it can be extended to entities not party to the contract containing it. The reasoning is understandable but impairs the security of legal relationships.

Such an extension of jurisdiction may be justified in special circumstances, such as succession.[13] Otherwise, it is liable to sap the countries' confidence in international arbitration. Hence, it is incumbent on investors to draft arbitration clauses with care.

Procedural problems

Mention should be made in this connection of the high number of cases of default arbitration awards. In addition to the three well-known oil cases involving Libya, these include the *Hedjaz Railway* case[14] the three ICSID proceedings between Jamaica and foreign companies, and the *Westland Helicopters* case. In that respect, arbitration between states and private parties does not differ from the ICJ in which defaults are tending to proliferate. This trend is regrettable since it interferes with the sound administration of justice.

It is therefore important for the arbitration clause to be carefully worded to enable the arbitration tribunal to function even if one of the parties refuses to

12 *Ibid*, at 1084.

13 See P Lalive, 'Criticism of Judgment of Swiss Federal Court in *SGTA* v *Bangladesh*', 89 *Revue de droit suisse* 529 (1970).

14 1972, unpublished award.

participate. This is particularly true of the constitution of the tribunal. In the three Libyan cases, the clause authorised the President of the ICJ to appoint a single arbitrator. But it appears to us that a tribunal of several arbitrators is more appropriate. In the *Hedjaz Railway* case, the arbitration clause authorised the President of the ICJ to appoint not only the umpire but the arbitrators of the party in default. However, it is certain that the institutionalisation of arbitration in the context of organisations like the ICC and ICSID has clear advantages, since such organisations can organise the arbitration down to the last detail.

This is especially true of the ICSID. Article 26 of the Washington Convention provides:

> 'Consent to arbitration under this Convention shall, unless otherwise stated, be deemed consent to such arbitration to the exclusion of any other remedy. A contracting State may require the exhaustion of local administrative or judicial remedies as a condition of its consent to arbitration under this Convention.'

This provision precludes the filing of an action in a local court. If such an action were filed, the court would have to disclaim jurisdiction especially since the clause, being contained in a treaty, prevails over any contrary provision of municipal law. Article 27 of the Washington Convention rules out any action based on diplomatic protection unless the country does not comply with the arbitration award. ICSID arbitration is thus completely autonomous and supersedes all other internal and international proceedings. This is not true of *ad hoc* arbitration, which is not exclusive of other remedies. In our opinion, these two clauses achieve perfect balance between the interests of states and companies.

As noted above, arbitration of the type we are considering need take no account of the company's nationality. As long as a contract contains an arbitration clause, there is an arbitration remedy. This statement must however be qualified in the case of ICSID established by the 1965 Washington Convention. The Convention does not apply to companies having the nationality of the state in which the investment is made, unless because of foreign control the parties have agreed that the company should be treated as a national of another contracting country.[15] In the *Holiday Inns* case, the plaintiffs undertook to act also on behalf of the four Moroccan subsidiaries. They contended that the Moroccan Government had treated them like foreign companies. The arbitrators ruled that the agreement referred to in Article 25 must be explicit, stating:

> 'The solution which such an agreement is intended to achieve constitutes an exception to the general rule established by the Convention, and one would expect that parties should express themselves clearly and explicitly with respect to such a derogation.'[16]

It appears that the parties may also agree on the nationality of a company which, because of the location of its principal office, would have the nationality of one country, but, by virtue of control, would have the nationality of another

15 Washington Convention, Article 25(2).
16 See P Lalive, *op cit*, note 7, at 141.

contracting country.[17] It is a general principle of law that arbitrators are competent to determine their own jurisdiction. In the ICJ, a preliminary plea to the jurisdiction has the effect of staying proceedings on the merits, and the Court disposes of the plea by a preliminary judgment. In our type of arbitration, there is no uniform practice. In cases as similar as the Libyan oil proceedings, the arbitrators, in the British Petroleum award, disposed of the issue of their jurisdiction in a six-line paragraph on the sole ground of the existence of an arbitration clause in the concession contract. But in the *Texaco* case, sold arbitrator Dupuy devoted a separate award to a detailed examination of Libya's objections set forth in a memorandum to the President of the ICJ.

The arbitration tribunal appointed under the auspices of the ICC in the *Southern Pacific Properties* case cited above disposed in the same award of the plea to its jurisdiction in a very circumstantial way and on the merits. Conversely, the ICC arbitrators in the *Westland Helicopters* case deemed it preferable to rule on their jurisdiction before taking up the merits.

This latter *modus operandi* strikes us as preferable. By staying the proceedings on the merits, it enables the parties to argue at length and the arbitrators to make a carefully considered award. And, above all, the defendant may, if the arbitrators sustain their jurisdiction, deem it preferable to forestall an award on the merits by reaching a settlement. It is of course hard to pinpoint the reasons prompting a compromise. But in the *Holiday Inns* case, for instance, the fact that the arbitrators had sustained their jurisdiction may have prompted the Moroccan Government to seek a settlement. The same thing may occur in the ICSID arbitration proceedings between Jamaica and foreign companies.

A question that sometimes arises in an arbitration proceeding is the arbitrators' authority to grant provisional measures. As the proceeding may take a long time, it is important to keep one of the parties from compromising enforcement of the award. In the absence of a specific provision, the arbitrators' power to make provisional measures is sometimes disputed.

Article 47 of the Washington Convention establishing ICSID is an improvement on that score, since it provides:

> 'Except as the parties otherwise agree, the tribunal may, if it considers that the circumstances so require, recommend any provisional measures which should be taken to preserve the respective rights of either party.'

Motions for provisional measures were made and granted in the *Holiday Inns* and *Agip* cases. ICJ practice shows that that court grants such relief only after determining that it has *prima facie* jurisdiction over the case. If the ICJ lacks jurisdiction, it cannot make interlocutory orders. In fact, the determination is a very superficial one, taking no account of the defendant's objections. It is confined to the question whether there is any basis for the ICJ's jurisdiction. In the arbitration proceedings discussed above, it appears that neither arbitration tribunal made a determination of *prima facie* jurisdiction. This may be regrettable, considering the sensitivity of countries, and it would be preferable in the future for the arbitrators to determine their jurisdiction. However,

17 Delaume, 'Le centre international pour le reglement des differends relatifs aux investissements', 109 *Clunet* 788 (1982).

according to the ICJ's decisions, the existence of a declaration accepting the optional clause suffices to establish such jurisdiction.

Is an interlocutory order granting ancillary relief binding? Legal authority concerning ancillary relief ordered by the ICJ is divided. Such orders by the Court in recent years have not been respected. The words 'may recommend' in Article 47 of the Washington Convention indicate that the framers of the Article considered the effect of such recommendations to be optional. In the *Agip* case, the Republic of the Congo did not consider itself bound by such recommendations. We have always deplored this state of affairs, provisional measures being closely linked to the proper administration of justice.

Much more could be said about procedural problems in international arbitration. However, in the limited context of this study it appeared to us to be more interesting to examine a few international arbitration awards on the merits.

Aspects of awards on the merits

International arbitration awards are not uniform. It is true that each case has its own characteristics which may account for the differing awards, but cases may involve the same legal issues. This is true in particular of nationalisations and of contracts containing stabilisation clauses.

Recent awards unanimously recognise the right of nationalisation. The scope of that right may vary according to the reasons, but the principle is settled. The nationalisation of BP's concession was held to be unlawful in the case of *BP* v *Libya*, but on the ground that it was discriminatory, which is contrary to international law. In other similar cases (*Texaco* v *Libya*, *Agip* v *Congo*), the unlawfulness of the nationalisation resulted from the existence of a stabilisation clause in the contract. It is therefore necessary to discuss those clauses.

As mentioned above, investment contracts are long in term, so changes in economic conditions may require adjustments. Such adjustments may be the result of an agreement by the parties, but may also be the result of action by the country pursuant to its prerogatives as a public authority, through the legislative branch. To protect themselves from such dangers, countries have included 'stabilisation' clauses in their contracts prohibiting unilateral amendment of the contracts.

The oil concession contracts with Libya provided:

> '1 The Government of Libya will take all steps necessary to ensure that the Company enjoys all the rights conferred by this concession. The contractual rights expressly created by this concession shall not be altered except by mutual consent of the parties.
>
> 2 This concession shall throughout the period of its validity be construed in accordance with the Petroleum Law and the Regulations in force on the date of execution of the agreement of amendment by which this paragraph 2 was incorporated into this concession agreement. Any amendment to or repeal of such Regulations shall not affect the contractual rights of the company without its consent.'

In the *Texaco* case, the arbitrators, having held for various reasons which need not be gone into herein that the concession was internationalised, found that there was nothing to keep a state in the exercise of its sovereignty from irrevocably binding itself by the clauses of the concession and granting a concessionaire irrevocable rights. In the arbitrators' opinion, such a stabilisation clause does not encroach on the state's sovereignty. It retains its prerogatives to make laws in regard to parties to whom it has not given such an undertaking. Hence, the stabilisation clause precludes a nationalisation which would otherwise have been lawful. This same reasoning is found in the arbitration award in the *Agip* case decided two years later.

But oddly, the arbitration award in the *Liamco* case relative to the same Libyan nationalisations, while recognising the validity of the clause and reaffirming the principle of the binding nature of the contracts, drew no inference therefrom, since it held that the nationalisation was lawful, but entitled the company to compensation.

In the *Kuwait–Aminoil* case, the arbitrators analysed the stabilisation clause differently and therefore refused to hold that the existence of the contract clause can preclude nationalisation proceedings. However, such a clause is undeniably valid:

> 'No doubt contractual limitations on the State's right to nationalise are juridically possible, but what that would involve would be a particularly serious undertaking which would have to be expressly stipulated for, and be within the regulations governing the conclusion of State contracts; and it is to be expected that it should cover only a relatively limited period. In the present case, however, the existence of such a stipulation would have to be presumed as being covered by the general language of the stabilisation clauses, and over the whole period of an especially long concession since it extended to 60 years'.[18]

Hence only an express clause prohibiting nationalisation can do so. The effect of such a clause being:

> 'by impliedly requiring that nationalisation shall not have any confiscatory character, they reinforce the necessity for a proper indemnification as a condition of it.'[19]

This award is probably more realistic than the one in the *Texaco* case. It does assign priority to the state's interests, but can it reasonably be considered that in a changing economic situation and over a very long period a country can be prohibited from nationalising without a specific undertaking? In any event, the general purport of this award should not be exaggerated. One of the arguments in support of the arbitrators' reasoning was that during its term

> 'the contract of concession thus changed its character and became one of those contracts in regard to which, in most legal systems, the State, while remaining bound to respect the contractual equilibrium, enjoys special advantages'.[20]

Many other cases could be cited in which the awards reflect differences of

18 21 *ILM* 976 (1982), at 1023.
19 *Ibid.*
20 *Ibid*, at 1024.

opinion. To avoid undue length of this paper, mere reference will be made to the redress allowed. In the *BP* case, the arbitrators held the principle of *restitutio in integrum* inapplicable for practical reasons. Yet that is the normal redress for the breach of contract in the *Texaco* award. In the *Liamco* case, however, the arbitrators held that

> '... *restitutio* presupposes the cancellation of the nationalization measures at issue, and such cancellation violates also the sovereignty of the nationalizing State.'[21]

Finally, the *Aminoil* award stressed the parties' legitimate expectations and the necessity of allowing the investor a reasonable rate of return.

Conclusion

At the close of this very brief study, the question arises whether our type of arbitration plays an important role in resolving disputes between states and companies. The low number of disputes referred to the ICSID (about 19 in 20 years) is surprising, but it must be noted that it is very difficult to determine the number of arbitration proceedings in other forums, as some awards are not published.

But aside from this, the problem cannot be discussed only in terms of the number of cases. It is probable that the mere inclusion of an arbitration clause in a contract, enabling the company to refer disputes to arbitration unilaterally, has strongly encouraged amicable settlements prior to any proceedings. Likewise, the commencement of a proceeding may stimulate such compromises. This occurred in six of the proceedings initiated in ICSID.

Finally, the existence of an arbitration award is calculated to persuade a state which did not participate in the proceeding to seek a settlement. Libya paid BP \$41,000,000 and delivered the equivalent of \$152,000,000 in crude oil to Texaco. So, on the whole, the inclusion of an arbitration clause may provide genuine security for companies which invest in foreign countries.

21 20 *ILM* (1981), at 64.

22 Disputes between states and foreign companies

A H Hermann

International arbitration of disputes between states and companies is a relatively recent phenomenon. The need for it springs from the increasing role played in the world economy by the multinational corporations, on the one hand, and by state traders, the new merchant princes, on the other. To this development, prominent since 1945, has been more recently added an unprecedented expansion of loans granted by banks to foreign states, and the inevitable defaulting on these loans.

The magnitude of these investments, developments and credit operations, makes political involvement of governments unavoidable; indeed, many of these transactions were preceded, stimulated and helped by governmental and intergovernmental actions, pursuing strategic and foreign policy objectives often in combination with an effort to secure export contracts by means of credits, guarantees or aid grants.

It would be good if the disputes generated by this development could be resolved in accordance with the admirable maxim coined by Dr Francis Mann:

> 'Public international law and private law ... are branches of the same tree. They apply in conformity with the demands of reasonable justice and practical convenience'.[1]

Unfortunately, we have the unenviable privilege of watching the forces at work which seem to be so violent and contradictory that it is almost impossible to say what is the shape of the tree and of its branches and that at times one fears it might be uprooted altogether. Both political and commercial interest in large international deals seem to be guided rather by General de Gaulle's *dictum*: 'I am for law as long as it is not contrary to our interests'.

The combination of commercial and political interests is more evident on the side of the state trader or the government granting or nationalising an oil concession; but it is no less real on the other side where the commercial and political subjects retain separate identities. This would by itself lead to an internationalisation of the contracts in which the relations between countries are materialised. Moreover, though multinational corporations may have more muscle than the state with which they contract, they are at a disadvantage when it comes to law. These companies need, therefore, to take the settlement of any disputes out of the territorial jurisdiction of the other party to the contract.

Even when it escapes the jurisdictional territory of the contracting state, the

1 F A Mann, *Studies in International Law* (Oxford 1973), at 239.

company is still at a great legal disadvantage: courts of most countries are slow to accept that the international contract, on the security of which the attainment of a better economic balance between East and West, and between North and South, depends, supersedes the traditional notions of 'sovereign immunity' and of 'act of state'. Hence the need to avoid as much as possible interference of courts in arbitration of disputes arising from such international contracts and the need for their assistance in the enforcement of awards.

But a few years ago such *desiderata* could be brushed aside as pious but unrealistic. Starting with the *Lena Goldfields* dispute in 1930,[2] and increasingly with the proliferation of disputes between states and the oil companies after 1950, arbitrators tried to solve these problems with great ingenuity and inventiveness but without much hope of success. A turning point came in 1981 when the conflict between the United States and Iran led to the establishment of a truly international arbitration tribunal, and the placing at its disposal of substantial funds for the settlement of claims by the nationals of the United States and Iran against the government of the other country.

In spite of the violent disruption of the tribunal's work last autumn – when two Iranian arbitrators manhandled and threatened to kill one of the neutrals – a Swedish judge – the experience is likely to be useful in the future. One expects that there will be a great need for such internationally agreed and funded tribunals in the course of the next few years as the financial squeeze is likely to oblige debtor countries to abandon many of their ambitions and unprofitable projects.

However, such better institutional arrangements modelled on the Iran–United States Arbitration Tribunal can hardly be attempted unless some measure of agreement is reached on the fundamental issues. Of these the question whether an act of state can be a *force majeure* defence for a state-controlled corporation seems to me to be the most important.

The state and its emanations

Two issues concerning the mode of the state in dispute with a company are of crucial importance for the decision to arbitrate and for the possibility of enforcing any award. The first is the question whether the behaviour by which the company is aggrieved can be classified as the state's governmental activity or its commercial activity. The second issue concerns the standing of government agencies, often incorporated in the form of trading companies: are they identical with the state, or do they operate at arm's length, so that either the government cannot be held responsible for them or they have a defence of *force majeure* if the government orders them to abandon or otherwise breach their contracts.

Polish sugar

By coincidence, the three recent English decisions trying, not quite

2 See Lena Goldfields 'Arbitration', reported in *The Times* (London), September 13, 1930; also in 34 *Cornell Law Quarterly* 42 (1950).

successfully, to illuminate these problems were all made in the course of reviewing arbitration awards concerning sugar contracts.

The House of Lords' decision in *C Czarnikow* v *Rolimpex*[3] rests on the finding of the arbitral tribunal that Rolimpex, one of the Polish foreign trade organisations, was an entity with separate will, following its own commercial strategies and, indeed, that at the critical time it pleaded that it should be allowed to fulfil its contracts.

The House of Lords decision in favour of Rolimpex had been at the time explained by this finding of facts from which the judges could not depart. Subsequently, however, this 'finding of facts' was given a general validity. Thus, in *I Congreso del Partido*, Lord Wilberforce said:

> 'State-controlled enterprises, with legal personality, ability to trade and to enter into contracts of private law, though wholly subject to the control of their state, are a well-known feature of the modern commercial scene. The distinction between them, and their governing state, may appear artificial: but it is an accepted distinction in the law of England and other states'.[4]

The dangerous consequences of this attitude are evident. In the *Rolimpex* case several western sugar merchants, of which Czarnikow was one, suffered losses amounting to some £40 million when the Polish Government decided not to honour its 1974 sugar contracts after a disappointing sugarbeet harvest and a substantial rise in the world price of sugar. The artificial distinction between the state and its trading agency, which I will call the Wilberforce Doctrine I, enabled Rolimpex to claim *force majeure*, and that it fulfilled its obligation to obtain necessary export licences though these were later nullified by an export ban. It is a threat to all contracts with state-controlled corporations, but it stands on feet of clay.

The arbitrators and all the judges involved were impressed by the fact that Rolimpex executives manifested a desire to honour the contracts and secured the backing of their immediate boss, the Minister for Trade. They were overruled by the Government. Both arbitrators and judges concluded that the distance between the trading organisation and Government was sufficiently demonstrated to justify the defence of 'government intervention'.

This conclusion reveals a misunderstanding of the theory and practice of state monopoly of foreign trade in Communist countries. The concepts of 'State monopoly' and 'government intervention' are mutually exclusive – the government cannot 'intervene' in its own business. Not only is the doctrine of the state monopoly of foreign trade part of the constitution of all COMECON countries, but it is one of the few fundamental rules which are meticulously followed in everyday practice. Every state trading agency is linked to the state budget and subject to directions, general or specific, formal or given over the telephone, by the Ministry of Foreign Trade. Moreover, it is quite unthinkable that a foreign trade organisation anywhere in COMECON could conclude contracts concerning the entire exportable surplus of a future harvest without being expressly authorised by its government to do so. Such speculative contracts are always a gamble. The *Rolimpex* decision of the House of Lords opened to Communist governments the possibility to gamble without any risk

3 [1979] AC 351.
4 [1983] 1 AC 244, at 258.

– as long as this possibility would not frighten away potential trading partners in the West.

Cuban sugar

The 'Wilberforce Doctrine I' was applied in aid of Cuba in its dispute with IANSA, the Chilean importer of sugar, after it lost the first leg of its defence based on the common law doctrine of sovereign immunity (the State Immunity Act 1978 did not yet apply) which continues to form part of the international law.

The dispute came before English courts twice, the first time[5] in the form of a case stated by the arbitral tribunal which awarded damages to IANSA for breach of contract and wrongful conversion of a cargo of sugar while it was being unloaded in Valparaiso from the *Playa Larga*. When about a quarter was discharged, the Communist Government of Chile was toppled and the Cuban Government ordered the master to sail out of the port immediately. The arbitrators also held that IANSA was entitled to damages for breach of contract and the restitution of money paid in respect of cargo on the *Marble Islands* diverted from its course to Valparaiso at about the same time. They declined to award damages in respect of the unshipped balance of the contract, holding that it was frustrated by the events in Chile.

Mr Justice Mustill affirmed this award with the exception of damages for the diverted cargo of *Marble Islands*. He held that a commercial contract, which would not be concluded if friendly relations did not exist between the exporting and the importing country, is frustrated if the regime of one of these countries is replaced by another which the other country disapproves.

His judgment was appealed, but before the appeal could be heard, another case arising from the same events reached the House of Lords – it concerned the arrest of the *I Congreso del Partido*, a sister ship of the *Playa Larga* and the *Marble Islands*, all owned by the Republic of Cuba. IANSA, as owner of the converted and diverted cargo on the two last named vessels had the *I Congreso del Partido* arrested in an English port as security for damages claimed from Cuba. Cuba answered the arrest with a defence of state immunity.

When this case reached the House of Lords, Lord Wilberforce said that, though a state remains capable at any time of acts of sovereignty, the instructions passed on to the master of the *Playa Larga* were in the nature of operational instructions issued by the owner of a ship through his agents. They were not an act done *jure imperii*. It followed from numerous decisions of English, United States and German courts, that an act done *jure gestionis*, as the instructions to the master were, could not be granted immunity only because it was politically motivated. Lord Wilberforce stated:

> 'If immunity were to be granted the moment that any decision taken by the trading state were shown to be not commercially, but politically, inspired, the 'restrictive' theory (of sovereign immunity) would almost cease to have any content and trading relations as to state-owned ships would become

5 *Empresa Exportadora de Azucar* v *Industria Azucarera Nacional SA* [1983] 2 Lloyd's Rep 171.

> impossible. It is precisely to protect private traders against politically inspired breaches, or wrongs, that the restrictive theory allows states to be brought before a municipal court'.[6]

I will call this the Wilberforce Doctrine II. It disposed of the view adopted by Mustill J that contracts concluded in view of friendship may be abandoned when the friends fall out. But his judgment was upheld by the Court of Appeal on December 2, 1982 on different grounds. Lord Justice Ackner said that the contract in respect of the cargo on the *Marble Islands*, and of the unshipped balance, was frustrated by the antagonism between Cuba and Chile and was made illegal by the Cuban Law No 1256, passed subsequently. There was no crucial difference between *Rolimpex* and *Cubazucar*, he said. Though it was subject to direction and control by the Cuban Government, *Cubazucar* had a separate legal existence. Thus, a judgment undone by the Wilberforce Doctrine II was rescued by the Wilberforce Doctrine I.

Kenyan sugar

Surprisingly *Rolimpex* v *Czarnikow* was not even mentioned by Mr Justice Parker when giving judgment in *Atisa* v *Aztec*[7] in 1983, although this case was eminently suitable for its application. There were even no need in this case to apply the Wilberforce Doctrine I as the independence of the exporter of the State was not in doubt. Atisa, the exporter, was a commercial company based outside Kenya, and if Rolimpex could benefit from the *force majeure* clause, Atisa had an even better claim to it. As in the Polish case, also here the government was the monopoly supplier of sugar and decided to repudiate a contract concluded with Atisa because of a bad harvest. However, in contrast with the Polish case, the arbitrators found that the Kenyan Government was at all times acting as a private trader. If they failed to deliver to Atisa, this was a private matter and did not entitle Atisa to a defence of *force majeure* against Aztec's claim of damages for breach of contract.

The *Settebello* case

Whatever hopes were raised by the Atisa case, these were dashed again when Mr Justice Hirst refused to allow an inquiry into the motives of the Portuguese Government, which by a special decree relieved its state shipyards of liability.[8] He was dealing with an application for letters of request to obtain evidence in Portugal. The applicant was Settebello Ltd, a Liberian outpost of Thyssen, the West German steel-making group, suing Banco Totta and Acores, a Portuguese bank with a branch in London, over a guarantee to pay £25 million in connection with the failure of the Portuguese state shipyards to deliver a 320,000-ton oil tanker on time. Under the terms of the contract the Thyssen-owned company was entitled to cancel the order and claim a penalty if the ship was not ready for delivery by April 30, 1982. Ten days before the cancellation date, the Portuguese Government made a decree enabling Portuguese companies, earlier declared to be in a 'critical economic condition',

6 *Op cit*, [1983] 1 AC 244, at 268–9.
7 [1983] 2 Lloyd's Rep 579.
8 *Settebello Ltd* v *Banco Totta & Acores*, *The Times*, June 24, 1985.

to suspend unilaterally for two years any right of their customers to cancel a contract when a total payment due exceeded Escudo 1 billion.

The ship was not ready and the shipyard lost no time in making the necessary declaration. The bank refused payment under its guarantee, claiming that, as a result of the new decree, no money was owed to the Thyssen group. Settebello argued that the Portuguese decree was discriminatory, applicable only to the one contract and made by the Government specially to extricate its own shipyard from a freely undertaken commercial liability, but Mr Justice Hirst refused to issue Letters of Request to obtain evidence in Portugal that the decree was made at the initiative of the shipyard and drafted by its lawyers. He said this would be meddling in the legislative business of a friendly power. He stated:

> 'If this effectively deprives the plaintiffs of obtaining the evidence that they need in order to sustain their plea, this is because their interests must yield to a higher legal principle – an unfortunate predicament, but similar to that in which the defendants in the *Buttes* case[9] were placed as a result of the House of Lords decision'.

Going even further, the judge said:

> 'I have formed the very clear provisional view that *Buttes* case, which is a unanimous decision of the House of Lords, effectively rules out evidence concerning the motives of a foreign legislature as a matter of principle on grounds of comity'.

This is an astonishing pronouncement, even if only 'provisional'. The *Buttes* case concerned several acts of Gulf states, defining their territorial and offshore rights. And the judge could not be persuaded that the House of Lords expressly acknowledged the need and propriety of obtaining evidence when Lord Wilberforce said:

> 'I am not saying that there may not be cases when it is so clear that a foreign government is taking action purely in order to extricate a state enterprise from contractual liability, that it may be possible to deny to such action the character of government intervention, within the meaning of a particular contract, but that result cannot, in my opinion, be achieved by means of the doctrine mentioned above: it would require clear evidence and definite findings'.

Mr Justice Hirst expressed the very gravest doubts whether the motive behind an act of state could ever be relevant in the present context. What was in question was 'not the foreign law in abstract but the results of its enforcement or recognition in England in the concrete case'.

This is very seductive, but unfortunately quite unworkable. A foreign act of state may be abhorred, but its results must be respected if it is non-discriminatory and genuinely part of governmental activities. But it is quite another matter if its only purpose is to extricate a government-owned enterprise from contractual liabilities.

To establish which of the two it is, the legislative aim must be considered. This was done in the House of Lords in the *Czarnikow* case when the Law

9 The *Buttes* case referred to is: *Buttes Gas and Oil Company* v *Hammer* [1982] AC 882.

Lords accepted the arbitrators' finding (wrong in my view) that a Polish state trader operated at arm's length from its Government. They accepted again the consideration of motives in the *I Congreso del Partido*[10] in June 1981, when they rejected the view that political motivation made a commercial act of the Cuban Government immune or that it justified the frustration of a contract.

The dangerous assumption that state trading agencies have a separate existence can be maintained only as long as legislative or executive measures apply indiscriminately but it must fall when a government acts to free its agency from liability under a particular contract. Evidently the question of motive is all-important when deciding about this type of *force majeure* defence.

Considered from a slightly different angle, the decree of the Portuguese Government amounted to confiscation of the $25 million due to the Thyssen group. It should not be recognised in international law if discriminatory – and here the question of motives reappears. But whatever the motive – whether discriminatory or not – the confiscation need not be recognised if no compensation is offered and to offer it would frustrate the very purpose of the Portuguese decree.

The unity of the state

The willingness of courts to ignore the legislation establishing a state monopoly of foreign trade, and to treat trading agencies of Communist countries as separate entities, encourages states occasionally to disclaim responsibility even for the acts of its government departments. Thus, in the *Topco/Calasiatic* case,[11] the Libyan government objected that arbitral proceedings were instituted against the Libyan Arab Republic while the deeds of concession were concluded by 'The Minister of Petroleum'.[12]

No need to say that the arbitrator, Professor Rene-Jean Dupuy, did not appreciate objections of this sort. He held that it clashed with the principle called 'the unity of the State', by virtue of which 'conduct of any State organ having that status under the internal law of that State shall be considered as an act of the State concerned under international law, provided that organ was acting in that capacity in the case in question'.[13]

The question which legal entities operating in France can be considered to be 'emanations' of the Libyan state was studied by 'three wise men' appointed by the Paris Tribunal de Grande Instance presided over by Mme Simone Rozes, when lifting attachments of the funds of Libyan companies obtained by LIAMCO under its award which received exequatur from a lower court. The study of the 'three wise men', however, was not concluded at the time the two parties reached a settlement and was, of course, discontinued then.

The most recent positive contribution to this issue can be found in the Algerian (Iran/US) Claims Settlement Declaration of January 19, 1981, which states in Article VII/3:

10 *Op cit*, note 4.
11 *Topco and Calasiatic – Libya Arbitration*, award published in 17 *ILM* 1 (1977).
12 A similar objection was made later by the Government of Iran when opposing a claim before the Iran/US Claims Tribunal: the contract in question, it asserted was not with the Iranian Government but with its Ministry of Defence.
13 17 *ILM* (1978), 1 at 23.

' "Iran" means the Government of Iran, any political subdivisions of Iran, and any agency, instrumentality, or entity controlled by the Government of Iran or any political subdivision thereof.'

The separateness of a state trader from the state owning and controlling it cannot be justified even on the formal criteria of municipal company law. The 'lifting of the corporate veil' or 'disregard of legal entity', well established in common law countries, is used particularly when a sole shareholder, or a small group of shareholders, use the corporate veil to enrich themselves on account of the company creditors or contracting parties. The doctrine of *Durchgriff* serves the same purpose in Germany and Switzerland. Does this doctrine apply equally to where the sole shareholder hiding behind the corporate veil is a state? The English *Rolimpex* case would suggest a reluctance to apply it. The United States courts, by contrast, see in the fact that the shareholder is a state, an additional reason for disregarding the corporate entity.[14]

The international variety of corporations and of rules applying to their 'unveiling' is much greater than that encountered within a single municipal system. The parties to international contracts, and arbitrators, may not be always familiar with the particular domestic law.

The issue is, of course, of particular importance when dealing with the state trading, mainly Communist, countries which operate a monopoly of foreign trade, but whose foreign trading agencies are in the form of separate corporations, sometimes even in the form of companies limited by shares. In the view of Professor Böckstiegel one should start with a presumption that these state trading agencies have a separate and independent existence. This presumption should be maintained in the face of general measures, legislative or executive, adopted by the state as long as these measures are motivated by general considerations – that is, not by considerations relating primarily and mainly to a contract which the government wishes to avoid. Such general measures should justify a defence of *force majeure* on the part of the state trading agency. However, the presumption of separate identity of this agency should be abandoned as soon as the measures taken by the state are addressed to the particular contract, or, at least, are clearly motivated by a desire to avoid its consequences. Such specific measures should, therefore, not be allowed to trigger a *force majeure* clause.

This view may sound well in theory, but is useless in practice, as even measures specifically designed for the evasion of contractual obligations will always be disguised and presented as being of a general nature. Moreover, even a general measure prompted by a bad harvest, and appropriate for the needs of the internal market, may be quite unnecessary in the international context when the commodity to be delivered under the contract in question is available on the world market and can be bought there either by the state trading agency or by the other party which then has a claim for any difference in price in comparison with the contract.

One can, therefore, conclude that it would greatly simplify matters if it was

14 See series of cases cited by Professor K H Böckstiegel, in 'The Legal Rules Applicable in International Commercial Arbitration Involving States or State Controlled Enterprises', in *60 Years of ICC Arbitration* 117, at note 32.

accepted that the rules of public international law prevent states from excusing breaches of contracts, concluded by themselves or by their agencies, by legislation or executive measures of their own.

The unmasking of the state traders

There is a general consensus that the state trading corporations should be treated as subject to the same rules as corporations owned privately, and that they should benefit in their day-to-day operations from the assumption of separate legal entity as long as they observe the rules of the game. In the vast majority of their dealings the state traders do observe the rules – they could hardly expect to be accepted as business partners if they did not. The same practical necessity dictates that courts should not hesitate to accept evidence disproving the assumption of separateness from the state and pull down the corporate mask if the state disowns its trading agency in order to avoid contractual obligations.

The principle that a state may not abuse legal technicalities to avoid its obligations was recognised by the Permanent Court of International Justice,[15] and by courts in the United States and West Germany. But even specific legislation designed to avoid contractual obligations is from time to time respected by national courts – for example Swiss.[16]

In a dispute concerning an abandoned project of hotel and tourist development agreed between *South Pacific Properties and Egoth*, the Egyptian state agency for tourism,[17] the arbitral tribunal held that Egyptian legislative and administrative acts which made the project impossible did not relieve Egypt from its liability for breach of contract which its Government endorsed. At the time of writing, the appeal against this award is still pending before French courts and an application for its enforcement before the High Court in London.

The applicable law

In many of the greatest arbitrations the problem of the state trading agency did not arise or was of no great importance. This applies particularly to disputes concerning concessions for the exploitation of mineral resources granted by the host state to a foreign company. Such disputes are invariably about a unilateral abrogration or modification of the concession by the government. The crucial issue before the arbitral tribunal can in most cases be boiled down to the question: which substantive law applies? If it is the domestic law of the host country, the foreign company has lost its case. It can only win if the concession contract can be brought, either under the public international law, or, unlikely, under the law of another state which does not recognise nationalisation or sequestration without compensation, and where the execution of any favourable award is not barred by sovereign immunity.

Public international law would, for all practical purposes, apply when the

15 PCIJ 1926, A 7 30 & 1930, A 46 167.

16 See Lalive, 'Arbitrage international et ordre public Suisse', 1 *Revue de droit suisse* 97 (1978).

17 ICC Award No 3493/1983, published in 22 *ILM* 752 (1983).

parties have agreed at least that the domestic law of the host country should apply insofar as it is not contrary to generally accepted principles of law, in which case it should be superseded by these principles or, better still, by the rules of public international law. The minimum safeguard is probably that which was used in the *Lena Goldfields* concession[18] which was made subject to 'any present or future Soviet legislation' with the exception that the Soviet Government may not modify the contract unilaterally.

No such exception was included in the concession contract between Saudi Arabia and the Arab American Oil Company (Aramco). When it came to the dispute, the arbitral tribunal, chaired by Professor Georges Sauser-Hall, held that as the Saudi Arabian law did not previously contain any specific rules for the exploitation of oil deposits, the 1933 Concession Agreement 'had the nature of a constitution'. The state, said the tribunal in its 1958 award, had the legal power to forbid itself to withdraw certain rights which it had granted.[19]

This reasoning seems to be somewhat thin on the ground, but the tribunal was even more daring when it concluded:

> 'Lastly, the Tribunal holds that public international law should be applied to the effects of the Concession, when objective reasons lead it to conclude that certain matters cannot be governed by any rule on the municipal law of any State, as is the case in all matters relating to transport by sea, to the sovereignty of the State on its territorial waters and to the responsibility of States for the violation of its international obligations'.[20]

The 'legal' acrobatics which the Aramco tribunal was obliged to perform to arrive at a fair award taught the next generation of lawyers to draft concession agreements more carefully. The Libyan concessions, for example, were at first drafted with a clause that the contract was governed by Libyan law insofar as this agreed with the 'principles of international law'. In more recent concessions the clause contains the further provision that in the absence of such conformity reference should be made to 'general principles of law'.

Such a clause enabled Professor Rene-Jean Dupuy to hold in the *Topco/Calasiatic*[21] case that the legal order from which the binding nature of the contract derived was international law, and that the law which governed the contract was the two-tier system provided by the parties – the first tier being Libyan law as long as it was not contrary to international law, and the second tier, the general principles of law.

The well-established principle of the public international law that a state cannot avoid its international obligations by reference to its municipal law is likely to remove the many problems damaging to trade, which originate from the contradiction between the commercial and the sovereign activities of a state whenever its contractual obligations are subject to a municipal law, even if this is not its own.

The question may be asked whether a private party can choose public international law to govern its contract, whether it can in this way promote itself to a level normally reserved for sovereigns. Dr F A Mann gives the following answer:

18 See *The Times* (London), September 13, 1930; 34 *Cornell Law Quarterly* 42 (1950).
19 27 *ILR* 117 at 152–3.
20 *Ibid*, at 172.
21 17 *ILM* 1 (1978).

> 'Nothing prevents a contract between the German state and a Dutch firm to be submitted to French law. Similarly, the fact that one party is not a state should not prevent the contract from being submitted to public international law.'[22]

This view is also supported by most arbitration awards concerning oil concessions, but there are more objections to be dealt with. The 1969 Vienna Convention on the Law of Treaties gives, by its Article 46, to a state the possibility to escape its contractual obligations if their fulfilment would be a manifest violation of an international law of fundamental importance. Nationalisation of industry may, of course, be taken for such an internal law of fundamental importance, but in that case also the other rule of public international law would apply which requires fair compensation to be paid for the nationalised property.

Enforcement

When it comes to enforcement of awards made against a state or its trading company, courts will hesitate to act; they fear – though they rarely admit it – that it may have unpleasant consequences for their own government or banks if they treated a foreign sovereign too harshly. Common law countries were particularly slow to abandon the doctrine of absolute sovereign immunity and relapsed into it gladly; but civil law courts, in Switzerland for example, were no less ingenious in achieving the same end. No one, however, displayed greater judicial inventiveness to protect foreign sovereign debtors when it suited domestic banks than the United States Appeal Court for the Second Circuit, making New York forum and law highly suspect for the creditors in international loan agreements.

Sovereign immunity

The restrictive interpretation of sovereign immunity – that in civil and commercial matters a sovereign is a private person in another's territory – was adopted in civil law countries in the course of the eighty years preceding 1960 when it was also embraced by Japan.

The United States courts had been moving towards excluding immunity in commercial issues since 1952, but the exclusion was completed only in 1977 by the Federal Sovereign Immunity Act. In the United Kingdom the restrictive theory of sovereign immunity was first recognised by the Privy Council in the *Philippine Admiral* in 1975,[23] but its definitive absorption by the common law was achieved only by Lord Denning's judgment in *Trendtex*,[24] approved by the House of Lords in *I Congreso* in 1982.[25] In the meantime Parliament adopted the State Immunity Act of 1978, which the courts have now interpreted for the first time in *Alcom* v *Republic of Colombia and Others.*[26] At issue was whether a

22 Mann, 'Contrats entre Etats et Personnes Privees Etrangères', *Revue belge de droit international* 562 (1975), at 564–5.
23 [1977] AC 373.
24 [1977] QB 529.
25 *Op cit*, at 261.
26 [1984] AC 580 CA & HL.

foreign government's bank account in the United Kingdom may be frozen by the courts, to secure the payment of the foreign government's commercial debts. The Court of Appeal said unanimously 'yes', but the House of Lords overruled that decision, again unanimously.

This is not the place to analyse in detail the reasoning by which the House of Lords and Court of Appeal reached such different results. When the convoluted text of the Act is unwound, it appears that a foreign state's property is immune against enforcement of a judgment if it is not used for commercial purposes, and that a declaration by the ambassador that it is not so used shall be accepted as sufficient evidence unless the contrary is proved. Such a declaration was delivered by the Colombian Ambassador, but the Court of Appeal held that it was disproved by the fact that the bank account was used to pay for air tickets and loans to stranded citizens which, in itself, was not an exercise of sovereign authority.

In taking the immediate application of the money rather than its ultimate aim, the Court of Appeal judgment was firmly based on the House of Lords decision in *I Congreso.*[27] It could have also referred to the 1975 Frankfurt Landgericht judgment in the Nigerian cement case, when it was held that a letter of credit was commercial by its very nature, and its purpose irrelevant.

Lord Diplock, by contrast, considered the ultimate purpose of the account and, in interpreting the 1978 State Immunity Act, substantially reduced the possibility of disproving the Ambassador's certificate. He held that the bank account was safe from execution

> 'unless it can be shown by the judgment creditor . . . that (it) was earmarked by the foreign state solely (save for *de minimis* exceptions) . . . for commercial transactions (such as) documentary credits for goods sold to the state . . .'[28]

The result is that foreign states' bank accounts will be open to enforcement of judgments only if the foreign governments' lawyers are particularly dim or negligent.

Special domestic relationship

The Swiss courts recognise in principle that sovereign immunity may not be claimed for a state's acts of a commercial nature or by its public or state-controlled corporations but the Federal Supreme Court developed two other obstacles to enforcement of awards or judgments.

One is the rule that assets of one state corporation must not be seized to satisfy a claim against another. The other, more serious obstacle, is known as the requirements of *Binnenbeziehung.* This means that Swiss courts will approve the enforcement in Switzerland of a judgment or award against a foreign state or its corporation only if the obligation was contracted or was to be performed in Switzerland. The assignment of a foreign private party's claim to a Swiss resident and even less the mere location of the debtor's assets in Switzerland, is not enough. The location of the arbitral tribunal in Switzerland is no help in this matter.

Thus, in the *Liamco* case the Swiss Federal Supreme Court lifted nine

27 *Op cit,* note 4.
28 *Ibid,* at 604.

attachment orders against Swiss banks holding Libyan assets because the award 'lacked sufficient domestic relatonship'.[29] In the *Bangladesh* case,[30] this court refused to recognise an award against the Bangladesh State though this State dissolved the debtor corporation by administrative measures which had the sole purpose of preventing the exposure of the corporation to arbitration. The court said that it would have decided differently if the claimant was a Swiss creditor: in such a case the court would have found it necessary to rectify those consequences of foreign law which were incompatible with the fundamental principles of justice respected in Switzerland – in the usual shorthand, it would have admitted the objection of public policy.

In this connection it should be noted that in *Arab Republic of Libya* v *Wetco Ltd*,[31] the court said it could not correct the effect of foreign laws by means of the public policy exception when the foreign state did not act with a discriminatory purpose as it did in the Bangladesh case. *Wetco* contended that LINOCO was an *alter ego* of the Libyan State and that it was consequently bound by the arbitration agreement concluded with LINOCO – a problem which appeared again in the already mentioned *South Pacific Properties and Egoth* case discussed above and now pending in London and Paris.

This attitude favourable to the state whose trading agency defaulted would be further reinforced by the passage of the 1981 Swiss Federal Enforcement and Bankruptcy Bill which would restrict pre-trial attachment to the assets directly owned by the foreign state trader. The measure would exclude any recourse to the assets of the foreign state or of its other corporations. On the other hand, the proposed code of Swiss private international law would preclude a successful pleading by a foreign state or its corporation of immunity or non-arbitrability on the basis of its domestic law.

Comity

The most outrageous novelty, however, has been invented by the US Court of Appeals for the Second Circuit (New York) in *Allied Bank International* v *Banco Agricola de Credito and others* on April 23, 1984.[32] Confirming the dismissal by the District Court of an action for the enforcement of payment under promissory notes payable in New York and subject to New York law, the court said that in prohibiting its state-owned bank to honour the bills, Costa Rica was acting as a sovereign regardless of any commercial component of the activity; and that comity required to recognise the action as analagous to the protection accorded to insolvent debtors who wished to reorganise their business under Chapter 11 of the US Bankruptcy Code.

The real reason behind this astonishing judgment, reversed on appeal on March 18, 1985[33] is probably the desire not to upset the second negotiation of the Costa Rican debt and to spare the banks agreeing to 're-scheduling' the embarrassment of having to call a default a default. The *Allied Bank*

29 20 *ILM* 1 (1980).

30 *Soc des Grands Traveaux de Marseille* v *Bangladesh*, May 6, 1976, 34 *Swiss Yearbook of International Law* 387 (1978).

31 37 *Swiss Yearbook of International Law* 446 (1981).

32 757 F 2d 516 (2d Cir 1985).

33 See, Financial Times Business Law Brief, April 1985.

International was the only one of some 39 banks holding Costa Rican promissory notes which was not willing to agree to a 'deferment' which, in reality, means to write off.

Conclusion

The emergence of large corporations, multinational in form and often transnational in their way of operation, and sometimes as powerful politically and economically as their sovereign partner, resulted in a qualitative change of the relationship between a state and a private company. The fundamental inequality derived from formal concepts of a sovereign, on the one hand, and the subject of another sovereign on the other, has been overshadowed by the more realistic assessment of the relationship between two different but not necessarily unequal subjects.

A relationship between partners who, for all practical purposes, are equal in the international arena, can hardly be regulated without reference to the public international law, or the general principles of law. International arbitration case law confirms[34] that a reference to the general principles of law always leads to the internationalisation of the contract, and each such reference stimulates the development of an international law of contract. This development was acknowledged in the *Topco & Calasiatic-Libya* award, where Professor Dupuy held that:

> 'States and private persons can, under certain conditions, come within the ambit of a particular and new branch of international law of contract.'

The growth of this international law of contract is fast because it is built out of prefabricated elements. Whole sections of English commercial law are being internationalised – a process which is obvious to English Commercial Court judges[35] – and there is a proliferation of multilateral international conventions and codes. Finally, international development projects lead to a new type of flexible contractual relationship, requiring a new type of legal management in which international arbitrators are playing an important role.

34 See Professor Dupuy in *Liamco Award* on the merits, January 19, 1977, in 17 *ILM* 1 (1978).

35 See Mr Justice Bingham and Lord Justice Goff on the internationalisation of the Lloyd's marine policy – but denied by the majority of the Court of Appeal and of the House of Lords in *Amin Rasheed Shipping Corp* v *Kuwait Insurance Co*, [1984] AC 60.

23 The strengths and weaknesses of international arbitration involving a state as a party: practical implications

Jeremy P Carver

At a superficial level, it may be asked whether the participation of a state in an arbitration makes any substantial difference. Resort to arbitration requires consent of the parties; and, given such consent, the state agrees to participate in substantially the same way as its private opponent. In theory, the state divests itself of those trappings of sovereignty which provide it with such immunity as is available from jurisdiction to suit in foreign municipal courts. It agrees, in principle, to be judged by the terms of the agreement by which the dispute is referred to arbitration.

However, as all lawyers who have ever been involved in such cases well know, the gulf between principle and practice is enormous. Arbitration, in practice, is often a far from perfect method of resolving commercial disputes between private parties from different countries. This paper seeks to address a few of the many such practical difficulties which are aggravated when a state is a party to an international commercial arbitration.

The political elements of consent

Definition of the difficulties in this area has to start with an appreciation of the differences between a state and a private party. Only in small part does this involve legal considerations.

The policy or decision-making of a corporation, however large, is driven primarily by commercial considerations. The board of a corporation, while answerable to shareholders, is vested with wide authority to act in the name of the corporation. If the financial analyses on the basis of which a particular contract was entered into prove to be substantially correct, the board will have every confidence that the shareholders will be more than satisfied. Even where things go wrong, provided the losses are contained and the board can demonstrate to auditors and shareholders that all reasonable remedial action is being taken, the board is unlikely to suffer serious sanction. And, if matters go seriously wrong, insolvency may extinguish the corporation; but the individuals involved can usually expect to find employment elsewhere.

How different are the workings of a state. Certainly, a government is accorded wide executive powers by the Constitution or otherwise. These powers devolve on various distinct departments of government or on entities established for specific purposes. The objects of such an entity may indeed be strictly commercial. But it is not just the different hierarchies of authority which make the formulation of decisions a vastly more complex matter than for a private corporation. Whatever political label may be applied to a state – capitalist or socialist, totalitarian or democratic, or whether its *per capita* GNP is measured in units or thousands – its government is ultimately answerable to people. When the willingness of those people to be so governed changes, those vested with authority to govern are subject to change: change which may be dramatic, and occasionally violent. Furthermore, there is no ultimate safety net of insolvency. Lawyers have debated in the context of international finance whether a state can undergo a process akin to private bankruptcy; but the obvious fact is that a state would rather that its citizens were fed than that its international creditors were paid.

This facile demonstration of difference bears particularly on the question of consent, which lies at the heart of any arbitral proceedings. As is well known, such consent to arbitrate can be evidenced by the original contract entered into for some wholly different purpose, often years before the dispute arose. Alternatively, it can be comprised in a specific *compromis* or agreement to arbitrate, which has as its sole or primary purpose the definition of the means of solving a dispute which has arisen.

In the original contract, the parties are for obvious reasons concentrating on the project or transaction to be undertaken. However hard the lawyers may try to impress upon the parties the need adequately to define a method of solving disputes, the parties have little desire to devote time and trouble to this remote, hypothetical issue. Even where the lawyers representing two private parties can agree some comprehensive and sensible formula for reference to arbitration, it would be a rash lawyer to advise his client that this formulation would sufficiently deal with every eventuality which might arise. But between lawyers from different jurisdictions and with different experience, the formulation ultimately agreed relies largely upon some institutional system of arbitration, and thus, when tested, on the imperfections in that system.

Even when represented by experienced outside counsel, a state tends to view the arbitration clause in a major project contract as of limited significance. Ideally, it seeks to be judged by its own laws, in its own courts. When this is recognised as being untenable, precedents – usually the product of previous lowest common denominators – tend to be far more significant than any formulation designed to deal with the particular characteristics of the project for which contracts are being prepared. The arbitration clause is usually agreed in the most general terms – providing for reference to ICSID or ICC or some other international body, before probably three arbitrators, according to the state's own or perhaps 'general principles' of law – and little else. Such a formulation is often virtually useless when the dispute actually arises and one party – whether it be the state or the private corporation – seeks to implement the clause.

This brings one to the need at the time when a dispute has arisen for a *compromis*, which essentially is a reaffirmation of consent. Between private parties, the degree of consent may be distinctly relative, one party having every incentive not to see a final award being entered against it. Whether claimant or respondent, a state will find greater difficulty in accepting the principle that some outside body should be empowered to decide issues which, in the eyes of the states, have, ultimately, internal political implications. The paucity of international disputes referred to the International Court of Justice underlines the reluctance of states to be judged by external, superficially objective, criteria. Governments prefer diplomatic solutions – or, of course, to be allowed to do exactly what they want.

Nevertheless, many arbitral tribunals have had to face the problems of deficient or relative consent to arbitrate between state and private parties. States have become increasingly aware that their sovereign freedom is conditioned by clear contractual obligations including an arbitration clause. The prevalance of unilateral awards against states who have refused to participate in arbitrations has probably increased the tendency of states to treat seriously a commitment to arbitrate. Private parties and practitioners might hope that the product of such awards was of a more consistent nature. There are, however, real incentives for a state not to be obviously delinquent in ignoring disputes.

Machinery of representation

Even when consent, however relative, to arbitrate an existing dispute is present, agreement on the procedure to be followed still depends in large part on agreement between the parties. Anyone who has been appointed arbitrator in a dispute between parties very differently organised and represented by lawyers from different backgrounds and jurisdictions knows how difficult it is to discharge the function of arbitrator fairly and impartially when the whole approach to the procedure to be followed is different. If the arbitrator himself tries to mediate some compromise between these different approaches, he runs the serious risk of compromising his authority as arbitrator before he has embarked on his substantive task.

Take, as an example, the elementary matter of a timetable for submission of written pleadings. The claimant wishes to hasten the process. It has good rapport with its lawyers, who maintain that only a few weeks are required for each side to prepare and submit adequate pleadings in writing. The opponent is more cautious. Not only does it not want an accelerated award; it recognises that preparation of its pleadings, assembling the evidence, procuring expert testimony which may affect the arguments to be presented, all will take time; and it insists upon a time-scale measured in months between written pleadings. It would be a rash arbitrator simply to direct a timetable halving the difference between the periods advocated on each side. To risk equal displeasure might seem tempting; but this would be to ignore what may well prove to be factors going to the substance of the dispute. A cursory appraisal might favour the claimant; while a more deliberate process would demonstrate that the respondent's defence was substantial. The arbitrator finds himself increasingly sucked into acrimonious procedural debate, undermining the respect which he must maintain for the award to be effective.

The likelihood for such procedural difficulties to form real obstacles to the arbitral process is enormously increased where a state is one of the parties. This is so not just because decisions tend to be taken against the backdrop of political considerations, but also because of the awkwardness of a state's representation.

Many states consider that their executive machinery includes sufficient lawyers competently to represent the state's interests and, for obvious reasons, prefer not to go outside that machinery. Not only can government lawyers be expected to understand the workings of the government better than any outsiders, but it saves money. But government lawyers tend to have only limited experience in this type of commercial arbitration; and, given its uncertainties, may decide to retain certain outside specialists, particularly as advocates in the oral hearings. Other states can recognise more easily the inexperience of their own government lawyers, and decide to retain outside counsel from the start. Either situation poses problems in effective communication: both internally between lawyer and client, and externally between the state's representatives and the tribunal or those representing the other party. A state usually imposes requirements of internal security which are inconsistent with the different confidentiality needs between private client and his lawyer. Modes of communication can be quite different. The large corporation and its lawyers may use the full panoply of devices, such as telecopiers, telex, telephone, etc; while the government departments may have to survive on more primitive methods: where even the telephone has only limited use and communication overseas has to employ the resources of the foreign ministry's diplomatic couriers.

Such elements, trivial in themselves, can present real difficulties in practice; particularly in the heat of an active case with deadlines approaching. Yet for an outside lawyer to try to persuade his government client at the start of a case that these and other similar, purely functional, matters need to be addressed, is often to invite disbelief, or even hostility given the unwieldy procurement processes which the officials concerned will have to follow.

Subjective experience suggests that there are various ways in which the state party and its lawyers can reduce these self-inflicted impediments to effective presentation. Within the state machinery, the departments and officials involved should be reduced only to those whose support, assistance or knowledge is absolutely necessary. Among these, there must be established a chain of command, with sufficiently clear areas of responsibility, leading up to the Minister or Chief Executive Officer ultimately responsible. Reporting directly to him, one person should be appointed as the primary point of contact of the state with the outside world, ie, the tribunal, the opposition and the state's own representatives. In public international litigation or arbitration, this individual is called the 'Agent'; and it has become more usual in international commercial arbitrations for such appointments to be made.

The state's outside lawyers must similarly forge a coherent structure, which can effectively channel the advice, expertise and product of the outside legal team, and can receive and ensure compliance with the Agent's instructions. The specialist, legally qualified or technically expert, whose role in the case is limited, can have little appreciation of the political significance of the case within the state. For him simply to follow his professional practices on behalf of the commercial client, may not be acceptable to the government client. The advocate who is used to preparing his own presentation to court may take exception to a client insisting upon knowing, and approving beforehand, exactly what he is going to say. But that is the sort of request he will often face when acting for a foreign government.

The tendency to multiply the individuals involved, whether within the state organisation, for political reasons, or in the external team, out of more basic considerations must be severely restrained. However complex the issues, few things distort the effective presentation of arguments to a tribunal more than a multiplicity of advisers. One unfortunate tendency of both state and private parties in large international arbitration is to appoint distinguished counsel for no other reason than that they are well known to a member of the arbitral tribunal. This may well be a factor when selecting outside lawyers, but it is surely subsidiary to established authority in the field or fields specifically engaged by the issues and practical efficiency in presentation of cases.

The size of a team can also impede the very necessary exercise of defining the issues. To provide the parties with an award which they can not only follow but respect, the tribunal needs a great deal of assistance from the parties. There have been cases where tribunals have thought that they understood the issues involved better at the commencement of the proceedings than at the end. Enormous written submissions, volumes of documents and weeks of oral argument and factual or expert testimony serve not so much to simplify the issues but to confuse them. Furthermore, as the case grows more complex, it becomes increasingly difficult to ensure that all members of a large legal team keep pace with the development of the case. Thus to leave behind members of the team, particularly if they are state officials, puts at risk the political support which is crucial for the arbitration to have an effective result.

Reverting to the role of the arbitrator or tribunal in procedural matters, the tribunal can often help the parties considerably by adoption of another device usual in international litigation. With the parties' consent, the tribunal can appoint its own clerk or registrar. The Registrar's function is partly to help the tribunal to manage and control the growing mountain of documents which major arbitration cases inevitably generate. Obviously, he organises the administrative aspects of oral hearings, accommodation, travel, secretarial facilities and many similar aspects for which the eminent arbitrator has neither the time nor inclination. Beyond this, the Registrar can play a vital role as communicator between the tribunal and each party, and, where the parties themselves find communication difficult, between the parties. The Registrar can discuss procedural *impasses* without risking the integrity of the tribunal. He can act as mediator between the parties. He can even indicate to parties substantive areas affecting the merits on which the tribunal would welcome more, or, sometimes, less, assistance. And he can also report to the tribunal points about which, in his opinion, a party feels particularly strongly and which the tribunal must deal with in its award, however little they may affect the outcome of the decision.

Effectiveness of the award

The ultimate test of the success or usefulness of any arbitral process is whether the award is effective. Too often, lawyers tend to equate 'effectiveness' with 'enforceability', a subject dealt with elsewhere in these papers.

It is hardly surprising that lawyers worry about the enforceability of arbitral awards. When clients face the prospect of, often, years of effort and expense in pursuing a dispute referred to arbitration, they need assurance that the 'piece of paper' they hope to receive at the end will be valuable. This approach, however, is essentially that of the party and his counsel embarking on domestic litigation, where the availability of assets of the opponent to meet a judgment for damages has significance. Similar considerations may properly arise in the approach to international arbitration between private parties.

In an international arbitration where a state is a party, other considerations must surely prevail. Insolvency or lack of assets of the state respondent is not really a factor. What should prevail in the adviser's mind is the willingness of the state to meet and pay the award. This requires a more fundamental adjustment to the way in which the arbitration is conducted.

It is axiomatic that an agreement to arbitrate, by original contract or by *compromis*, involves a commitment by both sides to accept and comply with the decision of the tribunal. Not only is this consent as noted above, distinctly relative at the time when the proceedings commence, it is a 'delicate flower' which requires constant nurture and encouragement. This puts a particular burden on the tribunal, and also on both sets of advisers. The burden is not discharged by the tribunal merely making an award which is a compromise for its own sake. If this is what the parties wanted, they could have expressly empowered the arbitrators to decide *ex aequo et bono*. It requires a great deal more care and hard work than a 'judgment of Solomon'.

Composition of the tribunal

First, it requires that both sides have confidence that the tribunal is capable of reaching a fair decision. A three-man tribunal, one appointed by each party with a 'neutral' chairman, seems at first sight to be a reasonable way of achieving this. But there are still difficulties.

Even with the party's own nominee, there are completely different approaches. The private party, when represented by experienced and reputable counsel, probably makes its selection on the basis of personality, distinction, authority and integrity. Once appointed, the arbitrator is left to get on with the case, without special pleading from the party which has appointed him. His duty is to the tribunal, and indeed he may not agree with many of the arguments which are presented by the side from whom he holds temporary, and often remunerative, office. The extent to which he 'represents' that side is to ensure that the tribunal take sufficient account of what it has submitted. And this is undoubtedly part of the process by which an award becomes acceptable.

Nevertheless, cases have been known where a party's nominee as arbitrator was far from being an impartial member of the tribunal; but was an active protagonist for his side within the tribunal, where, of course, the other side are excluded. Fear of such an appointment can arise particularly when a state is party to a case and where there is no restriction on its ability to appoint one of its own nationals. In those cases where this situation exists, the tribunal becomes distorted, and its award is often stillborn.

A simple solution, going some way to ease these anxieties, is for both sides to agree or accept that they will not appoint nationals of their own state: a situation which is implicit in certain arbitral rules.

The choice of neutral arbitrator is even harder. Many parties would prefer to select their own appointee only when the identity of the chairman, his outlook and personal prejudices, is known. But this can only be achieved when the *compromis* makes an express prior selection of chairman. Usually, the form of agreement is that each side appoints its own arbitrator and these two, when appointed, are required to agree the third; or, in default of agreement, some impartial body or individual has to make the appointment. The ICC may have statistics to confirm the impression that, in cases referred to it in which a state was a party, only a small minority had seen appointment of the chairman by the parties' own choice. In many more cases, the ICC court's own machinery for appointment will have been engaged. It must be doubted, in principle, whether a process so remote from the actual issues really ensures a sufficiently sensitive selection.

A divided tribunal is surely the worst way of arbitrating a complex dispute. Its members must have respect for each other, and must be able to work together in relative harmony. Possibly, the only time when such a situation might be sought is when the agreement to arbitrate is made and, probably, before the dispute has actually arisen. There is much to be said for a more elaborate arbitration clause, nominating either a panel of individuals who may be appointed, or, as precisely as possible, the qualifications and experience of all arbitrators.

Procedural rules

Second, acceptability of the award requires that the procedure followed takes sufficient account of the preferences of both sides. Here, as noted above, the Registrar can play a crucial role. Beyond this, the tribunal must try to understand the differences between the two sides, and, in its procedural directions, bring the parties together. Often, where lawyers from the same jurisdiction are acting on both sides in a case, this is not difficult. The formal or conventional rules of their domestic court practices should sufficiently mark out the 'ground rules'. When not only the parties but also their lawyers come from different backgrounds and jurisdictions, questions such as discovery of documents can be highly contentious. This is even more so when a state's own documents are in issue. Active and sympathetic patience on the part of the tribunal, its chairman and Registrar, is often the only way of overcoming these problems successfully. But these qualities are often in short supply.

Content of the award

Third, and most obviously, acceptability depends on the award itself. It is a mistake which some arbitrators make to suppose that all the parties really care about is the effect of the decision. Manifestly, this is important; but it is far from the whole story.

The ideal award leaves each side believing it has won. Some awards leave one side satisfied and the other dismayed. More often, both sides are disappointed. Perhaps unconsciously or not, arbitrators strive for a balance of dissatisfaction. There can be few merits in such an approach for its own sake, because arbitrators can seldom measure with any accuracy the real concerns of the parties before them.

In a national court, the judge deliberately seeks to inform counsel before him of the way in which he is thinking on particular issues. Judges ask questions, comment, criticise and otherwise intervene in the proceedings. Occasionally, they do so to excess. Most international arbitral tribunals conduct themselves quite differently. If questions are asked, they are posed formally, often in writing at an appropriate break in the proceedings. The responses are equally formal. The reticence of tribunals is the understandable product of the lack of familiarity between its members and those appearing before them. Where a state is a party, the complexity of decision-making, noted above, discourages an easy exchange of views between tribunal and counsel. One result of this awkwardness is the reluctance of parties in international arbitrations to settle their dispute amicably prior to issue of the award.

There are no easy solutions to the dilemma facing a tribunal. Its members need to be more constructively interventionalist, while at the same time respecting the factors which inhibit a quick and helpful reply.

The process of indicating responsibly to the parties the way in which the tribunal is thinking during the oral hearing is a vital element in ensuring acceptability of the award. It gives the parties the opportunity to address those aspects of apparent importance, and enables the tribunal to assess the reactions of the two contestants. There are few situations more unacceptable to parties than that the decision, when delivered, relies on issues or conclusions which were barely or never addressed during the hearings. By the time the hearings have ended, the parties should have a much clearer idea of the tribunal's approach, so that the award when issued contains few major surprises.

When the oral hearings have finally concluded, and the tribunal sits down to the main task of drafting its award, the arbitrators have to perform the most arduous part of their task with great tact and sensitivity. The award they produce has to be more than respectably reasoned. It must take account of and deal with all the principal issues raised. Even where the parties have wasted considerable effort in arguing a point of only peripheral relevance, an appreciation of the point, the relative merits of the arguments presented on it and the reasons why it is not relevant must be demonstrated. And the demonstration must be accurate. Few things annoy a party more than a misstatement of the submissions it has made on any issue, or, for example, the unreasoned adoption of one parties' contested translation of an important document.

Where a state is a party, the tribunal has in the award to take particular account of the political dimensions. Behind the Agent, there may be many with an interest in the outcome of the case, sometimes with mixed motives about the result hoped for. A careless award which trespasses on some taboo of national significance, of which the tribunal may be only dimly aware, can do irreparable damage to the effectiveness of the decision.

Conclusion

This paper has deliberately not dealt with the many legal issues which may be engaged by reason of a state or a state-controlled entity being a party to international commercial arbitration. Correct identification of the state party or parties implicated in the case may not be easy. The extent to which a state entity can plead as a defence *force majeure* brought about by the states' legislative or administrative acts often raises difficult 'Act of state' problems. Classification of issues and analysis of the applicable substantive law or legal principles is often made more complex by the fact that a state or one of its manifestations is a party.

Nevertheless, interesting as many of these legal issues undoubtedly may be, most arbitral decisions depend largely on the terms of the contract in issue and the weight of factual evidence presented.

Thus, analysis of the practical approach to their respective tasks of the arbitrators, parties and their advisers may be at least as significant for the success of arbitration in resolving international commercial disputes. The assessment here is largely subjective, based upon the author's observation of and participation in several major arbitrations in which states or other entities have been parties. To point to these or any other cases as justifying a particular conclusion would be invidious.

International arbitration between states and corporate entities: a cautionary note

24

Kenneth R Simmonds

Judge Huber, acting as sole arbitrator in the now classic *Island of Palmas* arbitration in 1928 said in his award:

> 'International law, like law in general, has the object of assuring the co-existence of legal interests which are worthy of legal protection'.[1]

When we consider the present condition of international adjudication, and the place of the international arbitral process in that context,[2] it is all too common to find the claim that voluntary recourse to arbitration, and the voluntary acceptance in advance of the binding character of an award, represents remarkable expression of faith and trust in an institution which continues to develop at a time when recourse to formal and permanent adjudication is becoming progressively more and more unpopular. Nevertheless, since World War II, instances of *ad hoc* arbitrations between states have been relatively few, even though many opportunities have existed for the use of this method of dispute resolution when the adversary model of procedure before a standing tribunal was inappropriate or it would have been easier to engage an opponent in this way rather than before the International Court of Justice. It is true that extensive reference to the arbitral process is made in the provisions of the 1982 UN Convention on the Law of the Sea on disputes settlement[3] – but the plethora of choice that is to be open to states parties to this Convention seems to me to reflect only the doubts and uncertainties that are prevalent in many states over their willingness to confide substantial issues to judicial or quasi-judicial adjudication.

The strengths of the arbitral process in international law have been the subject of a considerable literature.[4] It is a flexible and adaptable instrument for the resolution of certain kinds of dispute because it offers the parties the power to exercise a high degree of control over the proceedings and the selection of the terms of reference, as well as the composition, of the tribunal. The disadvantages of the process are equally clear; many *compromis* are ill-drawn and some awards have been ill-determined – there is a correlation, although not an inevitable one, between the two. In some there has been an

1 (1928) UNRIAA Vol II, 829; *US* v *The Netherlands*.

2 For a broad overview, and a valuable compilation of materials, see J Gillis Wetter, *The International Arbitral Process: Public and Private*, New York; Oceana 1979.

3 *UN Convention on the Law of the Sea, 1982*, Part XV and Annexes VII and VIII.

4 See Wetter, *op cit*, and see the listings in AM Stuyt, *Survey of International Arbitrations*, 1972, which surveys international arbitrations between 1794 and 1970.

exiguous control over the pleadings and the procedure. In others, arbitrators have shown tendencies to exceed their jurisdiction and to decide beyond the scope of the *compromis* or to attempt to resolve the dispute by a legal solution outside the submissions of the parties. Arbitration can also be complex, expensive and time-consuming – as can, of course, adjudication. I suspect that one of the principal reasons for its limited use (limited both geographically and in the subject-matter and content of disputes) is that many states look to judicial and quasi-judicial adjudication to settle disputes which are essentially concerned with *demands for a change in the law.*

The arbitral process is, however, a process of decision according to international law which is supported throughout by reference to appropriate procedural standards. International arbitration between states is essentially a *judicial* process distinguished from formal adjudication before a standing court by the *ad hoc* character of the tribunal and the extent of control exercisable over the process by the parties. The real variety and diversity for which the institution is noted lies in the terms of submission rather than in the procedures adopted. The concept of quasi-judicial arbitration is certainly unattractive to the majority of newly independent developing states and the capacity of the institution to resolve major political disputes of critical significance to the parties can easily be overstated.

If we turn to the recent history of the international arbitral process in disputes between states and corporate entities or individuals, we find, I believe, different reasons for the infrequency of recourse to it. Here very many disputes concern differing approaches to an understanding and interpretation of rules relating to the international minimum standard for the treatment of aliens and their property. Conflicts over the imputability of acts or omissions to the 'host' state; the nationality of claims; the exhaustion of local remedies; the nature, purposes and consequences of expropriation; and over 'disguised' or 'creeping' expropriation, very often stem from divergent philosophies of international law. Many of the principles and rules relating to state responsibility for economic injury are highly controversial and have been subjected in recent years to intensive re-examination and reassessment. The uncertainty over their present status and future direction has been very clearly reflected in a number of recent arbitral awards.[5] The criticisms provoked by these awards have mingled dissatisfaction with the law together with dissatisfaction with the arbitral process; that is a natural, if illogical, reaction which will increase the existing reluctance to have resort to arbitration in dispute situations where ideologies conflict. If resort to third party settlement of disputes is discarded when the parties are afraid of a crystallisation of the law then of course the future for *ad hoc* arbitration must be bleak. In his separate opinion in the *Barcelona Traction* case (1970) Judge Jessup advanced the view that the major controversial issue over the international minimum standard concerned that of compensation. Unhappily, subsequent events have indicated that the notion itself of an international minimum standard is widely challenged, even as to the substantive rights of investors, to say nothing of the existence of recourse as to international remedies.

5 See *BP Exploration Co (Libya) Ltd* v *Government of the Libyan Arab Republic* (Lagergren, Sole Arbitrator, 1973 and 1974) 53 *ILR* 297; *Texas Overseas Petroleum Co and California Asiatic Oil Co* v *Government of the Libyan Arab Republic* (Dupuy, Sole Arbitrator, 1977) 53 *ILR* 389; and *cf Saudi Arabia* v *Arabian American Oil Co* (1958) 27 *ILR* 117.

Some of the most significant work currently in hand by way of a reassessment of the status and content of these rules is that of the American Law Institute, which is revising the Restatement of the Foreign Relations Law of the United States. The revised Restatement, on which five tentative drafts have been issued since 1980, is intended to express American views on the rules which an international judicial or arbitral tribunal would apply if charged with the resolution of a dispute according to principles and rules of international law.[6] The existing Restatement of the Foreign Relations Law of the United States was developed between 1955 and 1962, adopted by the American Law Institute in 1962, and promulgated in 1965. It has since been regularly cited as authority in judgments, arbitral awards, briefs and opinions. The revised Restatement should be completed in time for adoption by the Institute and promulgation this year. The tentative drafts so far issued have dealt with subjects which include: the status of international law under US law[7]; limitations on jurisdiction[8]; sovereign immunity[9]; Act of state[10]; and the effect of foreign judgments and awards.[11]

The section of the revised Restatement most relevant to our present concern is that which deals with the law relating to state responsibility for economic injury. This provides as follows in Section 712:

> 'A state is responsible under international law for injury resulting from:
>
> 1 a taking by the state of the property of a national of another state, when the taking is not for a public purpose or is discriminatory, or when provision is not made for just compensation;
>
> 2 a discriminatory or other arbitrary repudiation by the state of a contract with a national of another state, or from any breach of such a contract when the foreign national is not given an adequate forum to determine the claim of breach or is not compensated for any breach determined to have occurred; or
>
> 3 other arbitrary or discriminatory acts or omissions by the state that impairs property or other economic interests of a national of another state.'

Both the text itself and the comments which accompany it have aroused considerable criticism. Section 712(1) of the revised Restatement indicates that something less than 'prompt, adequate and effective' compensation would be an accepted international norm today and that there has been a substantial modification of the traditional view as expressed in Sections 187–190 of the existing (1965) Restatement. It is understood that contrary positions have been put to the Reporters both by the Legal Adviser to the State Department and by the United States Overseas Private Investment Corporation. If questions of promptness, adequacy and effectiveness of compensation are to be subsumed into what is 'just' in all the circumstances of an individual case then we must expect major changes in the framing of bilateral investment treaties between

6 The Reporters for the revised Restatement include Professor Louis Henkin, Professor Andreas F Lowenfeld, Professor Louis B Sohn and Professor Detlev Vagts.

7 Tentative Draft No 1 (1980).

8 Tentative Drafts No 2 (1981) and No 3 (1982); see especially ss402 and 403.

9 Tentative Draft No 2 (1981).

10 Tentative Draft No 4 (1983).

11 *Ibid.*

states, in the adjudication of expropriation disputes and in the negotiation of settlements following expropriation.

In Comment (g) to Section 712(1) the Reporters deal with the very frequent problem of 'creeping expropriation' and put forward the view that:

> 'A state is not responsible for loss of property or for other economic injury that is due to bona fide general taxation or to regulation of the kind that is commonly accepted as within the police power of states, that does not discriminate against aliens, against aliens of particular nationality, or against a particular alien, and is not designed to cause the alien to abandon the property to the state or sell it at a distress price.'

A review of recent cases suggests that this takes too limited a view of what constitutes state action which may result in 'creeping expropriation'; so too does the Reporters' Comment (h) here which states that:

> '... a breach of contract may sometimes constitute "creeping expropriation" ... for example, if it makes impossible the continued operation of the project that is the subject of the contract.'

We have become all too familiar with situations of this kind where the continued operation of a project has been possible, but only *on an uneconomic basis*. Must therefore the foreign investor be forced to abandon a project before a claim for compensation may be made?

Section 712(2) deals with state responsibility for the discriminatory or other arbitrary repudiation of contracts with foreign nationals. The Reporters' Comment (h) gives here a number of examples of the application of this section to international contract practice. Example (iv) covers 'stabilisation clauses', which are very common in mining and other concessions contracts, and which prevent the host state from changing its taxation or other regulatory laws to the detriment of the foreign national. The Reporters suggest that such 'stabilisation clauses' may be resisted '... as an affront and an alleged derogation from the state's sovereignty.'

The comments on 'stabilisation clauses' that were made by the arbitrator in the *Texaco/Calasiatic–Libya* case may be recalled. Professor Dupuy in his award said at one point:

> '[The] emphasis on the contractual nature of the legal relation between the host state and the investor is intended to bring about an equilibrium between the goal of the general interest sought by such relations and the profitability which is necessary for the pursuit of the task entrusted to the private enterprise. The effect is also to ensure to the private contracting party a certain stability which is justified by the considerable investments it makes in the country concerned. The investor must in particular be protected against legislative uncertainties, that is to say the risks of the municipal law of the host country being modified, or against any government measures which would lead to an abrogation or rescission of the contract. Hence the insertion, as in the present case, of so-called stabilization clauses: these clauses tend to remove all or part of the agreement from the internal law and to provide for its correlative submission to *sui generis* rules.'[12]

12 *Texaco/Calasiatic–Libya* award, in 17 *ILM* 1 (1978) at para 45, p 17.

His analysis of 'internationalised contracts' in that award, and his conclusion that states and private persons could choose public international law as the law to govern their contractual relations – or that such internationalisation of contracts could arise from the very nature of the contract itself if it deals with the long-term economic development of a developing country – has attracted substantial criticism.[13] Yet the analysis does reflect developments long ago foreshadowed by Professor Wolfgang Friedmann, amongst others.[14]

Principles of public international law *are* being applied by a variety of tribunals on issues arising under long-term development agreements. Sometimes this has been achieved with substantial success and relative ease; examples include the ICSID arbitration awards in *Agip Co* v *Popular Republic of the Congo*, and in *Benvenuti and Bonfort* v *Popular Republic of the Congo*.[15] Yet in the recent *Kuwait* v *American Independent Oil Company* (Aminoil) *ad hoc* arbitration[16] the agreement to arbitrate prescribed 'principles common to the laws of Kuwait and the State of New York', and, in applying principles of international law the tribunal found that the UN General Assembly Resolution of 1962 on 'permanent sovereignty over natural resources'[17] was the '... most general formulation of the rules applicable for a law of nationalisation.' This is not a position that would find favour with many states who have argued for a radical revision of the public character relationships between developing countries and foreign corporate entities before, for example, UNCTAD or the UN Commission on Transnational Corporations in recent years.[18] Nevertheless, the practice of states continues to show, in a wide range of bilateral investment treaties, that governments which are parties to such agreements are legally bound to perform their obligations in good faith, can lawfully nationalise their contracts – as with other property – on payment of adequate compensation, and may also, in the exercise of their sovereignty, be prepared to divest themselves of the right to nationalise their contracts.[19] It is perhaps in this area that the prospects for international arbitration between developing states and corporate entities appears brightest.

Even so there is little ground for general optimism whether one considers *ad hoc* or institutional arbitration. The protection of foreign investment, and the legal standards applicable to that protection, was a subject that was exhaustively discussed during the negotiations which led up to the conclusion of the Second ACP–EEC Convention of Lomé of 1980. In the event all that was achieved was the attachment of an Annex to the Convention which called for bilateral inter-governmental investment agreements to ensure the effective non-discriminatory treatment of investments coming from European

13 See the review by Von Mehren and Kourides, 'International Arbitrations Between States and Foreign Private Parties: The Libyan Nationalisation Cases', in 75 *Am J Intl L* 476 (1981).

14 See GW Haight, 'The Internationalization of Development Contracts', in 3 *Public Law Forum* 69–78 (1984).

15 The two awards can be found in 21 *ILM* 726 and 740 (1982) respectively.

16 The award was handed down in Paris on March 24, 1982.

17 GA Res 1803 (XVII).

18 See K R Simmonds (ed), *Multinational Corporations Law* (Oceana, loose-leaf, 1979–), Introduction, *passim*.

19 Haight, *op cit*, n14 *supra*, 76–8, and see Böckstiegel, 'Arbitration between Parties from Industrialized and Lesser Developed Countries', in *Report of the 60th Conference, International Law Association*, 269 (1983).

Community Member States into the (then) fifty-eight co-signatory developing African, Caribbean and Pacific (ACP) States.[20] A similar pattern of discussion ensued during the recently concluded negotiations for the successor Third ACP–EEC Convention of Lomé of 1985. This time a Chapter on investment was actually included in the text of the Convention.[21] However, on examination, this proves again to be almost entirely exhortatory – with joint 'undertakings' and 'commitments' to accord investors fair and equitable treatment and to maintain predictable, safe investment climates.[22] There is also an affirmation of the principle of non-discrimination when regulating, applying and interpreting the recommended bilateral agreements. In the context of the development policy of the European Community this is disappointing enough; even more troubling is the absence in these provisions of any reference to relevant and applicable principles of international law.

20 See K R Simmonds, 'The Second Lomé Convention: The Innovative Features', in 17 *CML Rev* 99 (1980), at 115.

21 *Third ACP–EEC Convention of Lomé, 1985*, Title IV, Chapter 1, Arts 240–247. The Convention was signed in Lomé; Togo, on December 8, 1984, between the ten European Community Member States and 65 ACP States. It was the subject of an article published by the present writer in the September 1985, issue of the *Common Market Law Review*.

22 *Ibid*, Art 240.

Settlement of disputes within the framework of foreign debt rescheduling in Latin American countries

25

Bernardo M Cremades

It is often true that lawyers lag several years behind businessmen. Our point of view is much more static and, at times, our capacity to react is much slower. The issue of the moment in developing countries, particularly Latin American countries, is that of their enormous foreign debt. Both the initial loan contract and subsequent renegotiated debt agreements reflect, in their drafting, the exclusive use of ordinary legal criteria. These criteria are not always the most adequate for exceptional circumstances such as those posed by the foreign debt of developing countries. In other words, with respect to foreign debt, one must ask if the legal instruments ordinarily used for loan contracts or renegotiated debt agreements are appropriate, or whether alternatives must be found.

Economic and social background

President Nixon's decision to suspend the convertibility of the dollar to gold was based largely on the monetary crisis provoked by the extraordinary expansion of the United States' balance of payments deficit. This deficit was caused by the military expenses of the Vietnam war and the parallel investment of large amounts of capital abroad by large United States multinational companies. From the time of the abandonment of the gold standard the dollar was successively devalued, a fact which is often mentioned as the immediate cause of 'Black Thursday', October 16, 1973.

On 'Black Thursday', oil-producing countries set off the energy crisis and the 'oil shocks' that followed. In large part, this was a direct consequence of international economic policies carried out under the leadership of the United States. The repeated increases in the price of oil provoked the second phase of the crisis, the industrial crisis. The reaction of industrial nations, particularly in 1976–1977, was not long in coming and took the form of an energy-saving restructuring of their economies in order to reduce the demand for oil.

Monetary imbalances and further increases in the price of oil generated a third phase of the crisis, the financial crisis. Excess petrodollars belonging to OPEC countries were recycled through international banks between 1974 and 1982 and, in large part, loaned to less developed nations. The Third World's enormous debt was created at this time. The implications and consequences of the exaggerated debt in the Third World during these years are still an open book in contemporary economic history.

The foreign debt of Latin America has been subject to extensive politicisation. It is not infrequent to find posters in the strangest places with a text such as 'Foreign debt, no.' This politicisation is due in part to the lack of tact demonstrated by creditor countries in drafting foreign debt renegotiation agreements. The use of local lawyers is very scarce and may reflect a lack of confidence in their skills. Debt renegotiation agreements are often extraordinarily humiliating in their presentation and drafting, rather than in their content. It often seems as if the lawyers who took part in the negotiations were thinking more of the moral satisfaction of their creditor clients than in the enforceability of these agreements. In addition, the documents signed by debtor countries at moments in which their very economic survival is at issue are the exclusive product of Anglo-American contracting methods which are unfamiliar and, in many cases, incomprehensible to the Latin lawyer. The complaints which are made against debt renegotiation agreements in many Latin American parliaments are most often based on a lack of understanding of the clauses contained in these contracts.

The participation of states in international transactions

Recently there has been considerable legal progress concerning the issue of the participation of states or their government agencies in commerce or international transactions. Contrary to the clear-cut sovereignty of the past, we lawyers have made a definitive contribution toward making underlying philosophies more relative. Contrary to the traditional myth of sovereignty as a sacrosanct principle of international law, modern international economic law enters into a specific case-by-case analysis of agreements negotiated by sovereign states. It has been said that, today, sovereignty consists precisely in the ability to waive sovereign rights.

The legal consequences of the presence of sovereign states or their government agencies in international commercial contractual relations can be summarised as follows:

1 The theory of relative immunity has been increasingly gaining wider acceptance than the theory of absolute immunity. This is true in both the legislation and jurisprudence of developed nations.
2 In many developed nations express submission to a foreign legal forum or to arbitration proceedings almost automatically implies a waiver of the exception of sovereign immunity from jurisdiction at the time legal or arbitration proceedings are brought.
3 Sovereign immunity from execution is where the relative theory has taken a particularly strong hold. This issue may be summarised as follows:
   (a) State activity *iure gestionis* in international transactions does not coincide with the exception of immunity *iure imperii*. State activity of the latter type continues to be protected by public international law and prevents potential execution.
   (b) In many countries there is a distinction made between different types of foreign state property, depending on whether it is for public use or for use in commercial activities.
   (c) According to the relativity mentioned in (1) and (2) above, the courts of many developed countries do not hesitate to take precautionary

measures against foreign state property and to execute judicial judgments or arbitration awards.

Logically, all of these postulates are questioned by developing countries since they feel that, in most cases, they merely cover up, by means of fictitious arguments, the economic oppression by capital and technology exporting countries of countries which export raw materials or labour. In many of these latter countries, attempts are even being made to extend the definition of treason in their criminal codes so as to cover nationals who enter into agreements which may be considered extremely damaging to national interests. One president of a central bank in a well-known and important Latin American republic was imprisoned, while in office, as a result of a judge's opinion that acceptance of submission to a foreign legal forum was contrary to the national interest.

Major stages in renegotiating foreign debt

Renegotiation of foreign debt basically goes through three stages: agreement with the International Monetary Fund; renegotiation of the debt under the auspices of the Paris Club; and agreements with the international banking community.

Agreement with the International Monetary Fund

The crisis at the beginning of the 1970s was accompanied by numerous attempts to reform the International Monetary Fund. The abandonment of the gold standard was, to a large extent, parallel to the increased use of special drawing rights. Their tenuous implementation in 1968 as simple accounting entries culminated in June 1974 with their use as a type of accounting unit, based on a weighted basket of national currencies, meant to fix the value of the special drawing right. These rights thus became the basis for the international monetary system while the importance of gold and reserve currencies diminished progressively.

At the same time, the International Monetary Fund was assuming ever greater powers. The 1976 Jamaica Rules, which took effect April 1, 1978, introduced conditionality into the Fund's financing. Conditionality became a key factor in the reform of an international monetary institution forced to struggle with a profound crisis in the international economic situation. Conditionality serves a twofold purpose:

1 It determines, based on the provisions of the founding agreement, when the Fund should assist the country concerned.
2 It also refers to the country's obligation to draw up an economic programme aimed at attaining a viable balance of payments position at the end of the period being considered. These programmes set goals for certain macroeconomic variables, usually internal credit, financing of the public sector and foreign debt. Achieving these goals is a prerequisite for use of the Fund's financing.

In short, conditionality influences the Fund with respect to the possibility of providing financing through its resources. It also affects the soliciting country since it must present a viable economic programme and, at the same time, subject itself to the subsequent control of Fund officials.

Logically, presentation of a programme and subsequent supervision gives rise to varied reactions in debtor countries. They may feel that the reforms in the International Monetary Fund have gone too far. The Fund, in their opinion, has assumed strong powers, often to the detriment of what certain domestic social and political sectors consider an inalienable part of national sovereignty.

Renegotiation of debt under the auspices of the Paris Club

Once an agreement with the International Monetary Fund has been reached, renegotiation of debt between governments begins. Thus, the subject-matter of renegotiation is the debt which the debtor state has with the creditor states, directly or indirectly.

The so-called 'Paris Club' is an interesting institution. Although it has no institutional structure, it is effective in performing its renegotiating role. It is the result of the capacity of French financial authorities to bring together their equals from other countries. At these meetings commitments advising governments to act in a certain manner in their bilateral renegotiation of a debt with a certain country are entered into. The agreements of the Paris Club are reflected in minutes which set forth the commitments made. Afterwards, the various creditor countries sign bilateral agreements with debtor countries pursuant to what they agreed to in Paris.

The agreements of the Club relate to economic issues, leaving legal issues to the precision of bilateral agreements. For this reason, the minutes of the Paris Club do not usually include issues such as applicable law or the forum for resolving disputes. I should stress that no multilateral agreements are signed within the Paris Club. The proceedings are merely *procès-verbaux* and used as guidelines for the subsequent bilateral agreements containing legal details.

From an analysis of various bilateral agreements, it can be concluded that there is certain uniformity with respect to the following legal issues:

1 Applicable law is usually that of the creditor country which renegotiates the debt in the bilateral agreement. In all cases, the law of one of the OECD countries is chosen.
2 With respect to the selection of an arbitration forum, the International Chamber of Commerce holds a certain attraction. As an alternative solution, it is becoming more and more frequent to use the UNCITRAL Arbitration Rules which favour *ad hoc* arbitration whenever there is any reluctance to accept the arbitration of the International Chamber of Commerce.
3 An analysis of various bilateral agreements draws attention to the curious manner by which the negotiating states commit themselves. It is true that in many cases ratification is submitted to 'the competent authorities', but the identity of such authorities is left open. These agreements involve important commitments by states; yet they often are not subject to ordinary budgetary supervision as required by provisions which, in some cases, may be of constitutional rank. In some countries, this issue has posed serious problems, not only with respect to the enforceability of these agreements, but even to their very validity.

4 These debt renegotiation agreements are based on the concept of aggregating debt. In this way there is a break between present debt and the umbilical cord of its origin. These agreements attempt to be the purifying River Jordan for all sorts of problems which foreign debt may have had at its inception: the negligence of creditors and the possible corruption of those representing debtor institutions.
5 In some cases, the commitments of the debtor state may be conditional on the affected companies not being bankrupt or in moratorium. Thus, if at any given moment the situation of a debtor country worsens, it may make its bankruptcy laws more flexible as an indirect means of evading its commitments.
6 Among the resolutions of the Paris Club, there is usually a statement made concerning the desire for the debtor country in question to reach a comprehensive agreement with other creditors, particularly with foreign banks. Nevertheless, it is also provided that agreements based on commitments made under the auspices of the Paris Club must not receive less favourable treatment than that received by another creditor in a debt renegotiation under similar conditions. In other words, the Paris Club also requires a *pari passu* clause with respect to other renegotiations. Such clauses are aimed at reaching an overall and definitive solution for the debtor country with which the debt is being renegotiated. This has occasionally given rise to a race between banks and the Paris Club to see who signs first and who will thus receive more favourable treatment.
7 Renegotiation agreements under the auspices of the Paris Club are conditioned on the performance of the debtor country's commitments made with the International Monetary Fund.

In conclusion, under the auspices of the Paris Club debtor states reach an agreement on certain guidelines which are subsequently reflected in bilateral agreements with creditor states. In all of these agreements, the attractiveness of Paris is very often reflected in the choice of forum for resolving potential disputes. It is not infrequent for arbitration to be accepted, even the arbitration of the International Chamber of Commerce, although in recent years the tendency is toward *ad hoc* arbitration subject to UNCITRAL procedural rules.

Agreements with the international banking community

Agreements with the international banking community are the result of a laborious negotiation process between the debtor country and the many financing banks. In theory, these agreements are entered into by the debtor country's central bank with the guarantee of the state itself. In this way, the principal negotiator is the central bank which is both a sovereign entity and which, at the same time, has the agility of a commercial entity. Thus, it is not subject to the strict limitations often placed on government agencies as a result of parliamentary budgetary control. The state's participation as guarantor diffuses its participation although, if the principal debtor eventually fails in its commitments, the state will have to make good its guarantee. The agreements are negotiated by banks through a complex system of representation which allows for the creation of a negotiating committee and one or several agent banks.

Without entering into details concerning the various agreements negotiated by international banks in renegotiating their debts with Latin American countries, several important points can be outlined to assist in solving potential disputes:

1 In the express choice of the forum for resolving potential disputes which, as has been stated, implies an automatic waiver of sovereign immunity from jurisdiction, the judicial forums of countries other than that of the particular central bank are usually chosen for potential disputes with central banks. Arbitration is preferred for disputes with the guarantor state.

2 In choosing state jurisdiction for resolving disputes with central banks, the usual procedure followed is to domicile disputes in the country of the most important creditor banks and, particularly, in the country of the major currency of the loan. In some cases, the non-exclusive jurisdiction of one or several courts is chosen. This choice should be avoided since, in order to waive their own forum, Latin American procedural laws often require submission to a different but specifically stated forum.

3 Arbitration, as has been stated, is primarily chosen for contractual relations with the guarantor state. On many occasions the fundamental principle of neutrality in drawing up agreements is not strictly adhered to. In some agreements, and I am thinking specifically of the renegotiation of the debt with Brazil, it is required that the President of the Arbitration Tribunal be a licensed, practicing lawyer of New York. Though the President may in fact act impartially, this requirement may cast doubt on the neutrality of the proceedings.

   There is a certain tendency toward *ad hoc* as opposed to institutionalised arbitration. However, when used, arbitration institutions are usually of an Anglo-American orientation, such as the American Arbitration Association, the London Court of International Arbitration and ICSID.

   In some cases, and I am once again thinking of the Brazilian debt renegotiations, the parties provide that arbitration proceedings will be governed by certain articles of the 1965 Washington Convention. This provision raised great controversy in the Brazilian Parliament. It was felt that the executive branch had overstepped its powers by including in its renegotiation agreement the terms of an international convention which had been neither signed nor ratified by Brazil as required by its Constitution.

4 The various agreements renegotiated with Latin American countries repeatedly insist on the waiver by both the central bank and the guarantor state of immunity from execution against their property. The agreements reiterate the fact that these entities acted via *iure gestionis* and that their property was used in commercial activities.

   Also repeated throughout the clauses of these agreements is the possibility of seizure prior to trial or arbitration proceedings, as well as upon final judgment or award. Submission to the terms of the Immunity Acts of the United States or United Kingdom are also quite common.

   In conclusion, waiver of immunity from execution is one of the problems which most concerns the drafters of these agreements from a legal point of view.

5 In order to avoid procedural problems, these agreements usually include a provision concerning representation of the central bank and the guarantor

state for purposes of judicial or arbitration notifications. The central bank is usually represented by a financial institution with the same national origin which resides in the forum. The guarantor state is often represented by its diplomatic representatives in the country where the resolution of disputes has been domiciled. It is also frequent for the central bank or guarantor state to allow simple postal or telegraphic communication as a perfectly valid and effective means of notification.

6 All of these agreements specify the language in which proceedings will be held. This language is almost always English.

7 The applicable law is also chosen and is usually the law of the State of New York or of England.

8 Throughout the renegotiation agreements, the concern of creditors to guarantee the total and full enforceability of these agreements is apparent. The binding effect of the remainder of the agreement in the event of its partial invalidity is often mentioned, as is the survival of obligations.

Representatives of the debtor country sometimes certify the full legality and even the constitutionality of the agreement. Among the main waivers made, it is even possible to find one whereby the government agency waives its objections based on the nullity or unenforceability of the agreement. Such waiver is itself of questionable validity.

9 With respect to capacity to sue, banks reserve the alternative rights to act individually in their claims or to do so jointly through the agent bank. In addition, creditor institutions reserve the right to bring action against the central bank or directly against the guarantor state.

Banks reserve the right to freely transfer their rights, thus making possible the market for transfers of participations in bank loans in Latin American countries. Also mentioned throughout the renegotiation agreements is the joint, and not several, liability of banks to debtors, for any problems or damages which may arise in the management of the loans. It is also frequent to find clauses relating to the debtor country's obligation to make its commitments effective in the currency stated in the contract. This is true regardless of the currency in which judgment is rendered in the event of legal proceedings. There are also somewhat esoteric clauses concerning the potential diplomatic protection of the creditor banks.

Debt renegotiation agreements entered into with the international banking community reflect a contractual situation which goes beyond the ordinary participation of states or government agencies in international transactions. For the debtor country, accepting renegotiation agreements, particularly those subscribed with the international banking community, is vital and, to a certain extent, affects its economic survival. Given such circumstances, lawyers must question whether, in a world of international cooperation, sovereign immunity from execution may be validly waived *a priori*.

The magnitude of the amounts and the volume of the foreign debt being renegotiated, the political implications, the generalised awareness of the creditor institution's having negligently permitted the amount of indebtedness, corruption in those who assumed financial commitments in debtor countries, socialisation of foreign debt implied by aggregation of the debt by the issuing central bank with the guarantee of the state, the primarily social requirements which these commitments imply, and the economic programmes agreed to with the International Monetary Fund pursuant to conditionality, are very serious circumstances to which a lawyer must give specific and careful consideration when analysing the problems connected with the resolution of potential litigation arising from foreign debt renegotiation agreements.

Foreign debt renegotiation's departure from the ordinary forms of participation by a sovereign state or its government agencies in international transactions

The critical reaction in many political, economic and social sectors in Latin America to foreign debt renegotiation agreements draws attention to its underlying legal support. Fundamentally, the conclusions which can be reached are the following:

First, given the political, economic and social importance of debt renegotiation agreements, they should be distinguished from simple agreements for the participation of the state or its government agencies in international commerce. The central bank which renegotiates its country's foreign debt, or the state which guarantees such renegotiation, is not merely acting as a businessman without further implications. On the contrary, it is providing a primarily political response to a vital necessity of the human community it represents.

The best Brazilian legal doctrine correctly pointed out in the heated controversy following Brazil's debt renegotiation agreement that such agreements are actually legislative in nature. The actions of the central bank would seem to be very flexible despite parliamentary controls over its ordinary, and often extraordinary, activities. Agreements of this type require greater publicity and, above all, greater supervision by parliament. It has also been said that these activities of central banks may constitute an abuse of constitutional law in the sense that organic laws which regulate central banks are used to avoid parliamentary supervisory powers over decisions concerning crucial problems in the life of a country. Whatever the legal characterisation given to these agreements, they are placed at a different level from ordinary public participation in international transactions.

Second, as a result of the above, the validity and viability of the waiver of sovereign immunity, both from jurisdiction and from execution, poses a problem of limits. Relevant legal doctrine and jurisprudence developed in recent years cannot be applied to foreign debt renegotiations. It is one thing for a state or government agency to waive its sovereign immunity from jurisdiction or execution with respect to a particular commercial contract. It is quite another thing for a state to make such waiver with respect to all foreign obligations and commitments of public and private companies with whose political management it is entrusted.

Lord Wilberforce correctly stated, 'Once a trader, always a trader.' Nevertheless, once a state takes political decisions which affect all of its country's foreign economic relations, it is not acting as a trader or a businessman. Rather, it is clearly acting by virtue of *iure imperii*. This is true despite the contents of renegotiation agreements.

Third, the public law of the country whose debt is being renegotiated places limits on the applicable law of the agreement. The first limitation is public policy, since such agreements affect vital aspects of the nation. Moreover, the capacity of the persons who enter into renegotiation agreements on behalf of the central bank or the state in question is undeniably governed by the public law of the affected country. This public law is the law applicable to the capacity of the parties contracting on behalf of the central bank or the state.

The use of private contracting techniques in renegotiating debts will pose serious problems in the event of disputes. Specifically, the abovementioned abuse of constitutional law, with respect to the organic legislation governing the independence of the central bank, may raise doubts as to the very validity of renegotiation agreements.

Fourth, the waiver by a sovereign state of the right to invoke the potential nullity of renegotiation agreements does not coincide with international morality.

Fifth, the aggregation of foreign debt as a type of River Jordan used to purify the errors of the past is not easily justified. Irresponsible international financial behaviour may give rise to defences. Corruption as a serious defect in the creation of some foreign debt may constitute a just and logical defence for the debtor against his creditors. In the event of a dispute, aggregation of debt cannot set aside recent history.

Sixth, the submission by a state or its central bank to accept the jurisdiction of a judicial or arbitration forum may be defective if procedures for resolving disputes have been agreed to which lack neutrality, even though the impartiality of the parties is not questioned. In matters as important as foreign debt, there must be no doubts in this regard.

Conclusion

At the end of this road lies the doubt as to whether the employment of ordinary contracting techniques, well-suited to the business world, is useful in matters of this magnitude or whether, on the contrary, creditors and debtors have embarked on economic renegotiation with legal documents of doubtful validity and, in any event, questionable enforceability. Up to the present there have been no relevant precedents. Only the testing ground of judicial or arbitration proceedings can provide an answer to all of these unknowns.

Debtor countries and their lawyers are extraordinarily sensitive to these renegotiation agreements which are considered, in large part, humiliating. The agreements are written in a foreign language and their drafting is sometimes unintelligible even to the drafter. The repeated and, at times, contradictory waivers by the sovereign state are counterproductive and may well be unenforceable in practice.

In Latin America, the proliferation of posters against payment of foreign debt does nothing more than reflect the rather generalised feeling concerning three points:

1 Foreign debt is absolutely impossible to pay off based solely on the productive capacity of the countries concerned.
2 Foreign debt is understood in many places as a means for developed

countries to exploit developing countries. This is felt to be so because developed countries create their own currency, impose it generally on international trade and subsequently manipulate interest rates.

3 It is also felt that foreign debt has actually been paid by debtor countries, although not formally, due to the elevated interest rates already paid and the extensive spreads which have also been paid.

Renegotiation is often promoted by creditor banks for accounting and tax reasons, based on the requirements of their central banks and monetary and tax authorities. Many of these agreements give the impression that they have been negotiated and entered into not in order to be performed, but rather for purposes of delay. In some cases this delay may be due to international political reasons and, in other cases, it may be due to the commercial policies of creditor institutions. The latter will not hesitate to declare a debt unrecoverable if such is convenient for tax reasons. This is so even if such declaration technically indicates the debtor country's bankruptcy.

The generalised feeling is that debt renegotiation is neither humanitarian nor utopian, but merely technical, based on the pure logic of creditor entities who must meet certain requirements of the capital market in which they operate. All of this gives a very special character to the legal commitments entered into and, above all, raises questions concerning the postulates accepted until now for the ordinary participation of states and sovereign entities in international transactions.

Arbitration with foreign states or state-controlled entities: some practical questions 26

Pierre Lalive

I had proposed to limit my examination 'to practical difficulties arising from the special characteristics of international contracts involving foreign states or state-controlled entities (I do not like the outdated term "concession agreements") and of the fact that one of the parties is a state or state-controlled entity'. Within the very limited time at my disposal and forgetting about my original plan, I shall merely attempt to draw your attention to a few practical difficulties which may and do arise in contractual relations with foreign states or state-controlled entities – difficulties which should be kept in mind when negotiating and drafting an arbitration clause, and related clauses such as choice of law, *force majeure* and 'stabilisation' clauses.

I shall not deal with questions of drafting arbitration clauses,[1] except to make one general and rather trite remark: like most arbitrators, I have seen many arbitration clauses which are badly drafted, as if the experience of others was not known or was ignored by successive generations of practitioners! One feels bound to quote again, in this connection, the apt remark of Dr Kopelmanas that, when there were too few lawyers involved at the beginning of the life of a contract, there were too many at the end!

May I start with a general observation? Reading what a number of papers have to say about some arbitration cases I happen to know, I was struck, once again, by the considerable difficulty there is, not only of correctly summing up a complex case in a few lines, but also of properly understanding an award when the only information available is ... the text of the award itself!

With respect to the interesting discussion on publication of awards, I should like to add one, perhaps marginal, comment: even when an award is published or is available, it remains very difficult in most cases to assess or understand it when you do not happen to know exactly what the position and arguments of the parties have been (and they need not be fully reported in the award itself). Good illustrations of this point are the more or less famous final or partial awards given in the *Aramco*,[2] *Texaco*,[3] *Aminoil*[4] and *Westland*[5] cases. In all

1 The subject of arbitration clauses is dealt with by Markham Ball, in his paper 'Structuring the Arbitration in Advance – The Arbitration Clause in an International Development Agreement', Chapter 27 *infra*, at 297.
2 *Saudi Arabia* v *Arabian American Oil Co*, 27 *ILR* 117 (1958).
3 *Texaco Overseas Petroleum Co/California Asiatic Oil Co* v *Government of the Libyan Arab Republic* – 17 *ILM* 1 (1977).
4 *Kuwait* v *American Independant Oil Co*, 21 *ILM* 976 (1982).
5 *Westland Helicopters* v *Arab Organisation for Industrialisation* 23 *ILM* 1071 (1984).

these cases, comments have been published, sometimes by very learned writers, which show strikingly incomplete information in fact or a distinct lack of perception about the arbitrator's true position and function, in the context of the arbitration agreement and the respective claims and arguments of the parties.

To take the example of the *Aramco* award, given in 1958 by a tribunal under the chairmanship of Professor G Sauser-Hall, I confess I read with surprise Dr A H Hermann's remarks[6] which failed to take into account, among other things, the parties' express stipulations (eg, on the applicable law) in the arbitration agreement or the Saudi Government's contentions as to the 'much wider powers' (than in Aramco's view) possessed by the tribunal. Perhaps it is inevitable that an award, and even more a part of an award, should appear 'daring' or 'acrobatic' when taken out of context.

With regard to the *Texaco* award, it seems to have become fashionable, in some legal or political circles, at least on the Continent, to repeat that the single arbitrator's decision was much too bold and went beyond the present limits of international law. Now this is not the place to discuss whether this criticism is or is not justified but fairness would seem to require that some mention be made by the critics of two facts: (a) that the arbitration clause expressly provided for a 'period of grace', after the arbitrator's decision and until one party would be considered in default, and (b) that the award, 'bold' though it may have been, was directly instrumental in leading the parties to reach a friendly settlement.

The *Kuwait-Aminoil* decision may be, or has been, criticised by some as comparatively poor in legal contents, notably on the applicable law, but here again one should keep in mind that an arbitral award may be more a diplomatic piece of work than an exercise in jurisprudence; the published award is only, if one may use a rather worn cliché, 'the tip of the iceberg' and, after all, a measure of its success is the fact that both parties accepted it and even professed to be satisfied with it.

With regard, lastly, to the *Westland* case, which is attracting a lot of attention not only in this country but in all countries which are doing or intend to do business with Egypt, I should not have mentioned it, since it is still *sub judice*, but I simply cannot accept the totally incomplete and misleading presentations which, be it said with respect, have been made in his paper[7] by my distinguished French colleague Philippe Cahier, who has obviously fallen a victim of a not too skilful piece of 'disinformation'.

Mr Cahier presents an ICC award of March 5, 1984 as an illustration of an alleged 'trend by arbitrators to extend their jurisdiction to parties not formally privy to the contract'.[8] This statement is based on two affirmations, ie, that the four countries which created the Arab Organisation for Industrialisation (AOI) 'were not party to the contracts' concluded by Westland and that 'the arbitrators found that AOI was a legal entity distinct from the member countries'.

Regrettably, both affirmations are wrong or, at the very least, highly

6 'Disputes Between States and Foreign Companies', Chapter 22 *supra*, at 259.

7 'The Strengths and Weaknesses of International Arbitration Involving a State as a Party', Chapter 21, at 243.

8 *Ibid*, at 244.

controversial. Both have in fact been unanimously rejected by the arbitrators, apparently for good reasons (no trace of which is found in Mr Cahier's summary), and the three arbitrators happened to be in full agreement with a galaxy of the most famous international lawyers, including (to name but a few) Sir Robert Jennings, Professors R-J Dupuy, M Virally, D Bowett, etc. A brief quotation from Professor Jennings's opinion will suffice to illustrate my point: he writes about the AOI (which Professor Cahier, by the way, wrongly assimilates to an international organisation):

> 'The AOI has, apart from the Ministers of the Governments in Committee, in real terms no useful, separate existence. ... Its legal being is so interwoven with the Governments that there can be no clear legal distinction between the AOI and the Heads of the four states. ... The AOI is a legal device created by treaty, ... by means of which the states parties could the better conduct and co-ordinate their pursuit of the industrialisation programme. . . . The AOI is the four states, acting through a Committee of their Ministers ... It follows that the arbitration clauses of the Shareholders Agreement and its immediately associated instruments are provisions in which the states ... have submitted to the jurisdiction of this arbitral tribunal in respect, but only in respect, of the matters and purposes for which that complex was created by them'.

Now, commentators certainly remain free to share or not to share these views or to agree with the Tribunal. But they should not, it is submitted, venture to pass judgment on the basis of so incomplete and distorted information as to make any understanding of the case impossible.

Far from showing a 'trend of arbitrators to extend their jurisdiction to non-parties', the *Westland* case (which I happen to know well as one of the counsel for Westland) illustrates in the clearest possible manner, in my submission, the tendency of a minority of states or rather state administrations to go back on their obligations to arbitrate and even to resort to all possible means to paralyse the course of impartial adjudication. This is not, one should perhaps add, the biased view of one of the parties' counsel; the same view has been put forward by a well-known international lawyer of Egyptian nationality, Professor El-Kosheri, in a paper delivered in December 1984 in Paris (at the ICC Institute of International Business Law and Practice) who stated (I quote), *inter alia* that 'all possible techniques were utilised to prevent the Arbitral Tribunal formed by the ICC's Court of Arbitration from adjudicating the jurisdictional issue' and, after 'carefully reviewing the AOI case', he concludes that, whatever the political or other motives may have been, the tactics employed should be vigorously condemned.

Whatever the normal diversity of views may be on the merits of that case, all lawyers should and will regret that the Egyptian Government (at the same time when it is trying to develop Cairo as an international centre of arbitration!) should have been so ill-advised as to take part in one of the crudest cases of obstruction in the history of international arbitration.

With this brief discussion of the *Westland* case, we have touched upon one of the fundamental and most difficult problems of present-day international arbitration involving states, that of consent by the government or state entity, in particular in the case of so-called 'multi-party arbitrations' – a subject of its own which cannot be analysed here. On the proof of consent in general, reference has been made also to the so-called *Pyramids* case.[9] The award given on March 11, 1983 by a tribunal chaired by Professor Bernini has been described by Professor Cahier as another example of what he believes to be a 'trend by arbitrators to extend their jurisdiction' and we all know that the said award has been annulled by the Court of Appeals of Paris on July 12, 1984.[10] No doubt our colleague Bernini who is here will be able to comment and correct, if he wishes, such presentation. My own, admittedly superficial, impression, as just an ordinary reader of the two conflicting decisions, is that both are quite understandable and just happen to be based on a totally different interpretation of the facts relating to the conduct and intentions of the Egyptian Government in that case.

May I turn now to another, related, question that of the binding force of arbitration undertakings in the light of restrictions in the charter or by-laws of state-controlled entities, of the power of signatories and the duty of care and of good faith of the parties to a negotiation. I should like to refer in this connection to Professor Böckstiegel's excellent paper[11] where he discusses a recent 'Belgian' arbitration[12] and a 'Latin American' arbitration.

It seems difficult to overestimate the practical importance of the problem, having regard to the undeniable tendency of states and state-controlled entities, when sued in arbitration proceedings, to dispute jurisdiction, *inter alia*, on the ground of an alleged incapacity to arbitrate or an invalidity of the arbitration undertaking.

Parties wishing to enter into a contractual relationship with a state or state-controlled entity or corporation should be very careful, and more careful than they often are in practice (owing sometimes to over-eagerness to do business at all costs). It is impossible of course, within the limits of this paper, to do justice to the subject but I should like to draw your attention to the recent case of *Framatome* v *The Atomic Energy Organisation of Iran (AEOI)*.[13]

In its award on jurisdiction, the tribunal found that, as rightly contended by the Iranian agency AEOI, the conclusion of the contract in dispute (governed by Iranian law) was tainted by irregularities. It added (and this may serve as a warning to future negotiators) that:

> 'On the basis of the applicable Iranian law, one can and must regret, on the one hand, that the French co-contractor of AEOI, in a contract of such importance, did not take additional precautions ... in order to ensure the complete regularity of the operations according to the applicable Iranian texts and, on the other hand, regret that AEOI itself, its various organs and officers, did not respect the same texts better.'[14]

But the tribunal found that, under the applicable Iranian law, there was no question of any incapacity of contract on the part of AEOI itself (especially

9 *Southern Pacific Properties Ltd* v *The Arab Republic of Egypt and the Egyptian General Company for Tourism and Hotels*, 22 *ILM* 752 (1983).

10 23 *ILM* 1048 (1984).

11 'States in the International Arbitral Process', *supra*, at 40.

12 *Ibid* at 48. See also, *Journal des Tribunaux* 230, 1984, and 1 *Journal of International Arbitration* 184 (1984).

13 Decision of April 30, 1984, published in: 111 *Clunet* 58 (1984), and VIII *Yearbook: Commercial Arbitration* 94 (1983).

14 VIII *Yearbook: Commercial Arbitration* (1983), at 100.

since, in the present instance, its capacity had been exercised with the full approval and on the instructions of the Iranian Government). The tribunal also found that, in any case 'as a legal entity party to the present arbitration proceedings on jurisdiction, AEOI could not assert and take advantage of irregularities, infringement of statutes and violations of Iranian law which were committed by its own organs by omissions or commission'. Moreover, there existed in that case 'a decisive and independent reason which prevents the defendant from now contesting the validity of the contract: this contract was partially performed by both parties and for several months', ie, it had been ratified.

Another, equally or more important, aspect of this award on jurisdiction is its detailed treatment of the objection based, not on the lack of capacity or lack of power of the signatories of the contract but on the invalidity of the arbitration clause itself. The Iranian state agency relied, not only on the Iranian Code of Civil Procedure and on a statute of 1968 relating to undertakings by the Government or Government-financed agencies, but also on Article 139 of the (new) Constitution of the Islamic Republic of Iran (of 1979) which had been approved two years after the conclusion of the contracting parties had agreed that Iranian law would govern, the Iranian party, not unnaturally, contended that such choice of law clause referred to a 'living law', in its evolution, including therefore the new Constitution of 1979.

The question inevitably arose whether the Islamic Constitution did or did not apply to an arbitration clause contained in a contract made prior to it. Would an affirmative answer violate the so-called principle of 'non-retroactivity'? According to the award,

> 'in the absence of an express provision providing for retroactivity, it appears impossible to attach this characteristic to a constitutional text ... and in conformity with widely-accepted principles of public international law governing the relations between states, it is not possible, in the absence of explicit indications in the Article of the Constitution concerning its application *ratione temporis*, to presume any intention whatsoever of the Iranian state to question the validity of undertakings to arbitrate made previously, and presumably validly, by an Iranian public organisation at an international level'.[15]

Moreover, the tribunal found that, in the present case, the Iranian party which relied on the applicability of the Constitution, had failed to demonstrate, or even to attempt to show, any joint intention of the parties to submit the effectiveness of 'a contractual clause as fundamental as an arbitration clause ... to a sort of condition entirely within the power of one party, the occurrence of which would depend solely on the will of the state' of which the public organisation party to the dispute is an instrumentality.[16]

My last observation relates, not to the arbitration clause itself, but to the *force majeure* clause which is obviously of paramount importance and is fairly frequently involved, these days, by state corporations or state-controlled entities in particular. On the subject in general, may I merely refer you to what

15 *Ibid*, at 107.

16 See Oppetit, 'Arbitrage et Contrats d'Etat, L'arbitrage Framatome et autres c/ AEOI', 111 *Clunet* 37 (1984).

previous speakers have written or said here, in particular to Dr A H Hermann's extremely interesting and critical treatment of recent English cases, including of course the *Rolimpex* case of 1978.[17] Refraining from commenting on these cases or Dr Hermann's sharp and sometimes entirely justified criticisms, I should like to mention two or three very recent cases which illustrate some of the dangers involved in dealings with state-controlled entities.

In an (unpublished) ICC arbitration award between Western European companies and two Iranian state agencies (and this is *not* the *Framatome* case previously mentioned), it was submitted by the claimants that neither of the Iranian state entities (which had relied on *force majeure* to be excused from performing) could claim to be *exterior* to the Iranian Government; although one of them had a separate legal personality under Iranian law, it was, under its charter and by-laws, totally controlled by the Government. It is interesting to note that, having considered various concepts of *force majeure* in relation of course to the contractual provisions, the award refers to another concept of *force majeure* applicable only to state enterprises, in the case of which additional conditions must be simultaneously fulfilled:

(a) the act of state or government must be a political decision of national sovereignty;
(b) it must not have been taken in favour and the personal interest of the state or of its own enterprise; and
(c) it must be such that its effects would have been the same regarding private enterprises.[18]

Furthermore, the tribunal considered that, with regard to third (contracting) parties, the state enterprise and the Iranian state itself could only be considered as one single entity, so that there was no character of 'exteriority' and therefore no *force majeure* could be relied upon.

Let us not imagine that the claim of *force majeure* – as an excuse for failing to perform one's contractual obligations – is only, or mainly, raised by state enterprises of developing countries! In actual fact, a comparative study seems to reveal that states and state-controlled entities, all over the world, often find it difficult to behave like equal contracting parties and are prone to adopt a 'hierarchical' and 'authoritarian' attitude or merely to resort unilaterally to the *fait du prince* also with regard to foreign parties. Instances when such attitude borders on bad faith, to say the least, are also to be found with parties from industrialised countries supposed to have vast experience of arbitration and a long tradition of respect for law and justice.[19] A quite recent example is ICC Case No 4600 where a French company was acquired, shortly after the signing of an international contract with a developing country, by a French state organisation. At some later date, the French company was forbidden, by *confidential* ministerial instructions, both to perform its contract and to disclose the said confidential instructions to its foreign (here Asian) partner!

17 See *supra*, at 252.

18 See K H Böckstiegel, 'The Legal Rules Applicable in International Commercial Arbitration Involving States or State-Controlled Entities', in *60 Years of ICC Arbitration* 117 (Paris 1984); K H Böckstiegel, *Arbitration and State Enterprises* (Kluwer 1984), at 37–48.

19 On the attitude of practitioners in developing countries (which seems to sharply contrast with certain political statements), see an interesting and timely study by Paulsson: 'Le Tiers Monde dans l'arbitrage commercial international', [1983] *Revue de l'Arbitrage* 3.

And the question was raised in arbitration whether the French debtor could rely on the *force majeure* clause in the contract, having regard to its failure to prove the existence, contents and legality, under the applicable French law, of the alleged governmental prohibition to perform. One aspect of the problem was, of course, the question of 'exteriority', having regard to the domination exercised over the French company by the French Government, through its state organisation as well as directly, because of its special 'status'.

A peculiar and rather unpleasant aspect of the case was that, at the same time when the said Government, through its Minister of Industry, was confidentially instructing the company to stop performance, the same Government was giving repeated and formal assurances to the Government of the Asian creditor, that it would honour its treaty undertakings to encourage and facilitate the performance of the contract between the parties! Hardly surprisingly, the Asian creditor company had relied on a well-known French decision in the *Air France* case[20] where it was said that:

> 'It would be extremely shocking if a national company like Air France or, *a fortiori*, a public organisation, were allowed to protect itself behind its public law status in order to evade its contractual obligations. ... If such a solution were accepted, it would become all too easy for enterprises with a special (public) status to be excused from performing their contracts. It would suffice for them to provoke a withdrawal from authorisation and thereafter to rely on *force majeure*. There would then be no longer any balance nor security in juridical relations'.

The extraordinary conduct of the Government in that case, which I shall refrain from characterising here, has a certain analogy with the attitude adopted in the *Westland* case by the Egyptian Government, who had also undertaken by a treaty (a 'Memorandum of Understanding' with the United Kingdom Government) the international obligation to facilitate both the performance of the contracts and the arbitral settlement of possible disputes. The lesson to be derived from those two examples would seem to be that contracts concluded within the context of or under the protection of a treaty (or 'umbrella agreement') are no less vulnerable than 'ordinary' contracts, when a state has decided that its national interest justified the violation of public or private law undertakings.

To conclude, I should once more refer to the *Framatome-AEOI* case in connection with the question of *force majeure*, in order to emphasise a special feature of the case: the text of the contract expressly mentioned, among many instances of *force majeure* 'measures taken or neglected by the authorities'. It followed that, according to the arbitrators, the parties had agreed to consider the Iranian party (AEOI) as distinct from the Iranian authorities, at least for the purpose of the *force majeure* clause. The foreign claimants could hardly, therefore, rely on the well-known argument of lack of 'exteriority' of the Iranian organisation. For other, factual, reasons, the arbitrators came to the conclusion that the Iranian law invoked to excuse non-performance did not in fact make it impossible for AEOI to pay the instalments due. But one cannot

20 *Cour de cassation*, April 15, 1970, D 1971, 107.

help wondering whether, at the time of negotiating and drafting the contract, the non-Iranian parties had given sufficient thought to the risk of a governmental intervention limiting or prohibiting performance, if not (of course) to the possibility of an Islamic revolution!

Structuring the arbitration in advance – the arbitration clause in an international development agreement

27

Markham Ball*

This paper addresses the arbitration clause from the draftsman's point of view. It considers the principal points to be covered by the clause and the principal questions to be answered by the parties and their advisers when they draft the arbitration clause of a concession agreement or other long-term economic development agreement.

Contract terms must often differ from case to case to reflect differing circumstances and differences in the bargaining power of the parties. For this reason we do not here offer a model arbitration clause designed to fit all circumstances. Instead, the eleven points listed and discussed below are suggested as a checklist of the principal issues that the draftsman of an economic development agreement should consider as he or she prepares the dispute resolution clause.

To arbitrate or not to arbitrate

The first question is whether arbitration is the desirable means of dispute resolution. There are, of course, alternatives.

One alternative is to provide for the resolution of disputes in the courts of a named country, presumably the country where the economic activity is located. A second alternative is for the parties to include no dispute resolution provision at all. If a dispute arises, this course is also likely to lead ultimately to litigation (although not necessarily a judgment on the merits) in the courts of one nation or another. Which nation it will be, will be difficult to predict at the outset.

Proceedings in national courts are a viable alternative in many international contracts. Judicial proceedings are not necessarily more costly or time consuming than arbitral proceedings, and the parties may prefer the courts' more settled procedures, their power to compel the production of documents and witnesses, and their relatively strict rules of evidence. Courts, it can be argued, are less prone to judgments that 'split the difference,' and more likely to make decisions on the basis of strict legal rights. Certainly in many

* The author is indebted to his colleague Sydney J Kase of the law firm of Wald, Harkrader & Ross, Washington, DC, for her counsel and assistance in the preparation of this paper.

transactions, particularly those of a short-term commercial nature, the parties can justifiably rely on the impartiality and stability of national court systems as dispute resolution institutions.

In the case of economic development agreements, however, dispute resolution by international arbitration is singularly appropriate. These agreements typically extend over decades, during which much can change – including economic conditions, governments, governmental philosophies, and national judicial systems.[1] Many such agreements deal, furthermore, with vital natural and economic resources of the contracting state, matters on which a sovereign government is naturally reluctant to submit to the jurisdiction of another sovereign. For the private company, these agreements involve large, long-term investments and substantial risks. Both parties desire a neutral forum, one that is as free as possible from governmental pressure or national bias, and that is likely to operate with independence and objectivity for decades to come. Although international arbitration is frequently praised – or decried – for its 'flexibility,' a carefully drawn arbitration clause can do much to limit that flexibility to matters of procedure, and to provide in arbitration the stability and impartiality of judgment on questions of legal right that the parties to most economic development agreements desire.

Increasingly in recent years, the parties to such agreements have chosen to resolve their disputes through arbitration. As a result, there is a growing body of arbitral awards, many of which have been published, that, while far from ideal in quality or consistency, lends substance to the arbitral process, and an added measure of predictability.[2]

One other possible dispute resolution mechanism should be mentioned: that of conciliation. Transnational contracts frequently established conciliation mechanisms that the parties must exhaust before they commence litigation or

1 Many contracts between United States companies and Iranian entities that were entered into before the Iranian Revolution called for the resolution of disputes in the courts of Iran. Following the Revolution, a number of United States contractors and investors, claiming that Iranian courts no longer offer United States parties the prospect of a fair hearing, have sought to sue on their contracts in the courts of the United States and to file claims in the Iran–United States Claims Tribunal. See, eg, *Gibbs & Hill, Inc* v *Iran Power and Transmissioin Co*, Award No ITL 1–6–FT (Iran–United States Claims Tribunal, November 5, 1982); *TCSB, Inc* v *Iran*, Award No ITL 5–140–FT (Iran–United States Claims Tribunal, November 5, 1982).

2 See, eg, *SPP (Middle East) Limited, Southern Pacific Properties Limited* v *Arab Republic of Egypt and Egyptian General Company for Tourism and Hotels* ('Pyramids Plateau' Arbitration) 22 *ILM* 752 (1983), (Bernini, Elghatit, Litt, Arbs); *Kuwait* v *American Independent Oil Co (Aminoil)* ('Aminoil' Arbitration), 21 *ILM* 976 (1982), (Reuter, Sultan, Fitzmaurice, Arbs); *BP Exploration Co (Libya) Ltd* v *Government of the Libyan Arab Republic* ('BP Arbitration) 53 *International Law Reports* 297 (1979), (Largergren Arb); *Revere Copper and Brass, Inc* v *Overseas Private Investment Corp* ('Revere Copper' Arbitration), 56 *International Law Reports* 258 (1978) (Haight, Wetzel, Bergan, Arbs); *Libyan American Oil Co (LIAMCO)* v *Government of Libyan Arab Republic* ('Liamco' Arbitration), 20 *ILM* 1 (1980) (Mahmassani, Arb); *Texaco Overseas Petroleum Co/California Asiatic Oil Co* v *Government of the Libyan Arab Republic* ('TOPCO' Arbitration), 17 *ILM* 1 (1977), (Dupuy Arb); *Sapphire International Petroleums Ltd* v *National Iranian Oil Co* ('Sapphire' Arbitration), 35 *ILR* 136 (1963) (Cavin, Arb); *Saudi Arabia* v *Arabian American Oil Co* ('Aramco' Arbitration), 27 *International Law Reports*, 117 (1958) (Sauser-Hall, Badawi/Hassen, Habachy, Arbs).

arbitration. The rules of many arbitral institutions include conciliation procedures.[3]

Commitment to arbitrate

If the parties choose to submit their disputes to arbitration, their agreement must unequivocally express this intent. Language that clearly does so is found in suggested arbitration clauses that have been published with a number of sets of arbitral rules. The clause published with the UNCITRAL Arbitration Rules provides, for instance:

> 'Any dispute, controversy or claim arising out of or relating to this contract, or the breach, termination or invalidity thereof, shall be settled by arbitration in accordance with the UNCITRAL Arbitration Rules as at present in force.'[4]

This clause and other short-form clauses like it are, without more, insufficient for use in most economic development agreements, because – as the following pages will make clear – they fail to deal with many issues that the arbitration clause should cover. As an expression of a commitment to arbitrate, however, the UNCITRAL clause is clear and effective.

Parties that fail to make a clear choice between arbitration and litigation will most likely lose the opportunity to arbitrate. This was, in fact, the outcome of cases involving the following two arbitration clauses:

> 'In case of dispute (contestation), the parties undertake to submit to arbitration but in case of litigation the Tribunal de la Seine shall have exclusive jurisdiction.[5]
>
> All disputes arising out of this contract will be submitted in first instance to an arbitral tribunal of the German–Dutch Chamber of Commerce. If the decision is not acceptable to either party, an ordinary court of law, to be designated by the claimant, will be competent.[6]'

Arbitral tribunals can and should refuse to proceed in such an ambiguous situation, as there would be no assurance that the arbitral award would be enforceable.[7]

3 See, eg, Rules of Conciliation and Arbitration of the International Chamber of Commerce, Articles 1–5; Convention on the Settlement of Investment Disputes Between States and Nationals of Other States, Articles 28–35, Conciliation.

4 UNCITRAL Arbitration Rules. Similar clauses may be found in, eg, the Rules of Conciliation and Arbitration of the International Chamber of Commerce. The ICC recommends the following clause:

> 'All disputes arising in connection with the present contract shall be finally settled under the Rules of Conciliation and Arbitration of the International Chamber of Commerce by one or more arbitrators appointed in accordance with the said Rules'.

5 Craig, Park and Paulsson, *International Chamber of Commerce Arbitration*, No 9.02 (New York 1984), citing decisions of the *Tribunal de grande instance de Paris* (February 1, 1979 and October 16, 1979), [1980] *Revue de l'Arbitrage* 97, at 101.

6 *Ibid*, citing decisions of the Landgericht of Heidelberg (October 23, 1972) and Oberlandesgericht of Karlsruhe (March 13, 1973).

7 See, eg, Ruling of November 12, 1974, Case No 128/73, Arbitration Court at the Bulgarian Chamber of Commerce and Industry, reported in I *Yearbook: Commercial Arbitration* 124 (1976) ('An equivocal (ambiguous) arbitration agreement, which does not indicate beyond

Scope of the arbitration

The arbitration clause should specify the kinds of questions that will be subject to arbitration. The UNCITRAL clause set out in the preceeding section is a good example of a broad 'all disputes' clause. Covering 'any' dispute 'relating to' the contract or to its termination or invalidity, the UNCITRAL clause seems clearly broad enough to include not only claims based on alleged breaches of contract, but also claims of wrongful takings of rights secured by the contract, and claims based on theories such as *quantum meruit* or unjust enrichment.[8]

Narrower formulations are possible, but are generally not advisable. The parties might, for instance, provide for arbitration only of certain technical factual questions, leaving other questions of fact and law to the courts. One must be wary, however, of such attempted divisions of jurisdiction. They are far too likely to turn the dispute resolution process into a multiplicity of proceedings – arbitration of some issues, the litigation of others, and a great deal of dispute in a court or arbitral tribunal (or both) over which issues belong in arbitration and which in litigation.[9]

Institutional or *ad hoc* arbitration

The parties must decide whether their arbitration will be conducted within the supervisory and supporting apparatus of an arbitral institution. Such institutions include, among others, the Court of Arbitration of the International Chamber of Commerce (ICC), the International Centre for the Settlement of Investment Disputes (ICSID), the American Arbitration Association (AAA), the London Court of International Arbitration (LCIA), and the Arbitration Institute of the Stockholm Chamber of Commerce, as well as several regional arbitration centres. Parties that elect institutional arbitration obtain the benefits of established facilities, experienced staff and administrative support. The major arbitral institutions offer tested procedural rules and, in most cases, rosters of qualified arbitrators from which the parties may select. Parties that do not use arbitral institutions, but instead choose *ad hoc* arbitration, must make their own arrangements for procedures, the selection of arbitrators, and administrative support. By so doing, they are better able to control the procedural and administrative aspects of the proceedings and their cost.

---

doubt that the dispute is submitted to the Arbitration Court at the Bulgarian Chamber of Commerce and Industry, cannot be regarded as sufficient ground for its competence. The opposite standpoint risks complicating the enforcement of the award. It could be challenged as void because of the Court's incompetence.')

8 See, eg, *Morrison-Knudsen Pacific Ltd* v *Ministry of Roads & Transportation*, Award No 143–127–3 (Iran–US Claims Tribunal, July 31, 1984) (*quantum meruit* award); *Sea-Land Service, Inc* v *Government of the Islamic Republic of Iran and Ports and Shipping Organisation*, Award No 135–33–1 (Iran–US Claims Tribunal, June 22, 1984) (damages based on unjust enrichment).

9 See, eg, *United Aircraft International, Inc* v *Greenlandair, Inc* 298 F Supp 1329, 1330 (D Conn 1969) (on motion to restrain arbitration, court held that provision, 'Buyer is left to whatever remedies it may have at law for any claim of negligence,' was too ineptly worded to be regarded as a specific exception to provision that 'any disputes arising under this contract shall be settled and finally determined by arbitration').

Commentators generally recommend institutional arbitration, at least in the context of most commercial contracts.[10] In the case of economic development agreements, however, the parties appear, more often than not, to choose *ad hoc* arbitration.[11]

In fact, the differences between institutional and *ad hoc* arbitration may be more apparent than real. The rules of most arbitral institutions give the parties wide latitude to shape their procedures, and to control such matters as location of the arbitration and selection of arbitrators. Conversely, parties to an *ad hoc* arbitration have a number of well developed sets of procedural rules from which to choose for incorporation in their arbitration clause – most notably the rules of the United Nations Commission on International Trade Law (UNCITRAL). It is not difficult, furthermore, for the parties to an *ad hoc* arbitration to create a secretariat to manage the administrative aspects of their proceedings. The *Aminoil* Arbitration[12] is an example of this practice.

The parties' decision whether or not to choose institutional arbitration is not made in the abstract, but as part of their choice of an entire arbitral regime – a combination of institutional support and arbitral rules, backed up to varying degrees by international treaties and national laws. In the section that follows, we briefly describe three such regimes.

Choice of arbitral regime and procedural rules

The arbitration clause should name the institution, if any, that will administer an arbitration and the procedural rules that will apply. If an administering institution is chosen, the rules of that institution will generally, but not invariably, be chosen to govern the proceeding.[13] For present purposes, we concentrate on three arbitral regimes that seem particularly appropriate for use in the resolution of disputes under an international economic development agreement: institutional arbitration under the auspices and rules of the ICC and ICSID; and arbitration under the UNCITRAL Arbitration Rules.[14]

The ICC, ICSID and UNCITRAL Rules vary in their length and complexity – the ICC Rules being the briefest and the ICSID Rules the most lengthy and detailed – and in their treatment of a variety of procedural matters. For the most part, the differences are not very important. Many procedural details may be modified by the parties in the arbitration clause.[15] Some lacunae can be

10 See, eg, Craig, Park and Paulsson, *International Chamber of Commerce Arbitration*, New York 1984, at No 4.03.

11 See, Delaume, 'Foreign Sovereign Immunity: Impact on Arbitration,' 38 *Arbitration Journal* 34 (1983), at 40.

12 21 *ILM* 976 (1982).

13 The rules of the AAA and LCIA for instance, expressly provide that the parties may elect to have their proceedings governed by the UNCITRAL Arbitration Rules.

14 For detailed comparisons of various sets of rules, see Branson and Tupman, 'Selecting an Arbitral Forum: A Guide to Cost-Effective International Arbitration,' 24 *Virginia Journal of International Law* 917 (1984) (ICC, ICSID and UNCITRAL Rules); Stein and Wotman, 'International Commercial Arbitration in the 1980's: A Comparison of the Major Arbitral Systems and Rules,' 38 *Business Law* 1685 (1983), (AAA, LCA, UNCITRAL and ICC Rules).

15 Any of the provisions of the ICSID and UNCITRAL Rules may be varied by agreement of the parties (Washington Convention, Article 44; UNCITRAL Arbitration Rules, Article 1.1). The ICC Rules may be modified to fill gaps in the rules, but not to amend any provision (ICC Rules, Article 11).

filled adequately in the course of the arbitration by agreement of the parties or order of the tribunal. There are, however, a few major differences inherent in the nature of these institutions or in their rules that can have a significant impact on the course and outcome of an arbitration.

ICC

The well-respected ICC Court of Arbitration was established in 1922. Its headquarters and its administrative staff are in Paris. It has handled thousands of international disputes, and it is reportedly the preferred forum for arbitration between parties from industrialised and less developed countries.[16] The *Pyramids Plateau* Arbitration[17] involving an investment in Egypt, was recently concluded in Paris under the auspices of the ICC. In general, however, provisions for ICC arbitration appear to be used relatively infrequently in international economic development agreements.

Administrative charges and arbitrators' fees in ICC proceedings are assessed according to the amount of the claim, and, when a large amount is at stake, can be disproportionately high compared to the ICC's actual costs and the time expended by the arbitrators.[18] The requirement of an advanced deposit to cover anticipated charges[19] can also be burdensome. It may be possible, however, for the parties to negotiate for lower arbitrators' fees.[20]

ICSID

Created by the Washington Convention ICSID shares offices and staff with the World Bank in Washington, DC. As of January, 1985, 91 states had signed the Convention and 87 had ratified it. ICSID's jurisdiction includes legal disputes between a contracting state or state agency and a national of another contracting state that arise out of an investment. 'Investment' is not expressly defined in the Convention. If there is doubt whether a particular activity is 'investment,' parties may stipulate in their economic development agreement that its object is an investment within the meaning of the Washington Convention. ICSID will probably accept the parties' characterisation and accept jurisdiction, at least so long as neither party raises a jurisdictional objection in the course of an arbitral proceeding.[21] If either party does so object, the ICSID arbitral tribunal will determine its own competence.[22]

16 'Arbitration between Parties from Industrialised and Less Developed Countries' (Report to the 1982 Montreal Conference of the International Law Association, presented by the Committee on International Commercial Arbitration, K H Böckstiegel, rapporteur).

17 22 *ILM* 752 (1983).

18 The ICC's published schedule fixes the administrative charge in a claim of $100 million at $60,500 and the arbitrator's fees at between $50,450 and $184,000 for each arbitrator. See Branson and Tupman, 'Selecting an Arbitral Forum: A Guide to Cost-Effective International Arbitration,' 24 *Virginia Journal of International Law* 917 (1984), at 931.

19 ICC Arbitration Rules, Article 9.

20 See Goekjian, 'Conducting an ICC Arbitration, Part III,' *Middle East Executive Reports* 3, 20, n55 (April 1980).

21 Golsong, 'A Guide to Procedural Issues in International Arbitration,' 18 *International Lawyer* 633 (1984), at 634–5.

22 Washington Convention, Article 41.

In the nearly 20 years of its existence, only 19 arbitrations have been commenced under ICSID, and only five have resulted in arbitral awards. ICSID's caseload has increased somewhat in recent years.[23]

ICSID arbitration appears to offer distinct advantages to parties whose agreements come within the coverage of the Convention. ICSID's detailed and comprehensive rules were specifically designed for the kind of disputes that can arise under concession agreements. The costs of arbitrating a large claim are considerably lower under an ICSID arbitration than under an ICC arbitration. Administrative charges are assessed on the basis of the institution's actual expenses,[24] and arbitrators' fees are on a reasonable *per diem* basis.[25]

Furthermore, the ICSID Rules offer a unique benefit in relation to the enforcement of awards. Under the terms of the Washington Convention, an award, even if rendered in default, is entitled to recognition and enforcement in all of the countries that have signed the Washington Convention. Sovereign immunity is no defence in an enforcement action. The Washington Convention does, however, expressly preserve the defence of sovereign immunity from execution.[26]

An ICSID award may be reviewed, at the request of either party, by a committee appointed by the Secretary General of ICSID, and may be annulled by the committee on certain limited grounds going to the tribunal's jurisdiction or the fundamental fairness of the proceeding.[27] If not annulled through this process, however, an award rendered pursuant to the Washington Convention is final and binding within the territories of all contracting states.[28]

In contrast to the ICSID Rules, the ICC Rules provide for no administrative appeals. The UNCITRAL Rules provide that awards may be modified (by the arbitrators) only to correct manifest clerical errors.[29] A challenge to an ICC or UNCITRAL award must be made, if at all, in the course of judicial proceedings to enforce an award. The New York Convention provides that a court may decline to enforce an award on certain specified grounds, including invalidity of the arbitration agreement, lack of notice to a party, and other grounds related to the tribunal's jurisdiction and the fundamental fairness of its proceedings.[30]

UNCITRAL Rules

The UNCITRAL Arbitration Rules were drafted by the United Nations Commission on International Trade Law and promulgated by the UN General Assembly in 1976. The broad international consensus on which they are based, and their flexibility and technical soundness, have made them acceptable to

23 See Delaume, 'ICSID Arbitration', *supra*.
24 ICSID Administrative and Financial Regulations, Rule 14(3).
25 *Ibid*, Rule 14(1).
26 Washington Convention, Article 55.
27 The grounds upon which a party may request annulment of an award are: (1) that the tribunal was not properly constituted; (2) that the tribunal manifestly exceeded its powers; (3) that there was corruption on the part of a member of the tribunal; (4) that there was a serious departure from a fundamental rule of procedure; or (5) that the award failed to state the reasons on which it is based. Washington Convention, Article 52.
28 Washington Convention, Article 54.
29 UNCITRAL Arbitration Rules, Article 36.
30 New York Convention, Article V.

parties from both the developed and the developing nations. Despite their relative newness, they may well be the rules most frequently referred to in contracts being made today between states and nationals of other states. A modified version of the UNCITRAL Arbitration Rules is in use at the Iran–United States Claims Tribunal, which was established in 1981. Through the arbitration of the literally thousands of cases pending before that tribunal, a body of procedural lore and published decisions is developing that will provide substantial guidance in future arbitrations under the UNCITRAL Rules.

The place of the arbitration

Even though the arbitral rules discussed above make provision for the choice of an arbitral site if the parties fail to agree in advance,[31] the parties should, if possible, designate the place of arbitration in the arbitration clause. The question is too important, and the consequences of an ill-considered decision too drastic, for the question to be left to later agreement or even to decision by the arbitrators.

The place for the arbitration should be easily accessible and convenient. Interpreters, multilingual secretaries and adequate logistical support should be available. Although there are advantages to holding the arbitration in reasonable proximity to the place of contract performance, where witnesses, records and facilities related to the contract are likely to be found, the parties to economic development agreements usually choose not to locate the arbitration in the territory of the contracting state. They tend instead to look for a forum in a neutral third country.

The parties and their advisors must carefully assess the potential impact on the arbitration of the law of the state where the proceeding is held. Generally, the law of this state will be considered the *lex arbitri*, which will determine such important matters as the validity and interpretation of the arbitration agreement, interim measures available from national courts to aid the arbitration, the conditions under which the national courts will set aside an arbitral award, and, to a certain extent as described below the enforceability of an award in other countries.

The major forum states for arbitration have enacted internal legislation governing arbitration. The objectives of these national laws are to provide autonomy to the arbitrators and finality to the arbitral award, while at the same time ensuring the fairness of the proceedings and the integrity of the arbitral award. Parties desiring to arbitrate their disputes will want a forum state where local courts do not intervene unduly in arbitrations and where they accord finality to the arbitrators' conclusions of fact and law.

The United Kingdom and France in recent years have passed legislation strongly favouring resolution of international disputes by arbitration. In the United Kingdom, the 1979 Arbitration Act permits the parties to international contracts to exclude the jurisdiction of the English courts to review an arbitration award on points of law, as well as issues of fact in certain

31 See ICC Rules, Article 12; Washington Convention, Articles 62–63; UNCITRAL Arbitration Rules, Article 16.

situations.[32] In 1981, France promulgated an arbitration law limiting judicial intervention by setting forth the grounds upon which a party to an international arbitration may seek to set aside the award.[33] The grounds for setting aside an award under the United States Arbitration Act are equally narrow.[34]

The highest courts of England, France and the United States have denoted a special status for international, as opposed to domestic, arbitration. The House of Lords, in interpreting the United Kingdom's 1979 Arbitration Act, held that the policy favouring autonomy of the parties to adopt arbitration to resolve international disputes prevails over the policy favouring judicial review of domestic arbitral awards.[35] The highest court in France has held that the court's powers of intrusion into domestic arbitrations are not applicable to international arbitration.[36] The United States Supreme Court has held that the scope of arbitrability in an international arbitration should be greater than in a domestic arbitration, citing the need for a neutral forum in international commercial disputes.[37]

National courts can also act to facilitate arbitral proceedings by providing certain kinds of interim relief. For example, in England,[38] Sweden[39] and the United States,[40] courts will issue orders to prevent parties from dissipating or removing assets from the jurisdiction pending the outcome of arbitration. National courts can also compel the production of evidence for use in an arbitration,[41] enforce discovery orders,[42] or assist in the taking of evidence for the arbitral tribunal.[43]

32 Arbitration Act 1979, s3. See also, Shenton and Toland, 'London as a Venue for International Arbitration: The Arbitration Act, 1979', 12 *Law & Policy in International Business* 643 (1980).

33 Decree No 81–500, dated May 12, 1981. The five grounds on which an arbitral award may be set aside under Article 1502 are: (1) if the arbitrator decided in the absence of an arbitration agreement or on the basis of a void or expired agreement; (2) if the arbitral tribunal was irregularly composed or the sole arbitrator irregularly appointed; (3) if the arbitrator decided in a manner incompatible with the mission conferred upon him; (4) if due process was not respected; (5) if recognition or enforcement would be contrary to international public policy.

34 9 USC No 10. The grounds are: (1) where the award was procured by corruption, fraud, or undue means; (2) where there was evidence of partiality or corruption in the arbitrators; (3) where the arbitrators were guilty of misconduct in refusing to postpone the hearing or in refusing to hear evidence pertinent and material to the controversy, or of any other misbehaviour by which the rights of any party were prejudiced; (4) where the arbitrators exceeded their powers, or so imprefectly executed them that a final and definite award upon the subject-matter submitted was not made.

35 *BTP Tioxide Ltd* v *Pioneer Shipping Ltd & Armada Marine SA* [1982] AC 724.

36 Carbonneau, 'The Elaboration of a French Court Doctrine on International Commercial Arbitration: A Study in Liberal Civilian Judicial Creativity,' 55 *Tulane Law Review* 1 (1980).

37 *Scherk* v *Alberto Culver*, 417 US 506 (1974).

38 See *Mareva Compania Naviera SA* v *International Bulk Carriers Ltd* [1975] 2 Lloyd's Rep 509.

39 See, Craig, Park and Paulsson, *International Chamber of Commerce Arbitration*, No 31.02, citing Judgment of November 9, 1979, Sup Ct Sweden (reaffirming the authority of Swedish courts to order conservatory attachments in aid of arbitration).

40 See *Carolina Power & Light* v *Uranex*, 451 F Supp 1044 (ND Cal 1977); *Andros Compania Maritime* v *Andre & Cie*, 430 F Supp 88 (SDNY 1977); but see *Cooper* v *Motobecane, SA* 57 NY 2d 408, 414 (1982).

41 See, eg, 1929 Arbitration Act of Sweden, s15.

42 See, eg, English Arbitration Act 1950, s12(4).

43 See, eg, Concordat Suisse sur l'arbitrage (1974), Articles 3(d), 27.

Finally, the place of arbitration can have an important effect on the enforceability of an arbitral award. As noted above, the award in an arbitration subject to the Washington Convention is enforceable in the courts of any signatory state, regardless of where the arbitration takes place. With respect to other arbitrations, however, the principal bases for enforcement of awards outside the state where they are made are bilateral and multilateral treaties. By far the most important of these is the 1958 New York Convention. Under the New York Convention, a signatory country is obligated under prescribed circumstances to recognise and enforce arbitral awards made in the territory of other countries. Recognition and enforcement may be refused, however, where

> 'the award has not yet become binding on the parties, or has been set aside or suspended by a competent authority of the country in which, or under the law of which, that award was made.'[44]

It is important, therefore, that the courts of the state where the arbitration takes place do not hold unduly restrictive views of when an award is binding under that state's laws.[45]

Most states that have ratified the New York Convention have done so with the reservation that their obligation extends only to awards made in the territory of another contracting state. Many have also elected to limit their obligation to disputes arising out of relationships that are considered 'commercial' under their own national laws.[46] It is critically important, therefore, in all but ICSID arbitrations, for the arbitration clause to call for arbitration in the territory of a state that is party to the New York Convention and that has acceded without unduly restrictive reservations.

As of November 1984, 68 countries had ratified the New York Convention. The signatories include all of the states most commonly selected as arbitral forums, including the United Kingdom, France, the United States and Sweden.

Provisions for the appointment of arbitrators

Arbitral tribunals generally consist of either a single neutral arbitrator or a panel of three arbitrators. It is wise for the parties to specify in the arbitration clause both the number of arbitrators and their method of selection. If they do not, this lacuna will be filled by the arbitral rules chosen or the applicable national arbitration law, but not, perhaps, as the parties themselves would have chosen.[47]

44 New York Convention, Article V(1)(e).

45 Some scholars argue that under certain circumstances an award may be 'anational', that is, not tied to the laws of any state. Such an award, they argue, is not entitled to recognition under the New York Convention. See, eg, Hirsch, 'The Place of Arbitration and the *Lex Arbitri*', 34 *Arbitration Journal* 43 (1979), at 45.

46 New York Convention, Article I(3).

47 For example, the ICC Rules call for one arbitrator unless the Court of Arbitration decides on three (ICC Rules, Article 2(5)), and the UNCITRAL and ICSID Rules call for three – one appointed by each party and the third by agreement of the parties or, failing agreement, by a designated appointing authority (UNCITRAL Arbitration Rules, Article 7; Washington Convention, Article 37(2)). Under the United States and English Arbitration Acts, if neither the arbitration clause nor the chosen rules determine the method of appointment, the local court will make the appointment. US Arbitration Act, 9 USC No 5; English Arbitration Act 1979, s10.

A sole arbitrator may be the better choice if considerations of speed and cost are uppermost. On the other hand, a three-member tribunal is preferable for purposes of ensuring a thorough review of the dispute and avoiding error. If there are three arbitrators, it is possible for each party to name one.[48] Although a party-appointed arbitrator must be free from disqualifying bias or personal interest,[49] it is quite appropriate for a party to appoint an arbitrator who shares that party's general point of view and who comes from the same culture or legal system. Such an arbitrator can play a vital role in interpreting and explaining to the other arbitrators, who may come from different backgrounds, the position of the party that appointed him.

It is possible, but generally impractical, for the parties to designate arbitrators by name in the arbitration clause. It is also possible, and not uncommon in commercial contracts, for arbitration clauses to require that arbitrators possess certain technical qualifications. In economic development agreements, however, arbitration clauses generally make no provision as to the identities of the arbitrators or their technical qualifications. Arbitrations under these agreements usually involve complex issues of law and fact. When disputes arise, the parties tend to seek as arbitrators lawyers and jurists who are versed in international law and who have the capacity to resolve technical questions of fact by weighing the evidence of experts in the arbitral process. Perhaps the only restriction as to the qualifications of arbitrators that is common in economic development agreements is a requirement that at least one arbitrator – usually the sole arbitrator, or the chairman of a three-person panel – not have the same nationality as either party.[50]

Finally, the parties should always be sure that a suitable appointing authority has been designated to appoint an arbitrator or arbitrators if the individual parties fail to name their own or if agreement cannot be reached on a neutral or third arbitrator. Most, if not all, arbitral rules name appointing authorities to perform this function,[51] but the parties may prefer to designate a different appointing authority of their own choosing.

Language

Economic development agreements are frequently written in two languages, that of the contracting state and that of the foreign private party, with both versions stated to be of equal validity. It is wise to specify in the arbitration clause the language or languages in which any arbitration will be conducted, and, if possible, to specify a single language for that purpose. In the course of the parties' negotiations and in their dealings and written communications under the contract, a single language will tend to become the *de facto* language

48 The three sets of rules principally considered in this paper all provide that, when there are to be three arbitrators, each party will name one, unless the parties otherwise agree. ICC Rules, Article 2(4); UNCITRAL Arbitration Rules, Article 7; Washington Convention, Article 37(2).

49 ICC Rules, Article 2(7); UNCITRAL Arbitration Rules, Article 10; Washington Convention, Article 14(1).

50 Under the ICSID Rules, unless the parties otherwise agree, this requirement applies to the party-appointed arbitrators. ICSID Rule 3.

51 Eg, ICC Rules, Article 2(1); UNCITRAL Arbitration Rules, Article 6(2); ICSID Rule 4.

of the transaction. The parties should seek to identify that language and provide for its use in arbitrations.[52]

The difficulties with dual language proceedings are well illustrated in the Iran–United States Claims Tribunal. All principal filings in that tribunal are required to be submitted in both English and Farsi. There are simultaneous translations at the hearings. The process has proved burdensome and costly. The translations are of uneven quality. Often small mistakes in translation contribute to significant failures of communication.

Other procedural matters

There are a number of additional procedural matters that are not expressly provided for in most arbitration clauses, but that should nevertheless be considered by the draftsman for possible inclusion. Certain of these matters are expressly dealt with in some arbitral rules. If they are not covered by the rules chosen, or if the parties wish to deviate from the governing rules, they should consider dealing with these matters explicitly in the arbitration clause.

Matters of this sort include the imposition of time-limits for certain actions, the right of the tribunal to demand the production of documents or the testimony of witnesses,[53] the right of the tribunal to draw inferences from a party's failure to produce documents or witnesses,[54] the right of cross-examination,[55] and the consent of the parties to interim measures of judicial relief.

Provisions touching on a number of these points are included in the Rules of Evidence recently promulgated by the Council of the International Bar Association (IBA).[56] These are a comprehensive set of evidentiary rules designed to be incorporated by reference in the arbitration clause. Care must be taken, however, to avoid conflicts between provisions in the IBA Rules and comparable provisions in the arbitral rules chosen. For instance, the IBA Rules of Evidence include time-limits for filings and requirements as to the contents of particular filings that may not jibe with provisions in the chosen arbitral rules.[57] If the draftsman chooses to incorporate provisions from the IBA Rules, he may be well advised to do so selectively.

52 The ICSID Rules provide for the use of one or two languages, as the parties agree; if they do not agree, each is entitled to proceed in any of three specified languages. ICSID Rule 22. The ICC Rules (Article 15(3)) and UNCITRAL Arbitration Rules (Article 17) permit arbitrators to specify the language of the arbitration, if the parties have not agreed.

53 Existing rules differ in their treatment of this point. See, eg, ICC Rules, Article 14; UNCITRAL Arbitration Rules, Article 24(3); ICSID Rule 34(2).

54 The ICC and UNCITRAL Arbitration Rules do not specifically provide for this inference. But see ICSID Rule 34(3).

55 None of the major arbitral regimes explicitly provides for the right of cross-examination.

56 International Bar Association, Supplementary Rules of Evidence for Use in International Arbitration, May 28, 1983 ('IBA Rules').

57 The IBA Rules also provide, perhaps unwisely, that, in case of conflict between those rules and the chosen arbitral rules, the IBA Rules shall prevail: Article 1.3.

Enforcement of award

Questions of the enforcement of arbitral awards, and in particular the knotty question of sovereign immunity, are dealt with at length in other contributions to this Conference. We have discussed above the impact of the place of arbitration, and of the principal relevant international Conventions, on enforcement of awards. It is sufficient here to note that the draftsman will want to consider whether the arbitration clause should include a provision expressly waiving the governmental party's immunity in a suit for the recognition and enforcement of an arbitral award, and perhaps also its immunity from pre-judgment attachment or post-judgment execution against its property.

Choice of substantive law

Choice of the substantive law to be applied to the merits of a dispute can be one of the hardest points to agree on in the negotiation of an economic development agreement.

A threshold question for the draftsman is whether the arbitral tribunal is to be instructed to decide disputes according to law, or is to be authorised or directed to act as *amiable compositeur*, or to decide *ex aequo et bono*.[58] Decision according to such principles is perhaps most frequently suggested after disputes have arisen, when one or both parties believe that circumstances have so changed that it would be unfair to require them to perform the bargain they originally made. However, for parties seeking at the time of contracting to create a regime of clear rights and duties, a provision of the resolution of disputes on the basis of these principles introduces an element of uncertainty that is probably unacceptable.

Parties that wish their disputes to be decided by application of legal rules may select the law of a particular nation as the governing law. Typically, the law chosen is that of the host country. If they refer to the laws of the host country, the parties should consider whether the applicable law is that of the host country as it exists at the time of execution of the agreement, or the law as it develops over time. If the parties opt for the former, a so-called stabilisation clause should be inserted in the agreement. Such a clause directs the arbitral tribunal to disregard changes in host country laws made after the date of the contract, which might otherwise affect the foreign company's contractual rights or obligations.[59]

Ideally, the parties' agreement on choice of law will do more than identify the system of municipal law under which the parties' rights will be determined.

58 The two concepts are similar. The power to act as an *amiable compositeur* is the power to resolve a dispute without regard to express substantive rules of law and according to customary rules of equity and international commerce. The power to decide a case *ex aequo et bono* is the power to decide on the basis of fairness and good dealing. The arbitral rules here discussed expressly authorise the parties to elect settlement of their disputes according to these principles. ICC Rules, Article 13(4); UNCITRAL Arbitration Rules, Article 33; Washington Convention, Article 42(3).

59 See *Aramco* Arbitration where the arbitrators upheld the use of a stabilisation clause, noting that 'Nothing can prevent a State ... from binding itself irrevocably ... and from granting to the concessionaire irretractable rights': 27 *International Law Reports* 117 (1958) at 168.

In an international economic development agreement, it is also important to consider the extent to which international law will determine the resolution of disputes. In the typical expropriation case, for instance, the contractual rights of the parties exist under, and are defined by, municipal law, usually that of the state where the economic activity takes place. However, the claim of the foreign investor for the taking of those rights generally arises, or is claimed to arise, under international law (customary international law, treaty, or both) as well as under municipal law.

The Washington Convention deals with the need to consider both municipal and international law by providing that, in the absence of choice of law by the parties,

> 'the Tribunal shall apply the law of the Contracting State party to the dispute (including its rules on the conflict of laws) and such rules of international law as may be applicable.'[60]

The clause is a good one. In contrast, clauses considered in a number of reported arbitral decisions have dealt less simply with the relationship between municipal and international law, with results that are not entirely consistent.

For example, certain oil concession agreements concluded with Libya in the 1970's contained the following provision, which was required by Libyan law:

> 'This concession shall be governed by and interpreted in accordance with the principles of the law of Libya common to the principles of international law, and in the absence of such common principles then by and in accordance with the general principles of law, including such of those principles as may have been applied by international tribunals.'[61]

This clause was construed in three separate arbitrations arising out of the nationalisation of concession rights. The three sole arbitrators used three divergent approaches to the choice of law problem. In the *TOPCO* Arbitration,[62] the arbitrator applied Libyan law throughout the case; in the *Liamco* Arbitration,[63] the arbitrator applied Libyan law, except on the issue of damages, where he was not able to find a Libyan law common to the principles of international law; in the *BP* Arbitration,[64] the arbitrator applied general principles of law throughout the case.

Similarly, in the *Aramco* Arbitration the choice of law clause provided that disputes should be decided

> 'in accordance with Saudi Arabian law insofar as matters within the jurisdiction of Saudi Arabia are concerned, and in accordance with the law declared by the arbitration tribunal to be applicable insofar as matters beyond the jurisdiction of Saudi Arabia are concerned.'[65]

The Tribunal, eschewing Saudi law, relied instead upon 'general principles of law, ... the custom and practice in the oil business, and ... notions of pure

60 Washington Convention, Article 42(1).
61 *Liamco Arbitration*, 20 *ILM* 1 (1980), at 64.
62 17 *ILM* 1 (1977).
63 *Op cit.*
64 53 *ILR* 297 (1979).
65 *Aramco Arbitration*, *op cit*, at 153–4.

jurisprudence'[66] to find that Saudi Arabia had breached its concession agreement.

A surprising number of international agreements include no express provision on choice of law. The absence of a choice of law clause introduces an element of uncertainty into an arbitral proceeding. The uncertainty is undesirable, but it may not be fatal. Faced with agreements that are silent on choice of law, tribunals generally are able to find and apply choice of law rules that differ from case to case, but that are reasonable in the circumstances.[67]

Nevertheless, even if the parties cannot agree in advance on what system of law governs, they should at least make it clear that decisions are to be made according to law. To establish this minimum standard, the arbitration clause could provide, for instance, for decisions under 'generally accepted principles of law' or 'general principles of law.' The choice of law provision in the Accords establishing the Iran–United States Claims Tribunal reflects this general approach. Decisions by the Tribunal are to be based on principles of law, but the arbitrators have wide latitude in their choice of the applicable law:

> 'The Tribunal shall decide all cases on the basis of respect for law, applying such choice of law rules and principles of commercial and international law as the Tribunal determines to be applicable, taking into account relevant usages of the trade, contract provisions and changed circumstances.'[68]

On more than one occasion, the tribunal has declined to apply the municipal law that would govern under conventional choice of law principles, and has instead applied 'general principles of law'[69] see, eg, *CMI International, Inc* v *Ministry of Roads and Transportation*, Award No 99–245–2 (Iran–US Claims Tribunal, December 27, 1983) (declining to apply Idaho law).

The concept of 'general principles of law' is on its face somewhat vague. In fact, however, it may be no more difficult in a given case to discover and apply these principles than it is to find and apply a particular national law, which may be highly technical, or may not speak expressly to the point, and which may include idiosyncracies inappropriate in an international transaction.

Conclusion

The drafting of the arbitration clause in an economic development agreement is a complex task, requiring the evaluation of available arbitral rules and

66 *Ibid*, at 169.

67 See, eg, *Sapphire Arbitration*, 35 *International Law Reports* 136 (1963), at 164–5, where concession agreement made no mention of applicable law, arbitrator applied principles of law generally recognised by civilised nations; *Pyramids Plateau Arbitration*, 22 *ILM* 752 (1983), at 770–1 where agreements made no choice of law, arbitrators applied the laws of Egypt insofar as they do not contravene principles of international law; *Revere Cooper Arbitration*, 56 *ILR* 258 (1978), at 1331, where agreement was silent as to applicable law, arbitrators applied Jamaican law for ordinary purposes of the agreement and principles of public international law to the issue of breach of international concession agreements.

68 Declaration of the Government of the Democratic and Popular Republic of Algeria Concerning the Settlement of Claims by the Government of the United States of America and the Government of the Islamic Republic of Iran, Article V.

69 See, eg, *CMI International, Inc* v *Ministry of Roads and Transportation*, Award No 99–245–2 (Iran–US Claims Tribunal, December 27, 1983) (declining to apply Idaho law).

arbitral institutions, the study of municipal laws and international conventions that may be relevant, and the structuring of an arbitral scheme that is both practical and legally sound.

A careful effort will be well repaid. A well-crafted arbitration clause can establish a structure for arbitral proceedings that are efficient and fair. It can help insure that arbitral awards will be enforceable. Indeed, it can lessen the chance that the parties will someday find themselves in arbitration under the clause, for the very existence of the remedies it provides can serve as a deterrent to overreaching or unreasonable conduct by either party, and thus a deterrent to disputes that make arbitration necessary.

Sovereign immunity and transnational arbitration 28

Georges R Delaume

The presence of a state as a party to arbitral proceedings gives a particular colouration to the arbitral process. From the date of execution of the arbitration agreement throughout the proceedings and, ultimately, at the time of recognition and enforcement of an award, arbitration involving states raises a number of original issues.

Initially the threshold issues of the arbitrability of disputes involving states and of the authority of public officials to bind their principal must be faced. These are questions to which there is no uniform answer.[1]

Assuming that these questions are satisfactorily resolved, considerations of sovereign immunity may interfere with the conduct of the proceedings and their outcome. Thus, a state may raise immunity from suit as a bar to the enforcement of the arbitration agreement or to the proceedings for the recognition or confirmation of an award. Similarly, the state involved may plead immunity from execution to object to measures of execution against its property either in the form of provisional measures before the award is rendered or in the form of procedures intended to secure enforcement of the award after it is rendered.

These are issues which are well known, but are complicated by the lack of uniformity of immunity rules.

To be sure, recent trends in major western legal systems give increasing support to the restrictive doctrine of immunity. This is apparent from such treaty developments as the European Convention on State Immunity (the European Convention),[2] and certain bilateral treaties,[3] as well as statutory enactments, such as the Foreign Sovereign Immunities Act in the United States (FSIA),[4] the State Immunity Act in the United Kingdom (SIA),[5] and similar statutes in other countries.[6] Also, in other countries whose immunity rules remain uncodified, which is the case of western Continental countries, recent judicial pronouncements clearly endorse the restrictive notion of sovereign immunity.[7]

1 Delaume, *Transnational Contracts*, Chapter XIII, paragraph 13.07.
2 Reproduced in Delaume, *op cit*, Appendix I, Booklet D, p 5.
3 *Ibid*, Chapter XI, paragraph 11.02; Chapter XII, paragraph 12.06.
4 *Ibid*, Appendix I, Booklet D, p 69.
5 *Ibid*, p 51.
6 Such as Canada, Pakistan, Singapore, South Africa. See Delaume, *op cit*, Chapter XI, paragraph 11.01.
7 *Ibid*, Chapters XI and XII.

The fact remains, however, that, although the law of western countries evolves in the same direction, the immunity rules obtaining in individual countries are not always concordant. In the particular context of transnational arbitration, considerations of sovereign immunity may, therefore, be the source of dilatory tactics and expense that may hinder, if not altogether frustrate, the arbitration process.

Furthermore, the restrictive doctrine of immunity remains geographically confined to western countries. In contrast, socialist countries continue to adhere, at least in principle, to the absolute doctrine of immunity.[8] In this respect, however, it should be noted immediately that, in view of the extensive use of arbitration in socialist countries and of the record of these countries regarding compliance with arbitral awards, issues of immunity tend to recede in the background.

The situation is much less clear in regard to countries in the Third World. Only a few of these countries have clearly endorsed the restrictive doctrine of immunity.[9] In the absence of a comprehensive comparative survey, the law of other countries remains an unknown factor.

These are general remarks, which apply equally to *ad hoc* arbitration and to arbitration conducted under the auspices of specialised arbitration institutions, with one exception. This exception concerns arbitration taking place in the context of the Washington Convention[10] which is administered by ICSID.

The Washington Convention provides a self-contained machinery governed by truly international rules found in the Convention itself and the Regulations and Rules adopted for its implementation.[11] Under the ICSID Rules, a number of immunity issues, which, in the context of non-ICSID arbitration, may have an adverse effect upon the conduct of the proceedings and the effectiveness of the award, are either eliminated at the outset or take a different connotation when they are viewed in the context of the ICSID machinery.

Immunity from suit

Consent to arbitration as an implicit waiver of immunity

Non-ICSID arbitration

In the case of arbitration other than ICSID arbitration, and in the absence of an express waiver of immunity,[12] the question arises whether submission to

8 See, eg, Osakwe, 'A Soviet Perspective on Foreign Sovereign Immunity: Law and Practice', 23 *Virginia Journal of International Law* 13 (1982); The People's Republic of China: Aide Memoire of the Ministry of Foreign Affairs, February 3, 1983, 22 *ILM* 81 (1983); Sgro, 'China's Stance on Sovereign Immunity: A Critical Perspective of Jackson v People's Republic of China', 22 *Columbia Journal of Transnational Law* 101 (1983).

9 See eg, Pakistan and Singapore, n6 *supra*.

10 Reproduced in Delaume, *op cit*, Appendix II, Booklet B1, p 23.

11 The Regulations and Rules in effect on January 1, 1968 (as amended) have now been revised. The revised text was approved by the Administrative Council of ICSID on September 26, 1984. The text of the revised Regulations and Rules (together with that of the Convention) appears in Document ICSID/15. See also News from *ICSID*, Vol 2, No 1 (Winter 1985).

12 For examples of such waivers, see Delaume, *op cit*, Chapter XI, paragraph 11.07 and Chapter XII, paragraph 12.05.

arbitration should be regarded as an implicit waiver of immunity. Although states may be tempted to endorse the opposite view, the overwhelming weight of authority calls for an affirmative answer. Decisions of international and domestic tribunals, treaty and statutory provisions found in the European Convention and modern western statutes, all concur that a state party to an arbitration agreement is precluded from asserting its immunity in order to frustrate the purpose of the agreement.[13]

Although this principle is clear, its implementation is not always exempt from controversy. American decisions rendered in the context of the FSIA illustrate this point. In this connection it should be recalled that the legislative history of the FSIA mentions as an example of implicit waiver of immunity within the meaning of Section 1605(a)(1) of the FSIA, the case 'where a foreign state has agreed to arbitration in another country'.[14]

The question which has caused some divergence of opinion is whether by referring to 'another country', the authors of the FSIA had in mind only the United States,[15] or any country other than the state party to the arbitration agreement? The first and restrictive interpretation found favour, however only by way of dictum, in the *Verlinden* case.[16] The second interpretation prevailed in *Ipitrade*[17] and in LIAMCO,[18] before that case was discontinued following an amicable settlement.

It is submitted that the second interpretation is the one which should be preferred.[19]

In the same connection, the emphasis placed in American decisions on the fact that the United States, as a party to the New York Convention had a treaty commitment to give effect to awards rendered in other Convention states may be unfortunate.[20] Although treaty commitments may give additional reasons to uphold the general rule that consent to arbitration constitutes an implicit waiver of immunity, they should not detract from the general character of the rule. Both the contractual nature of arbitration and the need to uphold the binding character of arbitration agreements demand that the rule be applied equally in all cases, regardless of the existence or the absence of arbitration treaties.

13 *Ibid*, Chapter XIV, paragraph 14.02.

14 H Rep No 94–1487, p 18.

15 For a case concerning an award rendered in the United States, see *Birch Shipping Co* v *The Embassy of the United Republic of Tanzania*, 507 F Supp 311 (DDC 1980).

16 *Verlinden BV* v *Central Bank of Nigeria*, 488 F Supp 1284 (SDNY 1980), aff'd 647 F 2d 320 (2d Cir 1981), rev'd and remanded 103 S Ct 1962 (1983).

17 *Ipitrade International SA* v *Federal Republic of Nigeria*, 465 F Supp 824 (DDC 1978).

18 *Libyan American Oil Co* v *Socialist People's Libyan Arab Jamahiriya*, 482 F Supp 1175 (DDC 1980).

19 It has been held that a state does not waive its immunity by submitting to arbitration in its territory (*Chicago Bridge & Iron Co* v *Islamic Republic of Iran*, 506 F Supp 981 (ND 111 1980) or to litigation in its own courts (*Perez* v *The Bahamas*), 482 F Supp 1208 (DCC 1980), aff'd 652 F 2d 186 (DC Cir), cert denied, 102 S Ct 326 (1981). The issue was left undecided in *American Bell International* v *Islamic Republic of Iran*, 474 F Supp 420 (SDNY 1979).

20 See the *Ipitrade* and *LIAMCO* cases referred to above.

ICSID arbitration

One of these treaties, namely the Washington Convention clearly proclaims the binding character of arbitration agreements. Under the Convention,[21] consent to ICSID arbitration, once it is given, cannot be unilaterally revoked. For the purposes of the Washington Convention, therefore, consent to ICSID arbitration constitutes on the part of the state involved an irrevocable waiver of immunity from suit. Bound by its consent, that state is barred from raising any plea of immunity that would frustrate the proceedings or the recognition of the resulting award. In other words, within the context of the Washington Convention, immunity from suit is eradicated at the outset.

In exchange, the Washington Convention protects a consenting state from other forms of international litigation. Because consent to ICSID arbitration is equally binding upon the investor as it is on the state party to the dispute, that state is assured that the investor cannot bring action in a non-ICSID forum. The immediate consequence of this rule is that if the investor, in violation of its contractual commitments, sought to frustrate ICSID proceedings by bringing action in the municipal courts of a contracting state, the court concerned ought to stay the proceedings and refer the parties to ICSID arbitration. In other words, if a court in a contracting state becomes aware of the fact that a claim before it may call for adjudication under ICSID, the court ought to abstain from hearing the claim pending proper determination of the issue by ICSID. It is only in the event that ICSID would rule that, for some reason, the claim does not fall within its jurisdiction that the court in question could resume hearing the case, assuming, of course, that it would have an independent basis for entertaining jurisdiction over the parties and the subject-matter of the dispute.

This rule of judicial abstention is essential to the proper implementation of the Washington Convention. Failure by a court in a contracting state to observe it might expose that state to an international claim brought by the state party to the dispute.[22]

Recently, the rule of abstention was brought to the attention of US and French courts. The French courts' decisions will be considered below. In the United States, the issue arose in connection with the question whether consent to ICSID arbitration constituted a waiver of immunity for the purposes of the FSIA. The negative answer prevailed,[23] however, on considerations strictly based on the construction of the FSIA rather than, as they should have been, on the proper implementation of the Washington Convention.[24]

Immunity from suit and the recognition of arbitral awards

Non-ICSID awards

Assuming that an award has been rendered against a state and that the award creditor seeks recognition of the award in the form of a confirmation, an

21 Washington Convention, Article 25(1).

22 *Ibid*, Article 64. This argument was made by the United States in its Brief as Intervenor in the MINE case (see n23 *infra*). See Delaume, 'ICSID Arbitration and the Courts', 77 *American Journal of International Law* 784 (1983), at 785, n6.

23 *Maritime International Nominees Establishment* v *The Republic of Guinea*, 693 F 2d 1094 (DC Cir 1982), cert denied 104 S Ct 71 (1983).

24 Delaume, *op cit*, in 77 *Am J Int'l L* at 786–792.

exequatur, or similar proceeding, the award creditor may be faced with a plea of immunity filed by the state in the recognising court.

As a rule, pleas of immunity have been unsuccessful. When the issue arose, as it did in The Netherlands, the United States, and France,[25] the courts have held that when a state has waived its immunity by submitting to arbitration, the scope of the waiver extends to proceedings for confirmation or recognition of the resulting award.

This clearly is the correct solution, since otherwise sovereign immunity would make a mockery of the arbitration process. Nevertheless, the fact cannot be overlooked that pleas of immunity at the time of recognition have a nuisance value and can be the source of delays and expense.

ICSID awards

These problems are totally eliminated in the case of ICSID awards. The Washington Convention provides not only that the parties are bound by the award[26] but also that all contracting states must recognise ICSID awards and enforce the pecuniary obligations imposed by an award as if it were a final judgment of one of their domestic courts.[27] In addition, the Convention[28] makes the procedure for recognition as simple as possible. Any party to an ICSID award may obtain recognition of the award by furnishing to the competent court or authority designated in advance by each contracting state a copy of the award certified by the Secretary-General of ICSID.

This simple and expeditious procedure eliminates the problems attendant upon the recognition of foreign arbitral awards which subsist in domestic laws and under international conventions, including the New York Convention. Under the Washington Convention, there is no exception (not even on the ground of public policy) to the binding character of ICSID awards and to their recognition in contracting states.

More specifically, the Washington Convention removes from the procedure any issue of immunity since the competent court or authority is under a mandate to recognise an ICSID award in accordance with the provisions of the Convention. In the system of the Washington Convention, the contracting state party to the dispute is deemed to have waived any defense, including immunity from suit, which would interfere with the ICSID machinery and would be inconsistent with the consent given by that state to ICSID arbitration.

The effectiveness of this procedure has been acknowledged by the Court of Appeal of Paris, France in the case of *Benvenuti & Bonfant srl* v *Gouvernement de la République Populaire du Congo*.[29] In this case, which is so far the only decision in point and involved the recognition of an ICSID award against the Congolese Republic, the court acknowledged that the provisions of the Convention:

> '... offer a simplified procedure for recognition and enforcement (*exequatur simplifié*) and restrict the function of the court designated for the purposes

25 Delaume, *op cit*, Chapter XIV, paragraph 14.08.
26 Washington Convention, Article 53.
27 *Ibid*, Article 54(1).
28 *Ibid*, Article 54(1).
29 Paris, June 26, 1981, 108 *Clunet* 843 (1981).

of the Convention by each Contracting State to ascertaining the authenticity of the award certified by the Secretary General [of ICSID].'

The practical significance of this procedure is apparent. It means not only that the recognition of ICSID awards can be obtained with exceptional speed but also that, as soon as an award is recognised, it becomes a valid title on whose basis measures of execution can be taken, at least to the extent that such measures are possible under the immunity rules of the contracting state in which execution is sought.

Immunity from execution

Provisional measures (pre-award attachment)

Non-ICSID arbitration

Whether provisional measures, such as attachment, are available against the property of a state, is an issue which is not uniformly settled.

A negative answer is clearly given by the FSIA, which abolishes the earlier practice of prejudgment attachment for the purpose of acquiring *quasi in rem* jurisdiction.[30]

In other western countries, a distinction is made between execution against the assets of the state itself, as sovereign which is prohibited, and execution against the property of other public entities, which may be possible.[31] The same is true in regard to eastern bloc countries, since bilateral treaties allow execution against the property of trade delegations or similar entities engaged in transnational commercial activities.

ICSID arbitration

The situation is different under the rules applicable to ICSID arbitration. Under the Washington Convention, the only provisional measures to which the parties are entitled are those that can be recommended by an arbitral tribunal on its own initiative or at the parties' request.[32] In other words, by consenting to ICSID arbitration, the parties waive their right to seek interim measures of protection, including attachment, in domestic courts, whether before or after the institution of the proceedings.[33]

In the context of ICSID, the parties, if they wish to retain the option to seek

30 FSIA No 1610(c) and (d). Note also that American courts are not in agreement on the question whether, aside from immunity considerations, pre-award attachment is compatible with the spirit, if not the letter, of the New York Convention. See Delaume, *op cit*, Chapter XIII, para 13.14.

31 Delaume, *op cit*, Chapter XII, paragraph 12.06.

32 Washington Convention, Article 47; ICSID Arbitration Rule 39.

33 In this respect, the ICSID Rules differ from those of other arbitration institutions according to which requests for interim measures of protection addressed to a judicial authority are not deemed incompatible with the arbitration agreement. See, eg, in regard to the ICC Rules, Rule 8(5); Craig, Park and Paulsson, *International Chamber of Commerce Arbitration*, New York 1984, paragraphs 27.01 to 27.04. Comp, AAA Commercial Arbitration Rules No 46; UNCITRAL Arbitration Rules, Article 26.

judicial assistance with respect to provisional measures, must do so by way of express provision in the agreement recording their consent, which may take the form of a waiver of immunity.[34] In the absence of such an agreement, the exclusive character of ICSID arbitration requires the courts in contracting states, consistent with the rule of abstention, to refuse judicial assistance to the party seeking provisional measures.

République Populaire Révolutionnaire de Guinée et al v *Société Atlantic Triton*, a French decision,[35] illustrates this rule. In that case, Atlantic Triton, a Norwegian company, and the Republic of Guinea had entered into a contract for the conversion of vessels into fishing vessels and the training of crews. The contract provided for ICSID arbitration and Atlantic Triton submitted to ICSID a request for the institution of arbitration proceedings. The request was registered on January 19, 1984 and the ICSID arbitral tribunal was constituted on August 1, 1984. On October 12, 1983, ie, before the submission of the request to ICSID, Atlantic Triton obtained from a French commercial court an order of attachment concerning three Guinean vessels under repair in a French port. The order was confirmed on April 6, 1984, ie, after the registration of the request. On appeal, the Court of Appeal vacated the attachment on the ground that the arbitral tribunal had 'general and exclusive competence to decide not only in regard to the merits, but also in respect of any provisional measures' and that, consequently, the French courts had no jurisdiction in the matter.

This, clearly, was the correct solution. However, it should be noted that the court reached its decision solely on the basis of the exclusive character of consent to ICSID arbitration, irrespective of considerations of sovereign immunity. Indeed, a plea of immunity raised by Guinea in the same proceeding failed on the ground that the transaction had a commercial character.

Post-award execution

Non-ICSID arbitration

Whether an award can be enforced against the property of a foreign state or of other public entities is an issue on which there is no consensus. In this respect, the rules of immunity from execution are in even greater disarray than those concerning immunity from suit. Certain legal systems consider that when there is no immunity from suit, there should be no immunity from execution. Other systems, however, continue to deny execution even after recognition of a judgment or award against a state, or subject execution to the prior approval of the executive branch of the government, or distinguish between the property of the state itself and that of other public entities.[36]

The complexity of domestic rules of immunity is such that it is a direct invitation to forum shopping. This remark is nicely illustrated by the proceedings regarding attempts made by LIAMCO to enforce an award

34 Delaume, *op cit*, Chapter XV, paragraph 15.18. See also ICSID Model Clauses, clause XVI.

35 24 *ILM* 345 (1985).

36 Delaume, *op cit*, Chapter XII.

against Libya,[37] and to levy execution on Libya's assets in France, the United States, Switzerland and Sweden. In France, the award was granted *exequatur*, but attachments of Libyan accounts in Parisian banks were vacated, following intervention by the Public Attorney who claimed that under the doctrine of 'absolute' immunity, no measure of execution could obtain against the assets of Libya. Interestingly enough, however, the court, while vacating the attachments, took the unusual step of appointing a committee composed of three independent persons to ascertain whether the accounts attached were used for commercial or governmental activities.[38]

As already mentioned, in the United States, the District Court for the District of Columbia held that, by agreeing to arbitrate in Switzerland disputes with LIAMCO, Libya had waived its immunity and that the court had jurisdiction to recognise and enforce the award. However, the court declined jurisdiction on the basis of the Act of State doctrine. The United States Government in its *amicus* briefs to the United States Court of Appeals disagreed with that part of the lower court's decision based on the Act of State doctrine.[39]

In Switzerland, the Federal Tribunal, consistent with Swiss precedents, declined to exercise jurisdiction and refused to permit execution against assets of Libya located in Switzerland on the ground that the underlying transaction (a dispute over the nationalisation of LIAMCO's concession) bore no contact to Switzerland other than the fact that the sole arbitrator had elected to locate the seat of arbitration in Geneva. On the ground that this nexus with Switzerland was too tenuous to found jurisdiction, the tribunal vacated the attachment.[40]

The last proceeding took place in Sweden. The Court of Appeals of Svea (Stockholm)[41] held that by consenting to arbitration, Libya had waived its immunity from suit and execution. The court, however, did not explain whether execution was possible against all Libya's assets or only against assets used for commercial purposes. Appeal was taken to the Swedish Supreme Court.

The tantalising questions raised in the French, United States and Swedish courts remain, however, unanswered since a settlement ended the litigation.

37 *Libyan American Oil Co* v *Government of the Libyan Arab Republic*, 20 *ILM* 1 (1981).

38 TGI Paris, March 5, 1979, *Procureur de la Republique* v *Société LIAMCO*, 106 *Clunet* 857 (1979). The situation might be different today, following the latest pronouncement of the Court of Cassation in the *Eurodif* case. See Cass, March 14, 1984, *Société Eurodif et al* v *Republique Islamique d'Iran*, Juris-Classeur Periodique (also called Semaine Juridique) 1984, II, 20205), 111 *Clunet* 598 (1984). In that case, the court held that when the property sought to be executed against was used for the economic or commercial activity upon which the claim was based, there was no immunity from execution. This solution conforms to that which is provided for in No 1610(a)(2) of the FSIA. It is more restrictive than that which might obtain under the SIA since under s13(4) of the SIA any property of a foreign state used for commercial purposes may be executed against, even when that property bears no relation to the transaction out of which the claim arose.

39 20 *ILM* 161 (1981).

40 TF, June 19, 1980, *Socialist Libyan Arab Popular Jamajiriya* v *Libyan American Oil Co* (LIAMCO), 20 *ILM* 151 (1981).

41 CA Svea, June 18, 1980, *Libyan American Oil Co* v *Socialist People's Republic of Libya*. 20 *ILM* 893 (1981).

ICSID arbitration

As soon as an ICSID award is recognised in accordance with the simplified procedure described above, it becomes an executory title. As such the award could be readily enforced against the property of an investor, if the investor were the award debtor.

The situation, however, might be different in the event that the award be rendered against the state party to the dispute. The reason for this remark is that the Washington Convention does not purport to derogate to the rules of immunity from execution prevailing in contracting states.[42] In other words, and in contrast with its daring approach to issues of immunity from suit, the Convention does not alter or supersede the rules of immunity from execution in contracting states.

This solution could not be avoided in view of the opinions expressed during the drafting stages of the Convention by governmental representatives and of the lack of consensus on the meaning and scope of immunity from execution. Although this solution may be regretted, it does not mean that an ICSID award creditor cannot find in the Washington Convention greater protection than is available to him under other forms of arbitration. In this connection, it should be noted that in the system of the Washington Convention, issues of immunity cannot be considered in their individuality and must be considered in the context of the Convention as a whole. In particular, it is clear that if a contracting state party to a dispute invoked immunity from execution, either in its own courts or in the courts of another contracting state, in order to frustrate enforcement of an ICSID award, that state would violate its obligation to comply with the award.[43] In that case, the state involved would be exposed to various sanctions.

In the first place, failure to comply would restore the right of the contracting state whose national is the award creditor to give diplomatic protection to its national and to bring an international claim on its behalf. Under Article 27(1) of the Washington Convention, diplomatic protection is suspended during the period beginning with the date of consent to ICSID award. However, Article 27(1) provides expressly that diplomatic protection may be exercised again if the contracting state party to the dispute fails 'to abide by and comply with the award rendered in such dispute.'

In the second place, should the issue of non-compliance raise a question of interpretation or application of the Washington Convention, the contracting state whose national is involved would have the right to submit the question for adjudication to the International Court of Justice unless both contracting states agreed on another method, eg, by arbitration, of settlement.[44] In other words, even though the Convention does not purport to change rules of immunity from execution, it nevertheless imparts a new spirit to the rules by which the game may be played. In fact, it is interesting to note that none of the ICSID

42 Article 55 of the Washington Convention states that the original and expeditive procedure for the recognition of ICSID awards shall in no way 'be construed as derogating from the law in force in any Contracting State relating to immunity of that State or any foreign state from execution'.

43 Washington Convention, Article 53.

44 *Ibid*, Article 64.

awards on the merits which have been rendered so far,[45] has given rise to measures of execution.

There are several reasons for this situation. Exposure to the sanctions provided by the Washington Convention in the event of non-compliance with an award may be one of them, but is not probably the paramount consideration. One important factor to bear in mind is that, unlike in the case of well-known arbitration proceedings in which the state involved elected to default,[46] the history of ICSID shows a high degree of state participation in the proceedings. Although only one state acted as a claimant,[47] the states against which proceedings have been instituted have often formulated their own grievances in the form of counterclaims and have had, therefore, their full day in court. To the extent that these counterclaims have been successful, which has been the case in certain instances, the problem of enforcing the relevant award simply did not arise. In those cases in which awards were rendered against the state, the state's participation in the proceedings has certainly been a contributing factor to its willingness to comply with the award.

Finally, it should be noted that refusal by a state to comply with an ICSID award would deprive that state of any credibility in the international community. This is a risk that a state is not likely to assume lightly.

In the light of these considerations, the theoretically troublesome issue of immunity from execution, which has been the object of much scholarly discussion and regret, loses a great deal of practical significance.

Furthermore, the fact should not be overlooked that, in the case of ICSID arbitration as in that of other forms of arbitration with states, the investor, if his bargaining position is sufficiently strong, may succeed in providing expressly in the arbitration agreement that the state involved waives its immunity from execution in connection with the enforcement on an award.[48]

45 To date 22 disputes have been submitted to ICSID conciliation (2) or arbitration (20). At the time of writing, ten proceedings are pending. Of the twelve proceedings that have been terminated, seven were discontinued or amicably settled and only five resulted in awards. Only three awards have been published. See *AGIP SpA* v *Government of the People's Republic of the Congo*, 21 *ILM* 726 (1982) (English translation); *Société Ltd Benvenuti & Bonfant*, 21 *ILM* 740 (1982), with a correction at p 1478. *Klockner Industrie-Anlagen GmbH et al* v *United Republic of Cameroon et al*, 111 *Clunet* 409 (1984), and Paulsson, 'The ICSID Klockner v Cameroon Award: The Duties of Partners in North–South Economic Development Agreements', 1 *Journal of International Arbitration* 145 (1984). For a summary of ICSID cases, see doc. ICSID/16.

46 See, eg, *Sapphire International Petroleum Ltd* v *National Iranian Oil Company*, Award of March 15, 1963, 35 *International Law Reports* 136 (1967), at 170; *Texaco Overseas Petroleum Company/California Asiatic Oil Company and the Government of the Libyan Arab Republic*. Award of January 19, 1977, 53 *ILR* 389 (1979), paragraph 10; *BP Exploration Company (Libya Ltd)* v *Government of the Libyan Arab Republic*, Award of October 10, 1973, 53 *ILR* 297 (1979), at 311; *Libyan American Oil Company (LIAMCO)* v *Government of the Libyan Arab Republic* 20 *ILM* 1 (1981), at 78.

47 *Government of Gabon* v *Société Serete SA* Case ARB/76/1.

48 Delaume, *op cit*, Chapter XV, paragraph 15.28.

Sovereign immunity and arbitration 29

Hazel Fox

The plea of sovereign immunity in the sense of a procedural bar to jurisdiction based on the personal capacity of the litigant, has little immediate relevance in arbitration proceedings. Based on the assumption that states are equal, the essence of the plea is to correct the lop-sided situation where one state by reason of its control of the legislation and courts of the legal system operating in its territory has an unfair advantage over a foreign state which appears as litigant in these courts. Arbitration proceedings depend totally on the consent of the parties; without an arbitration agreement or a clause in an agreement agreeing to submit future disputes to arbitration, the arbitrator has no jurisdiction, no powers and the arbitral award has no binding effect. A party can never be brought before an arbitration tribunal without its consent. A plea that the tribunal has no competence is based not on the special status of the party but on a construction of the terms of the arbitration agreement in respect of issues such as the identity of the person signing the agreement, his authority to do so, whether the dispute falls within the matters agreed to be referred to arbitration and the extent of the jurisdiction conferred by the parties on the arbitrator.

An illustration is provided by the *Pyramids Plateau* case, a case concerning a commercial project to develop the plain adjacent to the Pyramids into a tourist complex. In that case the Paris Court of Appeals in 1984 annulled an arbitral award given in favour of the commercial developer, South Pacific Properties (SPP) on the ground that the Arab Republic of Egypt was not a party to the arbitration agreement.[1] SPP and The Egyptian Organisation of Tourism (EGOTH) were described as parties in the agreement containing an arbitration clause which they signed. The Egyptian Minister of Tourism appended his signature to the last page of the agreement. Egypt successfully challenged the arbitration not by pleading its status as a sovereign state but by establishing that it had never consented to be a party to the arbitration agreement.

Nevertheless, if not directly a bar to arbitration, the plea of sovereign immunity and the special position of the state which entitles it to peculiar rights as a litigant are matters which have important consequences for the arbitral process and require consideration at every stage of the arbitration. As Georges Delaume has written:

1 *Arab Republic of Egypt* v *South Pacific Properties Ltd*, 23 *ILM* 1048 (1984).

'The presence of the state as a party to the dispute gives a particular coloration to the arbitration process.'[2]

The plea of state immunity influences the decision to have recourse to arbitration. It is of direct concern whenever a local court's aid is required to back up the arbitration, whether by provisional remedies before or during arbitration, or by review or enforcement of the award after the arbitration is completed. Because of the public character of the state as 'the supreme protector of the general interest',[3] a preliminary question arises of the arbitrability of state contracts and the substantive law, applied by the arbitrator in his award, may have to take account and give some legal effect to the process of change which long-term state contracts undergo. Further, because, except for the truly 'floating' or 'delocalised' award, which is more talked about by learned writers than found in actual practice, the process of arbitration is linked with court adjudication, consent to arbitration may have implications for waiver of sovereign immunity before a local court. Let us examine each of these a little closer.

The risk of the plea of sovereign immunity and the obstacle it presents to bringing claims before local courts may well provide the motivation for recourse to arbitration; the parties' consent to arbitration may represent a compromise when no agreement to settlement by any one local court system can be achieved. The party which is a state is likely to want settlement by its own legal system; it knows the laws and may by retroactive legislation secure its interests. The private litigant, on the other hand, will prefer the laws of his home state with which he is familiar, particularly if they constitute a well-developed, stable and predictable body of commercial law as is the case with English and most United States state law. The choice of forum and applicable law depends largely on the bargaining power of the parties. In loans to foreign state borrowers, the courts and law of the country where the loan is funded or the major banks making the loan are located is likely to be chosen, not least for the reason that if the sovereign borrower defaults, its external assets will be available for attachment and set-off. Since the foreign state in this local forum can directly avail itself of the plea of state immunity, it will be necessary for the lender banks to anticipate this obstacle either by obtaining the states' consent in advance to submit to the local court jurisdiction or by structuring the transaction so that it falls within the commercial exception under the United States Foreign Sovereign Immunities Act 1976 (FSIA) or United Kingdom State Immunity Act 1978. These difficulties with local court jurisdiction and a state's unwillingness publicly to be seen to have its affairs decided by another state's legal system, may lead, particularly for state contracts other than loans, to the parties adopting some form of international arbitration.

Some writers and jurisdictions, particularly of courts in which the jurisdiction is defined by a civil code with no room for the exercise of discretion, treat the plea of state immunity as one of substantive law, going to the subject-matter of the dispute, not the person of the litigant. An example of the situation where it may arise between private litigants is to be found in the

2 75 *Am J Int'l L* 784 (1981), at 785.
3 *Kuwait* v *Aminoil*, 21 *ILM* 976 (1982), at 1001.

English and American litigation known as the *Buttes Gas* case[4]; where two oil companies were parties to private litigation, an essential basis of which turned on the validity of a maritime boundary proclaimed by the Emirate of Sharjah. The Anglo-American approach to these problems is to place them under the general heading of Act of State and to treat them as distinct from the procedural plea of state immunity which prevents a state from being impleaded by a local court. The scope of the substantive plea, Act of State, is still developing and case law is conflicting. The extent to which an arbitration tribunal has to take these matters into account in applying substantive law is uncertain. Whereas ordinary commercial contracts with the state may produce no special law, the recent *Aminoil* award and earlier arbitration awards involving states indicate, that in the absence of express provision, a state contract may be modified by the state without necessarily resulting in a breach of the contract.[5] So this is one aspect of arbitration where the special position of the state may produce a different outcome.

When the arbitration has been agreed to, if it does not itself produce a settlement, the successful party will want to enforce the award. At the present time he can only do this through national legal systems. This unavoidable link with national courts at the enforcement stage whether of provisional remedies or the final award, again makes state immunity directly relevant. There is little sense in engaging in an expensive arbitration if at the end of the day the sovereign status of the defendant will prevent recovery of any part of the sum awarded by the arbitrator. This linking of the arbitral process to adjudication by local courts also raises the possibility that consent of the state whereby it submits to one procedure may be construed as consent to the other procedure. Such a situation, for instance, may arise from the application of Section 9(1) of the United Kingdom State Immunity Act 1978 which provides that where a state has agreed in writing to submit a dispute to arbitration the state is not immune as respects proceedings in the courts of the United Kingdom which relate to the arbitration.

The statutory wording of Section 9(1) is ambiguous. Taken at its narrowest it gives supervisory jurisdiction to the local English court over any English arbitration to which the state has consented to be a party. As in most cases the arbitration will relate to commercial matters where, under the commercial exception to state immunity the local English court will exercise jurisdiction independent of the state's consent,[6] the extent of implied submission to the court is not an alarming one. But if the statutory wording is read at its widest it may mean that consent of a state to an arbitration held anywhere in the world will be deemed consent to enforcement of the arbitral award by the English courts. There has been considerable American case law in respect of a similar provision relating to express and implied waivers of state immunity under the FSIA.[7]

4 *Buttes Gas and Oil Co* v *Hammer* [1982] AC 888; *Occidental of Umm al Qaywayn* v *Buttes Gas & Oil Co*, 31 F Supp 92 (CD Cal 1971), aff'd 461 F 2d 1261 (9th Circ), cert denied 409 US 950 (1972); *Occidental of Umm al Qaywayn Inc* v *A Certain Cargo etc* 396 F Supp 461, 517 F 2d 1196 (5th Circ 1978), 42 US 928 (1979).

5 *Supra* n3.

6 State Immunity Act 1978, s3.

7 Foreign Sovereign Immunities Act 1976, s1605(a)(1). *Ipitrade* v *Nigeria* 465 F Supp 824 (DDC 1978); *LIAMCO* v *Libya* 482 F Supp 1175 (DDC 1980).

One interpretation derived from the wording of the European Convention on State Immunity 1972 would limit implied consent to the supervisory jurisdiction of the court of the country where the arbitration was held to questions relating to the validity or interpretation of the arbitration agreement, the arbitration procedure and the setting aside of the award.

Put simply, the issue is – is consent to arbitration confined to the arbitration proceedings or at most impliedly extended to the supervisory jurisdiction of the *local court*, or, alternatively is consent to arbitration to be construed widely to mean implied consent to the recognition and enforcement of the resulting arbitral award by *any court anywhere*? In favour of the narrow construction may be used my opening analysis that state immunity has no relevance to arbitration. If consent to arbitration is not concerned with the removal of any bar of state immunity before the arbitration tribunal it is difficult to extend it by implication to waiver of that bar before local courts. On the other hand it may be said that consent to arbitration involves commitment to accept the award as binding and that the obligation of good faith not to frustrate the purpose of the arbitration implies that the state consents to enforcement of the award by local courts. Whilst it is probably correct, that an arbitration which produces a legally unenforceable award is probably not an arbitration agreement according to English law it may be going too far to construe consent to arbitration as producing consent to enforcement anywhere. I would advocate a cautious approach. Bearing in mind that choice of arbitration may be a deliberate choice of a process alternative to that of resort to local courts, and that international law requires express waiver of a state's right to immunity, I would recommend the obtaining of express written consent to procedures of local courts whenever possible.

As the matter largely relates to enforcement of awards I need not deal with it further, save to stress that a state when deciding to consent to the arbitration process should not overlook the risk that its act may also be treated as a consent to local court jurisdiction.

The subject of state immunity is immense. I propose to confine myself to the early stages of the arbitration, and to consider the characteristics which distinguish a state party from a private litigant, and the special requirements as to capacity, authority and form of consent which that status imposes.

In the mixed variety of arbitration between private party and a state, a first issue will be the identity of the party to the contract and to the arbitration and whether the person consenting to the arbitration had authority to bind the party. What distinguishes a state from a private party? What difference does it make to the arbitration that a trading concern is owned by a state and not private shareholders? How can the arbitrator know whether the trading concern before it acts on its own behalf or as the agent of the state? How can the arbitrator be sure that it is the proper representative of the state and that it has capacity to bind the state as a party to the arbitration?

In answering these questions, there are a number of elements to be disentangled. The first is to identify the countries, territorial units or groupings of people which qualify as states or other entities for conferment of international legal personality. Second, to distinguish in these countries, political groupings (or, may I dare to use the words so popular with sociologists 'political elites'), the elements which are part of the state and those which enjoy sufficient factual or legal independence to be treated as private litigants. Third, if identified as a part of the state, the nature of the authority which permits the entity to consent on behalf of the state to an arbitration; and fourth and finally the form in which that consent is to be expressed. A general issue which has to be faced with all four elements is the proper law by which they are to be determined. Whilst the local law of the state, particularly its constitutional and administrative sections, is relevant to the structure and allocation of power in the state and the conditions of its exercise – in the words of Lord Denning, 'different countries have different ways of arranging their internal affairs' – it would seem difficult to allow the local law an exclusive say as this would permit a state and its emanations to come and go on the public scene as it pleased – again to quote Lord Denning, 'like The Cheshire Cat in *Alice in Wonderland.*'[8]

An example of such a coming and going is to be found in a case concerning an arbitration between a French company and a trading corporation of Pakistan. By the time it came to resort to arbitration East Pakistan had become the independent state of Bangladesh and had under its local law transferred the assets of the trading corporation to a new legal entity, the Bangladesh Development Corporation but not the obligation to resort to arbitration. The Swiss Court annulling the arbitral award against the Bangladesh Corporation held that the question of succession of the new legal entity to rights and obligations had to be decided by local Bangladeshi law and that consequently there was no obligation to submit to arbitration.[9]

English courts before the 1978 Act had similar problems. Shaw LJ gave this useful guidance in the *Trendtex* case with regard to the Central Bank of Nigeria:

> 'It is true that the constitution and powers of the Nigerian corporation must be viewed in the light of the domestic law of Nigeria. But its status in the international scene falls to be decided by the law of the country in which an issue as to its status is raised. In civilised states that law will derive from those principles of international law which have been generally accepted.'[10]

So far as the first element, statehood and international legal personality, international law provides a definition, independent of local law.[11] In parenthesis, it is as well to remind you that international law recognises legal persons other than states. You will be familiar with legal persons on the international scene such as United Nations, a universal international organisation, or the European Economic Community, a regional organisation. The rules of international law as to how such artificial personality may be created, maintained and dissolved are somewhat rudimentary. An arbitrator faced with a party which claims to be an international organisation may have difficulty in determining whether, like a limited company, it has a separate legal existence and independent obligations from its creator states. This was the problem which confronted the arbitration tribunal in the recent *Westland Helicopter* case,[12] where the company made its contract to sell helicopters with

8 *Trendtex Trading Corporation* v *Bank of Nigeria* [1977] 1 QB 529, at 559.

9 *Societe de Grands Travaux de Marseilles* v *Bangladesh* 1976, V *Yearbook: Commercial Arbitration* 217 (1980).

10 *Supra* n8, at 595.

11 Montevideo Convention 1933, Article 1.

12 Interim Award in the Arbitration between *Westland Helicopters* v *Arab Organisation for Industrialisation*, 23 *ILM* 1071 (1984).

the Arab Organisation for Industrialisation and not the four Arab states who established the organisation.

The more usual investigation, however, will be whether the party is a state. Where the issue comes before a local court, the international law definition is not always strictly observed. A broader view may be taken so as to allow local rulers and political sub-divisions including local government agencies to benefit from a plea of state immunity.[13]

Some conformity of the local court's attitude to the local executive's policy of recognition of foreign states and governments may also be observed. In the United Kingdom this conformity has in the past been achieved by the furnishing of an executive certificate from the Foreign Office to the English court stating whether Her Majesty's Government has recognised the state or government.[14] The State Immunity Act 1978, Section 21(a), expressly provides that a certificate of the Secretary of State shall be conclusive evidence for the purposes of the Act whether a country is a state or as to the person to be regarded as head or government of a state.

What is the position in an arbitration with regard to this issue? Is the law of the forum of the arbitration or the applicable law relevant? For example, in the case of an international arbitration held in London and governed by English law, should the arbitrator when considering the status of the Marshall Islands (a UN Trust Territory),[15] or the Palestine Liberation Organisation, as a party to the proceedings take account of the English court's or English government's attitude to these entities? The short answer is, probably, that, though these questions raise academic issues of great nicety, they will arise in practice rarely. Few are likely to undertake an arbitration against such a political controversial entity as the PLO unless it is backed up by guarantees from private litigants of sound commercial standing or by long established governments.

Yet the *Westland Helicopter* case provides a warning that such situations may arise. It also points to a solution, though one, which in my view, should be used with great circumspection if the certainty of commercial transactions is not to be undermined. That solution (which is also applicable to the second issue I am about to discuss, the distinction between organs of the government and separate agencies operating under private law) is the doctrine of tearing aside the corporate veil when overriding considerations of equity and justice require it. Recently the United States Supreme Court resorted to this doctrine in disregarding the separate legal entity of a bank set up by the State of Cuba and allowed claims against Cuba to be set off by the private litigant who had been sued by the Cuban bank for a commercial debt.[16] In the *Westland Helicopter* case, which is currently subject to proceedings at the suit of Egypt for annulment in the Swiss courts, the arbitration tribunal used this as an additional reason for its finding that the four Arab states were liable for the failure of their creature, the Arab Organisation for Industrialisation, to fulfil

13 Eg, *Duff Development Co Ltd* v *Kelantan* [1924] AC 797.

14 Eg, *Luther* v *Sagor* [1921] 1 KB 456. But see Lord Carrington's statement announcing that in future the British government would no longer expressly recognise governments. 1980, Hansard, House of Lords, Vol 408, cols 1121–1122. *Cf R* v *Sec of State for Foreign and Commonwealth Affairs, ex parte Trawnik, The Times*, April 18, 1985.

15 *Cf Marine Steel Ltd* v *Govt of the Marshall Islands* [1981] 2 NZLR 1 where the New Zealand High Court held the Marshall Islands not to be a state.

16 *First National City Bank* v *BANCEC 22 ILM* 840 (1983).

its contract. 'Equity, in common with the principle of international law, allows the corporate veil to be lifted, in order to protect third parties against an abuse which would be to their detriment.'[17]

The second element in the identity of the party to the arbitration, much more likely in practice to exercise the arbitrator, is the distinction between a department or organ of the state as the means by which a state acts, and the state trading agency fully subject to private law. An apparently private enterprise may on closer inspection reveal close links with a sovereign state. This is particularly true where the arbitration relates to a developing state. Owing to the socialist organisation of the economy in many developing states and to the absence of a developed private sector even in countries operating a mixed economy, it is likely that the state, as compared to the older industrialised states, will be more directly involved in large commercial transactions particularly those involving foreign funds and the participation of multinational corporations. The involvement of the state may take many forms, from direct participation as a party to the contract, as an institution enjoying factual independence from the state or separate legal powers, to legal entities incorporated under private law systems where the state has at most an interest as a shareholder or owner.

This type of issue arose in English courts in considering whether the incorporation as a separate legal entity of the Servicio Nacional del Trigo prevented it from forming part of the Spanish Department of Agriculture,[18] and whether the state trading organisation, Rolimpex was part of the Polish government and therefore responsible for the ban on exports which prevented it from fulfilling its sugar contract with Czarnikov.[19] Recent American cases decided under the FSIA illustrate the diversity of state involvement and the complex task of deciding which side of the line, public or private, the particular litigant falls. The German Information Centre (a section of the Consulate General of the German Federal Republic)[20] and the Novosti Press Agency 'owned' by the USSR,[21] were held to fall within the statutory definition of a state, but not a Yugoslav Workers' Organisation, incorporated for the purpose of operating a nuclear power station.[22]

Local jurisdictions have solved this difficult issue not by exclusive application of the law of the foreign state which creates or empowers these entities but by enacting objective criteria in local legislation which give advance notice to the foreign state of the likely treatment to be expected for its agents. So the FSIA employs an inclusive definition covering political sub-divisions, organs of the foreign state and entities in which the foreign state is the majority owner, whether separately incorporated or not, and a two-tier system of immunity which accords narrower immunities to state agencies or instrumentalities engaged in commercial activity in the United States.[23] The United Kingdom State Immunity Act 1978 operates a twofold definition; the head of state in his public capacity, the government and any department or

17 *Supra* n12.
18 *Baccus SRL* v *Servicio Nacional Del Trigo* [1957] 1 QB 438.
19 *C Czarnikov* v *Rolimpex* [1979] AC 359.
20 *Gittler* v *German Information Centre* 408 NY S 2d 600 (Sup Ct 1978).
21 *Yessenin Volpin* v *Novosti Press Agency* 443 F Supp 849. (SDNY 1978).
22 *Edlow International Co* v *Nuklearna Elektrarna Krsko* 441 F Supp 827 (SDNY 1977).
23 FSIA 1976, ss1063(a)(b); 1605(a)(3); 1610(b).

executive organ are included in the term, 'state' and enjoy equal immunity to the state. Separate entities capable of suing or being sued are made subject to private law except where they act for exclusively governmental purposes in circumstances where the state itself would be entitled to immunity.[24] Central banks of foreign states enjoy under both pieces of legislation special immunities from execution.[25]

Neither of these legislative schemes are simple as the cases already cited illustrate. With no accepted rule of international law to elucidate the problem – the International Law Commission in its draft articles on state immunity has not yet adopted any definition in this area – the arbitrator will have little to guide him but the intention and practice of the parties and accepted commercial practices. If the matter has not been dealt with by prior treaty arrangement, the private litigant is well advised to cover this point in advance by including in the agreement to arbitrate an express undertaking by the other party that the state entity, party to the transaction, is subject to private law and that it and the state which established it acknowledge its separate legal personality and that the matters in the contract concern a commercial transaction.

This brings me to the equally difficult question of authority to consent to the arbitration and the proper form of that consent. Consent to arbitration may take different forms, the actual acceptance of the tribunal's jurisdiction by appearance and taking a step in the proceedings relating to the merits, an agreement or *compromis* to submit an existing dispute to arbitration, or an agreement or *clause compromissoire* to submit future disputes when they arise to arbitration. Many states have administrative rules requiring a certain procedure and form to be observed when an agent commits a state to participation in an arbitration. Some ratification or counter-signature may be required. Must the arbitrator before exercising jurisdiction over a party be satisfied that actual consent in full compliance with the state's own laws be given, or is ostensible authority as judged by usual commercial practices, the law of the forum, or applicable law sufficient? The *Pyramids* project case already referred to, illustrates the problem. The Egyptian Minister of Tourism placed his signature with the date on the final page of the agreement containing an arbitration clause and the words 'approved, agreed and ratified'.[26] Was the act within the authority of the persons purporting to act on Egypt's behalf and sufficient to bind that state?

The American and United Kingdom legislation on state immunity does not provide much guidance here though the United Kingdom Act introduces an evidentiary rule that the head of the state's diplomatic mission in the United Kingdom shall be deemed to have authority to submit on behalf of the state to proceedings in the United Kingdom courts and that any person who has entered into a contract on behalf of and with the authority of the state shall be deemed to have authority to submit to local proceedings arising out of the contract.[27] It is still necessary, however, to satisfy the local court that the person making the original contract had authority to do so.

24 State Immunity Act 1978, s14.
25 FSIA 1976, s1611(b)(1); State Immunity Act 1978, s14(3)(4).
26 *Supra*, n1.
27 State Immunity Act 1978, s2(7).

Although no specific rule dealing with the problem appears to exist in international law, a similar problem of capacity arises in the signature and expression of consent by states to treaties. The solution to this problem has been codified and is to be found in Articles 7 and 46 of the Vienna Convention on the Law of Treaties 1969. Article 7(2) introduces presumptions as to certain agents of the state: Head of State, Heads of Governments and Ministers for Foreign Affairs are considered as representing their state for the purposes of all acts relating to the conclusion of a treaty. Heads of diplomatic missions are presumed to have more limited powers in respect of the adoption of the text of treaties made with the state to whom they are accredited. Article 46 provides that a state may not invoke the fact that its consent to be bound by a treaty has been expressed in violation of a provision of its internal law regarding competence to conclude treaties unless that violation was manifest and concerned a rule of its internal law of fundamental importance. The relationship of the two articles would appear to produce a rule that the designated office holders are *ex officio* entitled to perform the specified acts in relation to treaties, notwithstanding that, as a matter of internal law, they are not so empowered. In other words the Vienna Convention recognises in relation to the conclusion of treaties, a limited rule of ostensible authority of agents by which states may be deemed to give their consent to the conclusion of treaties. This approach would seem to offer some help in determining whether or not an agent of a state had authority to bind the state to an arbitration agreement. One way to safeguard the private party is to require any authority or special form of consent to be stated in the agreement, all other requirements or conditions of the law of the state not so stated to be deemed as waived irrevocably for the purposes of the arbitration.

30 Enforcement of arbitral awards in Eastern Europe

Werner Melis

This paper deals with enforcement of arbitral awards in Eastern Europe, geographically this refers to the member countries of the Council for Mutual Economic Assistance (CMEA), ie, Bulgaria, Czechoslovakia, the German Democratic Republic (GDR), Hungary, Poland, Romania and the Soviet Union. The limited space available does not allow a detailed systematic country by country analysis but only to develop the main aspects which are of special interest for East/West economic relations.

Enforcement of inter-CMEA arbitration awards

International commercial arbitration plays a more important role between socialist countries than between market economy countries: the arbitration courts at the Chambers of Commerce of CMEA-countries enjoy exclusive jurisdiction over disputes arising from commercial dealings between economic organisations in member countries of the CMEA on the basis of several multilateral agreements between member states.

CMEA general conditions of delivery

The first set of rules which concern the international sale of goods only were the General Conditions of Delivery of Goods between Organisations of the CMEA-countries in force as of January 1, 1958 (GCD CMEA 1958). They were followed by the General Conditions of Assembly (GCA CMEA 1962) and the General Conditions of Technical Servicing of 1962 (GCTS CMEA 1962) which are now valid in the versions 1979 and 1982 respectively. Paragraph 90 GCD CMEA provides the following:

> 'All disputes which may arise from or in connection with the contract shall be subject, without recourse to courts of law to consideration by arbitration in an arbitration tribunal established for such disputes in the country of the defendant or, by agreement of the parties, in a third member-country of the Council for Mutual Economic Assistance'.

These provisions are, as far as arbitration is concerned, mandatory as well for the economic organisations concluding foreign trade contracts as for the said arbitration courts.

The Moscow Convention

This competence has considerably been expanded by the provisions of the Convention on the Settlement by Arbitration of Civil Law Disputes out of Relations of Economic, Scientific and Technological Cooperation of May 26, 1972 (Moscow Convention) to all types of economic and technological cooperation Article I of the Moscow Convention provides:

> '1 All disputes between economic organisations resulting from contractual or other civil law cases arising between them in the course of economic, scientific and technical cooperation of the countries-parties to the present Convention shall be subject to arbitration proceedings with the exclusion of the above disputes from jurisdiction of the courts of law.
>
> 2 The term "cases" referred to in Paragraph 1 shall mean those arising from contracts of purchase, contracts on specialisation and cooperation of production, carrying out of building, industrial and construction works, on assembling projecting, prospecting, scientific-research, designing and exploratory development, transport-dispatching and other services, as well as other civil law cases arising in the course of economic, scientific and technical cooperation of the country-parties to the Convention.'

Article II, paragraph 1 of the Moscow Convention establishes the jurisdiction of the arbitration courts at the Chambers of Commerce in the country of the defendant as in paragraph 90 GCD CMEA. Article II para 2 provides in addition that where specialised arbitrations for the settlement of defined categories exist in the countries-parties such disputes can be submitted to such arbitrations with the consent of the parties. Such specialised arbitrations are the Maritime Arbitration Commission at the USSR Chamber of Commerce and Industry, the International Court of Arbitration for Marine and Inland Navigation in Gdynia, Poland, and two commodity arbitration courts for cotton and wool, also in Gdynia.

It follows from these provisions that arbitrations which fall under the Moscow Convention need not to be based upon a valid arbitration agreement unless the parties make use of the only possible choice, namely to have arbitration before the arbitration court of a Chamber of Commerce in a third member-country or one of the above-mentioned special arbitrations. Consequently the existence of an arbitration agreement is not a requirement for recognition and enforcement of an award. This does not, however, apply to foreign awards which shall be enforced under a multilateral convention, such as the New York Convention, or a bilateral agreement, or for domestic awards which do not fall under the provisions of the Moscow Convention, (for example, awards rendered in the territory of a CMEA-country in a litigation between an economic organisation and a western enterprise). In all these cases only awards which are based on a valid arbitration agreement will be recognised and, if necessary, enforced.

Recognition and enforcement of awards are dealt with in Articles IV and V of the Moscow Convention. Paragraph 1 of Article IV states that arbitration awards shall be final and binding and that: 'The parties shall enforce them voluntarily'.

Similar provisions can be found in paragraph 35 of the Uniform Rules of Procedure in the Arbitration Courts at the Chambers of Commerce of the

Council of Mutual Economic Assistance Countries, Moscow February 1974, and in the Rules of the Arbitration Courts in those countries which have all been amended during 1975 for the purpose of bringing them into line with these Model Rules. As all sources from socialist countries confirm, this principle of voluntary fulfilment of awards conforms with established practice of economic organisations. The provisions on enforcement have, therefore, not been used in practice. Similar observations can also be made for awards rendered in favour of parties from outside the CMEA-area.

According to Article IV, paragraph 2 of the Moscow Convention awards shall be recognised

> '... without further proceedings and shall be subject to enforcement in any country party to the Convention in the same order as entering into force judgments of the courts of law of the country concerned'.

An example of transformation of this provision into domestic law are the provisions of Section 27 of the Decree of the Council of Ministers of the GDR on Arbitral Jurisdiction of December 18, 1975: according to Section 27(1) final awards and settlements before a court of arbitration in the GDR having jurisdiction on the basis of special legal provisions (eg, the Moscow Convention), can be enforced in the same way as decisions of courts; awards and settlements which do not comply with Section 27(1) can be declared enforceable upon application of the creditor by decision of the Stadtbezirksgericht Berlin–Mitte (Section 27(2)). However, in countries where arbitral awards as such are not recognised as enforceable titles it is still necessary to obtain the necessary document, for example according to Article 339 of the Code of Civil Procedure (CCP) of the Russian Soviet Federative Socialist Republic (RSFSR).

Article IV, paragraph 3 of the Moscow Convention gives 'peaceful settlements confirmed by arbitration' the same status as for arbitral awards. This applies exclusively for settlements between economic organisations of member-countries before an arbitration court at a Chamber of Commerce in a member-country or before one of the specialised arbitration courts. Within its field of application this provision is wider than the provisions of any other multilateral instrument including the New York Convention which provides only for enforcement of 'arbitral awards' but not of settlements.

According to Article IV, paragraph 4, the provisions of paragraphs 1 and 2 apply also for the above-mentioned specialised arbitrations

> '... unless otherwise provided for by the national legislation of the country where the arbitration has its seat'.

Article IV, paragraph 5 of the Moscow Convention states that awards or settlements which have not been voluntarily enforced

> '... may be brought to execution by enforcement within two years. This statutory limitation shall be reckoned from the date of serving an award to the claiming party ... in relation to peaceful settlement ... from the date of agreement on such settlement'.

No such provision is contained in the New York Convention or in other multilateral conventions on arbitration. For the purposes of CMEA-countries, however, this provision is a step towards unification, as national provisions on the time-limits for application for enforcement differ largely from country to country: Czechoslovakia, GDR and Poland 10 years; Bulgaria and Hungary five years; USSR three months if all parties to the dispute are Soviet organisations, and one year, if at least one party is a foreign organisation or agency. This is also true for the calculation of the time-limits for limitation, which start, eg, in the GDR from the date of entry into force of the award and in Czechoslovakia from the date of maturity of the obligation expressed in the award.

Article V of the Moscow Convention limits the grounds for refusal of enforcement by the arbitral executive body in the country of the respondent to three, namely if

'(a) the award has been made with violation of the rules of competence, stipulated by the present Convention, or

(b) the party against which the award has been made proves that it was deprived of possibility to defend its rights owing to violation of arbitral rules of procedure or other circumstances, which it could not prevent and inform the arbitration about these circumstances, or

(c) the party against which the award has been made proves that this award has been annulled or suspended on the base of national legislation of the country in which it was made'.

Similar to Article V of the New York Convention these grounds are exhaustive. The grounds for refusal of recognition and enforcement of arbitral awards under the Moscow Convention are more restrictive than those under the national provisions of member countries and also *mutatis mutandis* as the pertinent provisions of Article V of the New York Convention.

In Article V, paragraph 2, it is expressly set out that in case of refusal of enforcement on the grounds (a) and (b), the party requesting enforcement is entitled '... to lay a new claim on the same grounds at the competent authority within the period of three months from the date of coming into force of this refusal.' No provision of this nature is incorporated in any other pertinent international convention. As regards the refusal of enforcement on the grounds of Article V, paragraph 2(c), the consequences will be determined on the basis of the laws of the country where the award has been made.

It must be stressed that the procedure for enforcement of awards which fall under the provisions of the Moscow Convention according to Article I, is the same for 'foreign' awards made in a member-country which shall be enforced in another member-country and 'domestic' awards made in the country where they shall be enforced. Due to the exhaustive enumeration in Article I, paragraph 2, nearly the totality of litigations arising out of commercial relations between economic organisation of CMEA-member-countries will be decided by arbitration under the rules of this convention.

Enforcement of awards from non-CMEA-countries

For commercial disputes between CMEA-countries and other countries the rules governing recognition and enforcement of foreign arbitral awards which shall be enforced in the territory of CMEA-countries are of interest.

As regards the distinction between 'foreign' and 'domestic' awards, the laws of all CMEA-countries consider awards which have been made outside their respective territory as 'foreign'. (The special situation for awards made in one CMEA-country and to be enforced in another, has already been pointed out.) Consequently awards made within their territory will be considered as 'domestic'. There is, however, one exception: in Hungary awards which have been rendered in Hungary are also considered as 'foreign' when the proceedings have taken place outside Hungary and the majority of arbitrators or the presiding arbitrator have not been Hungarian nationals.

For foreign awards two situations can be determined:

1 recognition or enforcement on the basis of multilateral or bilateral agreements;
2 recognition and enforcement in the absence of such agreements.

The New York Convention

All CMEA-countries have ratified the New York Convention. They have all made the so-called reciprocity-reservation (1st reservation); Hungary, Poland and Romania have also made the so-called commercial reservation (2nd reservation), both mentioned in Article I of the New York Convention. It follows that they will apply the New York Convention only to awards made in the territory of another contracting state. Those countries which have also made the 2nd reservation will apply the New York Convention only to disputes which are considered as 'commercial' under their national laws.

Recognition and enforcement of foreign arbitral awards made in another contracting state can, therefore, only be refused on the grounds of Article V of the New York Convention. As already mentioned in relation to awards which fall under the Moscow Convention, it is always stressed by authors from all CMEA-countries that the principle of voluntary execution of awards is respected by socialist economic organisations regarding any kind of arbitral awards which have been rendered against them. It is also true, that so far no decision of a court in a CMEA-country has been reported on Article V of the New York Convention. The fact that there has been, so far, no necessity to make use of the services of a court to get an award paid shall, however, not be misinterpreted in a way that it has in practice always been easy in the past for a successful party to have an award paid.

As a result of the quasi-universal application of the New York Convention other multilateral agreements which contain provisions on the recognition and enforcement of awards have become of less importance in this respect. The European Convention, to which all the CMEA-countries are party, refers in Article IX, paragraph 2, to the New York Convention and limits the application of Article V(1)(e) solely to cases of setting aside mentioned under Article IX, paragraph 1, in relations between contracting states that are also party to the New York Convention.

Other Conventions

There exists a variety of bilateral agreements between CMEA-countries and third countries (such as agreements on recognition and enforcement of court judgments or judicial assistance, trade and economic cooperation agreements) which contain also provisions concerning recognition and enforcement of arbitral awards rendered in the territory of the other contracting state. In particular, the Soviet Union has concluded more than 40 of such bilateral agreements. It would go too far for the purpose of this paper to go into details. It is noteworthy, however, to draw attention to the different approach taken by the Moscow Convention and the New York Convention for cases where a country in which an award is to be enforced is also a party to either of the above conventions (or both) and has also concluded a bilateral agreement with the country where the award has been made. According to Article VI, paragraph 1, of the Moscow Convention

> 'the provisions of previously concluded bilateral and multilateral agreements of the countries-parties to the Convention shall not be applied to the cases treated by this Convention with the exclusion of understandings in accordance with which certain categories of civil law disputes are subject to exclusive jurisdiction of competent authorities.'

On the other hand, Article VII, paragraph 1 of the New York Convention provides:

> 'The provision of the present Convention shall not affect the validity of multilateral or bilateral agreements concerning the recognition and enforcement of arbitral awards entered into with by the Contracting States nor deprive any interested party of any right he may have to avail himself of an arbitral award in the manner and to the extent allowed by the law or the treaties of the country where such award is sought to be relied upon'.

A similar provision is contained in Article X, paragraph 7 of the European Convention. Parties can, therefore, base their request on the provision of a bilateral agreement if this offers more favourable conditions than the New York Convention, such as more restrictive grounds for refusal of enforcement.

National laws

In the absence of bilateral or multilateral agreements, foreign arbitral awards will not be enforced in Bulgaria and in Poland.

A similar situation exists in Romania, where Article 375 of the Code of Civil Procedure prescribes reciprocity for enforcement of court judgments which, according to legal doctrine, applies also for arbitral awards, by agreement or by law. In the declaration made when Romania acceded to the New York Convention it is stated that the New York Convention is applicable to awards made in the territory of a state not participating in the Convention 'only on the basis of reciprocity established by joint agreement between the parties'.

In the other CMEA-countries enforcement of foreign arbitral awards is, according to the pertinent national legal provisions, possible even in the absence of any agreement with the country where the award has been made, if reciprocity can be ascertained.

The Presidium of the Supreme Soviet declared, on the occasion of ratification of the New York Convention, that:

> 'The Union of the Soviet Socialist Republics will apply the provision of this Convention with regard to awards made in the territory of the state not participating in the Convention, on the basis of reciprocity only'.

In Czechoslovakia, Section 30 of Article No 98/1963, 'On Arbitration in International Trade Relations and on Enforcement of Arbitral Awards', provides that awards rendered in a foreign country shall be recognised

> '... and enforced as Czechoslovac awards, if a reciprocity of treatment is secured. A reciprocity of treatment shall be deemed as secured also in the event when the respective foreign country declares foreign awards enforceable, subject to reciprocity of treatment'.

In the absence of an express declaration of the pertinent foreign country, Section 54 of the Act on Private International Law and Procedure of 1963 requires a Statement of the Ministry of Justice, issued with approval of the Ministry of Foreign Affairs and other appropriate Ministries, as a mandatory requirement for the event to assure reciprocity.

Also in Hungary reciprocity is required. Pertinent provisions are contained in Decree No 13, 1979 on Private International Law, Section 74, paragraph 2. Similar to the situation in Czechoslovakia the Hungarian Minister of Justice has to confirm to the court the existence of reciprocity.

No reciprocity is expressly required in the GDR. According to Section 27(2) of the Decree of the Council of Ministers of the GDR on Arbitral Jurisdiction of December 18, 1975 awards and settlements before an arbitration court can be enforced when they have been declared enforceable (exequator) by the Stadtgericht Berlin-Mitte.

It can be seen from this short review of the relevant rules in the CMEA-countries that it will, in practice, not be easy to obtain recognition and enforcement of an arbitral award in the absence of any agreement. It must be added, that in all countries concerned there are also other common requirements which will have to be satisfied, eg, that the award is final, or that it is not contrary to public policy.

Finally, the case has to be taken into account where an award has been rendered in the territory of a CMEA-country in favour of a foreign party having its place of business in a country which is not a member to the Moscow Convention, against an economic organisation in the country where the award has been made. With the exception concerning Hungary which has been mentioned above, such awards will be considered domestic awards and the relevant legal provisions in every country will apply in case of refusal of the loosing party to comply with the award voluntarily.

As in western countries there exist also in all CMEA-countries detailed provisions dealing with recognition and enforcement of domestic awards. There are, however, considerable differences regarding the procedure to be followed and the competent authorities, ie, courts or other state organs. Under specific conditions also settlements before arbitration courts are enforceable. It is beyond the scope of this paper to go into details here. In practice also here there has been a clear tendency in the past to avoid recourse to the available legal remedies.

To sum up: in all CMEA-countries there exists an effective legal framework based on national laws and on international bilateral and multilateral agreements to assure legal enforcement of arbitral awards in their territory. Although it has not in all cases been easy in the past to get awards honoured, it has not, as a general rule, been necessary to initiate enforcement proceedings.

Arbitration law in Eastern Europe concise selective bibliography in English

Organisation of Foreign Trade Arbitration in the CMEA-countries

Handbook on Foreign Trade – Arbitration in the CMEA-countries, general editor, S N Lebedev, Moscow 1983.

Main National Legal Provisions on Foreign Trade Arbitration

Bulgaria: Articles 9 and 237 CCP (1952); Article 25 Code of Merchant Shipping (1979);

Czechoslovakia: Act No 98/1963 Relating to Arbitration in International Trade and to Enforcement of Awards; Sections 47 and 48 of Act No 42/1980 on Economic Relations with Foreign Countries; Sections 251 – 354 of Act No 99/1963 (CCP);

German Democratic Republic: Decree of the Council of Ministers of the GDR on Arbitral Jurisdiction of December 18, 1975; Sections 185 and 198 CCP (1975);

Hungary: Act No III on Civil Procedure as amended by Decree No 26, 1972 Articles 360–364; Decree No 21, 1955, Articles 209–211; Decree No 13, 1979, Section 62, Chapter X;

Poland: Articles 695–715 CCP (1969);

Romania: Decree No 18 adopted by the State Council on February 5, 1976, Articles 341–370 CCP (1865) as amended 1948;

Soviet Union: Fundamentals of Civil Legislation of the USSR and the Union Republics (1961) Article 6; Fundamentals of Civil Procedure of the USSR and the Union Republics (1961) Articles 31, 41, 58 and 63; CCP of the Russian Soviet Federative Socialist Republic (1964) esp Articles 23, 27, 46, 129, 155, 219, 338, 339, 437.

31 The recognition and enforcement of foreign arbitral awards in the states of the Arab Middle East

Samir Saleh

An eminent author on international arbitration law has described the rules on the enforcement of foreign arbitral awards as being beset by uncertainty. According to that author, this uncertainty is fostered by the conflicting views of scholars and practitioners in each state. Faced with the need to formulate some general proposition about the situation in the Arab Middle East there are only two indisputable things one can mention. First, there are in certain states, in addition to where the New York Convention applies, domestic laws and a regional convention adopting, in the majority of cases, outdated concepts. Secondly, apart from the foregoing there is generally a lack of legislation. The statutory vacuum is potentially filled by Islamic law.

The conflicting views of lawyers in any particular state need not trouble us since little has been written on the subject.

To analyse the laws of each state in turn is beyond the scope of this paper. I therefore propose to give you a survey of the problems peculiar to the states of the Arab Middle East. Specifically we will consider the following questions:

1 Which Arab states have modern legislation on the recognition and enforcement of foreign arbitral awards?
2 Which Arab states do not have modern legislation and are still subject to Islamic law?
3 Which Arab states have adhered to the New York Convention or other international conventions relating to the recognition and enforcement of foreign awards?
4 Which states have adhered to the Arab League Convention of September 14, 1952 relating to the enforcement of judgments and awards?
5 What is the status of bilateral treaties in the regional context of the Arab states?
6 What are the peculiar obstacles to effect the enforcement of foreign awards?

Arab states with modern arbitration enforcement legislation

States with modern legislation dealing specifically with recognition and enforcement of arbitral awards are very few in number. Lebanese and Libyan laws have autonomous provisions applicable to foreign awards without any reference to their respective domestic laws on the enforcement of foreign judgments. Although Lebanon does not make reciprocity a condition of enforcement, Libya like Egypt, regards it as a fundamental prerequisite.

Syria, Egypt, Kuwait and Bahrain recognise the principle of enforcement of foreign awards and generally apply, in a somewhat literal manner, the same provisions relating to the enforcement of foreign judgments. As a result, the principle of reciprocity of treatment is required. For example, the laws of Syria, Kuwait and Bahrain require a foreign arbitral award to bear an enforcement order from the state where it was made. Doctrinal trends in certain states such as Egypt also impose this condition. The majority of legislative systems require an award to be final, *res judicata* and capable of being enforced. However, these are generally interpreted purely and simply as a requirement for enforcement in the state where the award was made.

While other states, such as Iraq, Jordan, The United Arab Emirates and North Yemen, are well furnished with modern laws dealing with the enforcement of foreign judgments, those laws contain no express reference to their application to foreign arbitral awards. In practice, the result is that an award which is not embodied in the judgment of a national court will not be enforceable in these states.

Except in the case of Lebanon, the essential characteristic of Arab national laws – and in this respect they differ from the New York Convention, and bilateral regional treaties – is that generally, they are concerned only with the *enforcement* of arbitral awards. The idea of *recognition* of arbitral awards is rarely mentioned in national laws owing to the fact that the Arab League Convention, which we shall analyse shortly, is solely concerned with the enforcement of judgments and awards, and that the Arab League Convention has served as a model, however outdated, for the draftsmen of domestic laws.

Another characteristic of those legal systems which have their own national laws is that the criterion of extraneity of the arbitral award is determined by the place where the award is made. The Explanatory Memorandum of Kuwaiti Civil and Commercial Procedure makes an illustrative case for the use of this criterion. Lebanon, however, while adopting the same principle allows an exception to the rule by deeming an award to be foreign if it was made in Lebanon but under a foreign law of procedure.

Most of the states with modern statutes have a common denominator. There is a distinction in the field of procedure between the enforcement of a domestic award and that of a foreign award: while domestic awards are generally enforced, *in camera*, without summoning the party to a hearing, the procedure of enforcement of a foreign award is subject to the rules of an ordinary case, ie, a public hearing and summoning the party against whom the enforcement is sought (eg, Syria, Jordan, Egypt, Kuwait, Bahrain).

It is evident that in those states with modern national laws the foreign award will not be subjected to any deep scrutiny. Accordingly the merits of the case will not be examined. However, exceptions are available when the concept of public policy is brought into play (for example, in Syria, Lebanon, Libya, Kuwait, Bahrain). The exceptions peculiar to arbitration, such as the question of the arbitrability of the case, are sometimes additional to the public policy requirements.

We shall see later how the public policy requirement demanded by the Syrian, Egyptian, Lebanese and Kuwaiti systems and modelled on those of the West, becomes intermingled in Saudi Arabia and some of the Gulf States (more strongly influenced by Islamic law) with an additional requirement that the award should not contravene the mandatory prescriptions of Islamic law.

Other matters which should be mentioned here are those relating to the validity of the arbitration clause and arbitration agreement, to the notification and hearing of the parties before an award is made and to the proper representation of the parties, and to the requirement that the judgment or award must not conflict with a judgment or award made in the state where enforcement is sought. These conditions are almost commonplace, and close to those of western systems.

Arab states still governed essentially by Islamic law

Saudi Arabia, Qatar and Oman do not have modern domestic legislation on the recognition and enforcement of foreign judgments and are therefore compelled to rely on principles of Islamic law in such cases. These principles, so far as Saudi Arabia is concerned, have already been breached insofar as Saudi Arabia has adhered to international conventions which adopt the principle of enforcement of arbitral awards in spite of the obstacle, created by Islamic law, of the territorial division of the world. This is an aspect to which we shall return below. The adherence of Saudi Arabia in 1980 to the Washington Convention which provides an arbitral procedure under the auspices of ICSID and which governs disputes between the foreign investor and the government or governmental agencies of the host State, has been in due course favourably received in certain circles in the United States. Although it includes a section on the enforcement of arbitral awards its scope is somewhat limited, as we shall see later.

The two other countries governed by Islamic law, Qatar and Oman, do not have their own national laws and have not adhered to a single international convention touching in any way upon the recognition and enforcement of foreign arbitral awards. But before proceeding any further with our analysis we must first decide which principle of Islamic law would apply to the problems of recognition and enforcement of foreign awards in the states under discussion.

Although Saudi Arabia's constitution does not make Islamic law a formal source of law, as is the case in many constitutions in the Gulf States (eg, Kuwait, the United Arab Emirates, Bahrain), Saudi Arabia is nevertheless influenced by Islamic law. The *two* sources of Islamic law which are mandatory are the Qur'ān and the Sunna, which is embodied in the *Hadīth*, the deeds and sayings of the Prophet. Other sources which are in fact a method of reasoning, such as the *qiyās* (reasoning by analogy) and the *ijmā'* (doctrinal propositions based on an unanimity of scholarly opinion) are more easily displaced by modern legislative provisions modestly termed 'Regulations' in deference to the sacred law of Islam. They are also frequently circumvented by contractual provisions which do not conflict with the two mandatory sources, the Qur'ān and the Sunna.

Oman is also strongly influenced by Islamic law and, more specifically, by the teachings of the Ibadi school, a school considered schismatic by the other so-called orthodox schools. With the exception of some laws promulgated on the authority of the Sultan and forming legislative islands for the use of foreigners, the Omani system is still dominated by Islamic law. Without entering into the details of the disputes between the various schools of Islamic law we can generalise by saying that in the absence of any texts the Ibadi school dominates in Oman, at least in so far as contractual matters are concerned, provided that their provisions do not contravene the Qur'ān and the Sunna.

Qatar, which is kept in a state of legislative lethargy, has constitutional provisions which stipulate that Islamic law is a fundamental source of law in this Emirate.

In view of this, what becomes of a foreign award, whether or not embodied in a judgment, when it is submitted for recognition and enforcement to a court in the three states governed by Islamic law? In order to answer this question properly (and to explain the negative aspects) it is necessary to be aware of the distinctive features of Islamic law in the realm of international relations. Islamic law basically divides the world into two parts: the *dār-al-ḥarb* or war territory, and the *dār-al-Islām* or Islamic territory. The states in which Islamic law is in force and which are ruled by Muslim leaders constitute the *dār-al-Islām*. The rest of the world is the *dār-al-ḥarb* the land of the infidels against whom, in theory at least, Muslims are in a perpetual state of war until the whole world is governed by Islam in the form of a *Pax Islamica*. This division of the world derives from the notion of the Holy War (*al-Jihād*). The precept of the *Jihād* is of paramount importance and constitutes a fundamental tenet of Islam.

This brief picture exempts us from answering the question since it clearly explains the major obstacle with which an arbitral award made in enemy territory will be confronted when enforcement is sought in Islamic territory, the *dār-al-Islām*. There will be no possibility of its recognition or its enforcement. It will not even have the value of written evidence. The whole case will have to be reheard and judged anew.

This wholesale rejection of the foreign arbitral award, this apparently insurmountable obstacle, has fortunately been ignored in at least one instance by Saudi Arabia, namely in its accession in 1980 to the Washington Convention: arbitral awards arising from disputes falling within the definition of investments under the Washington Convention are made under the auspices of ICSID. These awards are automatically enforceable in those states which have adhered to the Washington Convention without there being any further enforcement procedure.

Of course Saudi Arabia has also adhered to the Arab League Convention, which will be examined later, but its action in so doing was less significant on the international level since naturally all the signatories were states belonging to the *dār-al-Islām*.

Arab states party to the New York Convention

At the present time, only Syria, Egypt, Jordan and Kuwait have acceded to the New York Convention. Saudi Arabia may sign, if recent reports on the state of Saudi arbitration law are to be believed. We are not going to here enter into a close examination of the New York Convention as the subject has been well covered elsewhere and the literature on it is easily accessible. Instead we will deal with the traditional practice of the Arab states. What is important to bear in mind about the New York Convention is that it is a great step forward by comparison with the majority of the domestic legal systems of the Arab Middle East and the Arab League Convention.

1 The New York Convention sanctions the principle of recognition and enforcement of foreign arbitral awards and bestows on foreign awards the same status as domestic awards, while the domestic legal systems of the Arab Middle East draw a clear distinction between the treatment of national awards and the treatment of foreign awards.
2 The New York Convention recognises the principle of the binding arbitral award without the need for it to be embodied in a judgment, in contrast to the majority of Arab systems which, as we have noted in our description of the domestic laws, place the arbitral award on the same footing as a judgment either by making direct reference to laws relating to the enforcement of foreign judgments or implicitly through an absence of legislation. This has the consequence that an award must be embodied in a foreign judgment before it can be recognised.
3 The New York Convention avoids the double enforcement process (double exequatur) required in practice by the Arab League Convention and by most of the national laws.
4 The general thrust of the New York Convention centres around an extreme simplification of the documentation presented by the party seeking recognition and enforcement of an arbitral award: the two documents required are the original of the award or a certified copy, and the original of the arbitration agreement or a certified copy. The national laws of most of the states we are dealing with, as is the case with the Arab League Convention, work in the opposite way: the petitioner must first prove that the award is final and, in the majority of cases, that it is sanctioned by an enforcement order, that the award has been properly notified and the two parties have been properly summoned to the judicial proceedings.

Finally, the New York Convention is more comprehensive than the domestic laws of the states under study in that it includes both the recognition and the enforcement of arbitral awards whereas, in all but a few states, the domestic laws deal only with enforcement.

Arab states' adherence to Arab League Convention

Following our somewhat cursory treatment of the New York Convention and the analysis of it from the comparative view of the national systems of the Arab Middle East, we should like to pause a little in order to examine the Arab League Convention Relating to the Enforcement of Judgments and Arbitral Awards, of September 14, 1952, and proper to the Middle East.

The interesting thing about the Arab League Convention is not its provisions: they are not only commonplace, they are also outdated. They derive from the archaic regime laid down by the Geneva Convention on the Execution of Foreign Arbitral Awards of 1927. The Arab League Convention is of interest because of the number of relatively important states of the Arab Middle East which have ratified it: Syria, Jordan, Iraq, Egypt, Libya, Saudi Arabia, Kuwait and the United Arab Emirates. North Yemen and Lebanon have signed but not ratified it.

The states which have ratified it have generally modern national laws on enforcement of foreign judgments or awards, the exception being Saudi Arabia. We shall return to the strange position of Saudi Arabia, a state whose domestic laws do not allow enforcement without the necessity of trying the case anew, but which is nevertheless a party to a convention adopting a principle not recognised in its own internal legislation. We should also discuss some of the practical consequences of this odd situation.

What then are the provisions of the Arab League Convention?

1 *Ratione materiae*, the Arab League Convention applies to both civil and commercial disputes. It deals only with the enforcement of judgments and arbitral awards; no reference is made to their recognition.
2 The basic principle common to both judgments and awards is that the authority petitioned for enforcement cannot enter into a review of the case as a matter of substance (Article 3).
3 However, that authority can reject the petition for enforcement in any of the following cases:
   (a) if in the law of the state where enforcement is sought the subject of the dispute is not arbitrable;
   (b) if the arbitral award is not the result of a valid arbitration clause or arbitration agreement;
   (c) if the arbitrators have no jurisdiction under the arbitration clause or arbitration agreement or of the law on the basis of which the award was made;
   (d) if the parties were not properly summoned to appear;
   (e) if the award is contrary to public policy or to the moral order of the state where enforcement is sought;
   (f) if the award is not final in the state where it was made.

Lastly it is noteworthy that the documents which should accompany a petition for enforcement (which are the same for judgments and awards) imply the cumbersome condition of double enforcement in the state where the award was made and in the state where enforcement is sought (Article 5).

There are two points to be made about the practice which will illustrate certain paradoxical situations, and the divorce of law from reality which is to be found in many Arab states. The first is that the parties to the Arab League Convention are supposed to enjoy more favourable treatment because of their membership of a body which is essentially regional. Yet it is nothing of the sort since the four states which have ratified the New York Convention – Syria, Jordan, Egypt and Kuwait – are also parties to the Arab League Convention and therefore, because of the more favourable treatment of the New York Convention, in fact give greater advantages in the field of enforcement of foreign arbitral awards to countries as distant from them as Madagascar and Sri Lanka than to countries closer to them both in geography and culture. This paradoxical situation is typical of a region whose solidarity is more verbal than anything else.

The second point relates to Saudi Arabia which, it will be recalled, still does not have any modern law on the enforcement of foreign arbitral awards. A foreign arbitral award is only recognised in Saudi practice when it forms part of a judgment, and even then it is subjected to a new trial. Saudi Arabia's membership of the Arab League Convention can be regarded in some ways as a breach in the barrier which Islamic law has set up against the enforcement of the foreign arbitral award. Legal practitioners, mindful of the fact that an arbitral award embodied in a judgment of a court of an Arab League Convention member state is likely to be recognised more quickly and, in order to avoid a new trial, advise that an award should be embodied in a judgment issued in a court of an Arab League Convention member state. Thus, in spite of their archaism, the provisions of the Arab League Convention constitute an effective method of circumventing the difficulties presented by an even more archaic domestic system.

It should be reported that the Arab League Convention is being replaced by a new Convention signed in Ryad on April 8, 1983. The new Convention which is more comprehensive than the Convention of 1952 is called 'The Convention on the Judicial Cooperation between the States of the Arab League' was signed, *inter alia*, by Syria, Lebanon, Jordan, Iraq, Kuwait, Libya, UAW, Bahrain, Saudi Arabia, Qatar, Oman, North Yemen and the Democratic Republic of Yemen. The absence of Egypt is notable. We are not aware, so far, of a ratification other than that of Syria on October 27, 1983. Ratifications might be slow to come.

One of the characteristics of this new Convention which deals with enforcement of arbitral awards is that while it recognises the principle of enforcement of awards without examining the merits of the case and sets forth the classical conditions therefor, namely, the arbitrability of the dispute, the validity of the arbitration clause and arbitration agreement, the proper summoning and the non-violation of the public policy, morals and rules of the place where the enforcement is sought (Article 37). It also sets forth a condition peculiar to the states under study: the award must not violate either the provisions of the Constitution of the state where enforcement is sought or the tenets of Islamic law (Article 37). This rule is common to both judgments and arbitral awards (Article 30(a)).

Bilateral and regional treaties in the Arab Middle East

Our survey would not be complete without mention of the bilateral treaties relating to the recognition and enforcement of foreign judgments and arbitral awards.

These treaties sometimes replace, at the bilateral level, adherence to regional and international Conventions. For example, the treaties signed by Lebanon in some ways constitute a form of substitute for the New York and the Arab League Conventions. The treaties sometimes sanction the existence of closer economic relationships between the two states, for example the bilateral treaties of Syria with Bulgaria, Romania and East Germany. Sometimes they are the vestiges of a bygone age, for example the two treaties concluded by Libya in 1963 with Tunisia and Morocco, pre-dating the Libyan revolution of September 1969.

Obstacles to enforcement of awards in the Arab Middle East

This survey should have shown us what deserves a rather more thorough analysis. Middle Eastern laws are, on the whole, quite standardised: they reproduce with varying degrees of success and always somewhat belated provisions taken from western systems.

I propose to examine only those problems peculiar to the Arab Middle East as worthy of your attention. There are two: the concept of public policy and the arbitrability of the dispute. These two subjects are of interest in three ways. First, they are of practical interest since these two nations are often invoked to hinder the recognition and enforcement of foreign arbitral awards; secondly, they are of interest as a curiosity since their content is appreciably different from the principles of western law; and thirdly, they are of general interest since they emanate from four main sources: domestic laws, international and regional conventions and bilateral treaties.

Public policy

Public policy is the condition most commonly stipulated, in the domestic statutes in the regional and international conventions and the bilateral treaties to which the Arab states under examination have adhered. The national laws of Kuwait and Lebanon contain provisions concerning the arbitrability of cases in the state where enforcement is sought. Although there is no such express provision in Libya, doctrine considers arbitrability to be a prerequisite for the enforcement of a foreign award. The arbitrability of a case can be automatically invoked under the New York Convention. It is specifically mentioned as a precondition of enforcement in the Arab League Convention and various bilateral treaties.

The meaning of public policy

But what does public policy mean in this context? Some Middle Eastern systems adopt western thinking (Syria, Lebanon, Egypt and Kuwait). The concept of public policy is to be found in the laws relating to exchange control, the protection of tenants, illegal activities such as arms traffic and counterfeit currency, and in the statutory provisions which reserve to the exclusive jurisdiction of their national courts matters concerning labour law, commercial agencies and cases relating to immovable property including oil wealth. In Jordan the concept of public policy is inextricably linked to the arbitrability of a case; a strong Islamic faction in the Jordanian parliament would probably fill some legislative vacuum with provisions taken from Islamic law. In the United Arab Emirates and more specifically in Abu Dhabi, public policy is taken to be a judicial public policy conforming to Islamic law tenets. In North Yemen, public policy, in so far as it appears in the statutes applicable to the enforcement of foreign judgments, is quite simply the Islamic law concept.

It is noteworthy that most courts in the states we are discussing have not yet defined public policy. In these circumstances the classic distinction drawn by civil law between a domestic public policy and international public policy is not even relevant (except in judicial precedents to be found in the case of Lebanon, Egypt and Kuwait). In addition, Islamic law does not trouble itself with this distinction. It is opportune at this point to analyse briefly the Islamic concept of public policy since the arbitral award will come up against this obstacle in at least four states: Saudi Arabia, Qatar, Oman and North Yemen.

Public policy and Islamic law

Broadly speaking, there are two main aspects to the Islamic concept of public policy: a procedural aspect and a substantive aspect. As far as procedure is concerned three important principles should be borne in mind. These principles are not necessarily to be found in the Qur'ān and the Sunna, nevertheless they constitute the natural and immutable rules of Islamic judicial law. They are:

1 the strictly equal treatment of the parties to the judicial or arbitral action;
2 the prohibition against a judge or arbitrator deciding a dispute without hearing both plaintiff and defendant;
3 the prohibition against a judge or arbitrator making his judgment or award without giving the parties the opportunity to submit their evidence, pleas and defences.

When we come to the substantive aspect, the two main problems which are most likely to arise in practice in the procedure for enforcement of arbitral awards are the concepts of interest (*riba*) and aleatory or uncertain obligation (*gharar*). In contrast to the procedural aspect, the substantive concepts are deeply rooted in the scriptural source, the Qur'ān.

Interest and public policy

The prohibition of interest, strictly applied in Hanbali law (Saudi Arabia, Qatar) and Zaydi law (North Yemen) is linked in the minds of Muslim lawyers and economists with the rejection of the idea of the *homo economicus* as devised by the West, and with the integration of religious principles into the commercial life of the Muslim businessman. The separation of the sacred and the profane by the *homo economicus* of the West is rejected by Islamic orthodoxy. Its view is that while the businessman should be solvent he should also conform to Qur'ānic teaching, for although the Prophet did not condemn profit arising from sale or from a partnership he did prohibit the charging of interest on a loan. The underlying idea is the reprehensibility of the exploitation of a borrower by a lender. From this stems the modern notion of an Islamic bank operating as a partnership with the risk apparently shared between the bank and its partners, namely the depositors and the borrowers. Since interest could be an instrument of exploitation causing financial ruin it is treated as an unjustified increase in capital. The Hanafis, however, have managed for centuries to circumvent the prohibition of interest by a series of *ḥyāls*, the judicial ruses which endow the concept of interest with a semblance of respectability. But the Hanafis are of little interest to us in this context for the good reason that the countries in which their teaching prevails (Syria, Jordan and Egypt) have for a long time had laws relaxing the prohibition by regulating interest rates. It is important to note, however, that in Saudi Arabia, Qatar, Oman and North Yemen the prohibition of *riba* (usury), whose scriptural basis is unimpeachable, is strictly enforced. According to Hanbali teaching (eg, in Saudi Arabia, Qatar), the prohibition extends beyond the geographical boundaries of Islam.

To sum up, any arbitral award based on a contract containing a provision as to interest could come up against the prohibition of *riba* as contravening public policy, as laid down and enforced in Saudi Arabia, Qatar, Oman and North Yemen.

Uncertainty and public policy

Another prohibition which takes as its authority the concept of public policy is against uncertainty or risk (*gharar*) in particular kinds of contracts as well as in the terms of contracts. This prohibition also originated in the Qur'ān: there is no way around it or of mitigating its affect in Hanbali teaching (Saudi Arabia and Qatar) or in Zaydi teaching (North Yemen).

Gharar, uncertainty or risk, is thus prohibited by the scriptural sources. The underlying idea is that the parties to a contract must be fully aware of their obligations at the time they enter into the contract; an element of risk in a contract is the equivalent of a gamble and results in immoral gain. Such contracts would include such matters as insurance. It should be noted in passing that there are no insurance companies in Saudi Arabia, the quintessential *dār-al-Islām*; instead brokers or representatives of such companies (who must be Saudi nationals) arrange insurance most profitably abroad in the fiscal paradises of *dār-al-ḥarb* or enemy territory.

With a contract of sale or of hire, it is important to identify the object to be sold or rented. A contract which has as its object a *res nullius* or products whose existence is uncertain, such as unharvested crops, would be considered vitiated by *gharar*. The contract would not be void on the ground that its object did not exist but because of the state of uncertainty in which the parties found themselves at the time the contract was made and the risks that one of the parties would take concerning the delivery of the object of sale. It follows therefore that the price must also be fixed at the time the contract is made if it is not to be invalid.

An important exception to the *gharar* prohibition is the category of contracts which concerns the production and supply of materials not in existence at the time the contract is made (eg, construction). The Hanbalis, Zaydis and Ibadis (Oman) recognise their validity. It follows that every arbitral award upholding an aleatory contract or aleatory clause in a contract not conforming to the norms of Islamic law would be considered contrary to the concept of public policy as defined and still practiced in Saudi Arabia, Qatar, Oman and North Yemen.

Arbitrability

We now come to the final part of our survey: the arbitrability of a dispute. Here at least there is a degree of uniformity in the general principles adopted by the majority of states.

Even those judicial systems which take different views on the enforcement of awards seem to agree when it comes to the question of arbitrability: anything that cannot be the subject of conciliation cannot be arbitrated either. This principle is embodied in the provisions of Syrian, Lebanese, Iraqi, Egyptian, Libyan and Kuwaiti law. Those rights which cannot be conciliated generally include questions of personal status and criminal acts. An exception is that the financial consequence of cases relating to personal status and criminal acts are arbitrable. Some legislative peculiarities should be noted. Jordanian law enumerates non-arbitrable rights: any acts prohibited by law or regulation; acts contrary to moral or public policy or relating to personal status; the transfer of real property or *waqf* (a category of religious or family trust). Iraqi law adopts the principle of the equation, arbitrability = conciliation, but seemingly under the influence of Islamic law, requires the object of the conciliation to be identifiable and of market value. Finally, statutes in Dubai and Sharjah require that the dispute concerns the payment of a sum of money for it to be arbitrable.

However, the differences are most apparent in commercial matters. In fact these differences most often arise from special laws designed to protect a particular class of citizens or businessmen by excluding certain contracts such as the contract of employment or the contract of commercial agency or distributorship from the arbitral process. Thus future disputes between commercial agents or distributors cannot be made the subject of an arbitration clause in certain states but can be submitted to arbitration after the dispute has arisen (eg, in Lebanon). The same applies to an arbitration clause inserted in the printed terms of an insurance contract which the Libyan Civil Code renders null and void.

The respective positions of the states under examination also vary considerably, so far as bankruptcy, patent law and the invalidity of companies are concerned.

One other category of state remains governed, so far as the question of arbitrability is concerned, by principles of Islamic law. I refer to Bahrain, which has adopted the equation, arbitrability = conciliation, without there being any mention of the concept of conciliation in its Civil Code. Accordingly, Bahrain is forced back on to Islamic law. Islamic law still determines the question of arbitrability in Saudi Arabia. But parallel to Islamic law Saudi Arabia has promulgated special laws and standard form contracts for commercial agencies which in practice do not leave much room for arbitration abroad. Qatar, Oman and North Yemen (the latter in clear legislative provisions) remain governed by Islamic law.

Then what are the rules on arbitrability in Islamic law? They can be summarised as follows:

1 Products deemed *ḥarām* are not arbitrable, eg pork, alcohol, *res nullius*.
2 Rights falling within the jurisdiction of religious courts are not arbitrable, such as *ḥadd*, the penalties fixed by the Prophet which are irremissible, for example theft, adultery, consumption of wine or alcoholic drinks and apostasy. It is always possible to arbitrate on the financial consequences of offences other than *ḥadd*.
3 The arbitrability of matters relating to personal status such as marriage, affiliation, divorce and the guardianship of minors is subject to controversy between the schools.

This summary is necessarily simplified since there are countless controversies and subtle distinctions between the different schools. However all cases relating to religious law, *ḥadd* and any arbitration concerning *ḥarām* goods are absolutely prohibited.

Conclusion

We have finally completed our survey from which we can draw the following conclusions:

1 A considerable number of national laws relating to the enforcement of foreign awards require a foreign award to be embodied in a judgment. This does not encourage the enforcement of foreign awards.
2 The legislative vacuum filled by Islamic law discourages any attempt at enforcement since by virtue of that system the whole case must be tried anew by the courts of the state where enforcement is sought.
3 The New York Convention has only been ratified by four of the Arab Middle Eastern states.
4 The principles adopted by the Arab League Convention and the bilateral treaties are somewhat archaic.

Selected bibliography concerning arbitration in Islamic law

Comparative works

K Dilger, 'Arbitration, Enforcement of Foreign Judgments and Arbitration Awards, Clauses on the Choice of Law and Agreements on Jurisdiction of the Court of Egypt, Saudi Arabia and the Gulf States' (including Qatar), in *Proceedings of the Seminar on Middle East Law*, July 1–4, 1981, Hamburg, International Bar Association (1981).

S Saleh, *Commercial Arbitration in the Arab Middle East* (London 1984).

E Tyan, Emile, *Histoire de l'organisation judiciaire en pays d'Islam*, 2 vols (Leiden 1960).

Books: general and shari'a

J M Anderson, *Islamic Law in the Modern World* (New York 1959).

Y L de Bellefonds, *Traite de droit musulman comparé*, 3 vols, (Paris-La-Haye 1965, 1973).

G H Bousquet, *Du droit musulman et son application effective dans le monde* (Algiers 1949).

N J Coulson, *A History of Islamic Law* (Edinburgh 1971).

N J Coulson, *Conflicts and Tensions in Islamic Jurisprudence* (Chicago 1969).

N J Coulson, *Commercial Law in the Gulf States – The Islamic Legal Tradition*, (London 1984).

S Mahmasani, *The Philosophy of Jurisprudence in Islam*, (Leiden 1961), translation by F Ziadeh.

J Schacht, *An Introduction to Islamic Law* (Oxford 1975).

J Schacht, *The Origins of Muhammadan Jurisprudence* (Oxford 1959).

Books and articles state by state

Syria

El-Hakim, 'Syria', in VII *Yearbook: Commercial Arbitration* 35 (1982).

Lebanon

E Tyan, *Le droit de L'arbitrage* (Beirut 1972).

Iran

Yamulki, 'Iraq', in IV *Yearbook: Commercial Arbitration* 104 (1979).

Egypt

Chafik, 'Egypt', in IV *Yearbook: Commercial Arbitration* 44 (1979).

Libya

Buzghaia, 'Le litige international devant les tribunaux libyens', IV *Dirasa Qanuyya*, 33 (1974).

Buzghaia, 'Libya', in IV *Yearbook: Commercial Arbitration* 148 (1979).

Kuwait

Abu Zayyad, 'Kuwait', in IV *Yearbook: Commercial Arbitration* 139 (1979).

Y As'ad, *Commercial Arbitration and Legal Systems in Kuwait* (Kuwait 1978).

I Saad, *The Concept of Arbitration in Kuwaiti Law*, The Industrial Bank of Kuwait, (1981).

Bahrain

Al-Baharna, 'Bahrain', *Encyclopaedia of Comparative Law*, National Reports, pp B1–B4.

Saudi Arabia

A Lerrick, Alison and QJ Mian, *Saudi Business and Labour Law, Its Interpretation and Application*, (London 1982).

Van den Berg, 'Saudi Arabia', in IX *Yearbook: Commercial Arbitration* 7 (1984).

So far, so good; enforcement of foreign commercial arbitration awards in United States courts

32

Robert Coulson

United States courts have expressed an enlightened enforcement policy when dealing with commercial arbitration awards made in other countries. This is consistent with the obligations assumed by the United States in ratifying the 1958 New York Convention and reflects a supportive federal policy towards contractual arbitration, in general.

In this paper, I will discuss the enforcement mechanism contained in the New York Convention and how it has been applied in various federal court cases.

International commercial arbitration has been broadly utilised to obtain third-party decisions, avoiding the need to litigate in the local courts. In international trade, neither party may wish to submit to the jurisdiction of the national courts of the other party. Nor may it be feasible or agreeable to submit to the courts of a third jurisdiction. Therefore, arbitration is often an acceptable option, frequently utilised by contracting parties in world trade.

Many international commercial arbitrations proceed efficiently, at a quicker pace and at less expense than they might have in court litigation, but some arbitrations have been notoriously sluggish and expensive. Much depends upon the attitudes of the parties and their counsel. Sometimes, the arbitrators, an administrative agency or the general business climate can expedite that pace. Overall experience with arbitration has been satisfactory enough to persuade parties to favour it for international contractual disputes.

It is customary for arbitral awards to be satisfied voluntarily by the losing party, at least in countries that have adopted the New York Convention. In the United States, for example, very few awards need to be confirmed by the courts. Nevertheless, it is important, when courts are requested to do so, that they enforce arbitration awards to the extent required by applicable law.

International commercial arbitration would not flourish without the assistance of national courts. The New York Convention reflects that principle. Without good faith enforcement by national courts, the New York Convention would become emasculated.

The United States participated in the drafting of the New York Convention at a time when its own domestic policy towards commercial arbitration was being buttressed. Modern arbitration statutes were not passed by Congress or by the various states until the 1920s. Even in 1958, when the New York Convention became available, a strong national policy towards arbitration was yet to be enunciated. When the Federal Arbitration Act was amended, it contained the obligations imposed by the 1970 adoption of the New York Convention.

As the Supreme Court explained in the leading international commercial case of *Scherk* v *Alberto-Culver*[1]

> 'The goal of the Convention, and the principal purpose underlying American adoption and implementation of it, was to encourage the recognition and enforcement of commercial arbitration agreements in international contracts and to unify the standards by which agreements to arbitrate are observed and arbitral awards are enforced in the signatory countries.'

Most major trading countries have now ratified or acceded to the New York Convention, a significant step forward for international commercial arbitration. For the United States, adoption of the Convention represented a dramatic deferral to arbitration awards that might be rendered by foreign arbitrators, under foreign systems of arbitration and under foreign laws. It has not been customary for Congress to give *carte blanche* to foreigners in this way. Only the notion that international trade development would require federal recognition of the arbitral process, persuaded normally parochial legislators that it was in the national interest to adopt the New York Convention.

To be sure, Congress did invoke the 'commercial' and the 'reciprocity' reservations. By limiting the application of the New York Convention to 'commercial' disputes, the definition in Section 2 of the Federal Arbitration Act came into play: 'maritime transactions and contracts evidencing a transaction involving commerce.' Fortunately, this phrase had been expansively interpreted by a long line of Supreme Court cases extending jurisdiction of federal laws and regulations to cover commerce between the various states.

In *Fertilizer Corp of India* v *IDI Management, Inc*,[2] 'reciprocity' was construed to permit enforcement of an award under the New York Convention even though the losing party, a United States corporation, claimed that India had 'adopted various evasive devices ... to avoid enforcement of awards adverse to Indian parties.'[3] The court held that it was not necessary for the moving party to demonstrate that the award was not final and binding in India. It was enough to demonstrate that India had ratified the New York Convention.

The New York Convention, by its terms, was applicable to 'arbitral awards made in the territory of a state other than the state where the recognition and enforcement of such awards are sought,' and 'shall also apply to arbitral awards not considered as domestic awards in the state where their recognition and enforcement are sought.'[4]

Article III obliges courts to 'recognise arbitral awards as binding' and to enforce them under applicable laws and procedures. The relatively simple procedure for enforcing such an award is defined in Article IV. The moving party must provide a 'duly authenticated original award' and certified copies of the agreement to arbitrate.

1 417 US 506 (1973), at 520.
2 517 F Supp 948 (SD Ohio 1981).
3 *Ibid*, at 952.
4 Article I.

The New York Convention, in Article V, lists seven grounds for refusing enforcement of an award. A party resisting enforcement must prove that one or more of those grounds are applicable. Recent experience in the courts of the United States indicates that the burden on a resisting party will be onerous. So far, the courts have adopted a strong pro-enforcement bias consistent with the current national policy encouraging domestic arbitration. Often, awards would have been enforced under either the New York Convention or domestic law. Under both laws, United States courts currently favour enforcement.

The seven grounds given for not enforcing an international award are contained in Article V:

> '1 Recognition and enforcement of the award may be refused, at the request of the party against whom it is invoked, only if that party furnishes to the competent authority where the recognition and enforcement is sought, proof that:
>
> (a) The parties to the agreement referred to in Article II were, under the law applicable to them, under some incapacity, or the said agreement is not valid under the law to which the parties have subjected it or, failing any indication thereon, under the law of the country where the award was made; or
>
> (b) The party against whom the award is invoked was not given proper notice of the appointment of the arbitrator or of the arbitration proceedings or was otherwise unable to present his case; or
>
> (c) The award deals with a difference not contemplated by or not falling within the terms of the submission to arbitration, or it contains decisions on matters beyond the scope of the submission to arbitration, provided that, if the decisions on matters submitted to arbitration can be separated from those not so submitted, that part of the award which contains decisions on matters submitted to arbitration may be recognised and enforced; or
>
> (d) The composition of the arbitral authority or the arbitral procedure was not in accordance with the agreement of the parties, or, failing such agreement, was not in accordance with the law of the country where the arbitration took place; or
>
> (e) The award has not yet become binding on the parties, or has been set aside or suspended by a competent authority of the country in which, or under the law of which, that award was made.
>
> 2 Recognition and enforcement of an arbitral award may also be refused if the competent authority in the country where recognition and enforcement is sought finds that:
>
> (a) The subject-matter of the difference is not capable of settlement by arbitration under the law of the country; or
>
> (b) The recognition or enforcement of the award would be contrary to the public policy of that country.'

I will discuss them in order, although paragraphs 2(a) and (b) may be more important since they reflect policy considerations rather than mere procedure.

Paragraph 1(a) relates to the lack of capacity of the parties or the invalidity of the agreement under the applicable law. That law may be chosen by the parties or, if not, will be the law of the state where the award is made.

Paragraph 1(b) deals with 'proper notice' of the appointment of the arbitrator or of the proceedings and with having an opportunity to present the case. These are questions of due process. In *Parsons & Whittemore Overseas Co* v *Société General de L'Industrie du Papier (RAKTA)*,[5] the court said that the 'provision essentially sanctions the application of the forum state's standards of due process.' *Parsons & Whittemore*, in resisting a foreign award had claimed that the arbitrators refused to delay proceedings to accommodate the speaking schedule of a witness. Much of the witness's testimony having been supplied through affidavit, the court refused to consider that ruling to be an infringement which would justify refusal of enforcement. It was 'a risk inherent in an agreement to submit to arbitration.' The court found that the arbitrators acted within their power.

In a subsequent case, *Biotronik Mess-und Therapiegeraete GmbH & Co* v *Medford Medical Instrument Co*[6] the losing party claimed that it was unable to present its case because the transactions had not matured. The court dismissed that argument since it did not relate to the more limited question of notice and opportunity to be heard.

Paragraph 1(c) would deny enforcement if the award goes beyond the issues submitted to arbitration. This ground is found in virtually every domestic arbitration statute in the United States so that federal judges will not be nonplussed to encounter it. In the *Parsons & Whittemore* decision, where it was also raised, the court brushed it aside: 'This defence to enforcement of a foreign award, like the others already discussed, should be construed narrowly. Once again, a narrow construction would comport with the enforcement-facilitating thrust of the Convention.'[7] The court upheld damages for loss of production even though the contract specified that neither party shall have 'any liability for loss of production.' The paragraph 1(c) defence was denied on the basis that the arbitrators had interpreted the contract to authorise them to include loss of production in their award. Surely, this decision illustrates a positive attitude towards enforcement.

Paragraph 1(d) relates to the tribunal. Were the arbitrators selected in accordance with the parties' agreement or the applicable rules or applicable law of the forum? Here, the leading United States case is *Imperial Ethiopian Govt* v *Baruch–Foster Corp.*[8] After the award was rendered, Baruch–Foster learned for the first time that the chairman of the panel had once drafted a civil code for the Ethiopian Government. Nevertheless, the district court enforced the award and the court of appeals confirmed.

In domestic arbitration in the United States, the impartiality of neutral arbitrators has frequently been a source of litigation. Courts have imposed relatively strict requirements as to the arbitrator's duty to disclose and as to the need for independence and neutrality. The *Imperial Ethiopian* case may not be the last word on this provision, but it would appear that a more lenient attitude will be adopted under the New York Convention than would be applicable to domestic cases.

5 508 F 2d 969 (2nd Cir 1974), at 975.
6 415 F Supp 133 (DNJ 1976).
7 508 F 2d, at 976.
8 535 F 2nd 334 (5th Cir 1976).

Paragraph 1(e) requires that the award be 'binding on the parties' and shall not have been set aside where it was made. This defence was the main thrust in *Fertilizer Corp of India*, where the award was then being reviewed for errors of law. Indian courts being notoriously slow, the United States court rejected the defence noting that at some subsequent time, after final action in India, the question might be reviewed.

So much for procedure. More important, it would seem, are the substantive, public policy grounds. Paragraph 2(a) refers to situations where the court finds that the issues are not 'capable of settlement by arbitration' by local law. If the jurisdiction is one in which numerous categories of disputes may not be arbitrated, this defence has the potential of being expanded by judges. In the United States, this has not happened in spite of the fact that certain issues are not arbitrable under domestic law. The *Scherk* case involved securities issues that the respondent need not have arbitrated under domestic law. Nevertheless, the Supreme Court enforced the arbitration clause. Recent federal legislation has made it possible to arbitrate patent validity issues. Before that, the issue was not arbitrable.

A recent line of cases indicated that anti-trust issues are not arbitrable, although district courts may stay litigation while the parties resolve their contractual disagreements through arbitration. In *Mitsubishi Motors Corp* v *Soler Chrysler-Plymouth*[9] the United States Supreme Court held that anti-trust issues may be arbitrated under the New York Convention. The cases exempting anti-trust issues from arbitration in domestic cases are themselves now questionable. The issue raised in the *Mitsubishi* case involved an automobile dealership in Puerto Rico whose purchase agreement with a Japanese manufacturer contained an arbitration clause referring to the Japan Commercial Arbitration Association Rules, clearly a matter concerning international commerce.

Paragraph 2(b) raises the potentially troublesome defence that enforcement would be contrary to the public policy of the jurisdiction. Public policy is a broad concept, covering manifold subjects, constantly changing and likely to draw the attention of judicial activists. Public policy is subject to shifting interpretations depending upon political trends.

So far, at least, United States courts have exercised restraint. The defence has seldom been successful, but not for want of trying. For example, an award issued in Japan during the pendency of a corporate bankruptcy was at first rejected by the bankruptcy court, then enforced by a district court and by the Second Circuit Court of Appeals. After balancing the policy expressed by the New York Convention to enforce foreign arbitration awards against the bankruptcy law, the court construed narrowly the public policy defence.[10]

Several of the cases, earlier discussed, also raised public policy issues. For example, in *Fertilizer Corp of India*, the United States party claimed that the Indian Government had appointed an arbitrator who had previously acted as its counsel, which allegedly violated United States public policy. In fact, the policy as to party-appointed arbitrators in the United States is far from settled. A New Jersey state court has imposed an obligation on party-appointed arbitrators to disclose relationships with the appointing party, but that is

9 24 ILM 1064 (1985). See brief details, *supra*, Introduction, at 3–4.

10 *Fotochrome, Inc* v *Copal Co Ltd* 517 F 2d 512 (2nd Cir 1975).

hardly the majority view. Indeed, some arbitration systems in the United States utilise blatantly partisan, party-appointed arbitrators. At any rate, the court dismissed the alleged public policy defence in the *Fertilizer* case, relying on the strong policy in favour of the New York Convention.

In the *Imperial Ethiopian* case, where the chairman, a distinguished international arbitrator, had served as a consultant to the Ethiopian Government, the court also dismissed that defence.

One paragraph 2(b) case, *Laminoirs Trefileries-Cableries de Lens* v *Southwire Co*,[11] seems slightly less supportive. There, the court partially accepted the public policy defence. The arbitrators had issued an award against a United States party, including a relatively high rate of interest, based upon French law. *Southwire* claimed that the rates were usurious and against Georgia public policy. The purchase contract had designated Georgia as the applicable law, to the extent that it did not conflict with French law. The court accepted the initial interest rate of up to 10½ per cent, but struck down an even higher rate of up to 15½ per cent to be imposed two months after issuance of the award. That feature was viewed as a penalty by the court. In the United States, arbitrators are not authorised to order penalties or punitive damages. This untested district court decision illustrates what can be a continuing problem: From time to time, federal district court judges may refuse to enforce foreign arbitral awards which shock their conscience or, seemingly, violate ingrained judicial policies.

Recent domestic arbitration decisions also illustrate a trend towards enforcement. The Supreme Court has been strongly supportive of commercial arbitration, setting aside state statutes that stood in the way. The pro-enforcement policy of United States courts under the New York Convention is consistent with its support of domestic arbitration.

The case analysed in this paper may indicate that such a trend will continue. On the other hand, none of the above cases have amounted to flagrant violations of Article V. A hypothetical foreign award considered invalid in the country where it was issued and against a party who had insufficient notice of the appointment or the proceedings and who, therefore, was unable to present its case and which dealt with matters outside the terms of the agreement and was issued by an arbitrator who was partial to the winning party, would not be enforced by a United States court. Even one such defect, clearly established, might justify refusal.

The more substantive criteria of paragraphs 2(a) and (b), in appropriate circumstances, might also result in non-enforcement. Public policy is a broad and multifarious cloak. Only a few theories have so far been examined by the courts. Such vital concerns as defence policy, environmental controls and human relations are yet untested. The relatively few cases so far decided by United States courts indicate a pro-enforcement policy towards foreign arbitral awards under the New York Convention. I don't know whether the same attitude will persist when United States courts are faced with an arbitral award against a United States party where clear injustice has been done.

11 484 F Supp 1063 (ND Ga 1980).

The enforcement of arbitral awards against a state: the problem of immunity from execution 33

Giorgio Bernini and Albert Jan Van den Berg*

Legal rules relating to sovereign immunity in international commercial arbitration

This contribution to the survey of sovereign immunity issues in international commercial arbitration addresses the specific problems associated with the execution of an international arbitral award sought by a private party against a state. At the outset, we should stress that, in our opinion, only actual execution constitutes a separate phase from the arbitral proceedings. By contrast, recognition and enforcement of the award are the direct consequence and logical final step of the arbitral proceedings. Therefore, issues of immunity raised during recognition and enforcement procedures should be viewed as issues of immunity from jurisdiction.[1] Hence, we shall consider the case of a state claiming immunity at the moment of actual enforcement of an award, once jurisdictional issues have been resolved and the arbitral award has been recognised. We shall refer to this case as immunity from execution. The immunity plea would then refer only to the state's alleged immunity from enforcement by measures of execution against its property.

We must point out that such a 'pure' immunity from execution case seldom arises in practice, since the issue of immunity from jurisdiction tends to reappear at the stage of recognition of the award. This means that the state will more frequently rely on a plea of immunity from jurisdiction when recognition and enforcement of the award is sought, rather than wait until actual measures of execution are requested and raise the exception of immunity from execution.

We should also consider the role played in this field by diplomacy and out-of-court settlements. As we shall see in examining the *LIAMCO* case

* The authors wish to express their gratitude to Dott Silvia Borelli of the law offices of Van Doorne & Sjollema, Rotterdam, and assistant to the General Editor of the *Yearbook: Commercial Arbitration*, for her invaluable assistance in preparing this paper.

1 See the Swiss *LIAMCO* case, *Libyan American Oil Company* v *Socialist People's Libyan Arab Jamahirya*, decided by the *Tribunal Federal* on June 19, 1980, reported in VI *Yearbook: Commercial Arbitration* (1981). See also *Cour d'Appel* of Paris, June 26, 1981, *Benvenuti and Bonfant* v *The Government of the People's Republic of the Congo*, reported in G Delaume, *Transnational Contract*, (Dobbs Ferry 1978–1984), Vol V, Booklet F at 81.

below, settlement negotiations can achieve results that would be difficult to obtain in court.

The current state of affairs regarding immunity can be summarised as follows. Most nations distinguished between immunity from jurisdiction and immunity from execution. With respect to immunity from jurisdiction, a distinction is made between acts *iure gestionis* and acts *iure imperii*. Only as far as acts *iure imperii* are concerned can a state claim immunity. The doctrine of restrictive immunity is not applied to immunity from execution by most states. In this field, most states continue to apply an absolute immunity. In those states where the doctrine of restrictive immunity is applied to execution, different tests are either cumulatively or alternatively used for determining whether immunity from execution can be invoked, ie, the nature-of-funds test (use for sovereign or commercial purposes) and the nature-of-activity test (sovereign or commercial activity). Further, some states require that there is a connection between the legal relationship on which the award is based and the territory of the state where execution is sought.

As will be explained hereafter, we do not think that the distinction *iure imperii/iure gestionis* should be made for immunity from jurisdiction in matters relating to arbitration. By agreeing to arbitration, a state must be deemed to have waived immunity. For the same reason, we deem it inappropriate to distinguish between immunity from jurisdiction and immunity from execution in relation to arbitration. It is, in our opinion, illogical that by agreeing to arbitration a state would have waived its right to invoke immunity from jurisdiction only but not its right to invoke immunity from execution.

As mentioned, the dualism of immunity from jurisdiction and immunity from execution is accepted in the large majority of western legal systems. As far as sovereign immunity from jurisdiction is concerned, the theory of restrictive immunity has, beyond doubt, ousted absolute immunity principles. This change is shown in almost all western countries' legislation, doctrine and case law since the beginning of this century. The basic distinction between acts *iure imperii* and acts *iure gestionis*, on which restrictive immunity is founded, is still widely accepted and only the socialist countries reject it on the grounds of their own concept of state and state property.[2] We have already pointed out, and we shall return to the subject later, that this distinction should not be held valid in the field of arbitration, albeit for reasons different from those put forward by the socialist systems.

In principle, the theory of restrictive immunity is not applied to immunity from enforcement by means of execution measures. The reason for this much less enthusiastic response to the restrictive immunity theory in the field of immunity from execution is obviously political and economic. In this context prestige plays an even greater role than in the case of immunity from jurisdiction. Enforcement of execution is commonly felt to be a 'more intensive interference with the rights of the state'.[3] From the economic point of view,

2 See M Boguslavsky, 'Foreign State Immunity: Soviet Doctrine and Practice', 10 *Netherlands Yearbook of International Law* (*NYIL*) (1979), and F Enderlein, 'The Immunity of State Property from Foreign Jurisdiction and Execution: Doctrine and Practice of the German Democratic Republic', 10 *NYIL* 111 (1979). It must be mentioned that a slightly discordant opinion has been expressed as regarding Yugoslav law by T Varady, 'Immunity of State Property from Execution in the Yugoslav Legal System' 10 *NYIL* 85 (1979). However, the author also refers to Yugoslav doctrine to the contrary.

3 K H Böckstiegel, *Arbitration and State Enterprises* (Deventer 1984), at 50.

restrictive immunity principles applied to execution could result in foreign states refraining from investment in countries in which they know their property could be subject to execution.

We must anticipate now an incongruity that will become evident in the discussion presented below and from the examination of the statutes and case law. On the one hand we have the Executive, concerned with political and economic issues, and on the other hand the Judiciary, which incorporates the system's equally fundamental desire and necessity to base its activities solely on the law. In the field of immunity in general, and immunity from execution in particular, these two branches of the same tree inevitably conflict. A fair example of this internecine war is the Swiss situation, in which the courts are applying restrictive immunity from execution while the political authorities are seeking to codify the absolute immunity theory.[4]

The aforementioned delicate political and economic issues in the enforcement of international awards are reflected in some legal systems which require the intervention of political and administrative authorities of the state where execution is sought as a necessary step in the execution procedure, thereby implicitly recognising the dichotomy outlined above. In Italy, Article 1 of the Law No 1263 of July 15, 1926, states that enforcement proceedings against assets of a foreign state in Italian territory cannot proceed without the intervention of the Minister of Justice on the issue. The Minister's decision, however, can be challenged in civil and administrative courts.[5] The ultimate result of this provision is to shift the political responsibility of ruling on an execution against property of a foreign state from the courts to the political body.[6] This mechanism is particularly important since Italy theoretically does not recognise the existence of a principle of international law granting the states immunity from execution on assets located outside their territory. The Minister bases his decision primarily on reciprocity considerations, but since he is not obliged to do so, any political and economic aspects may be taken into account. Similar procedures exist in Greece,[7] in Yugoslavia, where execution is granted upon the consent of the Federal Secretariat of Justice,[8] and in The Netherlands, where the bailiff (*deurwaarder*) is prohibited from serving a writ against a state if the Minister of Justice has informed him that the service 'would be contrary to the obligations of the state under international law'.[9]

Mandatory intervention of political and administrative authorities at the stage of execution tends to frustrate the principles of restrictive immunity laid down by the judiciary. To recall again the example of Italy, the participation of the Minister of Justice in the enforcement against a foreign state's assets located in Italian territory appears incongruous as against a consistent weight of opinion, expressed by the courts, by which Italy 'in common with modern

4 JF Lalive, 'Swiss Law and Practice in Relation to Measures of Execution Against the Property of a Foreign State', 10 *NYIL* 153 (1979).

5 This is possible since the 1963 decision of the Italian Constitutional Court declaring unconstitutional the last paragraph of Article 1, which excluded such challenge.

6 L Condorelli and L Sbolci, 'Measures of Execution against the Property of Foreign States: The Law and Practice in Italy', 10 *NYIL* 197 (1979).

7 Law No 15 of 1938.

8 Yugoslav Law on Enforcement Procedure of 1978.

9 Article 13, paragraph 4, of the *Deurwaardersreglement*, as translated by C Voskuil, 'The International Law of State Immunity as Reflected in the Dutch Civil Law of Execution', 10 *NYIL* 245, (1979) at 261.

states, now allows herself to be sued'.[10] On the basis of this assumption, 'the courts have reasoned that the principle of equality of states is not violated by allowing foreign states to be sued in Italy on terms similar to those on which Italy may be sued in her own courts'.[11]

The Italian courts have therefore restricted the field of immunity from jurisdiction, thereby following the widely accepted tendency mentioned above. As we have already pointed out, the restrictive immunity theory is based on the distinction between acts *iure imperii* and acts *iure gestionis*. We believe that legislation and case law should go a step further and recognise that a state, by agreeing to arbitration, waives its right to claim immunity from jurisdiction independently from the nature of the activity carried out by the state in the underlying legal relationship. The fundamental principle of *pacta sunt servanda* should be the only relevant element in the issue. As pointed out by Luzzatto[12]:

> 'Sovereign immunity has been frequently invoked by states with a view to getting rid, either of the obligation to arbitrate, or of the duty to execute the award. There should be, however, no doubt, in this connection, that an agreement to arbitrate constitutes an implicit waiver and that therefore international or municipal rules granting sovereign immunity should not apply. This view, which had already been taken by some writers and courts, has been upheld recently by the United States District Court for the District of Columbia, in *Ipitrade International SA* v *Federal Republic of Nigeria*. The court relied upon the Foreign Sovereign Immunity Act of 1976 and on its legislative history, particularly on a statement in the Congressional Committee Report on the Jurisdiction of the United States Courts in Suits Against Foreign States of 9 September 1976, but the principle would seem to apply anyhow as a general rule. The *jure imperii* or *jure gestionis* character of the subject-matter of the agreement should therefore be irrelevant.'

The preliminary award in the ICC Case No 2321 (1974)[13] came very eloquently to the same conclusions:

> 'I must admit that I have found some difficulties to follow a line of reasoning that a state, just because of its supreme position and qualities, should be unable to give a binding promise. The principle of *pacta sunt servanda* is generally acknowledged in international law and it is difficult to see any reason why it should not apply here. A sovereign state must be sovereign enough to make a binding promise both under international law and municipal law. As to the latter aspect of the question I was informed by the Counsel of the First Defendant that according to both ... and English law the capacity of the state to enter into arbitration clauses was not restricted as such and that also the state could be sued in its own courts. To require or assume then that a promise of a state to submit to arbitration, in order to be binding, has to be confirmed in the face of the arbitrator, would probably impair the sovereignty of a state and its dignity more than the arbitrator's

10 Cappelletti-Perrillo, *Civil Procedure in Italy* (The Hague 1965), at 96.

11 *Ibid.*

12 M Luzzatto, 'International Commercial Arbitration and the Municipal Law of States', 157 *Recueil des Cours de l'Academic de Droit International* (1977), at 93.

13 Reported in I *Yearbook: Commercial Arbitration* 133 (1976), at 135.

> performance of his task, conferred upon him in accordance with what the parties once have agreed upon. The issue whether the subject-matter of the present dispute is a matter *jure gestionis* or *jure imperii* has also been argued by the parties on each side. From what I have said above it follows that this distinction is of no relevance once the parties have agreed upon arbitration.'

We have suggested that the so-called 'nature-of-the-activity test' (sovereign or commercial) should no longer be applied to establish whether a state is immune from jurisdiction. Once a state has agreed to arbitrate, the waiver of immunity implied in the signature of the arbitration agreement should not be confined to the realm of acts carried out by the state as if it were a private party.

As far as immunity from execution is concerned, however, we must consider two additional problems. First, most legal systems distinguish between waiver of immunity from jurisdiction and waiver of immunity from execution, ie, they do not imply the latter in the former. Second, the distinction between acts *iure imperii* and acts *iure gestionis* reappears almost unavoidably, at the state of execution, in the so-called 'nature-of-funds test'. As we shall see when examining statutes and case law more in detail, most legal systems prohibit execution against a state's property used for sovereign purposes, while they allow execution against property meant for commercial use. Consistently with our opinion that only the principle of *pacta sunt servanda* should be considered, we do not agree with this distinction, the last stumbling-block in the century-old frustration of the private party's claims towards a state.

It is a plain fact that the private party trying to execute an international arbitral award against a state encounters many obstacles, even if jurisdiction is no longer contested. If the state does not comply voluntarily with an award rendered against it, the private party can be left with no means of enforcing the decision in his favour. Lack of sanctions is actually a constant *leit-motiv* of public international law and takes, in commercial arbitration practice, the form of an almost total absence of means of enforcement. The feeble position of the private party has been improved, however, by the Washington Convention of 1965 which instituted the International Centre for the Settlement of Investment Disputes. A party who obtains an ICSID award enjoys a certain protection against the risk of the foreign state's assertion of immunity from execution. A contracting state does not waive its right to raise the exception of immunity from execution, as explicitly stated in Article 55 of the Washington Convention but it agrees to comply with the award[14] and to enforce the pecuniary obligations thereunder, in its territories, as if the award were a final judgment of a court of the state itself.[15] On the other hand, the Washington Convention provides that, in case the state does not abide by the award, the state of the private party has the right to exercise diplomatic protection, a right which is suspended during the ICSID arbitration.[16]

The ideal correspondence between immunity aspects of jurisdiction and execution, as pointed out above, is not so much real as desirable. As already noted, most legal systems distinguish between immunity from jurisdiction and immunity from execution, excluding that a waiver of the latter be implied in a waiver of the former. Many legal systems do not recognise that an agreement to

14 Washington Convention, Article 53.
15 *Ibid*, Article 54(1).
16 *Ibid*, Article 27(1).

arbitrate constitutes a waiver of immunity from jurisdiction. Most states also adopt in principle an absolute concept of immunity as far as execution is concerned, although admitting exceptions.

Socialist countries do not make this distinction, since they do not stray at any point from the absolute immunity theory. One author has stressed that it is only for the state itself to decide whether it is subject to the jurisdiction of a court, and whether enforcement should be granted: 'It is not the business of foreign courts to judge whether a certain object of state property enjoys immunity or not. The question is subject to regulation by the legal provisions of the GDR.'[17]

Among the countries that take an equal approach to the issues of immunity from jurisdiction and immunity from execution, it is in Switzerland that the extended theory of restrictive immunity has been most clearly applied. Swiss courts, albeit in the absence of a statute dealing with the issue, have consistently refused to distinguish between jurisdiction and enforcement from the point of view of immunity. Switzerland brings this theory to the point of implying a waiver of immunity from execution as well as a waiver of immunity from jurisdiction in an arbitration agreement signed by a state.[18] The Swiss Federal Supreme Court held[19] that, since powers of execution directly derive from powers of jurisdiction, there is no reason that Swiss courts should treat immunity from execution differently from immunity from jurisdiction. Once the jurisdictional issue has been decided and an award has been rendered, the state cannot be allowed to create a new obstacle for the private party by claiming to be immune from execution against property held for commercial purposes or simply for no specified public purpose. The distinction between commercial and sovereign nature, as we have stressed above, reappears when the character of the property to be executed is considered. Swiss case law also requires that there be a connection between the legal relationship on which the award has been rendered and Swiss territory (the so-called *Binnenbeziehung*) such as, for instance, Switzerland being the place of performance of the contract or the location in Switzerland of property of the foreign state.[20] This widens considerably the scope of the discretion left to both judiciary and political authority.

Austrian law also accepts the restrictive immunity theory regarding execution. Legislation permits enforcement by means of execution measures against a foreign state's immovable assets located in Austria, or its vested rights in domestic immovables belonging to other persons.[21] Case law has specified that the assets must be used for commercial purposes,[22] which confirms the observations made above on the nature-of-funds-test. In a decision of 1961,[23] the Austrian Supreme Court made an important statement advancing an additional step in the direction of restrictive immunity from execution. The Court held:

17 Enderlein, *op cit*, at 120.
18 See JF Lalive, *op cit*, at 162.
19 *United Arab Republic* v *Mrs X*, Tribunal Federal, February 10, 1960, *Clunet* 458 (1961).
20 See *SA Sogerfin* v *Yugoslavia* (1938), 61 Semaine Judiciaire 327 (1939), and *Kingdom of Greece* v *Julius Bar & Co* (1956), ATF 82 I 75.
21 Article IX of the Introductory Law to the Rules on Jurisdiction Law of August 1, 1895, as translated by I Seidl-Hohenveldern, 10 *NYIL* 97 (1979).
22 *Neustein* v *Republic of Indonesia*, August 6, 1958, case No 6.
23 Austrian Supreme Court, February 10, 1961, 84 *Juristische Blatter* 63 (1962).

'So far as concerns the lack of means to execute a judgment, we need only to point out that such means exist under international law within the framework of municipal law. There can be no violation of sovereignty because the binding force of a judgment operates only within the territory of the forum state and the judgment can be enforced only within that territory'.[24]

In the Federal Republic of Germany, the Constitutional Court has also accepted the restrictive immunity theory in the field of immunity from execution. In a 1977 decision,[25] it held that no international law principle prohibits enforcement against a state in cases in which the state is not immune from jurisdiction. The court relied on the distinction between sovereign acts and acts *iure gestionis*. In a 1983 decision, the court applied the nature-of-funds test, holding that immunity could be granted to a state's bank accounts only if the funds were used uniquely for governmental purposes.[26]

The United States Foreign Sovereign Immunities Act of 1976 (FSIA) heads in the direction of equality of treatment for immunity from jurisdiction and immunity from execution, without reaching that goal completely. In this statute the dualism of nature-of-funds test/nature-of-activity test is very clearly exemplified, and its provisions illustrate our observations on the issue. Immunity of a foreign state from enforcement by execution against its property in the United States is limited by a number of exceptions based on the commercial nature of that state's activity. The FSIA, however, provides for the further requirement that the property to be executed against 'is or was used for the commercial activity upon which the claim is based'.[27] The Act therefore endorses solely the criterion of the nature of the funds when the foreign state itself is the party claiming immunity. In contrast, when immunity from execution is claimed by an 'agency or instrumentality of the foreign state' a different criterion is used, which brings the FSIA closer to that ideal equality of immunity from jurisdiction and immunity from execution. Section 1610(b) draws an explicit link between them, stating that no immunity from execution can be claimed by an agency or instrumentality where there is no immunity from jurisdiction. This provision, by omitting the requirement that the property to be executed against be used for the commercial activity upon which the claim is based, makes use of the criterion based on the nature of the state's activity involved in the dispute.

The solution offered by the FSIA calls for some considerations. The statute provides that the state or state entity can waive its right to immunity from execution thereby distinguishing such waiver from a waiver of immunity from jurisdiction. However, the former can be made 'either explicitly or by implication',[28] which leaves the issue open. The FSIA further shows that the *iure gestionis/iure imperii* criterion still holds in the ambit of the nature-of-the-funds-test, although the application of this distinction is limited to funds

24 As translated by I Seidl-Hohenveldern, *op cit*, at 107.

25 Federal Constitutional Court, December 13, 1977, *Philippine Embassy Bank Account* case, 46 BVerfGe 342 (1977).

26 Federal Constitution Court, April 12, 1983, *National Iranian Oil Company* case, 37 Westpapier-Mitteilungen Zeitschrift fur Wirtschafts- und Bankrecht 722 (1983).

27 Foreign Immunities Act 1976, s1610(a).

28 *Ibid*, s1610(a)(1) and (b)(1).

owned by a state and not by a state agency or instrumentality. It is needless to say that the requirement that the funds to be executed against be used 'for the commercial activity upon which the claim is based' consistently limits the private party's chances against the state.

At this juncture it should be noted that the dichotomy nature-of-funds test/nature-of-activity test has been discussed thoroughly in an important French decision, *EURODIF*, which shall be examined in the second part of this paper. We can mention here that the FSIA has been closely followed in *EURODIF*.

Section 1611 of the FSIA lists certain types of property that are in any case immune from execution. By granting absolute immunity to the funds held by the foreign central banks or monetary authorities 'for their own account', the FSIA further defines its position concerning the complicated issue of the identity of the entities allowed to claim immunity, already extensively dealt with in Section 1603. Since the issue concerns immunity from jurisdiction as well as of immunity from execution, however, we shall only point out that the sovereign identity of central banks has been widely discussed in case law. The last part of Section 1611 further recognises the absolute immunity from execution of all property connected *lato sensu* with military activities. This exception recurs in all western legislation and can be said to be a logical consequence of the principle of absolute immunity for acts *iure imperii*. Since we cannot agree with the acts *iure gestionis*/acts *iure imperii* distinction once the state has waived its right to immunity by agreeing to arbitrate, we find it difficult to accept this distinction either. Once immunity has been explicitly or implicitly waived, the principle of *princeps in alterius territorio privatus* should be held fully valid. We should remember, however, that international treaties grant absolute protection to special categories of assets. Such is the case of the Vienna Conventions on Diplomatic and Consular Relations, and the Convention on State-Owned Vessels.[29]

A tempered recognition of absolute sovereign immunity from execution is the solution offered by the European Convention on state immunity.[30] This Convention states expressly that no measures of execution can be taken against the property of a contracting state without the state's consent.[31] However,

29 Article 22, paragraph 3, of the Vienna Convention on Diplomatic Relations of 1961 grants immunity from execution to 'the premises of the mission, their furnishings and other property thereof, and the means of transport of the mission'. Article 31, paragraph 4, of the Vienna Convention on Consular Relations of 1963, provides for the immunity of consular premises, property and means of transport from requisition. However, immunity from execution 'may be justified on the basis of the inviolability of the consular archives and documents'. Bouchez, 'The Nature and Scope of State Immunity from Jurisdiction and Execution', 10 *NYIL* 3 (1979). The Brussels Convention for the Unification of Certain Rules Relating to the Immunity of State-Owned Vessels, of 1926, prohibits execution against warships, government yachts, patrol vessels, hospital ships, auxiliary and supply ships, and on cargoes carried on board the said vessels, as well as cargo owned by the state and not used for commercial purposes, carried on board merchant vessels (Article 3). Aircraft used for governmental service (ie, also postal service), and on regular flights are immune from execution according to the Rome Convention on Precautionary Attachment on Aircraft 1933 (Article 3).

30 European Convention on State Immunity with Additional Protocol, done at Basle on May 16, 1972.

31 *Ibid*, Article 23.

Article 24 of the Convention on state immunity allows the contracting states to declare, when signing or ratifying the Convention, that

> 'its Courts shall be entitled to entertain proceedings against another contracting state to the extent that its courts are entitled to entertain proceedings against states not party to the present Convention'.

Hence, the United Kingdom and Belgium, for instance, which have both made this declaration, will be able to apply their restrictive principles of immunity from execution, although within the framework of Article 26. According to this article, property of a foreign state can be executed against in the forum state if such property has been solely used for the commercial activity upon which the claim is based. We have already mentioned that we shall find a recent discussion of this double criterion (nature of the property and of the activity) in the *EURODIF* decision of the French *Cour de Cassation* discussed below. As we have seen, the requirement of a link between the property to be executed against and the state's commercial activity is also accepted in the United States FSIA. Indeed, it is clear that the European Convention on state immunity sets out rules which were subsequently developed in both the FSIA and the United Kingdom State Immunity Act 1978.

The State Immunity Act bases its acceptance of the restrictive immunity theory on the distinction between property used for commercial and for public activities, ie, on the *iure gestionis/iure imperii* distinction applied to the nature-of-funds-test. The Act does not require that the property be used for the commercial activity upon which the claim is based, as do the European Convention on state immunity and the United States FSIA (only as far as the property of a foreign state is concerned). The property must be 'in use or intended for use for commercial purposes'.[32]

An interesting aspect in the United Kingdom Act, which is left open by the United States FSIA, is how the commercial or public use of the property to be executed against is to be determined. The Act provides for the issue to be decided by a certificate issued by the head of the state's diplomatic mission, unless the contrary is proved.[33] The United Kingdom can thus be said to be, since the Act has been enacted, one of the countries in which the ideal coherence in the treatment of sovereign immunity as a whole comes closer to reality.[34]

The French *Cour de Cassation* has criticised this nature-of-the-property-test, as applied independently from the nature-of-the-activity-test, in the EURODIF case. Indeed, the application of the former test alone tends to widen the field of immunity, as we have already pointed out. However, the French Court has followed the distinction between acts *iure imperii* and acts *iure gestionis*, a principle which, as discussed above, we do not hold applicable.

By way of conclusion of the first part of this paper, and before passing on to the examination of the relevant case law, we must mention that a general incentive to the voluntary compliance by states with awards rendered in connection with their commercial activities is given by the New York Convention. The contracting states must recognise and enforce (but nothing

32 State Immunity Act 1978, s13(4).
33 *Ibid*, s13(5).
34 See recent House of Lords decision, *Alcom Limited* v *Republic of Columbia* [1984] AC 580.

is said about actual execution) the foreign awards complying with the requirements of the Convention. Although awards to which a state is a party fall within the ambit of the New York Convention,[35] it is silent with respect to the actual execution of awards against a state, but does not impede it either.

This brief survey shows that the rules relating to immunity from execution are, as stated by Professor Delaume, in even greater disarray than the rules on immunity from jurisdiction.[36] Forum-shopping is the logical consequence of this diversity. A further element to be considered in this context is the existence of a 'territorial connection' in the legal systems accepting a restrictive immunity theory. We have already seen that Swiss case law requires a *Binnenbeziehung*, a contact between the legal relationship upon which the award is rendered and Swiss territory. The necessity of such a connection is also recognised by the United States FSIA, which requires that the commercial activity of the foreign state or state entity be performed in the United States.[37] In contrast, the United Kingdom State Immunity Act does not require any connection except that the assets be within the territory of the United Kingdom.

Case law concerning sovereign immunity in international commercial arbitration

We turn now to an examination of some cases that illustrate in practice some of the points made above.

LIAMCO is one of the most blatant examples of the problems created by the incoherence of the national and international rules on sovereign immunity. Seeking to enforce an award against Libya, LIAMCO tried to execute property of Libya in four different countries. In the country where execution would have been easiest, Switzerland, the courts refused to deal with the case since the legal relationship upon which the award had been rendered was not in any way connected with Switzerland. The fact that the sole arbitrator had been sitting in Geneva did not fulfil the requirement of the *Binnenbeziehung*.[38]

In the United States, the point of view was not sufficiently clarified, since only a District Court explicitly expressed its opinion on the suit.[39] The court refused to deal with the case on the ground of the Act of State doctrine. This reasoning was attacked in *amicus curiae* briefs to the Court of Appeals, filed by the American Arbitration Association and others. The United States Government took the position that it agreed with the District Court's statement that Libya had, according to the FSIA, waived its right to claim immunity from execution by submitting to arbitration in Geneva. The case was

35 A J Van den Berg *The New York Arbitration Convention of 1958* (Deventer 1981), at 51–3.

36 G Delaume, 'Foreign Sovereign Immunity: Impact on Arbitration', 38 *Arbitration Journal* 34 (1983) at 45.

37 A United States seat of the arbitration was held insufficient as a nexus in *Verlinden BV* v *Central Bank of Nigeria*, 488 F Supp 1284 (SDNY 1980). The decision was affirmed, but on different grounds by the United States Court of Appeals for the Second Circuit, on April 16, 1981. This decision is reported in 20 *ILM* 639 (1981). The Supreme Court reversed this decision on May 23, 1983, 22 *ILM* 647 (1983).

38 See *supra*, n1.

39 United States District Court for the District of Columbia, January 18, 1980, reported in VI *Yearbook: Commercial Arbitration* 248 (1981).

settled out of court, whereupon the *amici curiae* requested the Court of Appeals to vacate the order of the District Court. The order was vacated *per curiam* on May 6, 1981. Since the order of the Court of Appeals did not contain reasons, the reasoning of the decision can only be surmised.

The same uncertain situation was left open in France, where the *Tribunal de Grande Instance*[40] refused to grant any measure of execution, but nominated an independent committee to ascertain the public or commercial use of the funds (bank accounts) against which execution was requested. Finally, the Swedish Court of Appeal of Svea adopted the equation 'no immunity from jurisdiction: no immunity from execution', holding that Libya had waived both by submitting to arbitration.[41]

Another decision of the Paris *Tribunal de Grande Instance* should also be mentioned. This decision is one of the innumerable steps in the never-ending story of the case *SEEE* v *Yugoslavia*. On this occasion, SEEE tried to enforce in France the award obtained in Lausanne against Yugoslavia. The French court, while recognising that Yugoslavia had waived its right to claim immunity from jurisdiction by submitting to arbitration, held that a waiver of immunity from jurisdiction does not automatically result in the state's waiver of its right to immunity from execution as well. This principle was affirmed by the Court of Appeal.[42] The *Hoge Raad* came to the same conclusion in the Dutch proceedings between the parties.[43]

In the *Ipitrade* case in 1978,[44] again one small piece of the complicated litigation between Ipitrade and Nigeria, the French *Tribunal de Grande Instance* held that Nigerian bank accounts in France enjoyed absolute immunity from execution following the recognition in France of an arbitral award rendered in Switzerland.

The three French decisions examined above were lower courts' decisions. In 1984, the *Cour de Cassation* had the chance to define the French position on the subject, in the *EURODIF* case.[45] The facts of the case are, in a simplified version, the following. Within the framework of cooperation agreements stipulated in 1974 between France and Iran, the SERU (Uranium Research and Study Corporation), a subsidiary of the Atomic Energy Commission (CEA), and EURODIF, a French law corporation established in 1973 by SERU and similar organisations from three other European countries, entered into industrial cooperation agreements with the Iranian Government and the Iranian Atomic Energy Organisation (OEAI). The latter was replaced in 1978 by the OIAETI (Iranian Organisation for Economic and Technical Investment and Assistance). The OEAI and the CEA established in 1975 a French law corporation, SOFIDIF, which became in its turn a member of EURODIF.

40 Tribunal de Grande Instance of Paris, March 5, 1979, *Procureur de la Republique* v *Société LIAMCO*, 106 *Clunet* 857 (1979).

41 Court of Appeal of Svea, June 18, 1980, reported in VII *Yearbook: Commercial Arbitration* 359 (1982).

42 Tribunal de Grande Instance of Paris, July 8, 1970, *Societe Europenne d'Etudes et d'Enterprises* v *People's Federal Republic of Yugoslavia*, 96 *Clunet* 131 (1971), and *Court d'Appel* of Paris, January 29, 1975 [1975] *Revue de l'Arbitrage* 328.

43 Hoge Raad, October 26, 1973, in *Netherlands Jurisprudentie* No 361.

44 Tribunal de Grande Instance of Paris, September 12, 1978, *Procureur de la Republique* v *SA Ipitrade International*, 106 *Clunet* 857 (1979).

45 Cour de Cassation, *EURODIF Corporation* v *Islamic Republic of Iran*, in *Semaine Juridique* 1984, II, 20205.

EURODIF was to provide enriched uranium to SOFIDIF, and the latter would then distribute it between CEA and OEAI. Under these agreements, Iran lent CEA US$1 billion, the repayment of which was guaranteed by the French Government. Iran also lent EURODIF FFr943 million, to be paid in instalments, and agreed to advance FFr130 million to SOFIDIF to cover the operating costs of EURODIF. Following the Islamic Revolution of 1978, the third instalment of the loan to EURODIF (FFr400 million) and 70 of the 130 million advance to SOFIDIF were never paid by Iran; subsequently, Iran elected to discontinue the cooperation agreements.

EURODIF initiated ICC arbitration proceedings as provided for in the agreements between the parties, requesting an award determining the consequences of this unilateral breach of contracts. In the meantime EURODIF petitioned the President of the Commercial Court in Paris to attach the Iranian funds held by CEA (the US$1 billion loan) for the total amount claimed in the arbitration proceedings. The attachment was granted on October 24, 1979, but on April 21, 1982, the First Chamber of the Paris Court of Appeal quashed the order, holding that Iran could invoke immunity from execution. The Court of Appeal held that the funds on which attachment was asked were public funds since, if not attached, they would revert to Iran 'without any earmarking and the Iranian Government shall be free to decide as a matter of sovereign prerogative how to use them'. The Court of Appeal further stated that, once the public nature of the property was determined, it was useless to enquire whether the activity carried out by Iran had been sovereign or commercial.

This decision was appealed by EURODIF, and gave the *Cour de Cassation* the opportunity to define French doctrine on immunity from execution in general. The Concluding Statement by the Advocate General contains a thorough survey of the issue, as well as interesting remarks on sovereign immunity in general. The judgment of the *Cour de Cassation* follows the lines of the Concluding Statement and contains two main points of interest to this paper. It must be noted in advance that, since the decision is not explicitly limited to prejudgment attachments, its reasoning can be held to apply equally to execution as means of enforcement of a foreign arbitral award. First, the court states that immunity from execution is a matter of principle, but that it can be limited in exceptional circumstances. Second, it holds that immunity can be refused, by way of exception, when the property to be attached is intended to be used for the state's commercial activity upon which the claim is based. By doing so, the court followed the example of the United States FSIA. In the case at issue the adoption of the further requirement that the property to be executed against must be used for the commercial activity upon which the claim is based did not result in an enfeeblement of the private party's position. However, we should underline the evidently negative role that this principle can play in the field of immunity from execution.

The Court of Appeal applied the nature-of-funds test and disregarded the criterion of the nature of the activity. The French *Cour de Cassation* held that the Court of Appeal ought to have determined the exact nature of the activity carried out by Iran under the agreements 'in order to deal with the question of immunity from execution'.[46] The application of both the nature-of-funds and

46 As translated in 23 *ILM* 1062 (1984).

the nature-of-activity tests is explained by the court's further requirement that the funds to be executed against be used for the activity upon which the claim is based. According to the French *Cour de Cassation* therefore, three conditions must be fulfilled for immunity from execution to be denied:

- the state's activity must be commercial;
- the funds must have a commercial nature; and
- the funds must be used for the activity upon which the claim is based.

In this context, the application of both criteria has the positive result that the decision on the sovereign or commercial nature of the funds is not left to the discretion of the state, as pointed out in the Concluding Statement by the Advocate General, since

> 'it would suffice for a foreign government to refrain from assigning a specific use to the funds in dispute or even from making known its intentions as to the use of such funds, for its immunity from measures of execution to become totally unchallengeable.'[47]

This remark applies to the problems which could arise and have arisen on this issue under the United States FSIA and the United Kingdom State Immunity Act. Once again we stress that the only way to ensure actual execution of an award against a state is to abandon the *iure gestionis/iure imperii* principle in its last stronghold, the nature-of-funds-test. As we have seen, the French decision clung to the abovementioned distinction and even set a further requirement, following the FSIA example, which dramatically limits the private party's chances to actually enforce an award in his favour against a state.

Another interesting and recent case is the *SPP* case. In 1974 a Hong Kong company, SPP, undertook to build two tourist villages in Egypt. The identity of the other party to the agreement is the major issue in the legal battle which has followed the rendition of the award by ICC arbitrators in 1983. To summarise the issue as much as possible, we shall say that in brief, SPP claimed that Egypt was a party to the main contract, whereas Egypt contended that it was not. SPP tried to enforce the award in three countries, with contrasting results, the examination of which would go beyond the scope of this paper.[48] During the proceedings before the High Court in London, the issue of immunity from execution was considered, since SPP had asked the Court to grant a prejudgment attachment by way of security on funds held by Egypt in English banks, according to Section 5(5) of the Arbitration Act 1975.[49] We must stress that this is a very superficial survey of the case before the English Court, made with the sole purpose to provide a background to the issue of immunity from execution. On March 19, 1984, the Court of Appeal

47 *Ibid.*

48 The exequatur was granted in The Netherlands (President of the District Court of Amsterdam, July 12, 1984, reported in X *Yearbook: Commercial Arbitration* 487 (1985)), whilst in France the award was annulled on the same day (Cour d'Appel of Paris, July 12, 1984, reported in X *Yearbook: Commercial Arbitration*, 113 (1985)).

49 Arbitration Act 1975, s5(5) reads:

> 'Where an application for the setting aside or suspension of a Convention award has been made to such a competent authority as is mentioned in sub-section (2)(f) of this section, the court before which enforcement of the award is sought may, if it thinks fit, adjourn the proceedings and may, on the application of the party seeking to enforce the award, order the other party to give security'.

entertained the suit and held that it could order Egypt to give security under Section 5(5) of the 1975 Arbitration Act, 'were it not for the fact that the respondent is a foreign sovereign state'. The court expressed the opinion that, if it were faced with the issue of whether it is proper to make such an order, it certainly 'should want assistance from an *amicus curiae*'.

> 'In any event, before we could issue injunctive orders to the banks freezing the money, we should, it seems to me, have to be satisfied not only that SPP was arguably right in the relief it was seeking on appeal, but also that there was solid evidence that a major friendly foreign state with funds in this country was intending to remove them simply to avoid paying an arbitration award, albeit one for quite a large sum of money. For my part, I have seen no evidence which would justify my reaching any such conclusion.
>
> Accordingly, as I see it, it would be quite wrong for this Court to make an order of the type which SPP seeks, namely one freezing the assets of a friendly foreign state pending the hearing of this appeal, and I would decline to make such an order.'

The decision of the Court of Appeal specifically interprets the prejudgment attachment provisions of Section 5(5) of the 1975 Arbitration Act, but nevertheless presents interesting features for the discussion of the issue of immunity from execution is still considered independent of a waiver of immunity from jurisdiction, under United Kingdom legislation.

Finally reference is made to the recent English *Alcom* case.[50] According to Section 13(5) of the United Kingdom State Immunity Act 1978, the commercial or public nature of the state's property to be executed against is to be decided by a certificate issued by the head of that state's diplomatic mission in the United Kingdom, unless proof to the contrary is given. Alcom Ltd obtained a judgment by default against the Republic of Colombia, whereupon it sought execution against the Colombian Embassy's bank accounts in London. The Ambassador certified that the funds were 'not in use nor intended for use for commercial purposes but only to meet the expenditure necessarily incurred in the day-to-day running of the Diplomatic Mission'. The High Court set aside Alcom's request on these grounds, but the decision was reversed on appeal. The Court of Appeal held that 'the day-to-day running of the Mission' meant paying for goods and services, ie, including commercial transactions. Hence, the Embassy's funds could be attached. The Court of Appeal explicitly considered that the Ambassador's certificate itself supported the commercial nature of the funds. However, this decision was reversed by the House of Lords,[51] which held that funds used for defraying the day-to-day running expenses of a Diplomatic Mission are not on that account alone used for commercial purposes so as to be denied immunity from enforcement jurisdiction. For this it was necessary to show that (apart from *de minimis* exceptions) the funds were earmarked solely for the discharge of liabilities under commercial transactions. The Ambassador's certificate was conclusive evidence that in the case under consideration the funds were not so earmarked.

50 Court of Appeal, October 24, 1983, *Alcom Ltd* v *The Republic of Colombia*, [1984] AC 580 reported also in 78 *Am J Intl L* 451 (1984).

51 [1984] AC 580.

Conclusion

The foregoing survey of case law shows that: (a) the courts in general are reluctant to deny immunity from execution; (b) this situation can only be mended through the abandonment of the *iure imperii/iure gestionis* distinction, and the reliance upon the principle of *pacta sunt servanda*. Two of the decisions examined have explicitly or implicitly endorsed the theory of absolute immunity from execution (in *Ipitrade* and, to a certain extent, in *SPP*). The French decision in *LIAMCO* adopted as its cornerstone the *iure gestionis/iure imperii* nature of the funds to be executed against. The recent *EURODIF* judgment shows a development towards a further frustration of the private party's rights against a state, by holding that the general immunity from execution of a state can be exceptionally disregarded when the property against which execution is sought is used for the commercial activity upon which the claim is based. In Switzerland, where in principle a waiver of immunity from jurisdiction implies a waiver of immunity from execution, execution was denied in the *LIAMCO* case, on the grounds of lack of *Binnenbeziehung*.

Also the French and Dutch decisions in the *SEEE* case deny the existence of a necessary implication of the waiver of immunity from execution in the waiver of immunity from jurisdiction. Among the decisions examined, only the Swedish decision in *LIAMCO* explicitly endorses this theory, which is also followed by the *amicus curiae* brief of the United States' Government in the same case. We may also mention that the adoption of this principle is suggested, *de iure condendo*, by the Concluding Statement in *EURODIF* which recognises, however, its inapplicability *de iure condito*.

All these different approaches to the issue of immunity from execution (with the exception of the aforementioned Swedish decision) result in the weakening of the position of a private party *vis-à-vis* a state. The weakness of the private party has always been a feature in commercial transactions involving a state, in a situation which allows the state to violate the principle of *pacta sunt servanda*. We want to stress once again that, unless a state is held to have waived its right to immunity from execution together with its right to immunity from jurisdiction by signing the arbitration agreement, the main principle governing the commercial world, *pacta sunt servanda*, will always and undoubtedly be violated, and this confused and confusing situation will be perpetuated.

Index